LEGALLY VICTIMISING NATIONAL MONUMENTS

Role of Parliament, Union Government & Supreme Court

Dr. Krishan Mahajan

INDIA • SINGAPORE • MALAYSIA

Notion Press

Old No. 38, New No. 6
McNichols Road, Chetpet
Chennai - 600 031

First Published by Notion Press 2018
Copyright © Dr. Krishan Mahajan 2018
All Rights Reserved.

ISBN 978-1-64324-011-4

This book has been published with all efforts taken to make the material error-free after the consent of the author. However, the author and the publisher do not assume and hereby disclaim any liability to any party for any loss, damage, or disruption caused by errors or omissions, whether such errors or omissions result from negligence, accident, or any other cause.

No part of this book may be used, reproduced in any manner whatsoever without written permission from the author, except in the case of brief quotations embodied in critical articles and reviews.

DEDICATION

Dedicated to my parents, late (Smt.) Snehlata and late (Shri.) Ved Raj Mahajan, who sacrificed for their children all that they had, by deliberate choices of honesty, social responsibility and consequent poverty, to create upright citizens capable of withstanding suffering and adversity with a smile. That they could do this after the trauma of beginning life from scratch in post-partition India, is their everlasting tribute to the country wherein inevitability, easy lucre as virtue and constant resilience from pain, go hand in hand. This never dimmed their spirit of love and affection, sharing and helping in the suffering of one and all, including those who had inflicted on them undeserved trauma and pain.

CONTENTS SUMMARY

Preface . . . . *xvii*
Acknowledgements . . . . *xxix*
Table of Cases . . . . *xxxvii*
List of Abbreviations . . . . *xli*

Detailed Contents . . . . **v–xvi**

DETAILED CONTENTS

Part – I: The Legislative Framework

Chapter I: Legal Culture of Monuments 3
  1.1 The Study 3
  1.2 Study in Two Parts 4
  Part I: Legislative Framework 4
    1.2.1 Text & Context: Inter & Multi-disciplinary 4
    1.2.2 Relevant Constitutional Law 5
    1.2.3 Relevant Statutory Law 7
    1.2.4 Multi-disciplinary Linkages 8
    1.2.5 International Law 10
    1.2.6 First Part Ends 11
  Part II: Implementation Through Courts 12
    1.2.7 Supreme Court and High Courts Case Law 12
    1.2.8 Alternative 13
  1.3 Significance of Monuments 13
    1.3.1 What Governance of Monuments Tells 13
    1.3.2 Monuments as Identity Politics 14
    1.3.3 Religion & Monuments 15
    1.3.4 Ram Janam Bhoomi-Babri Masjid 17
    1.3.5 A German Example 19
    1.3.6 Cultureless Secularism, Monuments & Identity 20
  1.4 British India & British Monuments 21
    1.4.1 Analysis to Conclusions 22

1.5 Propositions 24
    1.5.1 The Legal Basis 26
    1.5.2 First Legal Problem: Past and Deeming Technique 27
    1.5.3 Second Legal Problem: Vague Ancient vs. Truthful
           History 28
    1.5.4 Third Legal Problem: Meaning of 'National' 29
    1.5.5 Uses of Legal Vagueness 30
1.6 Objectives of the Book 31
1.7 Growth In and Around a Monument 32
    1.7.1 Monuments of Fear 33
1.8 A Peep Into The Chapters 34
    1.8.1 Part I: The Legal Framework & Approaches to
           Preservation of Monuments 34
    1.8.2 Part II: Judicial Implementation 38

Chapter II: Correlation to History and Geography............... 43
    Doctrine of Partial Truth 43
    2.1 Partial Truth 43
    2.2 Verbal Constitutionalism 44
    2.3 Consequences 46
    2.4 History Shut-Out 48
    2.5 Article 29 as a Base for Article 49 50
    2.6 Correlation to Geography 51
    2.7 Essential Inputs 52
    2.8 Sustainable Development 54

Chapter III: Correlation to Economics........................... 56
    3.1 Developmental Model 56
    3.2 Consequence: Culture of Illegality 58
    3.3 Assumptions of Economics 61
        3.3.1 Assumption I 61
        3.3.2 Assumption II 62
        3.3.3 Assumption III 63

3.4 Culture of Darkness 63
3.5 Culture of Unaccountability 64
3.6 Corruption Blanket on Article 29 65
3.7 SC and CAG Reports 67
3.8 The Judiciary 67
3.9 SC: Development and Culture 69
3.10 Constitution and State Economics Dovetailed 71
3.11 Consequences of Dovetailing 72
    3.11.1 First Consequence 72
    3.11.2 Second Consequence 72
3.12 Western Law and Economics 76
3.13 Dams, Development and Damned 77
3.14 Difficult Existence – For Whom? 78
3.15 Kind of Development 79
3.16 Problem of the Judiciary's Role 79
3.17 Existing Law – Legality to Unconstitutionality 80
3.18 SC as Discoverer of the Public Good 81
3.19 SC as Problem-Solver 82
3.20 Cultural Illiteracy Ensured 84
3.21 Legal Cycle and Monuments 86
3.22 Effects of the Legal Cycle 87
3.23 Summing Up 87

Chapter IV: Constitutional Framework 89
  4.1 The 'National Importance' Brand 89
  4.2 Evolution: Central Control & National Brand 89
  4.3 Unconstitutional Branding: Model Regulations 91
    4.3.1 Andhra Pradesh 91
    4.3.2 Mumbai 92
  4.4 Conundrum of Art. 49 and Entry 67, List I 93
    4.4.1 Conundrum Resolution: Harmonious Reading ... 94
  4.5 Net Result 96

viii | Detailed Contents

Chapter V: State Control of Culture and Monuments 97
  5.1 Ancient Monuments Preservation Act, 1904 98
  5.2 Preceding Context 99
  5.3 Two Approaches 101
      5.3.1 Effects of a Choice 101
      5.3.2 Monuments – As-Objects Approach 102
      5.3.3 Monuments As Cultural Heritage Approach 102
      5.3.4 Execution of the First Approach 103
            5.3.4.1 The First Coup: Using "By a Law Made
                      by Parliament" 103
            5.3.4.2 Second Coup: From Parliament to
                      the Executive. 106
            5.3.4.3 Effect of the Second Coup 106
            5.3.4.4 Effect of the 7th Constitutional Amendment . . . 108
            5.3.4.5 Statutory Conclusion of the Coup 109
            5.3.4.6 First Effect: Shutting Out Public Debate. 110
            5.3.4.7 Second Effect: Hollowing out Art. 49 111
            5.3.4.8 Third Effect: Converting Art. 29 into a
                      State Right 112
            5.3.4.9 Net Effect: Unaccountability &
                      Lost Monuments 113
            5.3.4.10 Ancient Monuments Act, 1958 114
            5.3.4.11 Consequences of Conversion 115
            5.3.4.12 Amendments of 2010 116
                    5.3.4.12.1 Citizens Shut Out 116
                    5.3.4.12.2 Parliament Scrutiny Disabled 116
                    5.3.4.12.3 Oversight Disablement:
                                    Consequences 117
      5.3.5 Second Approach 118
            5.3.5.1 Nation of Cultural Minorities 121
            5.3.5.2 Cultural Heritage Approach Ignored 122

   5.3.5.3 Fundamental Duty 122
   5.3.5.4 Rootless Monuments 123
   5.3.5.5 Composite Heritage 127
   5.3.5.6 Citizen-Enabling Approach 128
   5.3.5.7 Sustainable Tourism 128
 5.4 International Law Ignored 129
 5.5 Economic Development vs. Protection 130
 5.6 State and Culture of Monuments 131
 5.7 Differential Application 131
 5.8 Divergence on Fundamental Duties 133

Chapter VI: The Constitutional Cleavage................ 135
 6.1 Monuments: Whose Culture? 135
 6.2 Culture: Citizen's Right & Duty 137
 6.3 Constitutional Cleavage 137
 6.4 Constitutional Archaeology 141
 6.5 Article 49, 29 and 51A(f) Cleavage 142
 6.6 First Cleavage: Art. 49 and 1958 Act 142
 6.7 Second Cleavage: Art. 49, 29 r/w 51A(f) 143
 6.8 The Ancient Monuments Act, 1958 144
   6.8.1 Act Reflects the Cleavage 144
 6.9 Consequences 147
 6.10 CAG Report, 2013 148
 6.11 Tourism Revenue Replaces Culture 149
 6.12 All India Cultural Heritage Service 150

Chapter VII: Constitutional Cultural Heritage Approach 151
 7.1 Cultural Fraternity, Identity and Unity 151
 7.2 Constitutional Scheme 152
 7.3 Monuments as One Art. 25 Religion 152
 7.4 Panchayat to Municipality: Monuments Gather and
    Unite Religions 153
 7.5 Constitutional Architecture: Culture Subsumes Religion ... 154

Chapter VIII: Statute vs. Constitution: Monuments as Objects 157
  8.1 Ignoring Difference between Monument and Object 157
  8.2 Act Defeats Article 49 158
  8.3 Unconstitutional Definition:
      Ancient – An Undefined Century 159
  8.4 Archaeological Interest 160
  8.5 How Objects-Approach Destroys Article 49 161
  8.6 Judicial Approach 165

Chapter IX: The Political Economy of Culture vs. Law 166
  9.1 Unquantified & Neglected 166
  9.2 Six Consequences 168
    9.2.1 First Consequence 168
    9.2.2 Second Consequence 169
    9.2.3 Third Consequence 169
    9.2.4 Fourth Consequence 170
    9.2.5 Fifth Consequence 170
    9.2.6 Sixth Consequence 171
  9.3 Citizens Torn Away from Culture & Monuments 172

Chapter X: Self-Defeating Conventions: The International Legal
          Framework for Monuments 173
  10.1 Consumption Creates The Effective Legal System 174
  10.2 People are the Heart of Monuments 175
  10.3 Problematic Efficacy 176
  10.4 Athens Charter 177
  10.5 Roerich Pact to Hague Convention 179
  10.6 1954 Hague Convention 180
  10.7 Duties of Contracting Parties 181
    10.7.1 First Duty 181
    10.7.2 Second Duty 181
    10.7.3 Third Duty 182

10.8   ICCROM 182
10.9   Venice Charter: Integrity of Monuments 183
10.10 ICOMOS 185
10.11 International Convention on Economic,
       Social & Cultural Rights............................. 186
10.12 Convention Concerning the Protection of
       the World Cultural & Natural Heritage 188
10.13 International National Trust Organisation (INTO) 190

Part – II: Judicial Implementation

Chapter XI: Supreme Court Saves a Protected Monument 195
11.1   First Assault: Green Belt 195
11.2   Second Assault: Hotel Near the Taj Monument 197
11.3   Third Assault: YANNI'S Concert 197
11.4   Fourth Assault: Wrong Data to SC 198
11.5   Fifth Assault: Taj Heritage Corridor Project 200

Chapter XII: Judicial Protection of Monuments through
             the Environment Route 204
12.1   Is Art. 32 for Monuments? 204
12.2   The MC Mehta Petition 204
12.3   On a Legally Rudderless Journey 206
12.4   A Unique Legal Journey Begins 206
12.5   Protection of Monuments – A Fundamental Right 211

Chapter XIII: Judicial Closure of Industries: The Loss of Reason... 214
13.1   SC: Permission Giving Authority 215
13.2   Which Equipment 216
13.3   Court: Incompetent and Then Competent 216
13.4   The Journey's Methodology 217
13.5   Reliance on Oral Statements 217
13.6   SC's Unit to Unit Permission 218

Chapter XIV: The Taj Heritage Corridor:
            Judicial Role in Using Criminal Law 222
14.1 Stages I–IV 223
14.2 SC: Investigate Without an FIR: Stage I 224
14.3 SC Lodges a Criminal Complaint 224
14.4 Amicus Prayers Ignored by SC 225
14.5 CVC Bypassed 226
14.6 SC's Silence on Relief after Dismissal: Stage II........... 226
     14.6.1 SC & Final Report Saga: Stage III................ 227
14.7 S.197 Cr.P.C. Sanction Refusal Defeats SC's Order 229
14.8 A Supreme Court of Benches 229
14.9 Domestic Inquiries 230
     14.9.1 Compulsory Waiting 230
     14.9.2 Let Time Pass 231
14.10 Disproportionate Assets Case Hived Off Suo Moto 232
14.11 Eco Restoration 232
14.12 SC Ignored Ancient Monuments Act, 1958 233

Chapter XV: Is Judicial Silence the Best Role?
           Neither Security nor Protection.................. 235
15.1 SC Allows Night Viewing 235
15.2 Khawasspuras: Replaced by Facilitation Centre 235
15.3 Rebuilding – No Conservation Principle 236
15.4 ASI Hits a Protected Monument Wall 237
15.5 SC's Order – Prior Permission 237
15.6 Questions Regarding Tourism 237
     15.6.1 First Question: Security 238
     15.6.2 Second Question: Carrying Capacity 238
15.7 I.A. for Carrying Capacity 239
15.8 Alternative Land for Facilitation Centre 239
15.9 ASI: Underground Passage to the Notified Taj Complex .. 240

15.10 Question of Judicial Will: Security Issue 241
    15.10.1 Four Questions for U.P. and Six for ASI 242
    15.10.2 Judicial Silence on U.P.'s and ASI's Replies 244
15.11 Judicial Silence: Shoes on Graves 245
15.12 Sustainable Tourism 246
15.13 Supreme Court's Waning Interest 247
    15.13.1 The Agra Master-Plan 247
    15.13.2 More Applications by Mehta 248
    15.13.3 Brick Kilns and Agricultural Top-Soil 249
    15.13.4 SC: Kiln by Kiln Permission 250
    15.13.5 Functioning of the TTZ Pollution
             Control Authority 250
    15.13.6 Low-Sulphur Diesel 251
    15.13.7 Shifting of Polluting Bus Stand at Bijli Ghar...... 251
    15.13.8 Night-View Monitoring 252
15.14 Tourism Takes over Monument Protection 253
    15.14.1 Memorandum and Manual: Agra Heritage Fund 253
    15.14.2 Solar Disappears 254
    15.14.3 Shah Jahan Park 255

Chapter XVI: Judicial Role: Tourism vs. Protected Walls in
               Taj Mahal Complex........................ 256
16.1 Khawassparas 257
16.2 Steps to Facilitate Tourism 258
    16.2.1 Notice in One I.A. and Reply in Another 259
    16.2.2 Silence on Internal Security of the Taj Mahal 259
    16.2.3 ASI Slips in a Facilitation Centre:
            The Taj Hotel's MOU 260
    16.2.4 Fait Accompli of Prepared Plans 260
    16.2.5 ASI Suppresses Further Facts 261
    16.2.6 Hospitality vs. Conservation 262

16.2.7 Tourism vs. Conservation 263
16.2.8 Reversible Illegality Approved 263
16.2.9 ASI Violates Its Conservation Manual 263
16.2.10 Questions on TMCC's Certificate to ASI 264
16.2.11 "Servants" vs. Monument Culture 264
16.2.12 Taj Mahal, Tourism and Toilets 265
16.2.13 Showing Entrances without Exits to
         Supreme Court 266
16.2.14 Undisclosed Entrance Construction
         without Exit 267
16.2.15 Supreme Court Saves the Taj Mahal Complex 267
16.2.16 Helpless Disclosure by ASI 268
16.2.17 Bridge of Half-Truths 269
16.2.18 Culture Buried 270
16.2.19 ASI's Truth, but Not the Whole Truth 271
16.2.20 SC's Committee Offers a Solution 272
16.2.21 Committee's People & Culture Approach 273
16.2.22 Committee's Alternative to ASI's Facilitation
         Centres 274
16.2.23 ASI Sticks to Its Facilitation Centres 277
16.2.24 SC's Mysterious Silence 278
16.2.25 The Whole Truth from ASI 278
16.2.26 ASI's Novel Pleadings & Suppression 280
16.2.27 Hiding UNESCO & ICOMOS Letters 281
16.2.28 Twenty Minute Hearings 282
16.2.29 Issues Defined: Another SC Committee 282
16.2.30 Full Truth Tumbles Out 283
16.2.31 Findings of the SC Committee 286
16.2.32 ASI's Lingering Reply 287

    16.2.33 Another ASI Attempt & SC's Mysterious Silence . . . 288
    16.2.34 Supreme Court Agrees to ASI's Underground
             Approach 289

Chapter XVII: Judicially Protecting Monuments without
                Reference to Any Law 291
    17.1 Victoria Memorial Hall Case 291
    17.2 Baljeet Singh Malik vs. Delhi Golf Club 292
    17.3 Wasim Ahmad Saeed vs. Union of India 292
    17.4 M.C. Mehta vs. Archaeological Survey of India........ 293
    17.5 Wasim Ahmad Saeed vs. Union of India 293
    17.6 Wasim Ahmad Saeed vs. Union of India 293
    17.7 M.C. Mehta vs. Union of India........................ 294
    17.8 M.C. Mehta vs. Union of India........................ 294
    17.9 M.C. Mehta vs. Union of India........................ 294

Chapter XVIII: Protecting Monuments: Role of High Courts...... 296
    18.1 Siri Fort Wall 296
    18.2 Bade and Chote Khan 297
    18.3 Red Fort Meena Bazar 297
    18.4 Church Cemetery 298
    18.5 Illegal Appellate Authority 298
    18.6 Jantar Mantar, Delhi 299
    18.7 Orissa: Churengagarh Fort 299

Chapter XIX: An Alternative Legal Approach.................... 302
    19.1 Unconstitutional Economics vs. Cultural Heritage 302
    19.2 Culture Since 1950................................... 304
    19.3 An Alternative Legal Approach 310
    19.4 Steps for a New Law.................................. 310
    19.5 Creating Jobs.. 314

Annexure I: List of Taj Trapezium Zone (TTZ) Monuments *317*

Bibliography *323*
    A. *Charters/Constitution/Statutes/International*
        Covenants and Conventions *323*
    B. *Case/Judgment Reporters* *325*
    C. *Dictionararies/Encyclopedias* *325*
    D. *Books.* *326*
    E. *Reports* *332*
    F. *Journal and News Articles* *333*
    G. *Public Lectures* *334*

PREFACE

Law and culture writing is rare in India. Even rarer is writing on law and culture specific to monuments. This is surprising.

Monuments symbolise religion, belief, customs and power. The legal book governing our lives, the Constitution of India, particularly recognises all that a monument symbolises. But it requires its filtration through fundamental rights of individuals, the fundamental specified ends of political power in the Directive Principles, the fundamental duties of citizens and the boundaries of legislative competence. The recognition given by the Constitution to custom, religion, religious institutions and culture as fundamental rights, turns the fundamental duty of the State to recognise and protect monuments of national importance into an inevitable struggle for a constitutional India that would attain the constitutional ends of fraternity and liberty based on the dignity of the individual in such a society. The Constitution calls for change and renewal. Monuments cannot change or renew themselves. Change and renewal are disruptive Monuments become a symbol of how those who manage India handle the disruption of several cultures.

The struggle is acute because the Constitution is silent on the link between protection of monuments of national importance, as an unenforceable Directive Principle, and the enforceable fundamental right to culture. Monuments and the people must suffer because of the constitutional silence on a compelling transparent accountability of public and private power and on information deprivation or the right to be informed by the State.

This turns our attention to what kind of document the Constitution itself is. It nowhere speaks of any effective accountability, of the managers of India that it stipulates. It adds to this, the legal protection, privilege and immunity of such managers without whispering anywhere the liability and the consequence if the managers at any level fail the principles fundamental in the governance of the country. This enables the managers of the change required by the Constitution to make either toothless laws or drastic laws with practically no provision for effective enforcement. In either case such a Constitution makes it possible for the managers to give de facto recognition to the very status and violence that was required to be changed. This gives a free run to the public and private power governing lives and monuments, regardless of the State law. Prostitution and dowry are the old examples of this. Equitable land distribution, opportunity of accessing constitutional public goods like education and health or organising for bargaining fair contracts in the Information Technology industry are the modern examples.

When the implosion (suicides) or explosion (public money scams and terrorism) in this struggle, makes the continuation of this operational matrix of the Constitution difficult, then a manager or two may be sacrificed while applying constitutional garnishing under the pressure of international creditors who make the life style of the managers possible. Lack of information renders the citizen helpless to meet the onslaught of public or private power, as there is nothing in the Constitution to give teeth to changing this culture. Hence instead of childrens' needs of survival, health, education and skills for a livelihood, being the first charge on India's money, the salaries and allowances of some of these managers exclusively get that privilege. A postmortem Parliamentary Committee or a Comptroller & Auditor General's report is all that a cultural change mandated by the Constitution, gets on a failure of that change. What about the Supreme Court meant to enforce fundamental rights like that of culture in which monuments have to survive?

The Supreme Court meant to enforce fundamental rights of children and their mothers, becomes merely a declaratory court of good wishes, since it refuses to take the Comptroller & Auditor General's reports as even a beginning for such enforcement.

The Ganges Pollution case Writ Petition 3727 of 1985 was typical of this. The Taj Heritage Corridor case in Writ Petition 13381 of 1984, still pending in the Supreme Court, went a step further with the Supreme Court accepting the refusal of sanction for prosecution of the erstwhile Chief Minister after having got the FIR registered on the basis of an investigation done step by step under its orders. The Supreme Court did not question as to why the CBI went to the governor to seek sanction on the basis of the order of the Special Judge, instead of coming to the Supreme Court which was still monitoring the case. The Supreme Court at least deserved that CBI inform it of the Special Judge's order on the investigation done under the Court's orders on the complaint filed by the Supreme Court against the Chief Minister. The Supreme Court could then have taken a call on the matter prior to the Governor pre-empting the entire case and the effort put in by the Supreme Court. But the Supreme Court kept silent, when this issue of prior information to it was raised specifically in the proceedings concerning the correctness and propriety of the Governor's refusal to grant sanction for prosecution of the Chief Minister.

In this very case the Supreme Court had earlier rebuked the senior CBI officer for stating that he cannot investigate till an FIR is registered, by telling him that he should realise that the Supreme Court was directing him to investigate in the absence of an FIR. The loud and clear message to the police was of lawless but binding law. In this aggregate constitutional culture of lawless law change, monuments as part of the fundamental right to culture can have little chance. The health of heritage stones and the way of recognising these gives away the health of citizens and of the operating constitutional culture.

Accordingly, the constitutional managers of India make this struggle painful. Almost all religions, communities, castes, families, professions and ways of livelihoods and living, as practiced, resist in multiple ways, the constitutional recognition of the dignity of every individual Indian, without which heritage stones cannot be protected. But this constitutional struggle is missing in the exercise of political-legal power to recognise monuments officially or not. This is achieved by simply ignoring the fundamental right to culture of individual citizens and then using the rest of the relevant constitutional provisions to exercise power to take over culture. The first Part of the book describes how this was done by Parliament and the Union Government, after explaining the linkage of monuments to History, Geography, Economics and Culture. The Second Part of the Book examines the role of the Supreme Court in this regard.

Tragically the story concerning accountability and the right to be informed is not remarkably different in the Supreme Court and the high courts, the constitutional institutions of last resort for finding the cultural meaning and effectively enforcing constitutional reason by analysing the use of power vis a vis citizens or their monuments.

Suffering monuments and people can have little effective space in a judicial culture wherein the rule of reason itself is in serious inter-se judicial conflict over judicial values. The Constitution of India becomes endangered, from the moment the distinction between the operating judicial culture and the extant political culture ends.

Does this distinction end when a sitting Supreme Court judge, breaking a court convention since 1950's, concludes his speech at Vigyan Bhawan with the ruling party's slogan ' Sabka Saath Sabka Vikas', in the presence of the Prime Minister, the Union Law Minister and the Chief Justice of India on the dias, during the ceremony for kicking off the Supreme Court's digitisation of court records programme. Did this judge take a cue from a previous Chief Justice of India, as head of proverbially the most powerful court in the world, publically weeping in the same Vigyan Bhawan before the same Prime Minister heading a powerful Executive of a huge electoral majority in Parliament. This Chief Justice of India was helplessly pleading for the issue of a notification by the Union Government to appoint the judges to the Supreme Court recommended by its collegium. No wonder Supreme Court's Justice Ranjan Gogoi concluded his speech at the digitisation ceremony by pointing out that someone earlier had referred to us as belonging to the good lot and the bad lot, but "I do not know to which lot we belong?"

Or, does the distinction end when in another break from Convention, the Supreme Court shuts the court for half the working day to be at the President of India's swearing-in ceremony when only the Chief Justice of India is required to administer the Constitutional oath of office. So far since 1950, Presidents and Prime Ministers had always adjusted the timing of their functions so as to never disturb the public time of the courts. Or, when the Supreme Court converts the one day holiday declared in its calendar, drawn up independently of the government's official calendar into a two working days holiday because of the government's confusion about the date of a religious day of a community. What is the impact of all this on the public perception of judicial independence? Does the perception of the little lawyer and the little judge in the littlest court working conscientiously and independently for the gods and hopes of little wo/men matter? The protection of monuments has to find a place in this culture.

In this the judges abiding by values suffer usually in silence. Judgeship in the constitutional courts is the only State appointment to a public office in India wherein the citizen has no assurance of the integrity or merit or both of those appointed as judges to deliver constitutional justice. Hence, the judiciary in the constitutional courts is not subject to bio-metric attendance or the right to information concerning making public the shares that judges hold, the list of their children, the names of their spouses, the persons or institutions whose hospitality the judge may have enjoyed, the list of major clients before the elevation of the judge, the political and financial connections, so that justice is not only done but seen to be done in the context of their constant lectures that technology be used to ensure access to free, fair and impartial justice. This disclosure should be the necessary public interest cost of becoming and being a judge. Technology itself is transparent only as it is made so by those who control it. Doesn't technology require inputs about a judge's life on a continuing periodic basis to ensure the public faith in the judiciary?

Of course the view on all this depends on the reference point used concerning such judicial conduct-institutional or personal, that is, what inures to institutional benefit or personal benefit or pleasure. One view of the film Padmavati (finally named Padmaavat) was that it reduced a woman to a vagina. Another was that it distorted history. A third was that it showed a fictional episode. The reference point can shift but the net result is that monuments become, like citizens, the victim of court arrears to the extent created by such a judicial culture.

The choice is between exercising authority by status combined with the potential violence of contempt power and authority by example of the judicial life actually lived.

The topping on this judicial culture is the institution of the Chief Justice of India. In view of the creeping addition by Parliament and the Union Government of an increasingly number of statutory non-judicial functions to the judicial functions of a judge and the rapid rise of litigation questioning the Government policies concerning the political economy, there is a compelling need to conceptualize the office of the Chief Justice of India for a radical overhaul. The Chief Justice of India apart from the court's judicial and administrative work today handles legal education, judicial diplomacy and the challenge of understanding governance, social change and his own colleagues. This requires a leadership that will create an internal team. Do we have the inter-se judge culture for this conceptual push driven by morality and public interest?

Constitutional culture is what it actually does and not what it proclaims. Monuments fall in the doing – proclamation gap. Probably that is why the caution, 'Mind the Gap'. The operating culture is one of alienation from oneself, others, culture and monuments. Citizens are missing from: the political administration of monuments, the distinct culture of citizens and operational court culture. The introduction and use of technology in the courts minus any concern as to what is needed by different classes of citizens accessing the court, messes up the court processes and administration. The question of those who should have access to the Court but are denied that access does not figure in court technology. The cultural perspective on technology is uniquely missing. Also missing is what happens with the increasing technological inputs into Courts to the judicial privacy/secrecy necessary to maintain judicial independence from the State providing the technology and from powerful private eyes ready to pay influence? The State is too ready to provide more and more security and the private sector more and more comfort.

We accordingly, come to the issue of the quality of access to justice for the citizen to protect one's distinct culture and monuments. The question that arises is as to why have national governments, with overwhelming electoral majorities in Parliament from 1950 onwards, not used their legislative power to bring in laws for ensuring this access for the enforcement of fundamental rights. Or, for ensuring even a fair distribution of work within the constitutional courts by fixing their internal subject divisions and the following of the seniority principles for such divisions? In the absence of this, issues on national heritage monuments like the Taj Mahal get tossed from bench to bench of the Supreme Court, be it under the Prevention of Corruption Act the Criminal Procedure Code or the environmental law. This invites in cases like that of the Taj Mahal, moves by other judges to check the flight of such matters from their bench by directing interim applications to be filed, instead of separate petitions which the Chief Justice of India could allot to any other bench. The judicial divisions so created in the highest court by cases of monuments and other subjects, suits politicians in power. The Supreme Court becomes a court of benches giving rise to the practising lawyers question 'Before which bench is the case?' That we have become comfortable with this question and treat it as normal, shows something about ourselves.

Yet there is an uncomfortable feeling that flows, when judges of the highest court have chosen to fight elections for high constitutional posts or accepted post retirement posts in commissions of inquiry, tribunals, the ICJ, task forces and Commissions, State governorships.

Post retirement arbitrations with a few retired judges monopolising the business is another troublesome venture of such judges. The late Justice A.C Gupta's refusal to charge more fees as an arbitrator than what his senior Justice H.R. Khanna was charging generally in arbitrations, is a judicial culture that is lost and even laughed upon. Inter-se deference to the duration of judicial experience seems to be a lost cause as is a consideration of its effect on the institution. The issue is of judges judging one another? How do monuments fit into this?

Monuments have little chance when corruption cases related to them become the subject of the interplay of critical voting support of the Centre in Parliament by another political party's MPs of the government of the State wherein the monument is located and that very Central Government is to decide the next Chief Justice of India. When this happens, should the judge concerned recuse himself from the case dealing with the monument of national importance?

Monuments of national importance also raise the issue of whether there is a Supreme Court of India as mentioned in the Constitution or a Supreme Court of Benches. Constitutional tension peaked when the Supreme Court bench had to decide the correctness and propriety of the Governor's order refusing sanction for the prosecution of the Chief Minister on an FIR registered against the Chief Minister on the complaint of the Supreme Court in the Taj Mahal Heritage Corridor Project. The investigation against the Chief Minister had been monitored step by step by the Supreme Court and it was still monitoring the case. Or, when a business house with a firm finger on the political economy of a State wherein the monument is located, takes over massive chunks of rich agricultural land for construction of express ways between the national capital and the monument, presents a fait accompli to the court and questions orally for days the very jurisdiction of the court to pass orders in public interest petitions concerning nationally important monuments like the Taj Mahal. It raised these questions in its own petition seeking sanction of the court for its constructions, on the basis of legal sanctions obtained by it already from the ruling politicians and their administrative departments.

After this its senior counsel again orally prayed for withdrawal of their own petition. After taking several days of the court's public time on the arguments of the counsel and the amicus, the court delivered no order even on the national loss of valuable top soil concerning the rich agricultural land. Its order kept quiet on the written submissions of the amicus.

In both instances the Supreme Court became a court of benches and not an integral institution as stated in the Constitution. In the first matter, it became so by an order of the court and in the second by the matter being transferred administratively, out of the bench fixed by a judicial order, to another bench.

This compels the question as to why no Union Government or Parliament has thought it fit under Art. 32(3) of the Constitution to legislate, for arming the district judiciary, (unfortunately named by the Constitution as the subordinate courts) with the power to issue the writs which high courts and the Supreme Court can issue and thereby give access to the justice of fundamental rights, including that of culture, to 1.3 billion.

The wealth process lobby for fast track commercial courts can get such courts, but for the billion in mofussil areas or villages there is no such movement by the governors of India for fast track fundamental rights courts. Fundamental rights today cover everything from childhood survival, health, education, skills livelihood to family life and culture, role of the police and the Union or State Ministries. But the absence of writ power to the nearest taluka courts for the villager, renders these judgments of the Supreme Court into mere declaratory ones when its constitutional duty under Art. 32 is to ensure **'enforcement'** of fundamental rights.

Can a majority population struggling for bare survival, despite Supreme Court's binding declarations on food, health, shelter and gender, ensure the protection and preservation of their distinct culture of monuments? Should they even be bothered about monuments which relieve their undeserved poverty by using these as free shelter? Except for the late Justice E.S. Venkataramiah of the Supreme Court, no other Supreme Court judge has raised this as a public issue at public forums. Yet, without such access to fundamental rights in the nearest taluka court, the ordinary villager can have little chance of seeking protection for his agricultural land, its top soil, his monuments and distinct culture. He has neither time nor money to run every time to the Supreme Court or the high court. He does not have the security of the Constitutional goods, like food, health, education and shelter, due to him being charged on the Consolidated Fund of India.

The struggle for a constitutional culture in courts is shown by the 1999 All India Chief Justices Conference followed by the Supreme Court's declaration through the Chief Justice of India of a 16 point Restatement of "Values of Judicial Life (Code of Conduct)" and its outright but binding judicial rejection by a two judge bench in 2003 for its application to high court judges in Indira Jaising vs. Registrar General Supreme Court.

Despite its own judgment the Supreme Court has taken to itself the administrative power of launching its own in-house inquiries on allegations against judges of high courts, with these reports being published in the media, when the Constitution does not give it any administrative power over the high courts. In the Indira Jaising judgment the court had declared, "In our constitutional scheme it is not possible to vest the Chief Justice with any control over the puisne judges with regard to conduct either personal or judicial." The judgment pointed out that the in house procedure is meant only for the 'personal information and satisfaction of the Chief Justice of India'. The judgment declared that the Code of Conduct has no legal sanction. But the aforesaid judgment left an in-terrorem weapon by stating that on acceptable allegations through the in-house procedure the Chief Justice of India could choose not to post cases before a particular judge against whom there are 'acceptable allegations'. A judiciary of fear can have little solace for what we have mentioned in the book as monuments of fear. It pits the culture and monuments of citizens who have been subjected to atrocities despite the Constitution and the courts, against the managers of the Constitution responsible for the culture that defeats the Constitution. Is there a need to rethink the structure of the Indian judiciary from the district court upwards and abolish the distinction between between Constitutional Courts and the other Courts which actually cater to the maximum number number of citizens? Can there be a Constitutional culture by keeping the district courts deprived of the power to enforce fundamental rights including that of culture itself?

Little seems to have been culturally learnt in the administration of the judiciary by the Supreme Court from the measured public rebuke given some years ago by the late Sabyasachi Mukharji, the then judge of the Calcutta high court, to the Supreme Court bench laying down specific time lines for a hearing and a decision for dealing with an electoral rolls case in that high court. Fear became palpable in this case.

While returning together from an All India Lawyers Conference on Legal Education at Agra, Justice Mukharji stopped at the Lord Krishna temple at Mathura to thank the Lord for his elevation to the Supreme Court. He told me, that on an earlier visit it is only in this temple, after passing the order at the high court and sending it to the Supreme Court, he had the intuitive message that his elevation would not stop because of the truthful stand he had taken on the Supreme Court order while complying with that order. God saves us and monuments. In this context, this book is a small and humble attempt to unravel through monuments of national importance, the political takeover of the fundamental right of citizens to their distinct culture and the approach of the Supreme Court to such monuments, particularly the Taj Mahal, which is the world's longest court monitored monument.

Constitutionally the fundamental right to culture and the dignity of the individual therein, form part of the constitutional component called social justice. But the Constitution required the social, economic and political to be taken together in all exercise of power. The political, business, administration and the professional class split this trinity of social, economic and political, especially in the wealth creation policies and processes through enacted and executive law. When such an approach of wealth and job creation, resulted in pollution that affected monuments of national importance, like the Taj Mahal, the Supreme Court too ignored the splitting of the trinity, the fundamental right to culture and its logical consequence. It is extremely rare to find the Supreme Court applying Directive Principles tests or the test of impact on ordinary citizens in taxation and revenue cases before it. Yet the Taj Mahal is an admitted revenue machine today inspite of the fundamental right to culture and the Directive Principle of the Constitution obliging the State to protect it.

The tragedy here is that the Supreme Court pursued this approach of not applying the social, economic and political as a trinity, in the cases on preservation and protection of monuments of national importance despite its attention having been drawn to the issue of sustainable development around, and sustainable tourism in, a monument. No advocate of the State or of a private party carrying on business in or near a monument would be paid to address all this to the court.

Monuments of national importance mirror the way we have worked the constitutional provisions to ensure fundamental rights for a few instead of all, under a Constitution that effectively disguised poverty, powerlessness and the lack of information for reducing these. The Constitution spelt out fundamental rights and freedoms from specific social evils, without requiring anywhere those commanding and enjoying State power, to tackle the causes of such evils, or to hold any one in the governance of the State accountable in terms of remedies. Accountability had to be on the basis of holding responsible the administrator and/or the elected politician for the denial of these rights to the citizens under his territorial jurisdiction with respect to which he enjoys extensive legal powers, status and comforts or from where the politician gets elected.

Under such constitutional governance of unaccountability, the preservation and protection of monuments suffers from the conversion of monuments into the wealth process of revenue tourism to make culture for a few instead of all. Like the malls, footfalls define the importance of a monument. The constitutional category of monuments of national importance gets divided into those with a heavy, medium and no footfall. The money available for their maintenance and protection is a correlation of this footfall. This effectively replaces the constitutional criteria for a monument of national importance in Art. 49, that of artistic or historic importance. It also replaces the legislative competence criteria for a monument of national importance in Entry 67 List I of the Constitution of India, that of ancient and historical. Worse, it hides the monument's background of suffering of the one sought to be made monumentally immortal in stone and of the condition of the people of that era, to contextualise any celebration that the monument is supposed to represent. The book examines this entire process, hoping that its awareness across a larger arena may help in examining ourselves, our cultures, monuments and our society in the struggle for a constitutional India, even under a Constitution drafted to hold no one accountable for even the dignity of bare survival. Deep inequality of suffering makes way for monumental illegality — both for humans and monuments.

This raises fundamental questions about the functioning, vis a vis monuments, of the three key constitutional institutions — Parliament, the Union Government and the Judiciary. What have Parliament, the Union Government and the Supreme Court done to our monuments of national importance? How has this been done? This book tries to answer these questions by showing how the fundamental right to culture under the Constitution has not simply been ignored but also harmed, in the case of monuments of national importance, which India is bound to protect as a fundamental principal of governance.

ACKNOWLEDGEMENTS

This book belongs to the legal-cultural genre. It is probably the first Indian law book which studies the impact on national monuments of law, as enacted, administered and adjudicated. It is based on the infinite area of culture and the finite area of specific laws concerning national monuments and court judgments, orders as also applications and pleadings. This enterprise, which commenced about six years ago with the nudge of my friend Prof. (Dr.) K.N. Chandrasekhran Pillai, former Director of the Indian Law Institute, owes much to many.

My thanks to former Supreme Court Justices Kuldip Singh, Saghir Ahmed, Ruma Pal, M.B. Shah, S.B Sinha, Chief Justices of India V.N Khare, R.C. Lahoti, S.H. Kapadia, for chiseling the architecture of legal thought through the thrust and parry of the various court proceedings that took place before them on issues relating to monuments of national importance. Chief Justice R.C. Lahoti quite often expressed his discomfort in open court, when the matter was mentioned before him, that the bench of the Taj Mahal case had already been decided by his outgoing predecessor's order before he took over as Chief Justice. So, he could not as Chief Justice of India do anything, when problems concerning orders passed by that bench were mentioned before him. This is especially true concerning the Taj Mahal, the case in which I was amicus for over a decade. The Taj Mahal remains the only international heritage monument which has been monitored for the longest period by the highest court in any Anglo-Saxon law country.

Post-retirement appointment of judges by a government do not happen instantly or overnight. Should a sitting judge be in touch with ruling politicians for such posts? And what happens if he is handling cases involving this very political class. The cost, both monetary and of values like independence, of the increasing judicial footprint of sitting Supreme Court judges in non-judicial fields remains to be calculated. And is it warranted by the Constitution? But this directly impinges on the Bar as shown by the free for all struggle to win howsoever in various bar elections or to create fiefdoms of various lawyer's associations for possible spheres of influence in the judiciary itself. What is a foolish amicus in cases of monuments doing with his time, is a question that hauntingly creeps up? My thanks to all those who enabled me to see this first hand in actual operation, both from outside and then from within the legal profession.

There are amicus who work so closely with the judges on a bench that they get to control access to the court on the subject matter being handled by them. They become empowered to decide which applications should be heard and which not heard by the bench without any provision for protesting to the bench against the unwritten decision of the amicus. An amicus who specifically tells the judges that he would not want to have this power bestowed on him by a judicial order, again belongs to the foolish class of advocates. What does being amicus or a friend of the court mean? Many times in the Supreme Court the distinction between being a friend of the court and being a friend of the judges on the bench seems to disappear. It appears, that an amicus is supposed to swim along with whatever the judges on the bench want. The amicus who does this seems to become an empowered amicus. The distinction between serving the institution of the court and serving the judges is fading away. Such a role as amicus is strong temptation with the chance of great fame as an effective counsel.

An example of this has been the Hawala or the Jain Diaries case. Every Friday the bench would clear out everybody from the court room — the lawyers, the litigants, the duly accredited legal correspondents and the interested public — except the amicus, the government counsel and officials. The doors of the courtroom would be shut. This was done without any order for in-camera hearing. There was not a word from the amicus on this complete negation of a court as a public court for a public hearing, unless specific orders to the contrary are passed, based on public interest. The irony of this being done in public interest litigation cannot be missed. But as practising lawyers we dare not publicly debate the role of an amicus in public interest litigation, which is the category that covers the cases of monuments in the Supreme Court. The judicial effect on such debate is chilling. My thanks to those who gave me the chance of working as amicus in the Taj Mahal protection, Ganges Pollution, Police Custody death, leprosy patients, bonded labour and carcass flayers cases in the Supreme Court.

The reason for the chilling effect is that the Supreme Court has become a place of judicial conflict, with sons, daughters and other close relatives of judges practising in the Supreme Court itself and the steady disappearance of the judicial spirit of firm disciplined tolerance while guiding young lawyers. Is this what happens when one increasingly relies for respect on the title of judge, no matter how you have arrived there, regardless of your ability or inability. The process of becoming a judge is a great leveller. But what happens to values? The late Chief Justice of India Y.V. Chandrachud during his tenure did not permit his lawyer son (now a Judge of the Supreme Court) anywhere near the Supreme Court.

I owe special thanks to the former Chief Justice of India Shri T.S. Thakur, Justices Arjun Sikri, Sanjay Kishan Kaul and two active Vice Chancellors in legal education, Prof. (Dr.) Mustafa Faizan and Prof. (Dr.) P.S. Jaswal, for their help in easing my switchover to academics, from an intense, monetarily richer court advocacy in a sharply deteriorating moral environment of legal business. Unfortunately, we hardly discuss the nature of legal business, its cross-country organisation from the district court to high court and the Supreme Court while discussing arrears, the doings of the creamiest section of lawyers in this regard and its corrosive effect on court administrations, and the independence of the judiciary.

The question is not one of knowledge of law. It is about integrity in many diverse ways beyond the mere monetary to social responsibility and accountability. Legal education today notoriously misses out on all this, since usually the actual practice of law is not brought into the classroom. There are hardly any full time law teachers with the necessary court experience, capable of bringing this truth into the lives of young law students. But our young law students catch on quickly to this from their first internship in a court. That drives several of them to seek refuge and a livelihood in the civil or judicial services and mistakenly in corporate rather than litigation practice. We are unwilling to face and even debate this truth, for any meaningful reform of the legal profession, the judiciary and legal education. So legal education has no course on the law of organising and managing legal business as a lawyer, even for a professional degree.

That this happens when retired Supreme Court judges practising lawyers and law academics are on the legal education committee of the Bar Council of India or in the curriculum committees of the UGC, which determine the subjects that must be taught in institutions conferring professional or a non professional law degree, speaks for itself. It is in this culture of law that the battle for saving heritage monuments must be attempted.

In the context of this overall pain over what some influential judges and the creamiest lawyers have done to the public interest in the Supreme Court, where I have spent over forty years in various roles or capacities, the solace during this study, was the constant presence of the spirituality of the former Chief Justice of India, Shri M.N. Venkatachaliah. He belongs to the school of rare Supreme Court judges who after being sworn in as the Chief Justice of India told the then Prime Minister in the presence of his Law Minister that there should be no back channel communication with him or his office. Predictably, he turned down approaches through influential advocates of the wealth process, to have his consent for the office of the Vice President of India. His response to the five star hotel accommodation offered by the Union Government to him as the Chairman of the Commission to Review the Working of the Constitution of India, working by giving up the monthly sum due to him, and the post retirement rejection by him of offers for a SEBI post or lucrative arbitration, is to remind ourselves of a living judicial sanyasi which may need a detailed narration on another occasion. Reverence is the only tribute to such self-denial in an environment of desperate judicial competition for posts, going to the extent in the case of a Supreme Court judge resigning to accept the offer of a political party's ticket to contest the election from Assam.

There has been conspicuous judicial silence, especially from the Supreme Court, on the increasing number of posts being statutorily created by ruling politicians at the Centre, making Chief Justices of India and other judges eligible for these. The political class having set up this race, then decides whom to pick. Some Supreme Court judges have conferred on themselves a freedom of speech during and beyond adjudication, to comment on anything and anyone that catches their fancy. This is unprecedented judicial freedom in any rule of law country. Yet one does not hear a judge of the highest court, inside or outside the court, in the judicial or retirement avatar, holding up the flag of independence of the judiciary, against this statutory progress of the political class vis a vis the judiciary. The late Supreme Court Justice Fazal Ali's words about the necessity of a judge being a sanyasi to maintain judicial independence, today sound remote, having been rendered irrelevant by many of his twentieth and twenty first century colleagues. My thanks to a line of exceptionally learned judges of humble rectitude from at least the late Justice Fazal Ali onwards, who exposed me to what a judicial culture means, when I entered the Supreme Court as a novice.

The writing process could become intensely thoughtful because of the excellent environment provided at GLOCAL University by the Chancellor Shri Mohd. Iqbal, the Pro-Chancellor Shri Mohd. Wajid, the Additional Pro-Chancellor Prof. (Dr.) Om Kumar Harsh, the Vice-Chancellor Prof. (Dr.) B. L. Raina, the Head of GLOCAL's Department of Law Mr. Ayaz Ahmad and all other Deans, Professors and faculty members of the esteemed University. My sincerest thanks to all of them. The mountain ranges, the morning breeze, sunrise, sunset and an excellent cuisine say peace be unto all.

The family is a challenge to crafting a book and the courage to complete it. But it is also a source of tremendous holistic help. My wife Dr. Saroj Mahajan, a dedicated teacher for about fifty years, of Physics, and I, have battled life and prejudice, hand in hand. My son,. Siddhant and daughter-in-law Ms. Arti and the two grand children, created the ambience at home, which compelled me to push this work into the silences of the night. There is a vast array of advocate friends in the Supreme Court and courts across the country, academic friends across several universities and disciplines, friends in industry, trades and chambers of commerce, in administrative positions of governance, who deserve my thanks for helping in myriad ways.

The librarians at the Ravenshaw University (Odisha), Ratan Tata Library at University of Delhi, Central Archaeology, National Law University, Odisha, Rajiv Gandhi National University of Law, Punjab and Vidya Jyoti, Delhi, deserve grateful thanks in the desperate search for relevant materials that such a book pushes one into. The National Archives is so organised and managed that it is impossible to access relevant information within a reasonable time. When you do not want to give information, then simply tire out the seeker. Our urban poor and villagers face this daily. They are compelled to pay for what they seek urgently, since time is the essence of the usefulness of relevant information. The right to be informed instead of the mere right to information remains a distant dream for citizens, especially those who are illiterate four times over in reading and writing — mathematics, English, law and the digital. These poor therefore become the living monuments of unconstitutionality at large and a valuable guide for making choices, personal and professional.

My brilliant colleagues Assistant Professor Dr. Nachiketa Mittal, Assistant Registrar, Centre for Research & Planning, Supreme Court, and Mr. Tathagat Chatterjee doing vital work in the Union Ministry of Commerce on India's international trade and service agreements, deserve blessings for saving me time on several counts that simply cannot be enumerated. They were extremely thoughtful in doing what needed to be done without saying so. I would take this opportunity to thank my student Mr. Sughosh Nirgundh for his help in assisting me in learning the techniques of footnoting, editing and formatting. I am grateful to all of them.

Last but not the least there is a deep debt of gratitude to my dear friend, Dr. Yogesh Pratap Singh, Associate Professor, National Law University, Odisha and Deputy Registrar, Supreme Court., for enabling me to earn my doctoral degree in law by working on this study. As the Supervisor for the doctoral degree, he provided the necessary mental comfort, especially after the atrocious experience with the Indian Law Institute after the thesis was ready for submission. The political economy of research academics remains an unwritten saga of the Indian academic universe. Profound thanks to him for rescuing the work done for this study, even while he was struggling with his own life as a legal academic.

I was humbled in the course of my research by the interest and encouragement of my colleagues at National Law University, Odisha and Rajiv Gandhi National University of Law, Patiala to whom I have offered little in return apart from a cup of tea at times. I thank all of them for providing support. I would love to reciprocate this whenever we meet. The camaraderie of doing constructive academic work is a lasting bond. My special thanks to all at the Notion Press for the work put in to bring out this book and make it accessible.

I have been fortunate therefore to have a diverse community that provided the ambience for the struggle towards this book. My thanks to those who chose to stop this study and profound thanks to those who still enabled me to complete it. Needless to say, the shortcomings and faults, of which I would be delighted to be informed, are entirely mine. I pray that the inner voice remains alive to guide me on. Temptation lurks seductively between chance and necessity.

– **Dr. Krishan Mahajan**

TABLE OF CASES

1. A.B. Bhaskara Rao vs. CBI (2011) 10 SCC 259.
2. A.K. Gopalan Vs. State of Madras AIR 1950 SC 27.
3. A.R. Antulay Vs. R.S. Nayak AIR 88 SC 1531.
4. A.S. Narayana Deekshitulu vs. State of Andhra Pradesh AIR 1996 SC 1765.
5. Acharya J. Avadhuta vs. Commissioner of Police AIR 1984 SC 51.
6. Andhra Pradesh Pollution Control Board vs. Prof. M.V. Nayadu, AIR, 1999 SC 812.
7. Andhra Pradesh Pollution Control Board vs. Prof. M.V. Nayadu, AIR 1999 SC 812.
8. Animal and Environmental Legal Defense Fund vs. Union of India, AIR 97 SC 1071.
9. Anju Johri vs. Union of India 118 (2005) DLT 418.
10. Archaeological Survey of India V. Narendra Anand, 144 (2007) DLT 794.
11. Arun Kumar Agrawal vs. National Insurance Co. Ltd.(2010) 9 SCC 218.
12. Ashok Kumar vs. Union of India and Ors. 2004 (111) DLT 230.
13. Aswini Kumar Ghose vs. Arabinda Bose AIR 52 SC 369.
14. Baljeet Singh Malik vs. Delhi Golf Club 1997 (1) SCALE (S.P.) 19.
15. Bandua Mukti Morcha vs. Union of India (1984) 3 SCC 161.
16. Bandhua Mukti Morcha vs. Union of India (1991) 4 SCC 177.
17. Bandhua Mukti Morcha vs. Union of India (1997) 10 SCC 549.
18. Commr. HRE vs. Lakhshindra AIR 54 SC 282.
19. D.K. Basu vs. State of West Bengal (1997) 1 SCC 416.
20. Dinesh Trivedi vs. Union of India (1997) 4 SCC 306.
21. Dinesh Trivedi vs. Union of India (1997) 4 SCC 306.
22. EMCA Construction Co. vs. Archaeological Survey of India, 2009 164 DLT 515.
23. Hill vs. Bank of San Pedro 107 P. 2d 399, 404, 41 Cal. App. 2D 595.

24. In re Central Provinces & Berar Sales of Motor Spirit and Lubricants Taxation Act, 1938, AIR 1939 FC 1.
25. Indira Jaising vs. Union of India 2003 5 SCC 494.
26. Indramani vs. W.R. Natu, A'63 SC 274 at 281 Para 15.
27. Ismail vs. union of India AIR 1995 SC 605.
28. Jagdev Singh Sidhanti vs. Pratap Singh Daulta AIR 1965 SC 183.
29. Kesvananda Bharati vs. State of Kerala (1973) 4 SCC 225.
30. L.N. Pandey vs. Union of India (1991) 4 SCC 33.
31. M.C. Mehta vs. Archaeological Survey of India 1996 (8) SCALE (S.P.) 11.
32. M.C. Mehta vs. Union of India (1998) 9 SCC 589.
33. M.C. Mehta vs. Union of India (1996)(1) SCALE (S.P.) 16.
34. M.C. Mehta vs. Union of India (1996)(2) SCALE (S.P.) 88.
35. M.C. Mehta vs. Union of India (1996)(3) SCALE (S.P.) 56.
36. M.C. Mehta vs. Union of India, CWP 3727/1985 (Ganges Pollution Case).
37. M.C. Mehta vs. Union of India, (1997) 3 SCC 715;(C.W.P. 13381/84, I.A. 376/2003.
38. M.C. Mehta vs. Union of India, (1998) 9 SCC 589.
39. M.C. Mehta vs. Union of India, (1996)(1) Scale (SP) 16.
40. M.C. Mehta vs. Union of India, (1996)(3) Scale (SP) 58.
41. M.C. Mehta vs. Kamalnath (1997) 1 SCC 388.
42. M.C. Mehta vs. Kamalnath (1997) 1 SCC 388.
43. M.C. Mehta vs. Kamalnath, A 2000 SC 1998.
44. M.C. Mehta vs. Union of India (1998) 1 SCC 471.
45. M.C. Mehta vs. Union of India AIR 97 SC 734.
46. M.C. Mehta vs. Union of India [CWP 13381/84](The Taj case).
47. Maneka Gandhi vs. Union of India AIR 1978 SC 597.
48. McKeon vs. Central Stamping.Co. C.C.A.N.J. 264 F.385;387.
49. Mohini Jain vs. State of Karnataka AIR 92 SC 1858.
50. N.D. Jaya vs. Union of India (2004) 9 SCC 362.
51. Nand Kishore vs. State of Punjab 1995 6 SCC 614.
52. Narmada Bachao Andolan vs. Union of India (2000) 10 SCC 664.
53. Nilabati Behera vs. State of Orissa (1993) 2 SCC 746.
54. Nilabati Behra vs. State of Orissa AIR 81 SC 746.
55. Orissa Industries Ltd vs. Archaeological Survey of India, Writ Petition © 20433/2009.

56. People's Union of Civil Liberties vs. Union of India 1997 1 SCC 301.
57. Prakash Singh vs. Union of India, Judgment dated September 22, 2006 in C.W.P. 310 of 1996.
58. Rajeev Mankotia vs. Secretary to the President of India, (1997) 10 SCC 441.
59. Ram Sharan vs. Union of India AIR 1989 SC 549.
60. Ram Sharan vs. Union of India AIR 1989 SC 549.
61. Reliance Petrochemicals Ltd. vs. Props of India Express AIR 1989 SC 190.
62. Roseline Wilson vs. Union of India, 2007 139 DLT 462.
63. S.P. Gupta vs. Union of India AIR 82 SC 149.
64. S.R. Bommi vs. Union of India AIR, 1994 SC 1918.
65. Samatha vs. State of Andhra Pradesh 1997 8 SCC 191.
66. SC Advocates on Record Association vs. Union of India (1993) 4 SCC 141.
67. State of Himanchal Pradesh vs. Ganesh Wood Products AIR 1996 SC 149.
68. State of Maharashtra vs. Sarangharsingh Chavan (2011) 1 SCC 577.
69. State of Orissa vs. Ganesh Chandra Jew (2004) 8 SCC 40.
70. Sudhir Goyal vs. Municipal; Corporation of Delhi. 2004 (112) DLT 249.
71. Sunil Batra vs. Delhi Administration AIR 1980 SC 579.
72. Supreme Court Bar Association Vs. Union of India AIR 1998 SC 1895.
73. TMA Pai Foundation vs. State of Karnataka AIR 2003 SC 355.
74. T.N. Godavarman vs. Union of India W.P. No. 202 of 1995.
75. Tamil Nadu vs. K. Shyam Sunder (2011) 8 SCC 737.
76. Unni Krishnan J.P. vs. State of Andhra Pradesh (1993) 1 SCC 645.
77. V.P. Singh vs. Union of India 2003 (102) D.L.T.72.
78. Vellore Citizens Forum vs. Union of India, (1996) 5 SCC 647.
79. Vellore Citizens Welfare Forum vs. Union of India AIR 1996 SC 2720–2727.
80. Vellore Citizens' Forum vs. Union of India, A'96 SC 2715.
81. Venkatarama Aiyar J. in Venkataramana Devaru vs. State of Mysore AIR 58 SC 255.
82. Victoria Memorial Hall vs. Howrah Ganatantrik Nagrik Samity (2010) 3 SCC 732.

83. Vineet Naryan vs. Union of India AIR 1998 SC 889.
84. Virender Gaur vs. State of Haryana (1995) 2 SCC 577.
85. Vishaka vs. State of Rajasthan (1997) 6 SCC 241.
86. Wasim Ahmad Saeed vs. Union of India, 1996(1) SCALE (S.P.) 19.
87. Wasim Ahmad Saeed vs. Union of India, 1996(6) SCALE (SP) 11.
88. Wasim Ahmad Saeed vs. Union of India 1997(5) SCALE 451.
89. Wasim Ahmad Saeed vs. Union of India and Others, (2002) 9 SCC 472 and 475.
90. Yashwant vs. Union of India CWP No. 10210/85.

LIST OF ABBREVIATIONS

Sr. No.		FULL FORM
	A	
1	AIR	ALL INDIA REPORTER
2	ASI	ARCHAEOLOGICAL SURVEY OF INDIA
	B	
3	BBC	BRITISH BROADCASTING CORPORATION
	C	
4	CAG	COMPTROLLER & AUDITOR GENERAL
5	CISF	CENTRAL INDUSTRIAL SECURITY FORCE
6	COS	COMMITTEE OF UNION GOVERNMENT SECRETARIES
7	CPCB	CENTRAL POLLUTION CONTROL BOARD
8	Cr.P.C	CRIMINAL PROCEDURE CODE
	I	
9	I.A	INTERIM APPLICATION
10	IAS	INDIAN ADMINISTRATIVE SERVICE
11	ICCROM	INTERNATIONAL CENTRE FOR THE CONSERVATION AND RESTORATION OF MONUMENTS
12	ICESCR	INTERNATIONAL COVENANT ON ECONOMIC, SOCIAL AND CULTURAL RIGHTS
13	ICCPR	INTERNATIONAL COVENANT ON CIVIL AND POLITICAL RIGHTS

14	ICOMOS	INTERNATIONAL COUNCIL OF MONUMENTS & SITES
15	ICTC	INTERNATIONAL CULTURAL TOURISM CHARTER
16	IMF	INTERNATIONAL MONETARY FUND
17	INTO	INTERNATIONAL NATIONAL TRUST ORGANISATION
18	INTACH	INDIAN NATIONAL TRUST FOR ART & CULTURE
19	IPC	INDIAN PENAL CODE
20	ITDC	INDIAN TOURISM DEVELOPMENT CORPORATION
	M	
21	MoEF	MINISTRY OF ENVIRONMENT & FORESTS
22	MOU	MEMORANDUM OF UNDERSTANDING
	N	
23	NEDA	NON-CONVENTIONAL ENERGY DEVELOPMENT
24	NEERI	NATIONAL ENVIRONMENT ENGINEERING RESEARCH INSTITUTE
25	NRICCP	NATIONAL RESEARCH LABORATORY FOR CONSERVATION OF CULTURAL PROPERTY
	R	
26	RFID	RADIO FREQUENCY IDENTIFICATION DEVICE
	S	
27	SCC	SUPREME COURT CASES
28	SCR	SUPREME COURT REPORTS

29	SCALE	WEEKLY SUPREME COURT REPORTS
30	SP	SUPERINTENDENT OF POLICE
	T	
31	TMCC	TAJ MAHAL CONSERVATION COLLABORATIVE
32	TTZ	TAJ TRAPEZIUM ZONE
	U	
33	UDHR	UNIVERSAL DECLARATION OF HUMAN RIGHTS
34	UNESCO	UNITED NATIONS EDUCATIONAL, SCIENTIFIC AND CULTURAL ORGANISATION
35	UNIDROIT	INSTITUTE OF THE INTERNATIONAL COMMISSION FOR THE UNIFICATION OF PRIVATE LAW

PART – I
THE LEGISLATIVE FRAMEWORK

Chapter I
LEGAL CULTURE OF MONUMENTS

Monuments. Who can declare these to be of "national importance?" Is there a fair, just and reasonable procedure to make such a declaration? That done, the State is constitutionally obliged to protect these. Does the obligation to protect make the Central Government ruling politicians the sole controllers of the monuments? Or does the fundamental right of citizens to their culture and their constitutional duty to preserve such monuments as their composite cultural heritage make citizens the prime controllers of such monuments? Have the ruling politicians at the Centre ever done something, since independence, to enable citizens to exercise their fundamental right to culture, of which monuments form a part. Is India a country of cultural minorities, regardless of religion, and therefore inherently a democratic country of myriad choices of composite culture or ways of life?

1.1 The Study

This book is a study of the role of Parliament, the Union Government and the Supreme Court of the method and manner by which the Supreme Court and some High Courts have tried to ensure the protection of monuments of national importance in the given framework of the Constitution of India and the laws thereunder. The study on nationally important monuments pertains specifically to Article 49 read with Entry 67 List I of the VIIth Schedule of the Constitution of India and the Parliamentary statute, the Ancient Monuments & Archaeological Sites and Remains Act, 1958.[1] This is sought to be understood in terms of how the cultural power of citizens on monuments was taken away by Parliament and Union Government's ruling political class, what they did with this power and ultimately whether the Supreme Court used its

---
[1] *Hereinafter 'Ancient Monuments Act' for brevity.*

power to protect the cultural spirit of such monuments and give back to citizens their fundamental right to monuments as part of their culture.

1.2 Study in Two Parts

The book is divided into two parts. The First Part examines the constitutional, statutory and international law framework. The second part examines the judicial implementation of this framework as shown by the judgments of the Supreme Court and the High Courts, to understand the role of the judiciary in the preservation of ancient heritage monuments.

Part I: Legislative Framework

1.2.1 Text & Context: Inter & Multi-disciplinary

The text for the study is the framework of constitutional, statutory and international law provisions. This makes the study interdisciplinary. The context is the relevant disciplines like history, geography and economics, embracing within them various other disciplines like sociology, to understand the meaning of the constitutional and legal provisions. Hence the work is multi-disciplinary. Both approaches raise the question as to what does a monument signify.

This initiated a widespread search for concepts, data and inter-linkages. Accordingly, the study has been carried out at the following libraries: Archaeological Survey of India, Delhi; Delhi High Court; Department of History, Delhi University; Department of Geography, Delhi University; Department of Sociology, Delhi University; National Law University, Odisha, Cuttack; Nehru Memorial Museum, Delhi; Rajiv Gandhi National Law University, Patiala, Punjab; Vidya Jyoti and Ratan Tata, Delhi; Ravenshaw University, Cuttack, Odisha, Parliament and Supreme Court. The study necessitated an examination of the case records of the Supreme Court and high courts, concerning protected monuments of national importance. It also required an analysis of the related judgments of the Supreme Court and several high courts.

The National Archives, Delhi, is so designed and managed that it is impossible to access relevant material within a reasonable time.

1.2.2 Relevant Constitutional Law

Since the Constitution of India is the prime legal source for the protection and preservation of monuments as described therein, the study takes a holistic approach to an understanding of the relevant Articles of the Constitution. The consequence of the aforesaid holistic approach is that the book has evolved into the larger constitutional concept of cultural heritage of which religion forms a significant part.

On this basis the book deals with Article 49 (national importance brand of monuments & consequences of the Seventh Constitutional Amendment in 1956), Art. 245(1) read with Entry 67, List I (kind of monuments — artistic, historic, ancient and historical — conundrum between Art. 49 and this Entry), Schedule VII; Art. 245(3) read with Entry 12 List II, (State brand of monuments in contrast to national brand under Art. 49) Seventh Schedule; Art. 245(2) read with Entry 40 List III, (Common area of Centre & States – non nationally important archaeological sites and remains, Seventh Schedule; Arts 25 (religious monuments e.g. Islamic funerary monuments and temples) & 26 (religious denomination monuments); Art. 51A(f) — composite cultural heritage; Art. 29 — fundamental right to culture and the Preamble (fraternity, unity and integrity) of the Constitution of India. It also deals with politically divisive monuments and monuments of fear, which though not monuments of national importance, yet can alter national and local politics of religion and culture.

Reference is made to Art. 21 of the Constitution also since the Supreme Court in the cases of monuments before it has never adopted the fundamental right to culture approach of Art. 29 with the cultural heritage approach under Art. 51A(f). Instead, when talking of culture, it has adopted the Art. 21 approach as shown by the Supreme Court's judgment in the Ramsharan case.[2] Can the Supreme Court decide

---

[2] Ramsharan Autyanuprasi vs. UOI, (1989) Supp SCC 251 (Alternately referred to as "Sawai Man Singh II case).

cases of monuments of national importance and of politically divisive monuments which have not been declared as monuments of national importance, by ignoring the fundamental right of citizens to their distinct culture and of the citizen's duty to preserve the rich heritage of India's composite culture?

The Supreme Court has nowhere addressed the question of what is the constitutional end that the fundamental right to culture or the preservation and protection of monuments of national importance is meant to achieve. The book points out that the constitutional end can only be the goals mentioned in the Preamble — fraternity, unity and integrity of India. A culture which goes against achieving this end by constitutional means is not constitutional culture. Legally, constitutional culture is the filter for India's past of custom, usage, tradition, ways of conducting life and treating monuments. Has the Supreme Court's approach and methods in cases of monuments, resulted in a national loss of building a constitutional foundation for understanding India through its culture of monuments?

The book focuses on shaping a holistic constitutional understanding of monuments from this network of Articles. Accordingly, it examines the key word in the Art. 29 fundamental right — culture, in the light of the broad international lines of thinking on culture. We examine further the choices available to the Congress Government and Parliament, at the time of the coming into force in 1950 of the major portion of the Constitution (Article 394), including Art. 29 and the approach adopted of ignoring Art. 29 and adopting the Entry 67 List I, VIIth Schedule of the Constitution approach to enact the Ancient and Historical Monuments and Archaeological Sites and Remains (Declaration of National Importance) Act, 1951.

The ignoring of Art. 29 is explained by the steady takeover since 1951, by the then Union of India, of culture, through a string of official institutions, since 1951. We also examine the constitutional coup by the Congress Government and Parliament in 1956 by enacting the Seventh Constitution Amendment to expand the declaration of monuments of national importance from the original "by a law" to such a declaration made "under a law," in Art. 49 and Entry 67 List I, VIIth Schedule of the Constitution. The follow up of this is examined in the statutory law enacted two years later, in 1958, The Ancient Monuments and Archaeological Sites and Remains Act, enacted "under a law" provision to convert the declaration of monuments as of national importance into an executive function from the original Parliamentary function prior to the 1956 Seventh Constitution Amendment.

The book does not cover monuments under Panchayats, which have a conditional power under Art. 243G read with Item 21 "cultural activities," in the XIth Schedule to the Constitution. The reason for this is that monuments of national importance are exclusively a subject for Parliament or the Union Government, in terms of Art. 49 and Entry 67 of List I of the VIIth Schedule to the Constitution. The power under Art. 243G is 'subject to the provisions of the Constitution', that is to Art. 49 and Entry 67 List I, VIIth Schedule of the Constitution. Further the panchayat's power to deal with any monument in its jurisdiction under the head "cultural activities," Item 21 in Eleventh Schedule, is dependent in terms of Article 243G on the State legislature enacting a law empowering them specifically with the authority, conditional or otherwise, to deal with such monuments. The States have no constitutional competence to legislatively or administratively deal with the subject of monuments of national importance, since Entry 12 of List II in the VIIth Schedule of the Constitution, clearly says, inter alia, "monuments...other than those declared by Parliament by or under a law to be of national importance." Entry 40 in List III of the VIIth Schedule of the Constitution deals only with the subject of archaeological sites and remains and not with monuments at all.

The same reasons, as in the case of Panchayats, apply to Municipalities power to deal with monuments under Art. 243W read with Entry 13 of the XIIth Schedule of the Constitution, under the head "promotion of cultural, educational and aesthetic aspects." Hence the book does not cover this area also.

1.2.3 Relevant Statutory Law

The statutory law examined is the Ancient Monuments Act, 1958, its amendments in 2010, in the context of the functioning of the Union

Ministry of Culture, which administers the Act. It also refers to The Water (Prevention & Control of Pollution) Act, 1974, the Air (Prevention and Control of Pollution) Act, 1981 and The Environment Protection Act, 1986, since the Supreme Court has largely taken the environmental approach to the protection of monuments or once in a while the cultural objects approach of the Ancient Monuments Act, 1958,[3] instead of the Art. 29 read with Art. 51A(f) and the Preamble approach of composite cultural heritage that ensures fraternity and the unity and integrity of India. Reference is also made to the Places of Worship (Special Provisions) Act, 1991, read with S.16, Protection of Places of Worship from Misuse, Pollution or Desecration, of the Ancient Monuments Act, 1958.

1.2.4 Multi-disciplinary Linkages

a) **History:** Monuments are mute spectators marking a territorial space in the continuum of time — past, present and future. They mark the instant and await as to how human beings treat them. So whether it is Art. 49 monuments (artistic or historical interest) or Entry 67 List I of the Seventh Schedule of the Constitution monuments (ancient and historical), a monument is part of history. But all history is not monuments alone. A monument of national importance, declared to be so by the State, is the view of the rulers of the history in which the monument is situated. Ancient is a temporal fact fixed by rulers for recognizing a monument. 'Historical' is a fact of the events evaluated by the rulers by which they give their meaning to a monument. A monument of national importance is a value judgment of the events in which a monument is located and for which it is recognized by the rulers. History therefore is the power to review and interpret events and mark these by a monument of that time. The evaluation bench mark is rarely stated by the rulers. But does Art. 49, creating on the rulers the obligation to protect monuments, declared by or under a law made by Parliament, take history as a symptom or a cause? Is a monument indicative of a historical symptom that is recognized

---

[3] Rajeev Mankotia vs. Secretary to the President of India, AIR 1997 SC 2766.

so that the cause of the symptom does not become visible or too visible, like the symptoms of various historical ills mentioned in the Fundamental Rights Chapter of the Constitution. Or is it the mark of a cause that should or should not have happened in time past. The answers depend on which history one recognizes and whether its recognition is derived or not from the culture or way of life at that point of time. These issues vis a vis monuments of national importance become an examination of the idea of history and whether it is linked to a stated aim of the kind of society the rulers want to create — one of fraternity, unity and integrity of the nation based on composite heritage of culture that works towards a culture of personal liberty, free speech and non arbitrary but transparent, public or private governance. The work herein deals with these issues, arising from the question as to what does a monument denote or symbolize?

b) **Geography:** Can the constitutional obligation to protect a monument of national importance be fulfilled without understanding as to why it was located at a certain place and how this original reason for the location can be used to preserve and protect the monument? This necessitates an examination of the physical, cultural, regional, economic, human and social geography and what it implies for the constitutional obligation of the rulers. The various kinds of geography necessarily bring in various strands of the sociological. If a monument is built and located to indicate the power of a conqueror over a subjugated people should it be recognised by the erstwhile subjects who are now independent, even though colonial rulers gave recognition to it?

c) **Economics:** The constitutional obligation to protect monuments of national importance has to be discharged in the ground reality of the structure of earning or livelihood opportunities, the pattern of spending and the conditions set up by the rulers for this purpose. In this context the book examines economics as a discipline for what it recognizes and what it does not. An objects approach, a cultural object approach and a cultural heritage approach to monuments entail different economic consequences for the idea of protection of monuments. If the rulers create an economic mechanism in which a national culture of illegality thrives and flourishes then what happens to monuments declared to be of national importance? Can monuments be protected when the economic system is worked by the rulers to negate the social order mandated by Art. 38 of the Constitution? Economic development is examined in the context of monuments.

1.2.5 International Law

The international commons of the cultural heritage in the form of monuments, located in nations, compels countries to get together for protecting this heritage. The international legal framework for the protection of monuments reveals that even in international law, the community has been replaced by the nation State *vis a vis* monuments. This is traced through the 1931 Athens Charter, the 1935 Roerich Pact to the 1954 Hague Convention for the Protection of Cultural Property in the Event of Armed Conflict, the 1957 agreement to set up under UNESCO the Centre for the Study of the Preservation & Restoration of Cultural Property and India becoming its member in 1961, the Venice Charter of 1964 on the Conservation and Restoration of Monuments resulting in the establishment of the International Council of Monuments & Sites (ICOMOS) and ending with the 1972 Convention Concerning the Protection of the World Cultural & Natural Heritage.

This brings in the kind of State that exists for the protection of monuments, because of the common internationally recognized threat to monuments, from economic development, modernization and globalization. Can India replace people by the State in the light of the fundamental right under Art. 29 of its Constitution and the problematic effectiveness of the Indian State in domestic law enforcement as compared to the economically advanced countries, which govern the evolution of international law. Though India is a signatory of several of these international norms, the Indian judiciary has not used these in cases of protection of monuments of national importance. No jurisprudence on monuments protection has emerged from the cases in the Supreme Court and the High Courts.

1.2.6 First Part Ends

The Indian legal system yields five kinds of monuments. They are monuments of: National Importance under Art. 49 and Art. 245 r/w Entry 67 List I, Seventh Schedule, Constitution and the Ancient Monuments Act, 1958; State importance under Art. 245(3) r/w Entry 12, List II, Seventh Schedule, Constitution; Heritage Committees Monuments under Development Rules of cities; Private Monuments and Orphan or abandoned monuments. An offshoot could be divisive monuments like the Babri Masjid/Ram Janam Bhoomi in Ayodhya, Uttar Pradesh. The book is generally confined to monuments of national importance under Art. 49 and Art. 245(1) Entry 67 List I of the Constitution plus the statutory law, the Ancient Monuments Act, 1958. An attempt has been made to understand such monuments in the context of history, geography and economics by correlating them to these disciplines. Does this legal classification lead to the establishment of a constitutional cultural heritage approach to the protection of ancient heritage monuments of national importance that will fulfil constitutional objectives as stated in the Preamble, by constitutional means. Or, are some of the classes of monuments unconstitutional, in the context of monuments of national importance? Has the Constitution missed out by not mentioning monuments of political significance as monuments of national importance? What has been the role of the judiciary with regard to these issues, while trying to preserve ancient heritage monuments?

The implementation of the statutory framework of the First Part has been examined in the Second Part, through judgments of the Supreme Court and high courts concerning monuments of national importance to discover the role of the judiciary in the preservation of ancient heritage monuments. The amicus curiae (court appointed lawyer or someone else for helping the court) has emerged as an important player in such cases coming under the rubric of public interest litigation. What is the role of the amicus — to be a friend of the court or of the judges? The question becomes important in the light of the judicial culture exhibited in the cases of monuments of national importance Can judges swing the court whichever way they want, regardless of the facts or the law? Can they rebuke and shut up counsel who resist to point out the legal path?

Part II: Implementation Through Courts

1.2.7 Supreme Court and High Courts Case Law

We point out three possible judicial approaches to monuments in terms of the Constitution — monument as an object (Art. 49, Entry 67 List I and Ancient Monuments Act approach), monuments as a cultural object (the first approach combined with its art or history) and monument as a composite cultural heritage approach to enable the fundamental right under Art. 29 in the light of Art. 51A(f) for achieving the Preamble's fraternity, unity and integrity of India.

Has any court adopted the third approach, even while taking an environmental approach to the protection of monuments. Environment is the net result of consumption and the production cum pollution it causes, or the way of life or of culture that it results in. The way of life can value a monument as a heritage or it can simply ignore it.

Further, whether even while adopting the environmental approach, international law has been applied for the protection of monuments. The star case is that of the Taj Mahal which has seen the maximum number of proceedings in the Supreme Court among the cases of monuments of national importance and is still pending since 1984. This reveals that the Supreme Court has been applying international law and common law norms in environmental cases, but has ignored these norms while adopting an environmental approach to the preservation of monuments of national importance like the Taj Mahal.

The implementation of the constitutional and statutory framework is seen through judgments and orders of the Supreme Court and high courts in cases concerning monuments of national importance and the approach in the case of other monuments. The book concludes by proposing the path for a new law that first recognises the fundamental right of citizens to their distinct culture, as the base for the emergence of monuments of national importance.

1.2.8 Alternative

After showing how, on the basis of well-established principles of interpretation, the constitutional provisions have to be read together for a constitutional end, the content for a new law has been indicated, to effectuate the citizen's fundamental right to culture and thereby recognise that India is a land of cultural minorities in terms of Art. 29. Even a religious or a linguistic minority is a cultural minority, since these have their distinct way of life. Monuments recognised by such cultural minorities should be the most enduring because of the community interest in protecting these. This opens a limitless area for sociological and other studies to contextualise any monument of a community.

1.3 Significance of Monuments

Our monuments tell about us. "Men must speak the truth, the truth living in their thoughts, not have a promise on their lips, and a lie in their hearts." So monuments become symbols of human behaviour at a point of time.[4] Monuments of national importance are the distillate of sociological and scientific studies of the monuments of cultural communities having a distinct culture of their own. It is to this distillate that the criteria of artistic or historic importance, in Article 49 or of ancientness in Entry 67, List I, VIIth Schedule of the Constitution of India, is applied for the emergence of a nationally important monument. The process becomes a public resource of public consciousness of monuments.

1.3.1 What Governance of Monuments Tells

The way we select some monuments as being of national importance tells about our political governance and the political economy context

---

[4] Guru Gobind Singh, translated by Navtej Sarna, Zafarnama, p.57, Penguin Books, New Delhi (2011).

of such monuments.⁵ The way we look at the selection of a monument for the legal status of national importance by the ruling political class and the way we protect our monuments tells about our legal and judicial governance in terms of citizens' participation in and access to such governance.

Shutting out debate on the Mughal and British pasts on India's monument of national importance, is to stultify the fundamental right to the culture of monuments and to create artificial monuments of national importance.

This raises the question of permitting foreign rich NGOs to engage in restoration of Indian monuments, associated historically only to a certain religion. Should such foreign NGOs or bodies determine the composite cultural heritage of India, simply because they have a cash chest to spend on monuments that they choose?

1.3.2 Monuments as Identity Politics

The way we pick out and pass on the past of the monuments of sections of citizens and of those selected by political rulers, tells us about the understanding of culture, structures of learning,⁶ of creating traditions and the identity or identities sought to be forged.⁷

The way we pick out and pass on the past of the monuments tells us this because past monuments make us experience the present differently "according to the pasts which we are able to connect that present". The

---

⁵ Frankel, Francine: India's Political Economy 1947–2004, p.776–777, 2ⁿᵈ edn, Oxford University Press, New Delhi (2006).

The economic development policy in the Congress manifesto of the Indian National Congress and the NDA for the 2004 Lok Sabha elections was the same. But the Vision Document of the BJP, the lead party of the NDA, called for a cultural nationalism to render justice without appeasement, which the Congress manifesto dubbed as obscurantist having the subversion of "our millineal heritage and composite nationhood as its objective."

⁶ Stein Burton, 'Cultural Changes, Education and New Classes' in A History of India, 1948, p. 264, 2ⁿᵈ edn, Oxford University Press, New Delhi (2010).

⁷ *Art. 29 of the Constitution is a forgotten, ignored or an en-passant Article in the teaching of Constitutional Law in our law schools, departments and universities.*

past is difficult to extract from a present monument not only because the present factors tend to influence or distort our recollections of the past, but also because past factors tend to influence or distort, our experience of the present.[8]

If what political rulers pick out and try to pass on is congruent with the monuments that sections of citizens understand, then a national identity through the culture of monuments becomes possible. But political rulers may have their own agendas. The Janata Government during May 1977 kicked up a major controversy on history textbooks for CBSE affiliated schools, because the then Prime Minister Morarji Desai was keen that readers do not get wrong ideas about various elements of our history and culture. Similarly, there was a movement to ban Ancient India written by Prof. R.S. Sharma.[9] Continuing this theme, Vinay Lal describes the "Disputes over Monuments: Historians in the Nation-State".[10] Hence culture and politics go hand in hand, as 'culture is more the product of politics, than politics is the dutiful handmaiden of culture'.[11] The use of political power to create traditions is demonstrated by the "shoe" controversy, "secular" education colleges in the Presidency towns and the British cultural-symbolic Constitution of India after the 1857 uprising.[12]

1.3.3 Religion & Monuments

Where the fundamental right to a monument spins off from the religious nature or background of the monument, it merges with the fundamental right to religion or that of a religious denomination. Since the fundamental right to religion is part of the fundamental right to

---

[8] Connerton Paul, How Societies Remember, Cambridge University Press, United Kingdom (2010).

[9] Lal, Vinay: The History of History, p. 107, Oxford University Press, New Delhi (2003).

[10] Ibid p. 113.

[11] Eagleton Terry, The Idea of Culture, p.59,, Blackwell, United Kingdom (Reprint 2000).

[12] Hobswam Eric & Ranger Terence, eds., The Invention of Tradition, p.176–178, Cambridge University Press, United Kingdom (1983).

culture,[13] such a monument becomes a fundamental right to culture under the Constitution of India. Or, stated directly, a monument of a section of citizens of India is part of their fundamental right to culture under Art. 29 of the Constitution of India.

The maximum number of cases that have come up before the Supreme Court relate to Islamic funerary architecture monuments, where the Muslim dead are buried and a garden structure is built to surround the tombs, usually with a mosque for prayers. These are the cases of the Taj Mahal, Sikandra[14] and Fatehpur Sikri[15] in Agra, all three being monuments of national importance under the Ancient Monuments Act, 1958.

This makes religion an important cultural factor[16] vis-a-vis monuments, especially in view of the fundamental rights of "all persons" to religion under Art. 25 and of religious denominations (their structures of worship, learning and rituals) under Art. 26.[17] Hence wherever monuments are a manifestation or expression of the fundamental right to religion or of a religious denomination, then sections of citizens under Art. 29 have a fundamental right to preserve such monuments. This is so because Art. 25, the fundamental right to religion, is subject to the fundamental right to culture in Art. 29 and under Art. 26 religious denominations have a fundamental right to establish and maintain institutions for religious purposes.

---

[13] Articles 29, 25 and 26.

[14] 'Supreme Court Monitoring Committee Inspection Report', dated February 25 2004, in M.C. Mehta vs. Union of India, (1997) 2 SCC 353 [*hereinafter* 'The Taj case' *for brevity*].

[15] Wasim Ahmed Saeed vs. Union of India and Others, (2002) 9 SCC 472 and 475: Orders dated May 12 and December 13, 2000.

[16] *The one thousand year old Chola temple, Brihadeeswarar on the U.N. World Heritage List is used as a platform for Bharatnatyam dancers, S. Ganasekran vs. ASI, Jan 25, 2011 Madras High Court.*

[17] *5,000 years of Indian Architecture, Publications Division, Ministry of I&B, GOI (Reprint March 1992)-Showing temples at Bodh Gaya, Ellora, Pattadakal, Kanchi, Mount Abu, Bhubaneshwar, Konark, Belur, Madurai; Jama Masjid, Ahmedabad, Mandu and Jaunpur; Churches at Kanjur (Kerala), Old Goa, Calcutta, Mylapore.*

The Himachal Pradesh High Court in Satinder Kumar vs. UOI,[18] held, in the case of an unused church in the Viceregal Lodge/Indian Institute of Advanced Study, Shimla, which had been declared to a be a monument of national importance, pursuant to a Supreme Court judgment in Rajeev Mankotia vs. Secretary to the President of India,[19] that S.3 of the Places of Worship (Special Provisions) Act, 1991 does not apply when conversion of a religious place is for a secular or non-religious purpose. The court declared that what this Section prohibits is the conversion of a place of religious worship from one religion or sect to some other religion or sect.

In Ramsharan Autyanuprasi vs. UOI,[20] the Supreme Court, while dismissing the petition as not being a pro bono public petition, held that "life" in Art. 21 "includes all that gives meaning to a man's life including his tradition, culture and heritage and protection of that heritage in its full measure" and in Jagdev Singh Sidhanti vs. Pratap Singh Daulta[21] that the right of citizens to conserve their language includes the right to agitate for the protection of the language since Art. 29(1) is absolute.

When the State ignores the homework that Art. 29 necessitates and Art. 29 itself, then even monuments which are legally not monuments of national importance, become monuments of religious identity and national division. This is shown by the Babri Masjid demolition event. We examine the manner in which this was dealt with by the Supreme Court.

1.3.4 Ram Janam Bhoomi-Babri Masjid

The Ram Janmabhoomi-Babri Masjid episode in Ayodhya, Uttar Pradesh, showed how divisive political monuments can be, so as to threaten the national fabric. On four consecutive days during the hearing of the Ram Janambhoomi Babri Masjid case, the Supreme Court bench of three judges refused to look into the intelligence reports handed over

---

[18] Satinder Kumar vs. UOI, AIR 2007 HP 77.

[19] Rajeev Mankotia vs. Secretary to the President of India, (1997) 10 SCC 441.

[20] Ramsharan Autyanuprasi vs. UOI, (1989) Supp SCC251.

[21] Jagdev Singh Sidhanti vs. Pratap Singh Daulta, AIR 1965 SC 183.

to the judges by Attorney General Milon Bannerjee. Finally, the Attorney General had to tell them that all the reports stated that the demolition of the Masjid was inevitable if the court did not curtail the number of Kar Sevaks to be permitted at the monument. The Supreme Court bench paid no heed to this. Instead, it appointed the District Judge (Lucknow) as its observer to inform it at once, if the Masjid was threatened with demolition. The SC provided two hotlines to the Observer for this purpose-one directly to the CJI and the other to the Court's Registry.

The Masjid was demolished on December 6, 1992 by 10:00 a.m., but the Observer reported nothing to the CJI or the Court's Registry. During the hearing of the case from evening till midnight on the day the masjid had been demolished, journalists pointed out that there was no report from the Observer. After initial futile attempts by the judges themselves to contact the Observer, in the presence of all those at the hearing at the CJI's residence, the Observer phoned back around midnight that the masjid had been demolished. The observer was never asked by the bench as to why he had not informed the Supreme Court, the Supreme Court Registry or the CJI on either of the two hotlines provided to him. In an ironical twist, the senior counsel of Uttar Pradesh's Chief Minister, who had given an undertaking to the Court that the Masjid would not be demolished, was declared by the bench to be henceforth the Amicus Curiae in the case.

At the commencement of the proceedings, the senior counsel Shri K.K. Venugopal (now the Attorney General of India) had declared that he hung his head in shame at what had happened, in spite of an undertaking by the Chief Minister of Uttar Pradesh, that the monument will not be harmed. Apart from a token jail sentence for the then Chief Minister, in the contempt proceedings by the Supreme Court, nothing else was done by the Court in terms of the Prime Minister and the President being passive spectators to a blatant violation of the Supreme Court's orders to prevent any harm to the monument, caught in a historical cultural conflict based on religion cum politics. The token contempt punishment sentence of one day's jail to Chief Minister Kalyan Singh, was without examining the reply filed by him to the Supreme Court's contempt notice. The reply virtually blamed the Supreme Court for the demolition.

No question was asked by the Supreme Court as to why the Central Forces, especially sent and stationed there, were not given an order by the State administration to prevent the demolition and compel obedience to the Supreme Court's orders and the Constitution, even while the monument was under the Supreme Court's supervision. No attempt was made by the Supreme Court to find out whether the Central Government, which was monitoring the entire situation, issued any direction to the State Government, on receiving information about the immobilization of its forces stationed there, to comply under Art. 141 and 144 and allow its forces to act to ensure compliance.

The court did not try to find out whether the Union Government pointed out to the Chief Minister of Uttar Pradesh, the consequence under Art. 365 of a failure to comply with its direction. In any event, the court did not ask the Union and the State Governments to explain as to why it should not treat such blatant and admitted violation of the court's order as a breakdown of the constitutional machinery in the State under Art. 356 of the Constitution. The Court did not call to account even its own Observer, a district judge, as to why he had not reported the events leading to the demolition and the demolition itself immediately when it happened, despite the court having ordered two hot lines connecting him to the court's registry and to the Chief Justice of India.

1.3.5 A German Example

To prevent the birthplace of Adolf Hitler, a house in Braunau am Inn on Austria's border with Germany, from becoming a neo-Nazi shrine, the Austrian Parliament on Dec 15, 2016, passed a law to expropriate the building from its 1912 owner, Gerlinde Pommer, who refused to sell the building to the Government. The Austrian Government told Parliament that it was taking over the building as "no other historical property exists in Austria that hold such a special, global and political meaning." The building cannot be demolished as it is in a heritage zone, wherein demolition is illegal. The owner filed a case in the Constitutional Court challenging the validity of the law itself. The court upheld the government's compulsory purchase as being in "public interest, commensurate and not without compensation."

Hitler's residence and command centre at Obersalzberg in the Bavarian Alps in Germany, was mostly destroyed during World War II. But after the war, the remains became a meeting place for neo-Nazis. The Bavarian Government dynamited the remains on April 30, 1952, which marked the seventh anniversary of Hitler's suicide. It put up "do not trespass" signs. But the number of visitors increased to make it the largest unadvertised tourist attraction and a shrine for neo-Nazis. The Government was then compelled to set up the Obersalzberg Documentation Centre near that location, thereby acknowledging its importance.[22]

1.3.6 Cultureless Secularism, Monuments & Identity

The problem is that the Constitution of India, which by recital of the sociocultural fiction of "we the people," has been legally given by the people of India to themselves, carves up between the political Centre and the States monuments of national and of lesser importance. This then raised the issue whether in determining monuments of national importance does political power urge a constitutional discourse among sections of citizens who are Art. 29 heirs to their specific cultures and gives them the freedom to deal with their history in terms of their traditions and monuments.[23] This leaves us with the problematic question as to whether the Constitution of India politically driven by an implicit or silent denial of Art. 29, is or can be a source of Indian identity by filtering culture through fundamental rights, to leave a cultureless secularism, which the Supreme Court judicially reinforces[24] without any

---

[22] Kenza Brayan, Seizure of Adolf Hitler's birthplace approved by Austrian court, *available at* www.Independent.co.uk/news/hitler birth place (last visited on 19.07.2017).

[23] Habermas, Jurgen: 'Struggles for Recognition in the Democratic Institutional State' in Guttman A (ed.), Multiculturalism: Examining The Politics of Cultural Recognition, p.215, 2nd edn, Princeton University Press, Princeton, United States of America (1994).

[24] S.R. Bommai vs. Union of India, AIR 1994 SC 1918.

reference whatsoever to the citizens fundamental right under Art. 29.[25] Can secularism minus the essential context of specific cultures and can monuments based on such cultureless secularism, that is cultureless monuments, yield a national Indian identity?

1.4 British India & British Monuments

Monuments of national importance are significant for understanding the creation of a physically defined India by the British, of a machinery for its administration for British objectives and the place of monuments therein of British recognised monuments. It is also significant to understand the place of monuments under the Constitution of India in independent India. Finally, the topic leads to an understanding as to how the Constitution of India has been worked by the Union Govt., Parliament, the Supreme Court and the high courts, concerning monuments.

The significance of the issue of monuments of national importance, is the establishment of a constitutional cultural heritage approach to the protection of ancient heritage monuments of national importance that will fulfil constitutional objectives as stated in the Preamble, by putting people at the centre of the constitutional, statutory and administrative steps for monuments, through Art. 29.

This defines the task for constitutional protection of monuments of national importance as:

1. Enable a cultural understanding of monuments i.e. spirit of monuments. (Monuments as culture approach).
2. With such understanding to evolve parameters of "national importance" for monuments. (Work out Art. 49 and Entry 67 List I, on basis of Art. 29).
3. To enable only sustainable tourism that which is compatible with the spirit of a monument. (Tourism as culture and not as revenue).
4. To facilitate citizens' fundamental right to a monument. (A law to work out Art. 29).

---

[25] Parekh B, 'The Constitution As A Statement of Indian Identity' in Bhargava R, ed.: Politics & Ethics of the Indian Constitution, p.43–58, Oxford University Press, New Delhi (2008).

5. To use the monuments as an emotive force of composite heritage that will enable the unity and integrity of India. (Purposive Art. 29 approach).
6. On this basis, to protect the spirit of a monument and not just its body or physical structure. (Replace monuments – as – objects approach by monuments as a cultural heritage approach).

This is important, since in the absence of a constitutional approach to the adjudication of ancient heritage monuments, the courts have adopted a limited approach of simply passing orders to save such monuments from imminent threats to their physical existence, or of treating the monuments as objects or as cultural objects under Entry 67 List I of the VIIth Schedule of the Constitution or Art. 49 under the Ancient Monuments Act, 1958 or simply taking an environmental approach without reference to the relevant constitutional[26] and statutory provisions.[27] Sometimes the judicial approach in the Supreme Court has also led to simply abandoning or ignoring the minimum discipline of law — basing orders on specific statutory provisions and on reasons.

This book should be useful to advocates and judges dealing with litigation on monuments and the need to protect monuments when dealing with litigation on development projects. It is expected to be useful to academic lawyers, teachers of social sciences and humanities, and policy makers to think out the relationship between State and culture in its different constitutional and legal dimensions so as to integrate the constitutionalism of "distinct cultures" with the fundamental rights of religion or language into actionable policy frameworks for monuments.

1.4.1 Analysis to Conclusions

There is no law book on the subject which has been dealt with by this study. Even all the orders of the Supreme Court concerning the monuments of national importance it has dealt with, are not available in the law reports.

---

[26] Preamble, Arts 29, 25, 26;49, 51A(f), Entry 67 VIIth Schedule, List I read with Art. 245 of the Constitution of India.

[27] Ancient Monuments & Archaeological Sites and Remains Act, 1958; Rule 5(1)(viii) of the Environment (Protection) Rules, 1986 of the Environment Protection Act, 1986.

The various reports and I.As concerning such monuments could be studied only in the registry of the Supreme Court and High Courts. The periodical literature on the topic deals largely with some Constitutional, statutory and international conventions provisions. So the net has had to be cast wide over a large number of libraries, original records of the Supreme Court, law reports, constitutional law commentaries, books and articles on culture and books dealing with associated disciplines of history, geography and economics. On the basis some of the pointers that arise on monuments and the role of the Supreme Court, are:

a. That the Supreme Court adopted an environmental approach, based on the fundamental rights declared by it in environmental law cases, to the issues of protection of monuments of national importance, instead of treating environmental protection of monuments as part of Art. 49 of the Constitution that obligates the State to protect such monuments from spoliation, disfigurement and destruction.

b. That even while taking an environmental approach independent of Art. 49, to the protection of monuments of national importance, it did not apply two key principles of environmental case law developed by it – Doctrine of Public Trust[28] and Sustainable Development[29] – to counter the effects of tourism and socio-economic change.

c. That even while taking such an environmental approach it did not seek the relevant inputs of history, geography and economics necessary for the protection of such monuments.

d. That in some cases the Supreme Court adopted the cultural objects approach under the Ancient Monuments and Archaeological Sites and Remains Act, 1958, instead of the constitutional cultural heritage approach.

e. That the Supreme Court departed from the minimal discipline of law while adjudicating issues raised by the protection of monuments of national importance – statutory provisions and reasons.

---

[28] M.C. Mehta vs. Kamal Nath, (1997) 1 SCC 388.

[29] Andhra Pradesh Pollution Control Board vs. Prof. M.V. Nayadu. (1999) 2 SCC 718.

f. That while expanding the ambit of its jurisdiction in relation to such monuments, the Supreme Court departed from the discipline of law in terms of recognised procedures by which major issues like questioning the very jurisdiction of the court are not allowed to be raised and argued only orally: directing Amicus to file replies to such oral pleadings; not directing the party to file a reply to the written submissions of the amicus; permitting a party to abandon its oral pleadings after having argued these; the court addressing itself to relevant issues, not raising irrelevant issues and answering relevant issues on the basis of facts and submissions.

1.5 Propositions

The relevant constitutional and statutory law, the multi-disciplinary linkages, the international law concerning Part I and then the implementation of the law concerning monuments by the Supreme Court and the executive agencies in Part II, leads to the following propositions:

The Supreme Court effectively protected some monuments of national importance from imminent danger through its orders but without referring to the relevant provisions of the Constitution, the statutes, and the other disciplines involved.

The Supreme Court in its entire adjudication concerning monuments of national importance never adopted the constitutional cultural heritage approach. The same applies to the High Courts. The constitutional approach based on a collective reading and interpretation of Arts. 29, 49, 25, 26 and 51 A (f), gives rise to the following chain of logic:

   a. That monuments are a part of cultural heritage.
   b. That cultural heritage of which monuments form a part belongs to citizens as their fundamental right under Art. 29, and additionally under Art. 25 and 26 to the extent a monument is part of a religion, giving rise to the fundamental duty under Art. 51(A)f.
   c. That the State has used Art. 49 and its power to amend the Constitution under Art. 368 to bring in the Seventh Constitution Amendment, 1956, to appropriate the entire process of determining

which monuments of the cultural heritage of citizens deserve to be classified as monuments of national importance on what basis.

d. That while enacting the Ancient Monuments and Archaeological Sites and Remains Act, 1958, in terms of the Seventh Constitution Amendment Act, 1956,[30] the Executive and Parliament, or the ruling politicians, have ignored the Art. 29 fundamental right of citizens to their culture to enact citizens out of their fundamental right by shutting them out in the entire Act.

e. That monuments cannot be protected by operating the Constitution and enacting laws so as to snap the link of citizens to monuments by disempowering them of their cultural heritage, since the monuments form a part of this cultural heritage.

f. That monuments which form a part of the citizens' fundamental right to cultural heritage can be protected only if their protection is seen in the historical, geographical and economic contexts in which the monuments are located.

g. That the kind of economics and economic development practiced by ruling politicians and their economists in the planning process of India is unconstitutional economics which inherently makes the protection of monuments a contradiction within such an economy.

h. That the law and economics movement in the West as reflected by the writings of Richard A. Posner and Eric Posner or in the international environmental field has ignored this aspect of culture or way of life of which monuments form a part.

i. That the Supreme Court has so far never seen monuments in a cultural context to link monuments to their history, geography and economic contexts in which monuments have been created and in which they continue to stand to effectively protect monuments. Instead it has got into an endless spiral of litigation of Interim Applications ('I.As') in a writ petition concerning each alleged threat to a monument of national importance.

---

[30] *See* 'First Effect: Shutting Out Public Debate' and 'Citizen's Shut Out' in Chapter VII at 7.3.4.6 and 7.3.4.12.1.

j. That unless the culture of citizens is made the basis for the recognition of monuments of national importance and the law used to construct a political economy, which does not displace, disempower, deculturalise and distress citizens, monuments cannot be protected from the admitted encroachments, unauthorised construction, vandalism, unsustainable tourism and environmental onslaught of human activity.
k. That unless there is data on the value of a monument, a threat perception profile and a management action programme for each monument involving the sections of citizens whose monument it is, the protection of monuments of national importance must remain a non-productive or wasteful cycle of court litigation, CAG and Parliamentary Committee reports.
l. That an enactment is needed to legally organize protection of monuments of national importance on the basis enumerated above by providing for the necessary organization, funds, technical, legal and administrative manpower and specific accountability to ensure meaningful and effective protection of monuments of national importance.

1.5.1 The Legal Basis

In this context the book has been thought out on four legal bases. Firstly, the provisions of the Constitution of India concerning the subject. In this Art. 29 has been treated as the foundational provision to state the composite cultural heritage approach to the protection of monuments of national importance. Secondly, the sole statute, Ancient Monuments and Archaeological Sites and Remains Act, 1958 which purportedly legislates, as per Art. 49 of the Constitution to enable the declaration of monuments of national importance by a notification, without stating how such monuments are to be protected and who is responsible for this constitutional duty. The Act is monuments – as – objects approach with no reference to their cultural context or heritage. Thirdly, the international legal framework for the protection of such monuments which shows the evolution from "community" to "States" for the legal protection of monuments. Fourthly, the judgments and orders of the

Supreme Court and some high courts concerning such monuments. The focus is on judgments and orders concerning the Taj Mahal which the Supreme Court has monitored for more than a decade, making it the world's longest court monitored monument.

A nation's present exists because of its past.[31] The past are its monuments. The preservation and conservation of monuments has spawned UN Conventions and international administration under UNESCO and national administrations under their respective statutes. But, there is no similar emergent consensus for the legal recognition of the past and its monuments. This is especially so in the post-colonial countries, which are relatively younger, free nations as compared to those in Europe or United States of America, which have had a stable religion, language, political and a legal system for hundreds of years already. Hence, younger nations, having most of the world's people, face an acute problem of which history of theirs they should recognize and accordingly which monuments symbolize this history. Yet, there is no national regional or bilateral forum for discussion and resolution on the legal parameters that should govern the legal recognition of history or the cultural heritage or monuments associated with such legal recognition. Consequently, there arise at least three legal problems.

1.5.2 First Legal Problem: Past and Deeming Technique

History is a troublesome subject for the younger free nations. The first legal problem that arises is how far back in time does such a nation go?[32] This essentially means how much history does a nation rake up when its prime objectives are of unity integrity, stability and economic

---

[31] Amartya Sen, On Interpreting India's Past, p. 38, The Asiatic Society, Calcutta, (1996) *While we cannot live without the past, we need not live within it either.*

[32] George Burton Adams (Revised by Robert L. Schuiler), Constitutional History of England, p.270, Jonathan Cape, London (Reprint 1956).
The historical argument is never of any validity against the results to which the living process of a nation's growth has brought it. However, far they may go beyond the beginning the past as made, if they are the genuine results of national life, genuine outgrowth of the past, they have a rightfulness of their own which History cannot question.

development. It is the problem of defining ancient in terms of time and in the context of building a nation.[33] India's Ancient Monuments & Archaeological Sites and Remains Act, 1958, recognizes history as only one hundred years into the past. But India has a cultural history of around five thousand years. The difficult and problematic question that even the history of these one hundred years may not be the cultural history of these years, or the conflict between the recorded history and the continuously visible culture, has been overcome in India's Act by using the legal technique of "deeming." Thousands of years of Indian history and its monuments have been deemed away by the Act, by accepting as deemed to continue to exist in independent India, what the British as colonial rulers recognized as ancient protected monuments.

1.5.3 Second Legal Problem: Vague Ancient vs. Truthful History

The second legal problem is who decides which monuments to legally recognize as a national protected monument even in the legally fixed time period for such recognition. Invariably the law leaves the final decision on this in the hands of the ruling politicians elected for a term, the reigning dictator or monarch. Nationhood or the process of forming a national identity is a political task and so may be the task is left to the rulers. This would be in keeping with the evolution of the international legal framework concerning monuments shifting from a "community" basis to a "State" basis. Hence, the use of the past or monuments in the process of making a nation depends on the kind of rulers that the young free country has. The rulers can proceed by the consensus rule or a participatory democracy that is responsible and responsive, or unilaterally. Hence, depending on the approach that the rulers adopt, the past and its monuments can become a means of national identity or divisiveness. Ruling politicians may feel that a nation in the process of forming a national identity requires to compromise history either by hiding it or not reopening it. The priority is nation hood and not

---

[33] Coupland R, The Indian Problem Report on the Constitutional Problem in India (Part I), p.33 (1944).: *"Nationalism feeds on memories..."*

truthful history. The legal techniques if "deeming," a fiction of continuity of the past into the new nation's present as well as future, and that of keeping vague the commencement of the time period legally defined as "ancient," help the priority of nation hood. India's Ancient Monuments Act, 1948 adopts both these legal techniques.

1.5.4 Third Legal Problem: Meaning of 'National'

The third legal problem is whether the law lays down any parameters for the guidance of the rulers in the task of deciding which monuments deserve to be nationally protected? Such laws normally define the attributes essential for a monument to be eligible for the label of being nationally important and so nationally protected. These are defined as its history, artistic or architectural value. But these words are invariably left undefined. Hence, these become words of unlimited content vesting vast discretion in the hands of the political rulers who will ultimately decide the issue of eligibility of a monument. However, what is missing in such laws is the parameter of whether a monument reflects the values enshrined in the young free nation's Constitution.

For example, one of the parameters of the Constitution may be the unity and integrity of the nation as a test for all governance, which includes the governance of the nation's past or its history. Does a monument reflect the new nation's unity or integrity or would it lead to disunity and disintegration by creating a law and order or even a national security problem.

If the monument reflects a celebratory triumph for one section of the young free nation's population but a sad conquest leading to subjugation for another section of its population,[34] then should such a monument be eligible for being considered as a nationally protected monument?

Another Constitutional value may be secular governance of the nation to ensure its unity and integrity or nationhood. Then should the process of considering monuments that are eligible for the "nationally protected" label, be an even-handed and transparent process between

---

[34] A. L. Basham, Martin S. Briggs, 'Muslim Architecture in India' in 'A Cultural History of India', Chapter 22, p. 310, OUP, New Delhi (1998).

various religions, faiths, languages, and cultures that exist in the young free nation? The answers to these questions may lie in the issue of the political use of history.[35] That depends on what political rulers think of the word "national" in the legal phrase monuments of national importance or nationally-protected monuments in Art. 49 of the Constitution and Entry 67, List I, Schedule VII.

1.5.5 Uses of Legal Vagueness

This lastly brings us to the issue of vagueness[36] in the laws concerning the recognition of monuments in a young free nation. The vagueness enables full political play in the recognition and governance of the nation's history. Legislative vagueness becomes a political tool to manage protest, discontent and resentment on an issue that can open emotional scars of the recent or distant past. If the nation has the institution of judicial review, then it also enables shifting of the problem from the political to the judicial arena, especially when the past becomes a political hot stove for the rulers. Legislative vagueness itself may enable the young free nation's unity and integrity by delay, through institutional shifting between government and the judiciary, and thereby buying time to play out or heal discontent or strife. Then the role of the judiciary becomes critical.

---

[35] Romila Thapar, Essay 1 – Ideology and the interpretation of early Indian History in History and Beyond, OUP (2010).

New Delhi as to how British administrators constructed the Aryan history of India to begin Indian history only from the Vedic age with Sanskrit as the language to suit British administrative interests, then the nationalist movement and then Hindu Revivalism and Anti-Brahmin movements. Proving from archaeological data this fallacy of this British historiographical base, she concludes at page. 18: "the insistence on ascribing Indo-European roots to all aspects of Vedic culture has acted as a restraint on the analysis of mythology, religion and cultural symbols from the historical point of view."

[36] K. A, Abbas vs. UoI, AIR 1971 SC 496.

If a law is vague, the court must, language permitting, put on it a construction in terms of the intention of the legislature and which advances its purpose. Where however the law admits of no such construction and the persons applying it are in a boundless sea of uncertainty and the law takes away a guaranteed freedom, the law must be held to offend the Constitution. The invalidity arises from the possibility of the misuse of the law.

1.6 Objectives of the Book

This study has been carried out with the following objectives:

1. To delineate the constitutional concept of culture in relation to monuments.
2. To examine the statutory framework of the Ancient Monuments Act, 1958.
3. To examine the international legal framework in relation to monuments.
4. To analyse the judgments and orders of the Supreme Court and high courts in the light of the legislative framework.
5. To suggest an alternative legal approach for the protection of monuments of national importance – the cultural heritage approach based on Art. 29 of the Constitution.

These objectives have two constitutional aims: a national identity based on composite cultural heritage and ensuring thereby fraternity, unity and integrity of India. Effective protection of monuments of national importance requires a cultural heritage approach based on the provisions of the Constitution. Only such an approach ensures participation of citizens in the selection of such monuments rooted in their respective cultures. The sum total of these monuments and cultures results in a composite heritage collection. The selection process from these monuments requires research, a comparative study and understanding of the diverse cultures of various sections of citizens having their own distinct language, script and culture. The debate and discussion across scripts, languages and cultures distils the factors for recognizing some of these monuments as being of national importance. The research and the process also create a large number of jobs by introducing the scientific spirit in the examination of cultures.

Such recognized monuments get rooted in the language, script and culture relevant to the monument and above all in the people whose culture the monument represents. This probably guarantees a preservation and protection of the monuments by the State with the support of the people. As the monuments become alive by this process, an Indian identity becomes possible to ensure fraternity, the unity and integrity of India.

1.7 Growth In and Around a Monument

It is essential to understand the development of a monument through the primary materials of the law: the Constitution, the relevant Act/s, rules, regulations, notifications, the international law texts to which India is a party and the case law as pronounced by the Supreme Court and the High Courts.

The understanding gets deepened and refined by discovering the relevant areas of history, geography and economics, since social history, social geography and the economics, law and society connectivity give meaning to the legal system of legislation and case law. This then gives depth and meaning to the places occupied by monuments as a territorial complex of human activity and the attempt by preservation to convert these places into legally regulated spaces.

A place grows organically around a monument according to the needs of the monument and the human beings around it finding their manner of living together. The legal regulation of the place, through enacted and judge declared law, converts the place into an inorganic space in pursuit of the constitutional goal of "protection". If the enacted law does not deal with who in the State will protect the monument and how s/he will protect it, then by default the constitutional function slips into the hands of the judiciary in the guise of public interest of fulfilling a constitutional duty, even without noticing that the constitutional duty (Article 49) as per the Constitution itself is not enforceable in a court of law. If the judicial approach is focused only on the monument or by adopting what we have called monuments as objects approach, then serious problems arise because under this approach the place is sought to be converted into a space by judicial dictum focusing only on the area of a monument instead of the historical geographical, economic and human activity place in which the monument was erected and stood.[37]

All socio-legal study is subject to the discipline of the legal framework and is recognized as a relevant fact or an irrelevant fact, with a view to

---

[37] Layard A.: 'Shopping in the Public Realm: A Law of Place,' p. 414, Journal of Law and Society 37 (2010); Blomley, N.K "Text and Context: Rethinking the Law Space Nexus," Progress in Human Geography, vol.-13, p.512–534 (1989).

understand the subject matter of the law, to test the application of the law itself in terms of its stated goals and to show its efficacy in achieving these goals.

If the study on the law concerning monuments, discovers that the law itself prescribes a socio-legal approach to the subject matter, for example the cultural heritage approach of the Fundamental Right in Art. 29 read with the Fundamental Duty in the context of the subject matter of monuments being studied, then it becomes mandatory to show how some social subjects are relevant.

The task of the study is done if the discovered approach satisfies the constitutional goals stated in the preamble, through the process described in the Fundamental duty as composite cultural heritage. This should fulfill what is stated by the Constitution to be "fundamental in the governance of the country" under Directive Principle in Art. 49 and be connected to the major cultural source recognized as a fundamental right, namely religion and religious denominations.

This done, the study has to apply this conceptual cultural heritage garland, threaded by gathering relevant constitutional beads, to the court decisions on monuments to test whether the court approach to tackling the problem has been according to the law. This is to test court decisions and orders gathered from the primary materials in the court's records, in the light of the constitutional and legal concepts discovered from a study of the Constitution and Statutory laws.

1.7.1 Monuments of Fear

This has been the thinking process of this study. Hence the study is of the judicial culture concerning monuments as reflected by the manner and method by which various High Courts and the Supreme Court approached the issue of protection of national heritage monuments. An evaluation of this can hopefully lead to a more meaningful judicial analysis of the constitutional and statutory framework of protection of monuments and consequently of the culture of India, the Indian identity, and accordingly act as a counter to the hegemony of the science-technology-innovation based modern economic development as only one way of living for unthinking consumption. It will also hopefully lead to an understanding that the monuments of the small man are equally worthy of national consideration as those of emperors and kings i.e. monuments of village heroes who gave up their lives to defend the distinct constitutional cultural right of their village culture to the might of the State apparatus, which admittedly denied them illegally the State funds for their declared entitlements under the Directive Principles. These monuments, which in several parts of India are kept hidden by the villagers, are the monuments of fear.

1.8 A Peep Into The Chapters

Based on this an analysis the book has been planned and presented in the following chapters.

1.8.1 Part I: The Legal Framework & Approaches to Preservation of Monuments

Chapter I – Introduction: This Chapter explains the division of the conceptual in Part I and the use or non-use of these concepts in Part II, called "Implementation." It outlines the relevant constitutional and statutory law, the multi-disciplinary linkages and the international law applicable. Concerning Part II, it outlines the three possible approaches the courts could take with various combinations done by the courts. The first is the monument – as – object approach combined with the environmental law approach. The second is the monument – as – a – cultural object approach. This can be seen in the single case of Rajeev Mankotia vs. Secretary to the President of India (1997)10 SCC 441. This case reveals that the court ignored the monument – as – cultural – heritage approach, required to be taken, by reading the constitutional provisions as a whole. The Chapter explains that the star monument is the Taj Mahal. This monument has invited the largest number of proceedings and orders of the Supreme Court, as compared to Fatehpur Sikri and other monuments of national importance before it. The court has been monitoring Taj Mahal since 1984 and the case is still pending in 2018.

The second segment of Chapter I explains the significance of the economic, legal and judicial governance of a monument and monuments as identity politics. It indicates how an Art. 29 approach or the cultural heritage approach makes religion an important factor for monuments and how a monument, which has not been declared to be of national importance under the Ancient Monuments Act, 1958 can be nationally divisive monument, in the absence of any homework by the State concerning Art. 29 of the Constitution. The Babri Masjid – Ram Janam Bhoomi case is analyzed concerning the role of the Supreme Court in its demolition. The significance of the topic is how to put people or citizens at the centre of constitutional, statutory and administrative steps for monuments through Art. 29, and its usefulness for various professionals, disciplines and policy makers.

The third aspect or segment of Chapter I states how the Supreme Court protected a monument of national importance like the Taj Mahal from imminent danger by its orders without referring to the relevant legal provisions. It did not read the relevant Articles of the Constitution together to shape a monuments – as – a – cultural heritage approach for the protection of monuments of national importance. The legal provisions required to be read together were: Art. 49 of the Constitution, Entry 67 List I of the VIIth Schedule, Arts 29, 25, 26 and 51A(f), with the Ancient Monuments Act, 1958.

Chapter II – Correlation to History and Geography: This explains how history has been used in our Constitution to declare the symptoms in the Fundamental Rights Chapter and not the causes for these symptoms, called social evils, to result in verbal constitutionalism; how history has been shut out by the Ancient Monuments Act, 1958 and then by the court to prevent the blossoming of the cultural identities of India. The importance of history and of geography in understanding a monument is given on the basis of the literature of these disciplines. It points out how Art. 49 becomes unworkable by ignoring these inputs and how the Supreme Court's environmental approach to the protection of ancient monuments of national importance, necessitates the use of history and geography.

Chapter III – Correlation to Economics. This chapter shows that there is international recognition that modern development constitutes the greatest danger to monuments. Accordingly, the Indian model of economic development, which is in line with the international model, is analyzed as to how it inherently spawns a culture of illegality to tear people away from monuments and monuments away from people. Hence unconstitutional economics which spawns a corruption blanket over Art. 29 raises the monumental problem of the judiciary ignoring this kind of economics in cases of the protection of ancient monuments of national importance. The Supreme Court handles cases which show deep structural problems. But it tries to find remedies without addressing itself to the structures which give rise to these problems. The structures of course are managed by political and economic heavy weights. Incorrect diagnosis can only result in unworkable remedies or cosmetic short term remedies.

Chapter IV – Constitutional Framework: The fourth chapter resolves the conundrum between the monuments mentioned in Art. 49 and those in Entry 67 List I, VIIth Schedule of the Constitution. The resolution is done by applying the principle of harmonious reading to provide protection to three kinds of monuments.

Chapter V – State Control of Culture & Monuments: The chapter details from 1950 onwards the State takeover of culture, that is Art. 29 and the consequences of that as shown by the Govt. of India's own report. In this context, it shows how the then Government executed a constitutional coup by the Seventh Constitutional Amendment to shift the branding of monuments of national importance from Parliament to the Executive. The effect of each of the steps in the coup concluding with the Ancient Monuments Act, 1958 is analysed to show how the fundamental right of Art. 29 was effectively taken over by the State, Art. 49 hollowed out by using the monuments as object approach under Entry 67 List I, VIIth Schedule, to leave rootless monuments of national importance. The result has been that the Supreme Court has allowed monuments like the Taj Mahal to be revenue machines instead of being one of sustainable tourism, the ignoring of the international law shift from community to State protection of monuments and the inherent conflict between economic development and protection. The chapter also shows the divergence in the Supreme Court's application of fundamental duties and the differential application by it of the environmental principle of sustainable development.

Chapter VI – The Constitutional Cleavage: The sixth chapter examines the monuments – as – objects – approach, instead of the constitutional approach of monuments-as-cultural heritage approach. It deals with the constitutional cleavage between Art. 49 on the one hand and Articles 29 plus Art. 51A(f) on the other when these Articles are read separately instead of collectively and how this cleavage is reflected in the Ancient Monuments Act, 1958. Three legal problems that arise in this context are discussed – how far back in time does a nation go, who decides which are monuments of national importance and parameters for guiding the decision of rulers as to which monuments are of national importance. It is suggested that the only legitimate guide can be constitutional values. The role of the Supreme Court in protecting the Taj Mahal against five assaults is examined.

Chapter VII – Constitutional Cultural Heritage Approach: The seventh chapter shows how the distinct cultures of India which include within it religion, constitute the composite cultural heritage that unites India into a fraternity with a cultural identity. The constitutional architecture of cultural unity is worked out till the panchayat level.

Chapter VIII – Statute vs. Constitution: Monuments as Objects: The eighth chapter deals with the problems of constitutional validity created by the definition of ancient monument in the Ancient Monuments Act, 1958 and by its monuments as objects approach which puts the focus on revenue, instead of on the historic or artistic interest of a monument. The 2010 amendments creating a toothless National Monuments Authority continue with this approach. The chapter examines the constitutional validity of a blanket ban on all private construction within 100 metres of a protected monument The amendments continue the non-accountability of the State in protecting national monuments of artistic or historic interest by making no Ministry or department responsible for finding out such cultural heritage and then preserving it.

Chapter IX – The Political Economy of Culture vs. Law: The ninth chapter shows how unconstitutional economics of the state creates a political economy which tears away Indians from their monuments and makes monuments meaningless for citizens. Economics does not consider anywhere the cost of this loss of culture either for individual citizens or for the nation. The chapter tries to show the inherent conceptual conflict between the discipline of economics and that of law due to which culture in developing countries has neither a value nor a price. Such a political economy for managing the people and the resources of the country retards the formation of an Indian national identity and thereby defeats the constructional goal of composite cultural heritage as well as the unity and integrity of India based on such heritage.

Chapter X – Self Defeating Conventions: The International Legal Framework on Monuments: The tenth chapter attempts to show that international conventions, treaties, declarations on monuments are not based on analysis as to why economic development becomes a threat to the protection of monuments. Economic development is not seen in the context of national cultures and whether protection of monuments can be ensured as part of the protection of national cultures or ways of life. Globalized economics resulting in a uniform matrix of economic development makes it difficult to retain the diversity of the monuments in every nation. Consequently, this global matrix has resulted in an international legal order wherein the legal framework for the protection of monuments has shifted from communities to States, just as in India and other developing countries the protection of monuments has shifted from citizens to the State. The State disempowers the citizen by information, accountability and effective remedy deprivation, to empower itself, albeit unconstitutionally.

1.8.2 Part II: Judicial Implementation

Chapter XI – Supreme Court Saves a Monument of National Importance: Five assaults were made on the Taj Mahal, notified since British times as a monument of national importance. All the five assaults were brought to the notice of the Supreme Court, which was monitoring the Taj Mahal by the Monitoring Committee appointed by the Court. In each case, the Monitoring Committee either filed a report or urgently communicated a desperate situation to the Supreme Court telephonically from the Taj Mahal itself. In all the five cases, the physical existence of the Taj Mahal was under threat. It was only because of the Supreme Court's immediate intervention that its longest monitored monument of national importance survived. If there is no monument, then there is nothing to protect. Under Art. 49 or under Art. 29, the cultural heritage of a section of citizens would be irreparably harmed or lost.

Chapter XII – Judicial Protection of Monuments Through The Environment Route: The Supreme Court's environmental approach was set by the petition filed before it concerning the protection of the Monument of National Importance, the Taj Mahal. The petition complained of environmental pollution, yellowing the Taj marble. The Supreme Court adopted this environmental approach of protection of the monument without any reference whatsoever to the cultural heritage which the monument represented and in which it was situated. It also accepted the status of "national importance" given to such British period monuments through the deeming provision of Ancient Monuments Act, 1958. Accordingly, it accepted the British appreciation of the monument which made it as one of national importance based on the story of an Emperor's love for his deceased wife.

If a cultural heritage approach had been adopted by the Supreme Court, even while adopting the environmental approach, then it would have become clear that the monument represents Islamic funerary architecture, the spirit of which is that those buried there have created for themselves a version of paradise in which they would like to be left alone in serenity, surrounded by greens, water, and prayers. Hence, through the environmental approach minus the context of Cultural Heritage and by implicitly accepting the British appreciation of the monument, the Supreme Court protected the body of the Taj Mahal, but not its spirit.

Accordingly, unchecked tourism was not seen even as an environmental danger to the monument itself. The environmental approach alone, to the protection of the monument, made the Supreme Court miss out on another aspect of cultural heritage, namely, that Hindus do not visit funeral grounds or burial sites as tourists. Yet, a recognition of this cultural heritage would again have resulted in protecting the spirit of the monument by putting a check on the environmental danger constituted by the hordes of tourists to the monument, who flagrantly violate the monument's own spirit and Cultural Heritage. This judicial approach inaugurated the era of protecting monuments simply through orders, without any reference to any provision of law.

Chapter XIII – Judicial Closure of Industries: The Loss of Reason: This chapter examines the methodology followed by the Supreme Court in protecting the monument of national importance, the Taj Mahal in which the Supreme Court became a Unit-to-Unit licensing Court to permit or prohibit the functioning of each industrial unit in Agra, wherein the Taj Mahal is located. The result of this methodology was that the polluting units using Coal as fuel were ordered to be shut down even though there were four official reports before the Court recommending the replacement of Coal by Gas. The shut down orders resulted in the loss of another heritage. Further, on oral statements by the U.P. Pollution Control Board that anti-pollution devices had been installed, the industries were allowed to function without any examination of the veracity of the reports filed by the Court. Hence, the foundational basis of the Rule of Law namely reason, seemed to be lost in the Court's rush to pass orders. But then there is the mystery of the missing or untraceable order passed in open court. By this order the Supreme Court bench superseded the Uttar Pradesh Pollution Control Board by the Central Pollution Control Board, when the amicus showed from report after report of inspections of industrial units, filed by the U.P. Board that some official had simply done a desk job of putting in figures in these reports without any actual inspection of the factory units.

Chapter XIV – The Taj Heritage Corridor: Judicial Role in Using Criminal Law: Judicial Role in using Criminal Law in relation to a Project named after the Protected Monument: This chapter examines the role of the Supreme Court in the Taj Heritage Corridor case against the then Chief Minister Mayawati of Uttar Pradesh wherein the Taj Mahal is located. It shows how the protection of monuments can result in State funds being used against the protected monument itself leading to action under criminal law with ultimately no accountability of those who managed the state funds. It also shows how ecological restoration of the damage done by such projects becomes as impossible as the accountability of the managers of the State funds, even though the Supreme Court is supervising the investigation as well as the ecological restoration.

Chapter XV – Is Judicial Silence the Best Role?: The Supreme Court protected monument, the Taj Mahal, was frequently swamped by thousands of persons collecting outside the entrance gates of the Taj and then forcing their way to do everything inside the Taj Mahal which was legally prohibited – bathing in the fountains, climbing the trees, heavy littering with leftover food and waste paper, burning of agarbatti fire on the marble platform of the monument itself and running over the Taj lawns, despite the contingency security plans filed by the U.P. Govt. before the Court for external security and the presence of the CISF for internal security of the Taj. The affidavits of the U.P. Home Secretary raised serious questions concerning the Supreme Court's earlier orders on the external security of the Taj by the UP Govt. The affidavit by the ASI raised serious questions about the internal security of the Taj Mahal. All these questions were specifically put in writing and raised before the Court. But there was complete judicial silence on these. There was also judicial silence on the specific application moved before the Court for directing the ASI to formulate a plan of Sustainable Tourism in the manner indicated in the application, to control the swamping and thereby the complete nullification of the constitutional concept of a protected monument, meant for the peaceful repose in death of Shahjehan and his wife Mumtaz.

Chapter XVI – Judicial Role: Tourism Vs Walls of Taj Mahal: This chapter analyses the manner in which ASI reconstructed a portion of the protected monument, the Taj Mahal complex, to facilitate tourism, by hiding information from the Supreme Court. The construction, done under the auspices of the ASI, in terms of an agreement with a private hotel, necessitated the breaking of internal walls of the Taj for enabling the tourists to move out from the newly constructed area to the exit point within that area. A short order by the Supreme Court put an immediate end to this proposed mischief and the use of the area newly constructed in violation of every conceivable principle of conservation. The chapter analyses from the Court record the "dubious" steps taken by the ASI, the Supreme Court's silence on accountability of officials concerned, and the Supreme Court's questionable in-principle approval to ASI's plan for a wholly new underground entrance to the Taj Mahal. The chapter shows how tourism took over the entire concept of a protected monument and its cultural heritage.

Chapter XVII – Judicially Protecting Monuments Without Reference to Any Law: This chapter analyses the various Supreme Court cases and orders wherein the Court has given judgments or passed orders without any reference to law or to facts from the record before it. The only explanation for this could be the urgency of disposal of matters.

Chapter XVIII – Protecting Monuments: Role of High Courts: An examination of the judgments and orders of various High Courts concerning monuments of national importance shows the complete absence of the Cultural Heritage approach and of the legal principle that orders cannot be against the record before the Court. The reasoning of judgments concerning the amendment of the Ancient Monuments Act, 1958 by which a blanket ban was put on any construction within 100 metres of a protected monument of National Importance, is examined in terms of the reasoning of the judgments and the rationale of the amendment itself.

Chapter XIX – An Alternative Legal Approach: This chapter sums up the lessons learnt from the judicial approach to the protection of monuments of national importance and recommends a cultural heritage approach in terms of the fundamental right under Art. 29 to enable citizens to discharge their fundamental duty under Art. 51A(f) and the State to discharge the principle of fundamental governance for monuments in Art. 49, with a view to fulfil constitutional values, especially that of the unity and integrity of India as a republican democracy that ensures the fraternity of the ways of life of all sections of citizens. Accordingly, the steps for a new law have been spelt out.

Chapter II
CORRELATION TO HISTORY AND GEOGRAPHY

Doctrine of Partial Truth

The words "every monument of historic interest," in Art. 49 of the Constitution, which imposes the obligation on the State to protect monuments of national importance, brings in the entire history of India.[1] The knowledge of history as a discipline in general and Indian history in particular also comes in because of the "ancient and historical monuments" mentioned in Entry 67, List I of the VIIth Schedule to the Constitution of India. It is history which pours meaning into Art. 49 and in Entry 67 List I of the Constitution. The additional legal requirement under the Ancient Monuments Act, of a monument being "ancient" makes history the foundation of a monument of national importance. The question therefore arises as to what is history? The Constitution itself indicates a doctrine of partial truth as history, in terms of what is recognized by it by way of specific mention and what is not recognized by it from the country's past. But then monuments exist legally under such a Constitution.

2.1 Partial Truth

By way of specific mention of the country's past the Constitution recognizes in the Fundamental Rights Chapter, human trafficking,

---

[1] Dipesh Chakrabarty: Bourgeois Categories Made Global: Utopian and Actual Lives of Historical Documents in India, EPW Vol XLIV No. 25 June 20, 2009, Page 67 at P.70.

For the problem of access to original records to write the history of India, the constitution in 1919 by the British of the Indian Historical Records Commission and the struggle to produce the pre- conditions that would enable the discipline of history to be part of the 'public sphere', forced labour, untouchability, entry to public temples being barred to large sections of citizens, the need for a power to make special provisions for women and children, child labour, equality of access to private spaces like public shops, bathing ghats and sources of drinking water and the prohibition of religious education in State funded educational institutions or the levy of any tax to promote or maintain any religion.[2]

The specific mention in independent India's Constitution, of these inherited social symptoms of India's past which need to be constitutionally remedied, is partial historical truth because the Constitution does not mention anywhere the historical causes of these symptoms – "land distribution," "religion," "colonialism," "poverty," "illiteracy" "information deprivation" and "unaccountability of those in power". Instead the Constitution continues specifically the entire colonial legal structure through Art. 372, without recognizing how that very legal structure was used by the British to ruin India's socio-economic structure, native industry, agriculture, imports, exports and to legally divide permanently India into two: one for the few in the presidency towns and the rest for the many in the mofussil.

There is no question of constitutional remedies for these causes, since the causes of the partial truth are not mentioned anywhere, as part of the history recognized by the Constitution. Monuments as objects or as cultural objects of the rulers reflect only the partial truth while either ignoring the monuments which are a culture of sections of citizens or by hiding the causes of the condition of the sections of citizens associated with or related to State-recognised monuments. Monuments and sites raised by the people themselves or reflecting their way or condition of life get no recognition from the rulers, such as villagers' monuments in naxalite areas, jain temples and gurudwaras. A history of the cultural minorities of India under Art. 29 is not part of the mainstream historical discourse.

2.2 Verbal Constitutionalism

Since history requires the selection and ordering of facts about the past in the light of some principle or norm of objectivity accepted

---

[2] Articles 15–17, 23–24, 27–28 of the Constitution of India.

by the historian which necessarily includes interpretation,[3] the Constitution reflects an interpretational choice of India's long history of suffering for most of its people. The choice made is that some of the historical symptoms of suffering were to be recognized but the causes and their constitutional remedies were to be ignored, while promising a constitutional future for the delivery of which none was to be responsible.[4] The failure of the highly educated elite, leading the Constituent Assembly, to recognise and tackle the causes in the drafting of the Constitution, necessarily led to complete unaccountability. The elite could sense the logical contradiction in what it was doing. Accordingly the Constitution became all length with little width or base for effective delivery of the length. Maybe the interpretational prism of national unity and integrity, led to this practical constitutional doctrine of partial truth as history by recognizing only half of the Indian historical truth. This made for a neat fit with the pattern of governance under the Government of India Act, 1935 and formally satisfied the "constitutionalism" requirements of the Anglo American constitutional systems. So, in terms of verbal existence, limited government through fundamental rights and the Federal division of legislative and executive power, the separation of governmental functions, a court structure and hence the rule of law exists, to indicate constitutionalism.

The constitutionalism is only verbal or apparent because of the absence in the lengthy Constitution of any mention of the necessary preconditions of a constitutional order of human dignity or just development of all: the citizens right to be informed, public

---

[3] E.H. Carr, What is History?, p.26, Penguin Books, United Kingdom (Reprint 1990).
Without this selection and ordering of facts about the past, "the past dissolves into a jumble of innumerable isolated and insignificant incidents and history cannot be written at all" R.G. Collingwood in The Idea of History states that history is a "special form of thought."

[4] *Article 75 (3) of the Constitution of India makes the Council of Ministers collectively responsible to the Lok Sabha without stating responsible for what. The Constitution does not make the elected representatives responsible and accountable for the implementation of the Directive principles and the Fundamental Rights which constitute critical components of the Rule of Law under the Constitution.*

consultancy both pre legislative[5] and pre-government schemes, the accountability of all politicians and administrators holding any public office to ensure delivery of the Directive Principles and the schemes thereunder by making their continuance in power, career growth and office dependent on this, the empowerment of the district judiciary with writ issuing power under Art. 32(3) to enforce fundamental rights in villages, systems of monetary and asset transparency for all those aspiring to and functioning in constitutional and administrative posts.

Since monuments exist in the constitutional context of partial truth pointed out above, a similar interpretational choice exists for monuments: their governance by the rulers is to be without people, information, transparency and accountability. The questions this raises is whether governance of monuments is to be done by treating the enforceable fundamental right under Art. 29 as the base of the unenforceable Directive Principle under Art. 49, empowering Parliament to state what shall be a monument of national importance and imposing an obligation on the State to protect such monuments.

2.3 Consequences

The consequences of ruling politicians ignoring Art. 29 in the discharge of the obligation under Art. 49, which is "fundamental in the governance of the country," become self-evident in the 2011 performance audit report of the Comptroller & Auditor General of India concerning the

---

[5] *The Committee of Union Govt Secretaries (CoS) at its meeting on Jan 10, 2014, under the Chairmanship of the Cabinet Secretary decided on a pre-legislative consultation policy both for principal and subordinate legislation by proactively publishing the proposed legislations with an explanatory note explaining the provisions in simple language, a feedback summary to be put on the website of the Ministry/Department concerned, the Law Ministry to ensure this has been complied with before vetting the Bill, a summary of this process to be put before the Cabinet along with the draft Bill and also before the relevant Parliamentary Standing Committee if the Bill is brought before it. If the Ministry/Dept. feels that this process is not feasible it must record reasons for the same in the note to the Cabinet. So far nothing has been done on this decision.*

functioning of the Union Ministry of Culture and its Archaeological Survey of India (ASI).[6]

In the Executive Summary, the report finds that governance from the Ministry of Culture was lax and deficient on aspects of adequacy of policy and legislation, financial management, monitoring of conservation projects and provision of human resources. Given the absence of accountability of anyone in the Constitution of India,[7] this report has not resulted in any consequence for the Union Minister and the Secretary of the Union Ministry of Culture, the particular officer in the Ministry basically in charge of monuments of national importance, the Director General ASI and the Director (Monuments) ASI. The CAG audit during joint physical inspections of the 1655 monuments, selected for inspection on the basis of their historical importance and geographic spread, 92 monuments or six percent were not traceable. Worse, this number was "far higher than the number communicated to the Parliament by ASI" which means that ASI furnished false information to Parliament. But not only there are no consequences for the Director General ASI and its Director (Monuments) but also none for the ASI Superintendents of these monuments that have disappeared. Of course, the Governors of the States where the untraceable monuments are located also go scot free as they are not accountable to ensure good governance of a State in terms of the Directive Principles in the Constitution. There is yet to be a Governor who has reported a breakdown of Constitutional machinery in a State in terms of the actual delivery of the Directive Principles, the Fundamental Rights and under the laws and schemes framed in terms of the Principles and the Rights. The majority of the people of India are constitutional consumers — that is, the State provides them under various laws and schemes, what they cannot afford to buy at market prices. The Governor, who is looked after by the State has no responsibility if scam after scam is revealed in the delivery of such goods and services meant for ensuring minimal human dignity.

---

[6] Performance Audit on Preservation and Conservation of Monuments and Antiquities, Report No. 18 of 2013.

[7] *But the Constitution provides privileges to MPs, protection to civil servants and immunities to the President.*[8] E.H. Carr: What is History?, p. 22 and 26, Penguin Books England (Reprint 1990).

2.4 History Shut-Out

Historians recognize that "all history is the history of thought" based on historical facts "refracted through the mind of the recorder" which necessarily requires interpretation.[8] But historians also recognize that for newly independent former colonial countries the interpretation of the past is a matter of "wider public concern" since history provides an ideological – cultural framework for national unity and growth.[9] Thus the facts extracted by a Government of a monument's past or the interpretation of a monument for it to be recognized as being of national importance, are crucial for the ideological cultural framework of national monuments and for national unity and growth.

But such an examination of Indian history is shut out by Section 3[10] of the Ancient Monuments Act, 1958. This deems away the history of the declaration by the British of Indian monuments as being of national importance by shutting out any examination of that history of monuments so declared under the Archaeological Sites and Remains (Declaration of National Importance) Act, 1951 and continues that into the States Reorganisation Act, 1956.

The colonial method and reason behind recognizing monuments for protection is not to be examined by an independent India in which citizens have a fundamental right to conserve their culture. This statutory black out shuts off the opportunity to discover the truth behind the colonial recognition by a notification in the Official Gazette, of ancient monuments in India as "protected monuments" pre and post the 1904 Ancient Monuments Preservation Act, which after independence were mechanically converted by the National Monuments (Declaration of

---

[8] E.H. Carr: What is History?, p. 22 and 26, Penguin Books England (Reprint 1990).

[9] Satish Chandra, Historiography, Religion and State in Medieval India, p.14, Har-Anand Publications, New Delhi (Reprint 2010).

[10] *All ancient and historical monuments and all archaeological sites and remains which have been declared by the Ancient and Historical Monuments and Archaeological Sites and Remains (Declaration of National Importance) Act 1951, or by Section 126 of State Reorganisation Act, 1956, to be of national importance shall be deemed to be ancient and historical monuments or archaeological sites and remains declared to be of national importance for the purpose of this Act.*

National Importance) Act, 1951 and S.126 of the States Reorganisation Act, 1956 into monuments of national importance and deemed to be so under the present Ancient Monuments Act, 1958.

Yet such an examination could yield learning lessons for the present monuments, since as part of its colonial policy the British Government in India appointed a Muslim as a Superintendent in the ASI for Islamic and British monuments and a Hindu as Superintendent for Hindu and Buddhist monuments.[11] The Official Gazette announcement declaring a monument as a protected monument under the 1904 Act did not state as to what was of "historical, archaeological or artistic interest" about such a monument, as per the definition of ancient monument in S.2(1). The policy of having Muslim and Hindu Superintendents was abolished after independence but the colonial policy continued of not declaring in the Official Gazette[12] as to what is historic, artistic or ancient about a monument declared to be of national importance under Art. 49 or Entry 67 List I of the Constitution or what is "historical or archaeological" about such a monument in terms of the definition of "ancient monument" under Section 2(a) of the 1958 Act.[13]

However, the judiciary has not considered it necessary to explore or engage itself with the geographic and socio-economic history of a monument in any case of the protection of a national monument that has come up before it. No judgment of the Supreme Court or of a high court concerning a monument of national importance has used the fundamental right under Art. 29 as a touchstone for testing political control and action viz.-a-viz. monuments. Accordingly, no court in cases of monuments of national importance, has questioned

---

[11] Archaeological Survey of India; "Preface" to the 1921–22 Annual Report.

[12] *The preamble to the 1970 UNESCO Convention on The Means of Prohibiting and Preventing the Illicit Import, Export and Transfer of Ownership of Cultural Property states that the true value of cultural property, which constitutes one of the basic elements of civilization and national culture, "can be appreciated only in relation to the fullest possible information regarding its origin, history and traditional setting."*

[13] *Archaeology can be defined as the anthropology of extinct cultures. It provides the means of learning about mankind's ways of life: P.378, International Encyclopaedia of the Social Sciences, David L. Sils Ed, The Macmillan Company and The Free Press.*

the constitutionality of Section 3 of the Ancient Monuments 1958 Act, which statutorily stopped Parliament from applying its constitutional mind to these monuments of deemed national importance. Using statutory power to block Parliament's constitutional power under Art. 49, is on the face of it impermissible in law. Further, mindlessness cannot be constitutional or legal.

2.5 Article 29 as a Base for Article 49

A harmonious and purposive reading of the Constitution to decide monuments of national importance is possible on the basis of the following constitutional architecture:

Ancient Indian history is seen and identified in terms of the sections of citizens under Art. 29 who have monuments as part of their culture. Nirmala Kumar Bose states that "Culture is a term of anthropology which comprises everything – from the traditional manner in which people produce, cook or eat their food; the way in which they plan and build their houses; or arrange them on the surface of land; to social, moral, and religious values which are generally accepted by men, and also habitual methods by means of which satisfaction is gained in respect of the higher qualities of the mind."[14]

This leads to a harvest of cultural identities[15] of India. Monuments will produce a national identity on the basis of the composite cultural heritage that evolves out of these sub identities based on monuments. Out of this composite cultural heritage the declaration of monuments of national importance must publicly specify in the draft or preliminary notification the art, the historic interest or the ancient history and the cultural sub identity that is considered to be of national importance from

---

[14] The Geographical Background of Indian Culture, p. 6, Vol. 1, The Cultural Heritage of India, The Ramakrishna Mission Institute of Culture, Kolkata (Reprint 2007).

[15] *Rabindranath Tagore, Nationalism, New Delhi Rupa Publishers (1994) p.77–99: Tagore stated that India's diversity was her nature and you can never coerce nature into your narrow limits of convenience without paying one day very dearly for it. The divide between Hindus and Muslims was largely due to cultural forces released by British colonialism which fractured the personality of every sensitive exposed Indian and set up the west as a crucial victor within the Indian-self.*

two constitutional standards: unity and integrity of India and composite cultural heritage.

2.6 Correlation to Geography

The instant of the present and the past of that instant occur in a specific space. The history constituted by the past-present continuum and geography[16] constituted by its space go together.[17] The logic of evolution of a monument is in a sense the history of evolution of its geography.[18] An ancient heritage or a protected monument is an ongoing history of interaction of the monument with its space, people and their activities that keep changing with technology, urbanization and new livelihoods or ways of living. Thus, the context of a cultural heritage monument is dynamic, that is, it keeps on changing. An Art. 29 approach to the discharge by the State of its obligation to protect monuments of national importance, propels it to cultural geography.

If culture is the distillate of human experience[19] then cultural geography tries to understand both the reactions of man to the physical environment of the occupied region and variable impact of man on the occupied environment, in terms of the cultural forms that he conceives and places on the landscape, as field systems, roads, settlements, crops, decorative plants and monumental structures.[20]

---

[16] American Geography, Inventory & Prospect, p.4, Syracuse University, (1954).

Geography is concerned with the arrangement of things on the face of the earth and with the association of things that give character to particular places.

[17] Freeman T.W., A Hundred Years of Geography, London (1961); James, P.E., All Possible Worlds: A History of Geographical Ideas, Indianapolis, Odyssey Press (1971); James P.E. and Martin G.J., A History of Geographical Ideas, 2nd edn, John Wiley, New York (1981).

[18] R.C. Majumdar, 'Chapter III, General Review of Archaeological Explorations & Excavations, Chapter IV, The Geological Background of Indian History and Chapter V, The Geographical Background of Indian History' in The History & Culture of the Indian People, Vol I, Bharatiya Vidya Bhawan, Mumbai (2010).

[19] Simon During edn, The Cultural Studies Reader, 2nd edn., Routledge, London (1999).

[20] Spencer, J.E. & Thomas W.L., Cultural Geography: An Evolutionary Introduction to our Humanized Earth, John Wiley & Sons, New York (1969).

Even a purely environmental approach, as the Supreme Court has adopted in several of its orders and judgments, or a cultural object approach adopted by the Supreme Court in a few cases, can protect the monument concerned through the dynamic concept of sustainable development in relation to the monument. Hence the geography of ways of living needs to be planned, restricted, prohibited or channelized by the use of law on sustainable development[21] to make the law an effective instrument for the protection of the monument concerned.

This is possible only after a detailed study of the monument to conclude how much of human activity and its effects, both within and outside the monument, can be sustained by it to prolong its life. That is how the monument is environmentally and/or as a cultural object, treated as a public trust resource, not only by the present but also by future generations and its use by the present generation for tourism or other purposes only in a manner that it is preserved for the future generations.

It is not only the environment of air, water and soil which is the result of geography but so also legislation. According to Baron de Montesquieu,[22] in his Spirit of Laws, Book XIV, Chapter 2, legislators must take cognizance of the effect of climate and soil on the character of a people as a guide for the making of laws. On this basis, he distinguished human types into people in Northern countries from those in Eastern countries.[23]

2.7 Essential Inputs

Accordingly, to make workable the constitutional concepts of protection under Art. 49 and the fundamental duty under Art. 51-A(f), the following

---

[21] State of Himachal Pradesh vs. Ganesh Wood Products, AIR 1996 SC 149; Andhra Pradesh Pollution Control Board vs. Prof. M.V. Nayadu, AIR 99 SC 812.

[22] The Spirit of Laws, translated by Thomas Nugent, revised by J. V. Prichard, based on a public domain edn., published in 1914 by G. Bell & Sons Ltd., London.

[23] Griffith Taylor edn, Chapter VI "Environmentalism & Possibilism" in Geography in the Twentieth Century, p.129, New York Philosophical Library, Methuen & Co., London (Reprint 1965).

geographical inputs become essential: physical geography to account for the spatial location, regional and economic geography to show the spatial location of the monument in terms of the manufacturing, trading or services of the area, human geography to show the nature of human activities around the monument, social geography to show the communities in the area and their relationship to the monument, historical geography,[24] to show the evolution of the area and activity around the monument, environmental geography[25] to show the changes in the air water and soil parameters around the monument and cultural geography to explain the change in the ways of living since the era of the monument.

The debate between the environmental deterministic approach which holds that man is the product of the earth's surface and the alternative approach which holds that man creates his own environment seems, for the moment, to have ended with the Fifth Assessment Report, Sept 27, 2013, of the Intergovernmental Panel on Climate Change. This report states that human activity is extremely likely the dominant cause of the rise in the earth's temperature.

The earlier Sept 5, 2013 Monitoring Report of National Oceanic & Atmospheric Administration, USA, states that "due to human activity the level of the most important heat trapping gas in the atmosphere, carbon dioxide, has reached the highest level in three million years." This scientifically determined climate change directly affects the security of a monument. But the ASI has no security plan for monuments of national importance.[26] Without this bench mark geographical data base the protection and preservation of a heritage monument simply becomes unscientific.

---

[24] Glacken C.J., "Man's Role in Changing the Face of the Earth," in Changing Ideas of the Habitable World, in W.L. Thomas edn, University of Chicago Press, Chicago (1956); Glacken C.J., Traces on the Rhodian Shore: Nature and Culture in Western Thought, from ancient times to the end of the eighteenth century, Berkley, University of California Press, (1967).

[25] Semple E.C., 'Man is the Product of the Earth's Surface' in Influences of Geographical Environment, Henry Holt, New York, (1911).

[26] Performance Audit on Preservation and Conservation of Monuments of Antiquities, Report No. 18 of 2013.

The result of ignoring geography is that monuments are sought to be protected regardless of the human organization around a monument for the whole range of the effects of anthropogenic or human activity on the monument. A monument cannot be preserved or protected if its legal custodians refuse to look beyond the monument itself i.e. the human ecological context in which it stands.

2.8 Sustainable Development

The Supreme Court in its environmental or cultural objects approach to the protection of ancient monuments of national importance has never thought it fit to take into account geography or even the legal concept of sustainable development.[27] This is most visible in the over one decade continuing protection sought to be given by it to the Taj Mahal. After recognizing that the Taj Mahal has become a tourism revenue industry, it has not passed any directions on pending applications seeking a direction to the Archaeological Survey of India (ASI) for taking steps to ensure sustainable tourism for its protection and preservation and on the pending applications against the changes in land use in Agra through executive orders of the Chief Town Planner. Even after the 2010 amendments to the Ancient Monuments Act, 1958 the ASI has not thought it fit to build up a data base of physical, human, social, historical, environmental, regional, cultural and other geographies of the areas of the monuments under its protection. Consequently, there is no geographical-ecological information system concerning these monuments. The Union Government has not moved any application concerning this, before the Supreme Court in the pending Taj Mahal matter (M.C. Mehta vs. Union of India[28]).

In March 2018, the ASI has capped at three hours, the time that a ticketed tourist can spend inside the Taj Mahal Complex. As in history, so in geography, ASI has chosen to recognise only partial truth — the

---

[27] Clark, G.L, The Geography of Law" in R. Preet and N. Thrift edn, New Models in Human Geography, p.310–337, Unwin Hyman, London (1989); Blomley, N.K. and Clark G.L, "Law, theory and geography," Urban Geography, p. 433–446, vol. 11(5) (1990).

[28] CWP 13381/84.

time spent in the Taj Complex instead of the number of tourists allowed inside the Complex in those three hours. The wear and tear of the marble and sandstone of the Taj Complex is dependent on the number of feet that scrape it daily for how much time. The application (I.A. 453 of 2009) for determining the carrying capacity of the Taj Complex, with ASI's promise to take steps to determine this, is pending for the last few years in the Supreme Court.

Thus the geographical information system with its ability to locate data in their spatial context, has not been taken forward by the courts as a technological input for adjudication, "by recreating heritage while maintaining its geographical specificity albeit in a digital environment."[29] The 2013 Performance Audit Report of the CAG has recommended that the ASI needs to enhance the use of modern scientific technology and that the ASI should frame a security plan of each monument taking into account its location, area, structure, footfall and other vulnerabilities. It has been specifically stated in the recommendation that the ASI should "ensure coverage of ground level realities" in each security plan.

---

[29] Matthew Fitzjohn, 'The Use of GIS in Landscape Heritage and Attitudes to Place' in Heritage Studies, p. 238, Marie Louise Stig Sorensen & John Carmann, Routledge U.K. (2009).

Chapter III

CORRELATION TO ECONOMICS

"Economic development,"[1] are two words that sum up modern India. But these two words have almost made it impossible to preserve monuments of national importance.

3.1 Developmental Model

For sixty five years since independence, the Indian State has adopted through the Planning Commission an international model of economic development.[2] This model treats a country as developed if more and more of its population shifts out from villages and agriculture to industries and then to services.[3] Under

---

[1] *For a history of the idea of development in Europe and its implications, see* Gasper Des and St Clair Asuncion Lera edn, Development Ethics, Ashgate Publishing Ltd, England (2010), *But none of the essays analyse the assumptions of this Eurocentric economics which play havoc with third world economies and in countries like India even against its Constitution. The concept of constitutional ethics is missing as is the concept of desire and the generation of desire into a need and a need into a want in Ancient Indian Jurisprudence.*

[2] *Academic imperialism of Eurocentric ideas brings foreign economics to India's development requiring India to travel through the same political and social disorder that Europe went through in its search for the meaning of progress amidst new technologies and new kinds of democracy, see* Hettne, B., Development Theory and the Three Worlds, Methuen, London (1990). *But Hettne deals neither with the assumptions of the economics of such academic imperialism, nor with the concept of unconstitutional economics that makes for unethical economics in countries classified by this foreign economics as third world and underdeveloped or developing. See also* Five-Year Plans: 1st to 12th of Planning Commission, Government of India.

[3] Kuznets Simon, Chapter 4: The Pattern of Shift of Labor Force from Agriculture, 1950–70, based on ILO estimates of the industrial structure of the labor force, in The Theory of Experience of Economic Development: ed. by Mark Gersovitz Carlos & Others, p. 43, George Allen Unwin, London (1982).

this model,[4] the shifting out of millions of rural citizens to cities is ensured by the State, causing massive rural distress by its failure to implement the land reform laws in the villages[5] doing development and creating educational, skill and job opportunities in cities instead of in situ in villages where the villagers and their culture, including monuments, exist. The failure of land reforms[6] and the absence of creation of job opportunities in villages by the State applying modern science and technology to existing jobs in the village itself, ensured that rural families could not continue to live in rural areas even for their meagre survival.

According to the Ministry of Agriculture in 2003, 86.1 percent of farmers were small and marginal, that is, holdings of 0.4 to 2 hectares, there is a gradual increase in land classified as uncultivable, only groups of farmer households possessing more than one hectare of land on an average were able to be above the poverty line resulting in migrations for livelihoods, the feminization and elderisation of farms, with rising numbers of agricultural labourers. Consumption expenditure accounted for 61 percent of the loans of sub marginal farmers and 43 percent for marginal farmers. The National Crime Records Bureau data show that nearly twenty lakh farmers have killed themselves between 1997 and 2008. The Supreme Court in State of Maharashtra vs. Sarangharsingh Chavan[7] declared that "Maharashtra can be called the graveyard of farmers." The position is so pathetic in Vidarbha region that families

---

[4] Achin Vanaik ed., Samir Kumar Das: General Introduction in Political Science, p. XXVII, ICSSR Research Service and Explorations, Vol. I, OUP (2013).

Where studies of 'modernisation' press in the direction of a political economy, explorations of 'modernities', can press more easily in the direction of cultural studies.

[5] Planning Commission: Report of the Committee on Land Ceiling Holdings, New Delhi (1961); Report of the Committee on Tenancy Reforms (1961).

[6] *The First Five Year Plan, 1951–56, had declared that "the future of land ownership and cultivation constitutes perhaps the most fundamental issue in national development. To a large extent the pattern of economic and social organization will depend upon the manner in which the land problem is resolved and that sooner or later the principles and objectives of policy for land cannot but influence policy in other sectors as well."*

[7] State of Maharastra vs. Sarangharsungh Chavan, (2011) 1 SCC 577.

are holding funerals and weddings at the same time and sometimes on the same day. In a moving show of solidarity the poor villagers are accumulating money and labour to conduct marriages and funerals of their poor neighbours. Agriculture employs 55 percent of the population contributes 17 percent of the Gross Domestic Product and provides 100% of the country's food.[8]

3.2 Consequence: Culture of Illegality

The consequences of this model resulting in disempowerment, displacement and deculturalisation of rural citizens, are three fold for monuments. Firstly, villagers are torn apart from their local cultures, monuments and languages. Secondly, the villagers land up in cities where nothing has been planned for them by the official economists even though they knew that the consequence of their model of economic development would be mass migrations to the cities.[9] The National Commission on Urbanisation, 1988 declared that despite the considerable achievements of the Five Years Plans very little constructive attention has been paid to the special aspects of the social and economic change taking place in the country. The report of the Commission nowhere dealt with the issue of how to deal with the inevitable migration arising from the model of economic development.[10]

Hence after being torn by sub-silentio State action, from their cultural context in the village, the villagers end up in a wholly alien cultural context of urban slums, since no legal space has been created by the State for them for this wholly foreseeable consequence of State action. The urban slum migrant villager's alienation of language, products and way of life does not make it possible for any connectivity between him and the monuments in the urban areas.

---

[8] State of India's Livelihoods Report 2010: The 4P report ed. Sankar Datta and Vipin Sharma, Sage Publications India Pvt. Ltd, New Delhi (2010).

[9] *UNESCO, Oct 17, 2013: Social Inclusion of Internal Migrants in India, New Delhi: A third of India's population are internal migrants for whom the Indian Govt has failed to provide legal or social protection.*

[10] Volume I, page 6.

Thirdly, the cultural message of illegality is impressed by the State on the migrant villagers[11] in terms of their own experience. The villagers recognize that they have been impelled to the urban slum condition of living on illegal land, in illegal housing, using illegal water and electricity without any toilet facilities, without their participation, consent or even information about this compulsive pushing out from their villages by the rulers. In any event this model of economic development or modernization has been adopted without any law, notification or even an executive order – the legal markers of the rule of law. With illegality writ large as the rule of law in their personal lives of uncertainty, discontinuity and disruption and none to ensure the constitutionality in their urban lives, the Constitution of India becomes a meaningless document for them. Their illegality grows into unauthorised colonies. It is the ruling politician who decides to regularise these and provide all civic amenities. The Chairman and the Deputy Chairman of the Planning Commission go scot free for inflicting this pain of national economic development on them by doing no planning for what was a fully foreseeable consequence of the kind of economic development launched officially by them. Further development by bringing in more villages into this development replicates the suffering on a larger scale and in an aggravated inequitable manner. Monuments also get worse inequitable treatment of neglect, encroachment and disappearance.

The net result is that the State has driven away people from their respective cultures and any monuments which form part of it. The State run by ruling politicians has done economic and social planning[12] by

---

[11] Olga Tellis vs. Bombay Municipal Corporation (1985) 3 SCC 571–573.

That which alone makes it possible to live, leave aside what makes life liveable, must be deemed to be an integral component of the right to life. Deprive a person of his right to livelihood and you shall have deprived him of his life. Indeed, that explains the massive migration of the rural population to big cities. They migrate because they have no means of livelihood in the villages. The motive force which propels their desertion of their hearths and homes in the village is the struggle for survival, that is the struggle for life. So unimpeachable is the evidence of the nexus between life and the means of livelihood. They have to ear to live. Only a handful can afford the luxury of living to eat. That they can do, namely, eat, only if they have the means of livelihood.

[12] Entry 20, List III, Seventh Schedule, the Constitution of India.

taking the social out of economic planning that is by making citizens as mere objects of economic planning instead of as the base and an intrinsic part of such planning. People become State objects. Monuments also become State objects. The State therefore knowingly does modernization and economic development by breaking up the preambular unity given by the Constitution in the Preamble[13] and reinforced in what is "fundamental in the governance of the country," Directive Principle in Art. 38.[14]

This unconstitutional approach[15] of the State or ruling politicians since 1950 through the Planning Commission[16] and the annual budgets[17] approved by Parliament, doves in neatly with their approach since 1950 of ignoring the fundamental right of all sections of citizens in India to

---

[13] *The Preamble to the Constitution of India gives primacy to social justice, followed by economic and political justice for the people of India. The Supreme Court in* Kesvananda Bharati vs. State of Kerala (1973) 4SCC 225 *has held that the Preamble is a key to the understanding of the Constitution of India.*

[14] Art. 38(1) of the Constitution of India.

The State shall strive to promote the welfare of the people by securing and protecting as effectively as it may a social order in which justice, social, economic and political, shall inform all the institutions of national life.

[15] The Hindustan Times, May 24, 2014, page 10.

On May 16, 2014 the outgoing Deputy Chairman of the Planning Commission submitted a note to the Prime Minister's Office which inter alia stated: "Ministries typically prepare programmes without explicitly exploring alternate programme designs to achieve the same results. Programmes are devised top down." The note pointed out the inability of ministries to judge whether programmes will deliver desired results and measure outcomes.

[16] Francine Frankel, India's Political Economy 1947–2004, p. 250–256, 2nd ed., OUP, New Delhi (1995).

Exercising its executive power under Art. 73 of the Constitution of India read with Entry 20 In List III of the Seventh Schedule of the Constitution of India, "Economic and Social Planning," the Union Govt. by a resolution on March 15, 1950 constituted the Planning Commission with functions inter alia of assessing the material, capital and human resources and determination of the priorities and allocation of resources for completing each stage of the Five Year Plans formulated by it. For conversion of the Planning Commission into a political body.

[17] Art. 112 of the Constitution of India.

their culture, including monuments, in Art. 29 while discharging their constitutional obligation under Art. 49 to declare monuments of national importance and to preserve such monuments.

Citizens are ignored under the Directive Principles for economic development.[18] Citizens are ignored under Directive Principles for declaring monuments of national importance and preserving such monuments. The cycle of rule of law as the rule of illegality is complete – unconstitutional compelling of citizens from villages to cities to make them lead illegal lives and the unconstitutional recognition and protection of monuments. The State destroys culture through economic development by compelling people out of it and the State then takes over the culture of monuments under Art. 49 and the Ancient Monuments Act because now there are no sections of citizens left with their culture. In both cases this is done by the State simply ignoring Art. 29 in particular and the Constitution read as a whole in general.

3.3 Assumptions of Economics

This has been possible because the unconstitutional action of the State in ignoring Art. 29 and doing economic planning without any social planning for the consequences of such economic planning, dovetails with the normally unstated assumptions of economics. These assumptions pit economic development against monuments.

3.3.1 Assumption I

Economics assumes that what cannot be quantified does not exist. So the fundamental right to culture and its loss is not quantified. The harm or injury caused by the compelled migration of tens of thousands of villagers due to economic planning minus social planning is not quantified. The harm caused to cities and their already existing population of citizens by this compelled migration, so as to result in a breakdown of the town planning and municipal law is not

---

[18] Samatha vs. State of Andhra Pradesh, (1997) 8 SCC 191.
The right to development has become part of Art. 21, 38, 39 and 46.

quantified.[19] The social harm caused by which fifty percent of the population of cities lives in slums is not quantified. The failure of the State to ensure in these slums the fundamental right to shelter, health, education of children and their nutrition is not quantified. Hence, for economics, this population is non-existent. India has the statistical expertise and organizations that can quantify this. But Indian planners will not do it because then the unconstitutional economics[20] on which economic planning is based becomes established, as does the national break down of the rule of law and the loss of culture.[21]

3.3.2 Assumption II

The second assumption of economics is that it does not recognize something which carries no monetary figure. So the fundamental right to culture of sections of citizens, especially where it is part of the fundamental right to religion, gets no monetary valuation and therefore

---

[19] EAS Sarma, former Secretary in the Union Finance Ministry, in The Indian Express Nov 17, 2013 'Meeting Urban India's Growing Environmental Challenge' *The urban share in India's population has steadily increased from 17% in 1951 to 31% in 2011, In 1951 there were only five cities with more than a million people. Today, there are 56 such cities, three among them with more than then million residents each..., In reality however, the way urban growth is planned and regulated in India has raised serious questions on its sustainability and its adverse impacts on environment and the quality of life of the people.'*

[20] *In violation of Art. 38(2), which requires as a principle fundamental in the governance of India, that the State shall in particular strive to minimize inequalities of income, such inequalities have only increased sharply under this model of economic development. The Managing Director of IMF, Christine Lagarde at the Feb 4, 2014 BBC Richard Dimbleby Lecture London, stated inter alia, "In India the net worth of the billionaire community increased 12 fold in 15 years, enough to eliminate absolute poverty in this country twice over."*

[21] *The Indian State has done nothing to implement the Supreme Court's ruling in* Arun Kumar Agrawal vs. National Insurance Co. Ltd (2010) 9 SCC 218 *that the census definition of work by which housewives are categorized as nonworkers reflects gender discrimination. Nothing also has been done on its suggestion that it is high time that Parliament does a rethinking for properly assessing the value of homemakers and householders work. Since the housewives work is not quantified they do not exist for purposes of the State's economic planning.*

no recognition from economics. Monuments have no monetary figure or price. So, for economists, these do not exist, like the house wives.

3.3.3 Assumption III

The third assumption of economics is that of ceteris paribus or other things being equal or constant.[22] The Indian state's economic eye is shut to the palpable consequences of economic planning in which other things are not equal. Of course, other things can be deemed to be equal by simply not quantifying those other things and not putting a monetary value on them. These assumptions of the discipline of economics on which Indian economic planning is based so as to unconstitutionally divorce it completely from the constitutional principle fundamental in the governance of the country, a social order[23] of justice social economic and political, dovetails with the way the Constitution is worked by the Indian State. Monuments are a part of this kind of working of the Constitution.

3.4 Culture of Darkness

The State in India does not grant to Indian citizens, by law or executive order, the right to be informed[24] of the State's laws, orders, schemes and plans which would impact their lives. The State does not recognize this right in the Indian context of general, legal and English illiteracy. The harm caused by this illiteracy to the fundamental rights of citizens and thereby to the economics of his life is not quantified or monetized. Hence in the absence of this right it becomes possible for the State to implement an economic policy and plans which compel citizens to uproot themselves from their hearth and home to city slums and live as

---

[22] David Begg, S. Fischer, R. Dornbusch, A Final Look at the Problem of 'Other Things Equal in Economics, p. 26, 4th edn, McGraw Hill Cos England (2002).

[23] Art. 38 of the Constitution of India.

[24] Reliance Petrochemicals Ltd. vs. Props. of Indian Express, AIR 1989 SC 190.

People at large have a right to know in order to be able to take part in a participatory development in the industrial life and democracy.

illegal city entities without demanding an alternative economic planning which will ensure them in situ equality of opportunity to constitutional goods-education, skills, homes, health, dignity of their way of life, culture and monuments in the village and recognition of the unquantified and non-priced public interest.

The State in India either by law or by executive order does not implement the basic principle of the rule of law – accountability of its Ministers and administrators who do such unconstitutional economic planning and execute it in known violation of the citizens fundamental right without informing them of such economic policy. Despite the vast media, public relations departments and Information Service officers at their command. The advertised brightness or shine of the Indian State leaves the majority of its people, their way of life, culture and monuments, in darkness.[25]

3.5 Culture of Unaccountability

The bench mark of accountability is given by the Constitution in the Directive Principles which are declared to be "fundamental in the governance of the country" and in the fundamental rights which prohibit the State from creating the kind of society mandated by the Directive Principles in an arbitrary, unfair, unjust or unreasonable manner. But the Indian State does not provide for the career progression of any administrative officer on the basis of how far that officer has implemented, at least from the Collector upwards, constitutional good governance in this manner. An outstanding example of this is that not a single District Collector, who is an Indian Administrative Service Officer, has been held accountable by the higher politico-bureaucratic machinery or even the Supreme Court under the Prevention of Bonded Labor Act, despite the specific statutory duties imposed on the District administration under the Act. The Supreme Court has done nothing to

---

[25] In a bunch of Writ Petitions led by Common Cause, C.W.P. 13 of 2003, the Supreme Court on May 13, 2015 and March 18, 2016 permitted Government advertisements in print or electronic media to carry the photos of the President, Prime Minister, Chief Justice of India, Governors, Chief Ministers and Cabinet Ministers.

enforce these statutory duties in cases like Bandhua Mukti Morcha vs. Union of India,[26] despite the reports to it of its Amicus.

There is no public reporting requirement as to how far Governors and Chief Ministers in each State have so fulfilled these good governance principles given in the Constitution itself. Thus, human development indexes do not carry the harm or damage caused to the rule of law, to the citizens and their way of life or culture by those managing the State machinery, politically or administratively.[27] This damage is not quantified and priced.

Hence the State managers formulating and executing an economic policy that silently deprives citizen villagers of their fundamental rights to hearth, home, culture and monuments by an unconstitutional economic policy that knowingly pushes them to cities for further deprivation of their fundamental rights and mandatory constitutional governance, does not result in any compensation from the State for the violation of these fundamental rights.[28] The way of life or culture, in this manner of the working of the Constitution, finds no mention – politically, administratively, educationally or by way of public information. Monuments are simply victims of this unconstitutional culture.

3.6 Corruption Blanket on Article 29

The Indian State has not laid the information and accountability basis of its constitutional, legislative and executive agencies and agents, to

---

[26] Bandhua Mukti Morcha vs. Union of India, (1984) 3 SCC 161.

[27] *United Nations Development Programme, Human Development Report, 2003, p 341, Oxford University Press, New York. The Human Development Index (HDI) is a summary measure of human development. It measures the average achievements in a country in three basic dimensions of human development – A long and healthy life, as measured by life expectancy at birth; knowledge as measured by the adult literacy rate (with two-thirds weight) and the combined primary, secondary and tertiary gross enrolment ratio (with one third weight) and a decent standard of living (as measured by the Gross Domestic Product per capita).*

[28] Nilabati Behera vs. State of Orissa (1993) 2 SCC 746, *Supreme Court declared that citizens are entitled to compensation from the State for violation of their fundamental rights by the State, its agencies or agents.*

even think of creating a competitive market of Directive Principles and Fundamental Rights supported by a financial and taxation policy tailored for this purpose. The fundamental right to culture of all citizens can have little viable chance in a State run by ruling politicians cum administrators, who for their survival and for being re-elected to office must keep on pleasing the powerful rural landowner on the one hand and the powerful industrialist on the other which constitute a dominant coalition, not of any constitutional development for all citizens, "but one preoccupied in a spree of anarchical grabbing of public resources."[29]

Instead of culture and compensation, the State ideated and implemented development provides extensive and endemic corruption. S.Y. Quraishi, former Chief Election Commissioner of India, in a public lecture stated that money for political parties comes from "a nexus with black money, money of the criminals with a specific purpose of wanting a return on the investment. Obviously, the day such a Member of Parliament becomes a Minister, he will call his bureaucrats and say, I have spent Rs. 5–10 crore for an election and have to return this money, so please start paying me. Obviously a bureaucrat who will collect money for the minister will pocket some and that is how the nexus between the bureaucracy and the politician begins. When this happens there is no stopping corruption. Unfortunately and ironically, election has become the root cause of corruption."[30]

At the same lecture the main speaker Subhash C. Kashyap, former Secretary General of Parliament, stated inter alia: "People have seen so-called democratic governments become governments of the corrupt, by the corrupt, for the corrupt, often surviving tough politics of brinkmanship, bluff and blackmail." A study by the Centre for Media Studies, Nov 23, 2013 concluded that Rs. 22,000 crore bribe is paid on roads every year by truck drivers, with 90% of it going to policemen and transport department personnel.

---

[29] Bardhan, Pranab The Political Economy of Development in India, Oxford: Basil Blackwell (1984).

[30] Vajpeyi Memorial Lecture, April 1, 2013, Media India Centre for Research & Development, Gurgaon, Haryana.

3.7 SC and CAG Reports

For constitutional reports on illegalities in spending of public monies, the Comptroller & Auditor General's Reports are Illustrative: Report No. 22, 2012–13 Union Govt.;[31] The Performance Audit of Integrated Child Development Services (ICDS) scheme; Report No. 6, 2013, Union Govt.;[32] Performance Audit of Mahatma Gandhi National Rural Employment Guarantee Scheme; Report 21 of 2011–12, Water Pollution in India;[33] Report No. 7, 2012–13, Performance Audit of Allocation of Coal Blocks & Augmentation of Coal Production.[34]

After the arguments of the Amicus that the Union Ministry of Environment and Forests affidavit in answer to the Comptroller and Auditor General's report concerning the spending of funds for the Ganga Action Plan under the Prime Minister, the Supreme Court expressed its dissatisfaction with the affidavit and directed it to file another one. Till today that has not been complied with by the Union Govt. The Supreme Court took no action on this despite the Amicus pointing out the non-compliance and gradually the Supreme Court would pass over the matter when it came up for hearing. Ultimately the Supreme Court circulated *suo motu* a draft order to which the Amicus filed his reply pointing out that official reports disclosed an alarming state of infections from the Ganga especially for those using its waters for bathing drinking, cooking and irrigation. There was no response or hearing.[35]

3.8 The Judiciary

The statutory committee constituted by the Chief Justice of India and headed by a retired judge of that very court, under the Judges Inquiry Act, found Justice V. Ramaswami of the Supreme Court guilty of judicial

---

[31] Ministry of Women & Child Development.

[32] Ministry of Rural Development.

[33] Union Ministry of Environment & Forests.

[34] Union Ministry of Coal.

[35] M.C. Mehta vs. Union of India, [*hereafter* 'Ganges Pollution Case' *for brevity*].

misbehavior. But nothing could be done about him as under the voting procedure in Parliament for his removal on the basis of the statutory committee's report, as the requisite number of votes under the Judges Inquiry Act, were not cast by the Members of Parliament, since the ruling Cong-I had directed its MPs not to vote.

In 1996, at the All India Chief Justices Conference, the Chief Justice of India, and senior judges of the Supreme Court with the Chief Justices of all High Courts formulated a 16-point "Restatement of the values of judicial life." On May 9, 2003 in Indira Jaising vs. Union of India,[36] the Supreme Court of India struck these down as illegal in their application to judges of the High Courts and Supreme Court since these did not have the sanction of the law.

Chief Minister of West Bengal, Mamata Banerjee stated during the Platinum Jubilee celebration of the Legislative Assembly, "At times favourable verdicts are given in return for money. These days, judgements are purchased. There is corruption among a section of the judiciary. I know there can be a defamation suit against me for saying this. But this must be said and I am ready to go to jail for saying so."[37]

Ananda Mohan Bhattacharjee, originally a judge of the Calcutta High Court was forced to resign in 1995 while he was the sitting Chief Justice of Bombay High Court after it was found he had received Rs. 70 lakhs as an advance amount for a book by him from a publishing house to have links with the underworld. Justice Soumitra Sen of the Calcutta High Court was charged for the misconduct of misappropriation of funds in capacity of Court Receiver in 1983. When Parliament was proceeding with motion for impeaching him, the judge resigned to render the impeachment proceedings infructuous.[38]

---

[36] Indira Jaising vs. UOI, 2003 5 SCC 494.

[37] Some-times-quote-verdicts-are-purchased-mamata, last visited on http://ibnlive.in.com/news/sometimes-quote-verdicts-hour-purchased-mamata/282322-37-64.html, (last visited on July 4, 2017).

[38] Judges-impeachment-procedure-and-justice-soumitra-sen's-case, last visited on http://indiancurrentaffairs.wordpress.com/2011/12/11/judges-impeachment-procedure-and-justice-soumitra-sen's-case/, (last visited on July 4, 2017).

In its 230th Report 2009, the Law Commission recommended that in order to eliminate the practice of "Uncle Judges," the judges whose kith and kin are practicing in a High Court should not be posted in the same High Court.

The Supreme Court bench of Justice M. Katju and Justice Gyan Sudha Misra on November 26, 2010 declared that most judges of Allahabad High Court are corrupt and collude with advocates.

The N.N. Vohra Committee Report dated 5 October 1993 noted that the growth and spread of crime syndicates in Indian society has been pervasive and that "The criminal elements have developed an extensive network of contacts with bureaucrats, government functionaries at lower levels, politicians, media personalities, strategically located persons in non-governmental sector and members of the judiciary."[39] In 2011 the Supreme Court declared: "Corruption by public servants has become a gigantic problem. It has spread everywhere. No facet of public activity has been left unaffected by the stink of corruption".[40]

How can a culture of corruption of citizens in power managing the State's resources and citizens subsist with a constitutional protection of citizens' culture and monuments?

3.9 SC: Development and Culture

The managers[41] of the State, public and private, are both the problem, and if they choose, the solution to unconstitutional economic development and consequent deculturalisation of languages,[42] scripts, the formal education system and the manifold ways of living of Indian citizens which gives cultural meaning to the unenumerated ways of life of the sub-continental territory called Bharat. The Indian State has enacted a Biological Diversity Act, 2002 for protection of diversity of Bharat's

---

[39] Dinesh Trivedi vs. UOI, (1997) 4 SCC 306.

[40] A.B. Bhaskara Rao vs. CBI, (2011)10 SCC 259.

[41] Rudolf Lloyd I and Rudolf Susanne Hoeber, in Pursuit of Lakshmi: The Political Economy of the Indian State, Chicago III. University of Chicago Press (1987).

[42] *The People's Linguistic Survey of India conducted by the Gujarat based Bhasha Trust states that 220 languages of India disappeared in last 50 years and 150 could vanish in next 50 years.*

plants, animals and micro-organisms but made no statutory provision for Bharat's human diversity. Accordingly, "vernacular heritage," the effect of modernization especially in agriculture and on rural culture figures nowhere in any official planning on economic development, culture or monuments, even though this is recognized by ICOMOS, the International Committee on Monuments and Sites, of which India is a member.[43]

Unfortunately this breakdown and deculturalisation of the rule of law by pursuit of unconstitutional economics by the State has not been noticed by the Supreme Court and not been argued by any of the senior advocates appearing in cases related to monuments, culture or construction of dams which simply drown Art. 29.[44] The Narmada Bachao Andolan,[45] judgment concerning construction of a dam on an inter State river and involving huge submergence of villages as also uprooting of villagers and indigenous citizens[46] does not record a single argument on the drowning of cultural heritage. In the Tehri dam case, N.D. Jayal vs. Union of India,[47] cultural heritage and monuments figured nowhere in the concept of sustained development. Accordingly there was no question of raising the issue of unconstitutional development based on such unconstitutional economics. This is normally treated as a question of political policy and therefore out of bounds for a court. But the Supreme Court has itself held that constitutional questions maybe political questions but that does not take these out of the court's constitutional jurisdiction of fundamental rights.[48]

---

[43] ICOMOS, Heritage at Risk: Vernacular Heritage, available at http://www.international.icomos.org/risk/isc-verna_2000.htm (last visited June 17, 2014).

[44] India is a party to the Charter on the Protection and Management of Underwater Cultural Heritage.

[45] Narmada Bachao Andolan vs. UOI, (2000) 10 SCC664.

[46] *As to how the State has denied the displaced tribals their legal rights, See Aug 4, 1994 Socio-Legal Field report on rehabilitation of Narmada Dam tribes of the advocate given to the Supreme Court.*

[47] N.D. Jayal vs. UOI, (2004) 9 SCC 362.

[48] State of Rajasthan vs. Union of India, AIR 1977 SC 361.

3.10 Constitution and State Economics Dovetailed

Unquantified and non-monetized protection of monuments as part of an unquantified and non-monetized fundamental principle of constitutional governance under Art. 29, along with an unquantified and non-monetized fundamental right to culture gets no recognition from the State's unconstitutional economic planning and execution which because of its inherent assumptions of economics enables the State to simply ignore the unquantified and non-monetized severe harm caused by such State driven economics to: the citizens, the rule of law, the public interest and to cultural heritage. Protection of monuments of national importance falls in the hands of such a State and thereby becomes an impossibility.

The performance audit report by the Comptroller and Auditor General concerning the Union Ministry of Culture and its Archaeological Survey of India only confirms this consequence of the working of the Constitution and the economic system in India joining hands in unconstitutional economics.[49]

But a performance audit without pinpointing who is responsible for such serious abandonment of performance only adds to the unconstitutionality of a State creating victims of unconstitutional governance without any one accountable for the same. Such management of the Constitution dovetails with the State economics wherein the involuntary costs of compelled migration, conversion from law abiding citizens to non-law-abiding ones, the loss of culture and family of the victims are externalities[50] and hence that cost is not to be counted as part of the State run project of development.

---

[49] *The 2013 report of the Comptroller & Auditor General of India states about India's most touristic monument of national importance, the Taj Mahal, that twenty three unauthorised constructions dot its surroundings, that encroachers have squatted even near the Khan e Alam garden on its premises, that cracks and cement fixes are aplenty on the mausoleum's stone walls, that designs and inlay works done with precious stones on the main edifice are missing and in their place are shoddy patchworks, and the ceilings of the mosque and mehramkhana in the complex are seeping.*

[50] David Begg, S. Fischer and R. Dornbusch, Economics, p. 264, 4th edn, McGraw Hill Companies, England (2005); Paul A Samuelson, William D Nordhaus, Indian Adaptation p. 44, 19th edn, McGraw Hill Education (India) Pvt. Ltd, New Delhi (2011).

3.11 Consequences of Dovetailing

In this context, famous revenue producing monuments like the Taj Mahal of national importance get further victimized in terms of the constitutional duty of the State to protect monuments of national importance.

3.11.1 First Consequence

Firstly, the rising cost of the land or real estate on which the monument stands is quantified and monetized unlike that of the monument. The real estate value is therefore visibly more against a zero-monetary value of the monument. Real estate is the fastest growing economic sector and also one of the fastest growing and highest employment sectors. Unconstitutional economics with its underbelly of corruption[51] makes real estate more attractive to a State managed on the basis of such economics, than a monument and the fundamental right to culture of the citizens.

3.11.2 Second Consequence

Secondly, the more visitors that a monument attracts, the more monetarily attractive becomes the land around it for construction of hotels, tourist facilities, residences and markets. Land use and the legal discretionary powers under a Town Planning Act or Urban Development Act, become huge illegal monetary prizes for ruling politicians and urban development administrators, who control the exercise of the discretion to exempt land from the use fixed for it under a master plan or an urban law. Accordingly, the State-that is the specific Ministers in charge, the specific administrators and the specific technical personnel – have an economic interest in cultural degradation that results from the illegal economic development around a monument.

---

[51] Mahajan Krishan, Sustainable Development in a State of Unconstitutional Economics, p. 53, Vol. II, National Green Tribunal, International Journal on Environmental Law, New Delhi (2014).

Or, to put it another way, why should these specific agents of the State agree to an economic policy based on cultural heritage or for that matter of environmental improvement around monuments when such agents will not benefit from such protection and instead lose out on the benefits flowing in from big projects, infrastructure development and real estate around a monument to enable more and speedier tourism. There is no market for monuments in stark contrast to the market for the real estate on which a monument stands and that which is around it. Hence monuments of national importance are those which have tourism and those which have none. The touristic monument will be protected to the minimal extent necessary for the growth of the tourist industry.[52] The monument is used to create the market that victimizes it. The non-touristic or less touristic monuments, which are the majority, are a mere uncompensated social expense which only contributes to the fiscal deficit.

This puts the protection of cultural heritage and of monuments of national importance on the same textual constitutional status as environmental protection – even though in the Constitution culture under Art. 29 is a specific fundamental right unlike environment which, despite the Supreme Court having declared as a fundamental right, continues to be a mere Directive Principle in Art. 48-A.

But environment has a market and monuments of national importance do not. The land around monuments especially touristic monuments of national importance has a market but the non-touristic monuments do not. The legal system reflects this market and market duality in two ways.

On the one hand, the Urban Development and Town Planning Acts contain discretionary provisions for exemption from the prescribed land use of lands near or around monuments and on the other hand the Ancient Monuments Act, 1958 nowhere recognizes in relation to

---

[52] Performance Audit Report of CAG on the Preservation of Monuments & Antiquities, p.211 (2013):

The Moily Committee in 2010 had stated that large amount of conservation work is confined to ticketed monuments and world heritage sites and that there are several hundred monuments which have not received a single rupee towards conservation in the last twenty to thirty years.

monuments, the doctrines of public trust, sustainable development and of cultural heritage. Cultural heritage of monuments is a collective non-profit public goods concept.[53] The markets around monuments are an individual profit-seeking concept.

The discretionary powers for change in land use under the Urban Development Act, enabling departure from a master plan under that Act prohibiting land uses around a monument, becomes a lucrative legal channel for ruling politicians, administrators and town planners that finances representative democracy in the wards and constituencies around a monument. The research work shows that the Supreme Court while monitoring the Taj Mahal paid no heed to the report of its Amicus Curiae concerning this exercise of discretionary power exemption by the Chief Town Planner of Agra. Monuments thus contribute to the pricing of the land around them but themselves become endangered because they are not a piece of the market economy generated by them for that land. In economic terms persons would like to steal the land. No one would like to steal the monument erected on that land.

That which is desirable to be stolen is worth protecting. That which is not so desirable does not deserve protection. Hence according to the 2013 Performance Audit Report No. 18 of the CAG on Preservation & Conservation of Monuments & Antiquities, out of the sample of 1655 centrally protected monuments of national importance 92 monuments were not traceable; there was no centralized data base of the notifications of monuments which define the area of a monument and are crucial for establishing encroachment or unauthorised construction, the encroachment of monuments and unauthorised constructions were widespread; inspection notes on the condition of monuments were not being prepared by the ASI officials; there was poor documentation of the conservation works; even basic records such as measurement books, log books and site registers were not being maintained properly so as to make it impossible to find out whether monuments selected

---

[53] Husain, S. Abid, The National Culture of India, p. xxiv, National Book Trust, India (2006).

Culture is a sense of ultimate values possessed by a particular society as expressed in its collective institutions, by its individual members in their dispositions, feelings, attitudes and manners as well as in significant forms which they give to material objects.

for conservation works were need based as also the propriety and genuineness of the expenditure incurred on the conservation works. The audit report pointed out that the supervising Union Ministry of Culture had not developed any Comprehensive Conservation Policy, the ASI did not have a conservation policy as the draft policy was being finalized since August 2011, and that all the red signals raised on the working of the ASI by the Parliamentary Standing Committee on Transport, Tourism and Culture, by the Supreme Court and High Court had been ignored by the Union Ministry of Culture. Worse, though the notification declaring the ASI a Scientific and Technical Institution was issued in 1990, it was never implemented and according to the Parliamentary Moily Committee, 2010, threats to the monuments had been ignored by the understaffed and underfunded ASI. Sixty six cases of unauthorised construction in the protected area of Jaisalmer Fort, Rajasthan could not be removed by the ASI despite the judgment of the Rajasthan high court in Feb 2004.

In Civil Appeal 16899/96, of the ASI, the Supreme Court on April 16, 2004 annulled the Karnataka Government's 1976 notifications declaring 43 monuments of national importance as Karnataka Waqf Board properties. After this judgment the Karnataka Government notified in August 2005, further six monuments of national importance, as Waqf properties. Instead of implementing and enforcing the Supreme Court judgment, the ASI requested the Karnataka Government for a joint survey of these monuments from 2008. The Union Ministry of Culture simply kept quiet in this regard.

In 2005, the Supreme Court directed that at the Tenkailasanatha temple, a monument of national importance in Trissur, the chemical composition of each fire cracker burst during the rituals in the festival season, should be such as not to exceed 125 decibels. This was to protect the mural paintings of the temple which were being destroyed by the fire crackers. ASI did nothing to enforce the judgment. The CAG Performance Audit team in 2012[54] found that fire crackers being used in the function were "still damaging the roof of the protected monument."[55]

---

[54] *Audit was completed in Dec 2012.*

[55] Performance Audit Report No. 18 of the CAG, p. 217 (2013).

This extraordinary phenomena of the wanton and willful destruction[56] of cultural heritage of monuments of national importance during peacetime by the very State charged with a constitutional duty to protect such monuments, explains itself only through the kind of economics, as explained above, practiced by the State in India, with which dovetails the complete absence of accountability under the Constitution of India of Ministers and their bureaucrats, in a situation where the Ministers and bureaucrats in the name of the State have taken over the fundamental right of citizens to their monuments.

3.12 Western Law and Economics

Law and Economics writings by economist turned lawyers like Richard Posner of non-developing countries, predictably, do not deal with non-economic entities like culture and monuments.[57] They ignore culture or the way of life as determining Biology and Economics. This is the approach in the 'Radical Feminist Critique of Sex & Reason', while advocating the enterprise of "law and economics" as an ethic of scientific inquiry, pragmatically understood.[58] He ignores culture even while trying to answer why people confine themselves to social norms.[59] While discussing the Epistemology and Ontology of Law, he ignores the cultural habit of appraising things and the interaction of the increasingly empirical with the history of meanings set by a cultural

---

[56] *Since 1961, India has been a member of ICCRON (International Charter for the Conservation and Restoration of Monuments – Venice Charter) and under it of the International Centre for the Study of the Preservation and Restoration of Cultural Property established at Rome in 1959, pursuant to the 9th UNESCO General Conference in New Delhi in 1956. Under Art. 1 of the Convention concerning the Protection of the World Cultural and Natural Heritage, 1972, monuments are a "Cultural Heritage" whose protection under Art. 5 must be integrated into comprehensive planning programme, giving it a function in the life of a community.*

[57] Richard A. Posner, Overcoming Law, Universal Law Publishing Co., New Delhi (reprint 2007).

[58] In Law & Social Norms," 2009.

[59] Richard A. Posner, The Problems of Jurisprudence, Universal Law Publishing Co., New Delhi (reprint)

evolution of thousands of years.⁶⁰ Posner ignores the split cultures that a lawyer represents while working the legal system to earn therefrom while realizing that the entire legal process is against the culture that the lawyer inherits, unless that culture has been effaced by his upbringing. In "How Judges Think" (2011), while treating a judge as a rational self-interested utility maximizer he gives nine theories of judicial behaviour which discuss everything except the culture shaping a judge's choices.

Hence culturally Western economics or its law and economics movement cannot see the twin pillars of unconstitutional economics and a Constitution of unaccountability of those who create these twin pillars of economic development, resulting in a crisis of people and resources summed up in non-economic cultural phrases like disempowerment, deculturalisation and non-quantified suffering.

It seems the conceptual basket of Western economics is unable to cope with the new phenomena of the results of the application of such economics in developing countries, which results in any event to produce sufficient markets for advanced economies goods to support the life style of resonating citizens within the developing countries, especially those who are in charge of the State.

3.13 Dams, Development and Damned

Accordingly, in the analysis by western professionals of dams vs. cultural heritage controversy in developing countries like Egypt, Sudan, Romania and Turkey there is no reference whatsoever to the kind of economics pursued by these countries for "economic development" in the context of their respective Constitutions and whether such Western economics that justifies a dam, takes into account the effects on the way of life of those whom a dam would displace and disrupt without their consent, without any informed participation in the State's decision to have a dam and an interrogation of the legal processes by which a dam is decided upon by a State.

---

⁶⁰ Richard A. Posner, Frontiers of Legal Theory', Universal Law Publishing Co., New Delhi (reprint 2010).

The culture or the way of life is assumed away and a dam is assumed to be economic progress without questioning that the progress is for whom in each of these countries as the concern is only to save the visible cultural objects threatened by these dams without reference to the way of life of the communities who may be associated with such cultural objects.

Hence an assertion is made by such analysis that "it is not morally defensible to condemn people to a difficult existence in order for the world to have a museum" without an examination of the morality and constitutionality of the process by which a decision to have a dam is taken by a State and its consequences on the unquantified, unmonetized and therefore economically irrelevant way of life. Such a way of life or culture is damned.

3.14 Difficult Existence – For Whom?

On the other hand, the assumed cultural meaning of "difficult existence" by Western standards is assumed to apply to a wholly different culture of living which is probably a way of living with nature instead of against nature. In this context mitigation of injury and exploring of alternatives after the event become meaningless for those whose way of life has been wiped out by the dam for no reason that they can understand and about which agencies financing the dam have no monetary concern. There is no suggestion in such analysis for a mandatory post dam verification of the claims which resulted in the dam and for a fair empirical investigation into who benefits how much from the dam. There is also no suggestion that international and domestic financing agencies be bound down in international law to comply with a proven absolute necessity principle in changing the way of life of people and thereby destroying the inherent component of cultural heritage.[61]

How cultural heritage, despite international pressures of modernization in what and how to build, can be preserved is shown by Laurie Baker, a Britisher who demonstrated in Kerala what could be done with traditional local materials and building techniques.

---

[61] Wangkeo Kanchana, Monumental Challenges: The Lawfulness of Destroying Cultural Heritage During Peacetime, vol. 189, Yale J. Int'l L. (2003).

Out of that experience he says: "In the building world our current sacred cow – word is "modern". Any building labelled modern, however ugly or mistaken, is accepted. But where are our so called modern Indian styles? Alas they are mainly poor imitations of other countries' efforts to use present day materials and techniques. How wonderful it will be when our architects and engineers combine the lessons learned from our own traditional building styles with the honest undisguised use of our regionally plentiful, inexpensive materials."[62]

3.15 Kind of Development

The fundamental right to culture in Art. 29 of the Constitution interrogates economic development as currently pursued. This is so because the issue is not development. The issue under our Constitution is what kind of development: development based on citizens' cultural heritage or without it; development with or without citizens' participation; development sustainable for all citizens or for a few citizens; development with or against nature; development which includes or ignores social cost and suffering; development with or without corruption.

Then only the fundamental right to development acquires any meaning in which alone monuments can be protected. For those uprooted from their hearth and home in the name of development and already torn away from their culture or monuments into alien slums, a monument is more valuable as a shelter than an abstract luxury of a supposed heritage with which the deliberately displaced, deculturised and distressed citizen has no connection, understanding or belonging.

3.16 Problem of the Judiciary's Role

The problem therefore concerning the role of the judiciary in the protection of ancient heritage monuments is the absence of understanding the kind of economics which drives the process of modernisation of a developing

---

[62] Banerji, Mridula, 'Colonial Architecture & Indian Rationalism' in The History & Culture of the Indian People, p.245 at 251, Vol 8, 7th edn, Bhawan's Book University, Bharatiya Vidya Bhavan, Mumbai (2001).

country like India and in which the issue of constitutional protection of monuments arises. Added to this is the problem of judicial understanding of the role of the judiciary itself in general. This role is analysed in the context of the legislative framework, the disciplines of history, geography and economics and the judiciary's judgments and orders in the cases relating to monuments that come up before it for a decision.

The Taj Mahal is a protected monument,[63] which has taken up the largest amount of time of the judiciary in the Supreme Court since 1984. The only legal jacket to explain this is the writ of continuing mandamus.[64] But there is no specific order of the Supreme Court to this effect, even though the Supreme Court still continues to monitor the Taj Mahal on the presumed legal jacket which at various times was referred to orally by Justices S.B. Sinha, S.H. Kapadia (as he then was) while sitting as a special bench consisting of Sinha, Kapadia and Justice D.K. Jain.

Behind the issue of the role of the judiciary in the protection of ancient heritage monuments lies the persistent clash between three viewpoints on the judiciary's role under the Constitution.

3.17 Existing Law – Legality to Unconstitutionality

The first viewpoint is that the Constitution permits the judiciary only to direct various authorities' subject to judicial review, to perform their legal duties or to quash the illegality in such performance and thereby declare the law on the basis of existing legislation. The high culmination of this is to declare an existing law itself as unconstitutional.

This is based on the silences or the unspoken assumptions of constitutional governance: firstly, that the executive governs as a constitutionally limited government.[65] The changes in laws or in

---

[63] Ss. 2(a) & 2(j), Ancient Monuments Act, 1958.

[64] Vineet Narayan vs. UOI, AIR 1998 SC 889.

[65] *Under the Constitution of India constitutionalism or limited government consists of separation of legislative, executive and judicial functions, the control of executive and legislative power by the vertical division between the Centre and the States in List I, II and III in the Seventh Schedule of the Constitution read with Articles 245, 73, 162 and 253 and the overall horizontal control of all the powers and functions through fundamental rights and directive principles, backed by judicial review as part of the basic structure of the Constitution.*

governance are left to socio-political movements and political parties, or to politics and the forces of society in the management of resources and people by a particular government.[66]

The second approach does away with these assumptions so as to cause change through the use of the instrument of interpretation. This second approach is considered as an activist approach in contrast to the first conservative or traditional judicial approach.

3.18 SC as Discoverer of the Public Good

The second approach became visible in the Supreme Court's interpretation on locus standi for relief on violation of fundamental rights or statutory obligations,[67] to fill in an area on which the Constitution was silent. In interpreting the word "Life" in Francis Coralie Mullin vs. Union Territory of Delhi while interpreting Art. 21, wherein neither the petitioner pleaded Art. 21 as the basis for her grievance nor Art. 21 was required to be interpreted, the Supreme Court transplanted wholesale the Directive Principles into the Fundamental Rights Chapter of the Constitution without dealing with specific Constitutional words that the Directive Principles are "unenforceable in a court of law."[68] The Supreme Court in Maneka Gandhi vs. UOI,[69] followed by Sunil Batra vs. Delhi Administration[70] interpreted "procedure established by law"

---

[66] In re Central Provinces & Berar Sales of Motor Spirit and Lubricants Taxation Act, 1938, AIR 1939 FC:

A broad and liberal spirit should inspire those whose duty it is to interpret the Constitution; but I do not imply by this that they are free to stretch or pervert the language of the enactment in the interests of any legal or constitutional theory, or even for the purpose of supplying omissions or of correcting supposed errors. See also A.R. Antulay vs. R.S. Nayak, AIR 1988 SC 1531, Paras 38.40 and 81, wherein the Supreme court held that a court cannot confer jurisdiction on itself which was not provided by the Constitution or statutory law and that a judicial order made without jurisdiction is a nullity.

[67] S.P. Gupta vs. UOI, AIR 1982 SC 149.

[68] Francis Coralie vs. Union Territory of Delhi, AIR 1981 SC 746.

[69] Maneka Gandhi vs. UOI, AIR 1978 SC 597.

[70] Sunil Batra vs. Delhi Administration, AIR 1980 SC 579.

in Art. 21, as having the same content as "due process of law" of the U.S. Constitution.

It gave this interpretation without reference to the Constituent Assembly Debates which had specifically rejected this proposition. It ignored the earlier binding Constitution bench judgment of the Supreme Court in A.K. Gopalan vs. State of Madras[71] which had specifically pointed out the Constituent Assembly debates plus it also ignored the grammatical structure of the Article itself. It did this without any finding that there was any ambiguity, absurdity or perversity in the clear words of Article 21. Accordingly, in 1995, the Supreme Court declared in Nand Kishore vs. State of Punjab:[72] "Their Lordships decisions declared the existing law but do not enact any fresh law, is not in keeping with the plenary function of the Supreme Court under Art. 141 of the Constitution, for the Court is not merely an interpreter of law as existing, but much beyond that. The court as a wing of the State is by itself a source of law. The law is what the court says it is."

This activist approach of the Supreme Court demolished the traditional or conservative approach of the rule of legal reason being based on language, pleadings, principles of interpretation or precedents, since those who interpret are constitutionally armed with the power of all India binding finality to declare the public good by pouring new meaning regardless of text or context.

3.19 SC as Problem-Solver

The third approach does away with the legal cover of using the instrument of interpretation to discover the meaning of constitutional provisions in the adjudication of cases before it. After initiating the process of laying down law by guidelines, without any claim to judicial power to do so, this approach now outright claims the power of interim legislation by laying down mandatory enforceable guidelines, till Parliament makes a law on the subject. This approach had its probable first manifestation

---

[71] A.K. Gopalan vs. State of Madras, AIR 1950 SC 27.
[72] Nand Kishore vs. State of Punjab, (1995) 6 SCC 614.

in L.N. Pandey vs. UOI,[73] wherein the Supreme Court laid down guidelines for inter-country adoptions from India, without reference to any constitutional or legal principle enabling it to lay down guidelines on an issue on which admittedly there was no law. Two years later this approach saw the creation of a collegium in the Supreme Court for the selection and appointment of high court and Supreme Court judges in SC Advocates on Record Association vs. UOI,[74] when no such institution exists in the Constitution. This was followed four years later by Vishaka vs. State of Rajasthan[75] wherein the Supreme Court claimed the power, without mentioning any source of such power, to make interim legislation for sexual harassment at the workplace till Parliament made a law.

The Supreme Court created a duty on the executive to fill in a 'vacuum' of legislation which 'vacuum; will be discovered by it and filled in by it pending Parliament making a law to fill such discovered 'vacuum'. The same year the Supreme Court laid down guidelines on police arrest in D.K. Basu vs. State of West Bengal.[76] In 1998, in Supreme Court Bar Association vs. Union of India[77] a Constitution bench of the court held "Indeed, this court is not a court of restricted jurisdiction of only dispute-settling. It is well recognised and established that this Court has always been a law-maker and its role travels merely beyond dispute settling. It is a problem solver in the nebulous areas, but the substantive provisions dealing with the subject matter of a given case, cannot altogether be ignored by this court, while making an order under Art. 142."

By 2006, in Prakash Singh vs. Union of India[78] the Supreme Court advanced to laying down a complete new structure of police organization in India.

This approach simply does away with the constitutional assumption of the separation of powers principle that courts do not legislate. What was initially being done by way of guidelines and reading words into

---

[73] L.N. Pandey vs. UOI, (1991) 4 SCC 33.

[74] SC Advocates on Record Association vs. UOI, (1993) 4 SCC 441.

[75] Vishaka vs. State of Rajasthan, (1997)6SCC241.

[76] D. K. Basu vs. State of West Bengal, (1997) 1 SCC416.

[77] Supreme Court Bar Association vs. Union of India, AIR 1998 SC 1895.

[78] Prakash Singh vs. Union of India, (2006) 8 SCC 1.

constitutional provisions, under the cover of or by reference to the power to interpret as an essential component of the power to adjudicate constitutional cases, now became a free-wheeling judicial exercise to remedy the problem posed before it by a case.

The problem of protection of monuments of national importance fell into this category of free-wheeling exercise of judicial power without any constitutional or legal exposition in the judgments and orders concerning the acquisition of this power by the Supreme Court. The most outstanding example of this are the Taj Mahal judgments and orders. This judicial approach may be called supra-constitutional or a meta-legal approach. This approach sought orderly change, without the social, political or economic movements for bringing about this change, in a case subjected to the meta-legal methods of the Supreme Court. This made the enforcement of judgments and orders in these cases questionable.

This approach is unprecedented in the history of any country in the Anglo-Saxon legal system derived from common law. In England law and legal institutions evolved over a thousand years from the village upwards with participation of the villagers in a common language understood by all of them. The judiciary travelled down the villages to mark its presence and authority.[79] Similarly, in the United States it is people's political movements that shaped the law and the judiciary. For about ninety years the U.S. Supreme Court judges travelled on horseback holding circuit or camp courts throughout the country to make justice accessible and to mark their presence and authority amongst the citizens.[80]

3.20 Cultural Illiteracy Ensured

With citizens involvement missing, the Indian public's silence and lack of protest becomes understandable at the manner in which Parliament has defeated through Art. 21(A) inserted by the Constitution

---

[79] Adams, George Burton, revised by Robert L. Schuyler, Constitutional History of England, Jonathan Cape, Thirty Bedford Square, London (Reprint 1956).

[80] Nowak, John E. & Rotunda, Ronald D., Constitutional Law, 4th edn, Hornbook Series, West Publishing Co (1991); Minnesota and Raymond Arsenault, ed., 'Crucible of Liberty' in 200 years of the Bill of Rights, The Free Press, Macmillan Inc., New York (1991).

(Eighty Sixth) Amendment Act, 2002 the right of children to free primary education by nullifying the Supreme Court judgment in Unni Krishnan J.P. vs. State of Andhra Pradesh.[81] Art. 21A grants the Fundamental Right to free and compulsory education from the age of six when at that age no school will admit a child. Primary education is the first step that opens the possibility of understanding your own way of life or culture and its symbols like monuments. It is the first step to discover your own identity.

Inequality, in violation of the fundamental governance (Art. 37) principle Art. 38(2) has been increased by enabling those having money to put their children into play schools from the age of two upwards till entry into primary school and the majority without money to live with the hope that suddenly at the age of six the child will start studying without any preparatory input in a playschool or otherwise. The majority of children can only await the states' "endeavor" under Directive Principle Art. 45 to provide "early childhood care and education for all children until they complete the age of six years." In this context it is ironical that citizens have been loaded with the fundamental duty under Art. 51-A(k) to provide opportunities for education of their children between the age of 6–14 years. Hence, the dim chance of education providing a culture of understanding of monuments is lost constitutionally to an unknown future. This has been done by making education of the child till the age of six (Art. 45) an unenforceable directive principle under which the State "shall endeavor" to give education to the child.

An activist and then a free-wheeling justicing Supreme Court has also kept quiet by taking no *suo motu* action on these amendments which wipe out the public interest reasoning for free primary education given in Mohini Jain vs. State of Karnataka,[82] namely, that there cannot be a democracy based on illiterates. In addition, what can illiterates understand about cultural heritage or monuments and the Union Govt's economic planning that uproots them from villages to slums and from their heritage.

The role of education in creating a code of common culture has been emphasised by the Supreme Court stating in State of

---

[81] Unni Krishnan J.P. vs. State of Andhra Pradesh, (1993) 1 SCC 645.
[82] Mohini Jain vs. State of Karnataka, AIR 1992 SC 1858.

Tamil Nadu vs. K. Shyam Sunder:[83] "Uniform education would achieve the code of common culture, removal of disparity and depletion of discriminatory values in human rights. It would enhance the virtues and improve the quality of human life, elevate the thoughts which advance our constitutional philosophy of an equal society. In future, it may prove to be a basic preparation for the Uniform Civil Code, as it may help in diminishing opportunities to those who foment fanatic and fissiparous tendencies."

3.21 Legal Cycle and Monuments

The problem of enforcement of judicial orders and judgments as in Bandhua Mukti Morcha vs. Union of India[84] and Taj Mahal case[85] orders, brings about an impasse in the legal structure under our Constitution. Parliament enacts law declaring rights and entitlements for social, economic and political justice. The Government or ruling politicians operationalise that law by notifications, circulars, orders, to make social, economic and political justice available to citizens by using its constitutional power under Art. 73 to govern administratively over all subjects in the Union List. None of it gets implemented or is implemented so as to leave the citizens problems in an aggravated form. As police and administrative remedies fail or are unavailable, resort is had to the courts. The courts pronounce orders and judgments which remain unenforced by the same ruling politician, police and administration. The people and their problems of mis-governance or non-governance remain where they are.

Monuments, despite good intentions, become part of this legal cycle. Currently this is the problem of governance through judicial orders and judgments on monuments which must be implemented and enforced by the very same government and administration that compelled an individual or an NGO to resort to the court.

---

[83] State of Tamil Nadu vs. K. Shyam Sunder, (2011) 8 SCC 737.

[84] Bandhua Mukti Morcha vs. Union of India, (1984) 3 SCC 161.

[85] M. C. Mehta vs. UOI, (1991) 4 SCC 177.

3.22 Effects of the Legal Cycle

Consequently, it is not surprising that Report No. 18 of 2013, by the CAG on Performance Audit of Preservation & Conservation of Monuments & Antiquities, finds that the Union Ministry of Culture and the ASI simply ignored court rulings and the red flags raised on their functioning by expert and Parliamentary committees. In all the functions – excavation, conservation, keeping count of its monuments and antiquities, encroachments and unauthorised construction in, near or over monuments, relevant data bases, notifications, security, manpower and funding – were found to be in grave default.

The Report pointed out that the National Mission of Monuments and Antiquities lacked "direction, vision and appropriate strategy" and had failed to fulfil its purposes in a time bound manner. Despite the Antiquities and Art Treasure Act, the "illegal export of antiquities was rampant" and the "proposed legislative amendments to the Act were pending for years."

The ruling politicians, that is the Union Ministry of Culture, was lax and deficient in all this to the extent that there was no policy, no data and no count. The ASI under the Ministry simply showed no interest in all this.

3.23 Summing Up

The monumental problem therefore concerning the role of the judiciary in the protection of monuments of national importance is the ignoring of the fundamental threat of unconstitutional economic development which creates major monetary incentives for violating monuments; the political and administrative collapse concerning legal duties vis a vis such monuments; the non-compliance with court orders; the non-accountability under the Constitution and the relevant laws of those who govern such monuments.

The judiciary has ignored the foundational problem of citizens completely missing from these monuments in the process of their selection as monuments of national importance, in their protection and conservation and in their cultural heritage contextualization by forgetting that there is an Art. 29 which gives citizens a fundamental right to their culture in which alone monuments can find an effective place. We analyse this by the well settled discipline of law – finding the relevant law, the relevant facts, relevant supporting documentation, the legal holistic diagnosis and then the alternatives.

Chapter IV
CONSTITUTIONAL FRAMEWORK

4.1 The 'National Importance' Brand

The Constitution's Directive Principles of State Policy state in Article 49 the "obligation of the State to protect every monument...of artistic or historic interest, declared law by or under a law made by Parliament, to be of national importance......"

Monuments of national importance are exclusively a Parliamentary/Union Government, Seventh Schedule List I Entry 67 subject, under the Constitution. This is reinforced by Entry 40 in List III of Schedule VII and Entry 12, List II, Seventh Schedule. Under Entry 40 of List III of Schedule Seven only "archaeological sites and remains other than those declared by or under law made by Parliament to be of national importance, maybe legislated both by the Centre and the States under Art. 245(2)". Under Entry 12, List II only "ancient and historical monuments and records other than those declared by or under a law made by Parliament to be of national importance." In all the three Entries, the Union Government, by the Constitution (Seventh Amendment) Act, 1956, introduced the words "under a law" as an addition to the already existing words "by a law." The effect o this is analysed in detail in Chapter V Para 5.3 onwards.

4.2 Evolution: Central Control & National Brand

Monuments regulation began locally along with the local evolution of British trading activity and then rule in Bombay, Bengal and Madras. The Bengal Regulation of 1810 in the Bengal Code and the Madras Regulation VII of 1817 in the Madras Code, were issued to empower the Governments in these two provinces to take action when any ancient or historical building was threatened by private individuals. The conservation of monuments was kept outside the scope of the first Director General of ASI, Alexander Cunningham. For some time from

1881 onwards conservation of monuments came under Central control with the appointment of Major H.H. Cole as the Curator of Ancient Monuments under Governor General Lord Ripon (1880–1884).

But on the post of Director-General being abolished in 1883 the British Govt. again left the conservation task to local governments. Central control on monuments returned in 1885 under Director – General James Burgess. Again, after Burgess the conservation work reverted to the local governments. With John Marshall's work as the Director General from 1902 onwards, the necessity of centralized control was expressed by the British government enacting the Ancient Monuments Preservation Act, 1904. Finally following the Montague – Chelmsford reforms in 1919, the Devolution Rules, 1921 clearly stated archaeology as a Central subject. There was no concept of monuments of national importance.

The Government of India Act, 1935 strengthened this legal position by putting ancient and historical monuments, archaeological sites and remains in the Union List without any entry on this subject in the Provincial List. This enabled Director General Mortimer Wheeler in 1944 to take over the execution of monuments conservation work from the Public Works Departments of local governments and put it under the Archaeological Survey of India (ASI).[1] From Jan 26, 1950 Indians as citizens instead of subjects inherited this legacy under a Constitution that gave exclusive control to the Centre[2] over ancient and historical monuments of national importance and left other monuments under the control of the respective States through the State archaeological department.[3]

Thus, the constitutional brand of monuments of national importance belongs only to those monuments which have been declared by Parliament by a law, or which have been so declared by the Union Government under a law made by Parliament.

---

[1] Marshall J.H., 'Introduction' in Inaugural Issue of ASI's archaeological "Annual," p. 3–11. (1902).

[2] Entry 67 List I, VIIth Schedule of the Constitution of India.

[3] Entry 12, List II of the Constitution of India.

4.3 Unconstitutional Branding: Model Regulations

Despite this clear constitutional position that has evolved from 1810 onwards, the Model Heritage Regulations, 2011 framed by the Town and Country Planning Organisation, Union Ministry of Urban Development create monuments of national importance, for monuments which are not under the purview of ASI or the State Archaeological Department. These are called Grade-I Buildings under Para 7.1 of the Model Heritage Guidelines. Under Para 5, the list of such buildings in a State is to be prepared by the Commissioner/CEO, Municipal Corporation/Municipal Council/Nagar Panchayat or Vice Chairman, Development Authority or District Collector as the case may be, on the advice of the Heritage Conservation Committee to be appointed by the State Government. Before finalizing the list, objections and suggestions from the public are to be invited and considered.

All this stands in stark violation of the Constitution which unequivocally makes 'monuments of national importance' exclusively a subject for Parliament under Art. 49 and for Parliament as also the Union Government under Entry 67 List I of the Seventh Schedule of the Constitution read with Art. 245(2) of the Seventh Schedule to the Constitution.[4]

However, it seems that even prior to the issuing of the Model Heritage Guidelines by the Central Government in 2011, some States had already incorporated such guidelines in their urban development or municipal statutes. One such State is that of Andhra Pradesh.

4.3.1 *Andhra Pradesh*

The Municipal Administration and Urban Development Department of Andhra Pradesh vide G.O.Ms No. 542, M.A. dated December 14, 1995 granted approval to the Hyderabad Urban Development Authority to add a new regulation to the existing Hyderabad Urban Development Authority Zoning Regulations, 1981, for the Conservation of Historical Buildings and areas in Hyderabad City as annexed to this Order.

---

[4] Art. 73, of the Constitution of India.

The annexure stated that in terms of this order, after Zoning Regulation No. 12, the Conservation of Historical Buildings Regulation is added under S.59(1) of the Andhra Pradesh Urban Areas (Development) Act, 1975. The new regulation classified "buildings and precincts of national or historical importance" as Grade I, specifying that these "richly deserve careful preservation" as distinct from Grade II buildings which "deserve intelligent conservation" and Grade III which "deserve protection of unique features and attributes."

Pursuant to this new regulation, vide G.O.Ms. No. 102 M.A. dated March 23, 1998, the Hyderabad Urban Development Authority, on the recommendation of the Heritage Conservation Committee, issued in Annexure I a List of 137 buildings in which 24 were mentioned as Grade I buildings of national importance. But the provision of the Constitution from which the State Government derives the power to empower the Hyderabad Development Authority to declare buildings as being of "national importance" is nowhere mentioned or explained. No reference whatsoever is made to Schedule VII Entries 67 List I, 12 List II, 40 List III, read with Art. 245 of the Constitution or to the Ancient Monuments and Archaeological Sites and Remains Act, 1958 enacted by Parliament.

4.3.2 Mumbai

The same legal situation prevails under Development Control Regulations for Greater Mumbai, 1991, in Regulation 66 Para 3 in Part V. The Regulations were notified on February 20, 1991 by the Maharashtra Urban Development Department under the Maharashtra Regional and Town Planning Act, 1966.

Any question, as to the constitutional source for all such Regulations, would probably elicit an answer based on the Model Heritage Regulations issued by the Central Government, which state that the Regulations apply to non-Archaeological Survey of India buildings.

But the answer is not constitutionally tenable because the power under Article 49 and the subject matter under Entry 67 List I do not divide historical buildings of national importance into ASI administered and non ASI administered buildings. The constitutional provisions apply to all buildings and no building can be declared by a State Government to be historically of national importance as the Constitution does not give such competence to States. Only Parliament, under Art. 49 or in terms of Entry 67 List I, is empowered to do so by or under a law made by it. These provisions exhaust the constitutional power to declare historical buildings of national importance. No power whatsoever has been conferred on State Governments or their instrumentalities to declare any building of 'artistic or historic interest' or which is 'ancient and historical' in their State to be of national importance.

It is strange that the Union Ministry of Culture and its agency, the ASI, have kept quiet about the unconstitutional legal action of the States concerning the declaration of "monuments of national importance." The national importance brand has been unconstitutionally hijacked by the States.

4.4 Conundrum of Art. 49 and Entry 67, List I

The Constitution's Directive Principles of State Policy state in Article 49 the "obligation of the State to protect every monument. of artistic or historic interest, declared by or under a law made by Parliament, to be of national importance." However, the subject matter of legislation pertaining to Art. 49, speaks in Entry 67 List I of "ancient and historical monuments......declared by or under law made by Parliament to be of national importance."

Thus the subject matter for the Parliamentary law concerning the selection of a monument to be of national importance, is "artistic or historic interest" under Art. 49, whereas it is "ancient and historical" under Entry 67 List I of the VIIth Schedule to the Constitution.

The subject matter of Parliamentary law under Art. 49 must be art — the manner or style of depiction or use of materials constituting the monument. Or, it should be an event in the past concerning the monument, to make it of historical interest. On the other hand, when Parliament makes that law by exercising its power under Art. 246(1) of the Constitution the subject matter of such law in terms of Entry 67 ListI, must be a monument that is by itself history or part of past event/s and in addition the span of time concerning that monument must go back to the beginning of the country's history that is "ancient".

The two constitutional provisions speak differently and thereby raise the conundrum of what is it that is protected as a monument by the Constitution.

While dealing with monuments of national importance, the judiciary has remained silent on this conundrum of the interpretation of the Constitution created by the language used in Art. 49 and in Entry 67 List I. The conundrum arises because in any event Parliament has to make a law either in terms of the Directive Principle Art. 49 or in exercise of its legislative power under Entry 67 List I, Schedule VII read with Article 246(1). We try to resolve this conundrum here.

4.4.1 *Conundrum Resolution: Harmonious Reading*

In making this law Parliament must apply the Directive Principle Art. 49, since Art. 37 requires it to do so on the ground that it "shall be the duty of the State to apply the directive principles in making laws".[5] So the conundrum may be resolved by treating Art. 49 as one source of legislative power for monuments of national importance with reference to the kind of monuments mentioned therein and Art. 246(1) to be another source of legislative power for monuments of national importance with reference to the kind of monuments mentioned in Entry 67 List I. Art. 49 would apply to either exercise of legislative power by Parliament to declare monuments of national importance, since that is the mandatory requirement of Art. 37, which states that "it shall be the duty of the State to apply these directive principles in making laws," the principles being "fundamental in the governance of the country."

If all legislative power for declaring monuments of national importance were to be referable only to Art. 246(1) read with Entry 67 List I, then "artistic interest" monuments under Art. 49, like the Taj Mahal would cease to be monuments of national importance. This would be an absurd result and the rules of interpretation require that

---

[5] *The Fundamental Rights chapter of the Constitution defines "State" in Art. 12 to include inter alia "the Parliament of India" and in the Directive Principles chapter of the Constitution Art. 36 declares that the word "State" has the same meaning as in Art. 12, unless the context requires otherwise.*

such interpretation be abandoned. As stated in T.M.A. Pai Foundation vs. State of Karnataka,[6] by the six majority judges in the eleven judge bench, "When constitutional provisions are interpreted, it has to be borne in mind that the interpretation should be such as to further the object of their incorporation. They cannot be read in isolation and have to be read harmoniously to provide meaning and purpose. They cannot be interpreted in a manner that renders another provision redundant." Hence the key substantive words concerning monuments in the Constitution are "national importance," occurring in Art. 49.[7]

If we apply the principle that a subject matter entry, Entry 67 List I of the Schedule VII of the Constitution cannot prevail over the substantive provisions in Art. 49 of the Constitution, then the subject matter entry will become surplus and otiose. This is not permissible by the interpretation rule which requires that all words in an enactment must be given their full meaning and no words can be treated as surplus or superfluous. As Patanjali Shastry, C.J.I. stated in Aswini Kumar Ghose vs. Arabinda Bose:[8] "It is not a sound principle of construction to brush aside words in a statute as being inapposite surplusage, if they can have appropriate application in circumstances conceivably within the contemplation of the statute."

The approach of treating Art. 49 and Entry 67 List I read with Art. 246(1) as enabling legislation concerning monuments of national importance to the kinds of monuments mentioned in their respective fields as stated in the Article and the Entry respectively, overcomes these problems of interpretation.

As stated by Venkatarama Aiyar J. in Venkataramana Devaru vs. State of Mysore,[9] "The rule of construction is well settled that when there are in an enactment two provisions which cannot be reconciled with each other, they should be so interpreted that, if possible, effect

---

[6] T.M.A. Pai Foundation vs. State of Karnataka, AIR 2003 SC 355 at 415 Para 148.

[7] *This is reinforced by the fact that only archaeological sites and remains which are not of national importance find mention in Entry 40, List III of the Seventh Schedule to the Constitution.*

[8] Aswini Kumar Ghose vs. Arabinda Bose, AIR 1952 SC 369 at p. 377.

[9] Venkataramana Devaru vs. State of Mysore, AIR 1958 SC 255 at p. 268.

should be given to both. This is what is known as the rule of harmonious construction."

4.5 Net Result

The net interpretative result of reading Art. 49 and Entry 67 List I of the Seventh Schedule of the Constitution is that monuments are of three kinds: those of historic interest and those of artistic interest under Art. 49; those which are ancient and historical under Entry 67 List I. So what is protected are these kinds of monuments, "by or under a law made by Parliament."

Chapter V
STATE CONTROL OF CULTURE AND MONUMENTS

Prior to Independence, the British through their education and language policy had already taken over the official and urban livelihood culture of British India for their administration and governance. Having taken this policy decision, the British logically treated the work of preserving and protecting the rich treasure of monuments, officially recognized by them, as one of preserving monuments as objects. There could be no official space for understanding and preserving monuments in the context of Indian cultures of the time, space and ways of life around a monument. This approach expressed itself in the Ancient Monuments Preservation Act, 1904. But after independence, it was expected that under a Constitution which in Art. 29 gave Indians a fundamental right to their distinct culture, script and language, there would be a cultural approach to the State's obligation in Art. 49, to determine and protect by a Parliamentary law, monuments of national importance. Art. 29 carried the seed of India's cultural renaissance with far-reaching effects for India's polity, languages, educational systems, livelihoods and equality of opportunity for all this.

However, independent India's first Government and ruling party, the Indian National Congress, not only ignored citizens in terms of their fundamental right to culture but also carried out a constitutional coup to firmly put the entire process of declaration and preservation of monuments of national importance under Central Government control. Independent India, despite Art. 29, has continued the colonial British policy of State control of culture through the entire constitutional process of recognising monuments of national importance and a monuments – as – objects approach.

5.1 Ancient Monuments Preservation Act, 1904

The British Act clearly showed that citizens of India were to have no say or role in the determination of ancient monuments of "historical, archaeological or artistic interest, declared to be protected by the Central Government." Section 3 empowered the Central Government to notify an ancient monument as a protected monument, through the Official Gazette., after hearing within thirty days of the notification, any objection to such a notification. The definition of ancient monument in Section 2(1), did not refer to any indication of time to determine 'ancientness'. Hence ancientness of a monument had no criteria for its determination. No reasons or documentation was required to be given for declaring a monument of India as "ancient" Ancientness was what the British Government in India decided And under Section 3(4) the notification was conclusive evidence of the fact that a monument was ancient. From proposal to expiry of the notified proposal's objection period, a monument was a protected monument simply because the British Government in India had said so. This rendered meaningless, the provision for objecting to the Notification within thirty days of the issue of the Notification.

There was no definition or criteria in the Act of the words historical, archaeological or artistic, qualifying an ancient monument under the Act. There was no requirement on the part of the Central Government to state as to the category in which the proposed protected monument belonged out of the three categories of historical, artistic or archaeological. The Act did not require any reasons to be given in the Notification proposing an ancient monument to be protected. The notification could be withdrawn, as and when the British Government wanted, without any duty to give a reason for the withdrawal.

The words 'national importance' were missing from the Act. Any monument in India could be notified as a protected monument for the entire country, regardless of whether it was of national importance or not.

In short,. the British Government had complete and total power to decide which monuments of British India qualified to be protected and preserved under the Act. The Archaeological Survey of India, constituted as a professional archaeological wing by the British Government, simply masked this unreasoned and undefined British control over monuments in India, just as the Act created an image of rule of law for monuments to mask the complete and absolute power without any criteria or guidelines conferred by it, in choosing monuments that needed to be protected. Accordingly, there is no public document of law available under this Act as to why or on what basis or attributes a monument had been recognised for protection.

Would Indians get a better deal concerning their monuments of national importance in an independent India, under a Constitution which gave them a fundamental right to their distinct culture, language and script? It seems not from the manner in which the Constitution was used by free India's first government of the Indian National Congress, concerning monuments of national importance. We analyse and examine that manner in the preceding context of what was already being done to culture in music, literature and drama.

5.2 Preceding Context

In the independence cum partition turmoil, citizens were concerned with the survival and recommencement of life by searching for shelters & livelihood. This combined with the general illiteracy and the lack of awareness of a Constitution conferring rights on them as citizens, left a huge space for the Indian State to show its protecting hand of safety to such citizens in the wake of the world's largest communal migration. The protecting Indian State which offered security, filled the Art. 29 cultural space by a series of State created cultural institutions — the Indian Council for Cultural Relations (for foreign cultural relations) in 1950; the Sangeet Natak Akademi (Indian music and dance) in 1953, established by a resolution of the Union Ministry of Education on May 31, 1952 and registered as a society on Sept 11, 1961); the Lalit Kala Akademi (For Indian modern and contemporary art, set up in 1954 and registered as a society on March 11, 1957); the National Gallery of Modern Art in 1954 (Administered as a subordinate office of the Department of Culture, GOI); the Sahitya Akademi in 1954 and the National School of Drama in 1959.

Many of these State sponsored institutions became reflections of the Union Ministry of Culture's role of control and of artists and administrators with political linkages. The 2016–17 Citizens Charter of the Ministry is focussed on Finance and Fellowships and its document on "National Mission on Cultural Mapping & Roadmap" seems to aspire to record the present without the past. Accordingly, it speaks of art forms and artists but without a word on the substantial tangible heritage of monuments, religion or role of citizens therein in terms of Art. 29 of the Constitution.

The May 2014 'Report of the High Powered Committee on the Akademies and Other Institutions under the Union Ministry of Culture' stated: "No culture has survived without patronage. In the past, such support came from royalty and the nobility. In modern society, it must come from the Government of the day. But is the State machinery able to appreciate the nuances of creativity, and to encourage, and harmonise, the many voices of human endeavour? The representatives of Government often believe that theirs is the power and the right to receive obeisance. On the other hand our ambassadors of culture are sometimes so uncultured in their ways; some of them do not know the difference between self-actualistation and self aggrandisement. In public positions, they must realise that they are answerable to the public, to the ordinary citizen; they are responsible for the honest utilisation of the tax payer's money."[1]

The Committee "delved" into the three previous reports of October 22, 1964, July 31, 1972 and July 1990 (Bhabha Committee; Khosla Committee and Haksar Committee) and stated: "It is unfortunate that the efforts of previous High Powered Committees do not seem to have been reflected in any significant changes in the bureaucratic systems and the style of functioning of our institutions. As we wrestled with the formalisation of our recommendations there was a feeling that it has all been said before."[2] It concluded: "What is most crucial today is that the Ministry of Culture accepts that it is stuck in antediluvian systems and that change is inevitable. Indeed it must guide that change assiduously, else the bureaucratic control centre would be out of sync

---

[1] P.3 of the Report.

[2] P.6 Para 2.5 of the Report.

with the outside environment………. There is indeed the need for political and administrative will to bring about change; the sustenance of the hearts and minds of people must go beyond politics into the realm of statesmanship and governance."

Hence the future of the line of the Union Government's line of action for monuments in the context of Art. 49, Entry 67 List I, VIIth Schedule and Art. 29 was set from 1950 onwards.

5.3 Two Approaches

Whether the subject matter called a monument located in ancient history is "ancient and historical" under Entry 67 List I or is of "historic interest" or "artistic interest" under Art. 49, to qualify to be a monument of national importance, raises the question as to how this is to be decided. With the commencement of the Constitution, two approaches were available to the Union Government on January 26, 1950 with regard to monuments: to treat these as objects[3] (First Approach) or as a cultural heritage (Second Approach).

5.3.1 Effects of a Choice

The constitutional choices in determining monuments of national importance are firstly between history as a State determined past or history as a State determined culture and secondly, history as a pulsating, felt truth of what people preserve as their distinct culture. Culture is a social construct and any aspect of it, including monuments, cannot be protected if the "social" is ignored or taken out of this construct. Monuments will be preserved only when ordinary citizens realize the historical importance of a given monument, know that with its destruction something irreparable will be lost and are aware of their joint responsibility in preserving or protecting it.

The first is a non-Art. 29 approach. Under this approach the State continues with the colonial path of non-participation of citizens, in

---

[3] *The possible Constitutional justification for this would be that in Art. 49 itself the word 'monument' was mentioned along with the word 'object' by stating: "It shall be the obligation of the State to protect every monument or place or object of artistic or historic interest……"*

spite of Art. 29, and hence continues with the same pre-independence organization called the Archaeological Survey of India (ASI) for selection, appropriation and protection of citizen's culture, as suits the State, that is, the ruling politicians, at a point of time. The second is an Art. 29 approach or a citizen's participation approach.

5.3.2 Monuments – As-Objects Approach

If the first course, of monuments as objects were to be adopted, then that would continue the pre independence colonial tradition of ignoring completely the culture of the Indian people, including its languages, vernacular literature and monuments. This would mean reading independent India's Constitution concerning monuments as limited to only Art. 49 and Entry 67 List I of the VIIth Schedule. Under this approach monuments were artistic or historic objects under Art. 49 or ancient and historical objects under Entry 67 List I of the VIIth Schedule. This would be akin to the Govt of India Act, 1935 which in Entry 15 List I stated: "Ancient and historical monuments; archaeological sites and remains."

This was politically comfortable since by virtue of Articles 374378.311(2), 277, 294 and 118(2) the Constitution continued the British laws, administration and the personnel and the power on monuments remained in the hands of the ruling party that constituted the Union Government. The only change was that independent India's Constitution required under Art. 49, a monument to be recognized "**by a law made by Parliament**" as being of national importance. Hence in terms of independent India's elected representative government in Parliament, each monument to be recognized as one of national importance had to be brought to the notice of the representatives of the people of India elected by them to Parliament. The proposal would be discussed and voted upon to be made into a law.

5.3.3 Monuments As Cultural Heritage Approach

If the second course of monuments as a cultural heritage were to be adopted, then that would require the then Union Government to recognise Art. 29 of the Constitution of India. It would require reading

Art. 49, Entry 67 List I of the Seventh Schedule to the Constitution with Art. 29 which for the first time in India's history recognized in a modern Constitution the fundamental right of Indians to their distinct culture, language and script. The Union of India, in constitutional terms and the principles of interpretation, had actually no choice but to so read the provisions concerning monuments in Art. 49 and Entry 67 List I of the Constitution. This was so because of the well established principle that the provisions of the Constitution, concerning a subject matter, have to be read as a whole.

5.3.4 Execution of the First Approach

We now examine how the first, monuments-as-objects approach, was handled by independent India's first government and Parliament.

5.3.4.1 The First Coup: Using "By a Law Made by Parliament"

The change as compared to the pre independence colonial situation was that independent India's Constitution required under Art. 49, and Entry 67 List I, VIIth Schedule of the Constitution, a monument to be recognized **"by a law made by Parliament,"**[4] as being of national importance. Hence in terms of the Entry and the Article, independent India's elected representative government had to bring before Parliament, each monument to be recognized as one of national importance. The proposal would be discussed and voted upon to be made into a law.

The first choice required to be made by independent India's first government at the Centre was to decide whether to follow the Art. 49 route or the Entry 67 List I route. Under Art. 49 the area of consideration of artistic or historic monuments was very wide due to the words "every monument." Since these words are not present in Entry 67 List I, the area is narrowed down to simply ancient and historical monuments. Art. 49 monuments of "artistic or historic interest" raised the question that the monument should be of artistic or historic interest to whom? Hence Art. 49 compelled a data base for which the State would be pushed to

---

[4] Indramani vs. W. R. Natu, AIR 1963 SC 274 at p. 281, para 15: *"By an Act would mean by a provision directly enacted in the statute in question...."*

the fundamental right to culture in Art. 29. The State would have to map "every monument of artistic or historic interest" and then decide which ones deserve to be granted the brand of national importance. All these problems did not exist in taking the Entry 67 List I where the only controlling factor was an undefined time, "ancient" and an event "historic" available from recorded history. There was no need to resort to Art. 29 in taking the Entry 67 List I route for making a law to confer the brand of national importance on an ancient and historical monument. The question that this raises is whether out of two constitutional paths for legislation can the State take a path that enables it to ignore a fundamental right, in this case Art. 29. Or, is the State bound to choose that legislative path which will facilitate a fundamental right? This remains an unresolved question of the scope of judicial review of legislation, involving issues of policy making and its impact on fundamental rights.

Given what the Union Government had done already from 1951 onwards with music, dance, drama, literature and arts, by way of Akademies, as shown by the Hi — Powered Committee Report of 2014, the choice between the two approaches had to be the first monuments-as-objects approach, ensuring the State's political control over the question of recognition of monuments of national importance, through the ruling party in power. This was reflected clearly by the Bill moved by it in Parliament, The Ancient and Historical Monuments And Archaeological Sites and Remains (Declaration of National Importance) Act 1951, (hereinafter Declaration of Importance Act, 1951)[5] which Parliament passed. The title and all the three Sections of the Act used the Entry 67 List I words "ancient and historical monuments" instead of the Art. 49 words "every monument of artistic or historic interest." The Act legislatively expressed the Union Government's intention to be concerned with only Entry 67 List I monuments — "ancient and historical" – and not Art. 49's "every monument of artistic or historic interest." Under Section 2 a Schedule was provided for "ancient and historical monuments."

---

[5] The Ancient and Historical Monuments And Archaeological Sites and Remains (Declaration of National Importance) Act 1951, Act No. LXXI of 1951.

The Act did not define the words "ancient and historical" or the words "national importance." So no one knew the content of these constitutional words, the fulfilment of which is a mandatory condition, in conferring the status of ancient and historical monuments put in Schedule I. This was reinforced by the Indian Parliament Act 3 of 1954, which amended the Schedule to add and subtract "ancient and historical monuments" of national importance. The Amendment Act in Section 2 required the Schedule in the 1951 Act to be amended to carry the following Explanatory Note: "The entries in this Schedule are intended only to identify the ancient and historical monuments…referred to ro specified therein……." Hence the Amendment Act clarified that the 1951 Act was only an Act for naming the ancient and historical monuments of national importance and not for giving any criteria by which these monuments had been considered to have fulfilled the constitutional requirements of being ancient, historical and such as to be of national importance.

The problem of continuity with the past monuments mentioned in the 1904 Ancient Monuments Preservation Act, was resolved in Section 3 by stating that these would be 'deemed' to be of national importance, even though the words 'national importance' were non existent in the 1904 Act, The question that this analysis raises is whether the words "by a law" in Art. 49 and in Entry 67 List I, VIIth Schedule, were meant to be used in this manner. In using these words there was a choice between tabling a Bill for each monument being proposed by the Government for the status of national importance or to move in Parliament a Bill defining the content of the constitutional terms — ancient, historical, national importance—and showing their applicability to the monuments proposed to be put in the Schedule as such monuments of national importance. Neither of these two courses were adopted. Instead the Act was reduced to an executive order which simply declares the order or the monument without any criteria or reasons.

So the first constitutional coup was to use the constitutional mandatory requirement of the words "by a law made in Parliament" to use the overwhelming majority in India's first Parliament of the ruling party to get through and enact a constitutionally and legally meaningless law which left nothing to be debated in Parliament and shut out any examination of the monuments proposed to be of national importance. The citizens's fundamental right to monuments as part of his fundamental right to culture, thus stood eliminated, quietly but effectively. But it seems that even such an Act with such a result irked the then ruling party, the Indian National Congress.

5.3.4.2 Second Coup: From Parliament to the Executive

The clearest intention of the 1956 Union Government and ruling party to keep citizens out of the process of determining monuments of national importance by following only and only the Entry 67 List I, Schedule VII of the Constitution route, instead of the Art. 29 read with this Entry and Art. 49, was exhibited by its moving the Constitution (Seventh Amendment) Bill, 1956.

So far, both Art. 49 and Entry 67 List I required monuments of national importance to be declared "by a law made by Parliament." Pursuant to this the Union Government had enacted through Parliament the Declaration of Importance Act 1951. Now the Constitution was sought to be amended to add the words "or under" after the word "by" in Art. 49 and in Entry 67 List I, VIIth Schedule. This was achieved through Section 27 of the Constitution Seventh (Amendment) Act, 1956 to replace monuments of national importance "declared by a law made by Parliament" with "declared by or under a law made by Parliament." The coup was the giving of a choice to the Union Government to declare monuments of national importance either through Parliament or bypass Parliament completely and declare such monuments by an executive order.

5.3.4.3 Effect of the Second Coup

The pre-amendment Art. 49 and Entry 67 List I, permitting the declaration of monuments of national importance only "by" a Parliamentary law, brought Parliament's oversight specifically on each declaration, could now be done by moving a Bill to amend the Schedule of such monuments in The Declaration of Monuments of National Importance Act, 1951. The Bill also revealed as to whether the legislative power conferred by the aforesaid Act, on the basis of the pre Seventh Constitution Amendment Act, was being exercised in terms of the test under Art. 49 — "every monument of artistic or historic interest," or whether it was being exercised under Entry 67 List I read with Art. 246 (1), concerning "ancient and historical monuments" mentioned therein. If Art. 49 is read all alone, the way the Union Government was reading its legislative power under Art. 246(1) over the subject of monuments in Entry 67 List I, VIIth Schedule, by ignoring Art. 49 and Art. 29, then the constitutional obligation of the State to protect monuments of national importance stood limited only to the artistic and historic monuments in Art. 49. Hence it is significant that the Declaration of National Importance Act did not provide for any obligation to protect the monuments and did not specify who in the Union Government was obliged to do so for the monuments put in Schedule, Part I of this Act which are stated to be "protected monuments" in the recital to Part I of the Schedule. The Act nowhere defines the word "protected." Hence there was no constitutional or legal basis for protection of the monuments of national importance declared in terms of Entry 67 List I as "ancient and historical." The Seventh Constitution Amendment Act did not deal with this issue of protection of monuments of ancient and historical national importance.

Now this Parliamentary oversight could be avoided by the Union Govt, since it could choose to pass an executive order "under a law made by Parliament" for declaring a monument to be of national importance. The words "under any law" would mean that which is not directly found under the statute itself but is conferred or imposed by virtue of powers enabling this to be done.[6] Hence the words "under any law" made it possible to apply Art. 73(1)(a) to Entry 67 List I so as to extend the executive power of the Union Government to Entry 67 List I. Art. 73(1)(a) states: "Subject to the provisions of this Constitution, the executive power of the Union shall extend to (a) to the matters with respect to which Parliament has power to make laws."

The first Central Government of independent India used its majority in Parliament to amend the Constitution to nullify Parliament scrutiny over monuments sought to be declared by it of national importance, to shift this power for such a declaration by it entirely to itself by a notification issued by it and make such declarations without any

---

[6] Indramani vs. W.R. Natu AIR 1963 SC 274 at 281 Para 15.

parliamentary scrutiny. The base for total political control by the ruling party or the Executive was ready.

5.3.4.4 Effect of the 7th Constitutional Amendment

Consequently, the same pre-independence Archaeological Survey of India without any change and not subject to any public scrutiny continued to be the administrator of the monuments in India. Hence, post Constitution independent India had now the same legal framework for monuments as pre-constitution colonial India. Clause 24 of the Seventh Constitution Amendment Act altered the original constitutional architecture of monuments of national importance by shutting out the principle of representative governance from such monuments, without explaining or pointing out this consequence.

This sub-silentio constitutional coup at the very threshold of India's independence journey was explained by Clause 24 of the Seventh Constitution Amendment Bill, 1956 merely in terms of the "cumbrous procedure" of each time an Act being required for any alteration or addition to the Schedule of monuments of national importance in the 1951 Act. The national importance of a monument had been reduced to a play of political parties in power at the Centre by ruling politicians of 1950s completely altering the original constitutional intent of public control through a public debate by its duly elected representatives in Parliament.[7] This would also be subversive of the only possible constitutional purpose behind the original "by law" Art. 49 and Entry 67 List I namely, the unity and integrity of India. This would be the purposive interpretation of Art. 49 and Entry 67 List I on a reading of these provisions of the Constitution in the light of the Preamble. The citizen's opportunity to a public debate through their representatives in Parliament, as to whether the monument proposed to be declared as one

---

[7] *Articles 81 and 326 of the Constitution of India. The 1976 UNESCO Recommendation on Participation by People at Large in Cultural Life and Their Contribution stated in its Preamble: "Culture is not merely an accumulation of works and knowledge which an elite produces, collects and conserves in order to place it within the reach of all; or that a people rich in its past and its heritage offers to others, as a model which their own history has failed to provide for them; and that culture is not limited to works of art and humanities.*

of national importance would ensure the unity and integrity of India or otherwise, was now lost after the Seventh Constitution Amendment's introduction of the words "under a law" in Art. 49 and Entry 67 List I of the Seventh Schedule of the Constitution.

5.3.4.5 Statutory Conclusion of the Coup

The Union Government exercised the choice created by the Seventh Constitution Amendment 1956 of declaring monuments to be of national importance either "by" or "under" a "law made by Parliament," by using the "under a law" provision. It did this by tabling in Parliament a Bill on August 28, 1958 the Ancient Monuments, Archaeological Sites and Remains Bill. This was passed by Parliament and the enacted law was brought into force from October 15, 1959. Under S.4 of the Act, if in the opinion of the Central Government a monument, not already deemed to be of national importance, is of national importance then it may declare it to be so after a two-month period to file objections.

The coup was now complete. The power to declare monuments of national importance had shifted from Parliament to the Union Government or the Executive. Since there was no need now for the Declaration of National Importance Act, 1951 the same was repealed by Section 39 of the Ancient Monuments Act, 1958. The coup had finally resulted in citizens losing completely the possibility of a debate in Parliament on monuments proposed to be declared of national importance, as was existing earlier under the Declaration of Importance Act, 1951, prior to the Seventh Constitution Amendment, 1956. Section 3 deemed the monuments in the Schedule to the 1951 Act and under S.126 of the States Reorganisation Act1956, as continuing to be of national importance. Under S.2(j) all monuments of national importance were protected monuments.

The Act clearly stated in its preamble the language of Entry 67 List I, Schedule VII namely ancient and historical monuments of national importance. There was no reference to Art. 49 "every monument of artistic or historic interest." Instead the Entry 67 List I approach was used to convert Art. 29 or the fundamental right to a monument as a cultural right into a State right and hollow out Art. 49. We now examine the effects of this statutory conclusion.

5.3.4.6 First Effect: Shutting Out Public Debate

Prior to the three-step process from 1951–1958, Declaration of National Importance Act1951, the Seventh Constitution Amendment 1956 and the Ancient Monuments Act, 1958, the Union Government of independent India adopted the same approach as that of the Ancient Monuments Preservation Act, 1904. So on January 26, 1950, as per Art. 394, when Art. 49 and Entry 67 List I came into force, the1904 Act continued because Art. 372 permitted the continuance, subject to the provisions of the Constitution and till it was altered, repealed or amended. There were no fundamental rights or Directive Principles in 1904, the British Act for the preservation of ancient monuments did not look at monuments as a part of the Art. 29 fundamental right of Indians to culture or as monuments of national importance, as in Art. 49 Directive Principle. But this monuments as objects approach continued till 1951, when the Declaration of National Importance Act was enacted and subsequently, by ignoring Art. 29 or the fundamental right to culture. 12 The possible constitutional justification for this would be that in Art. 49 itself the word 'monument' was mentioned along with the word 'object' by stating "It shall be the obligation of the State to protect every monument or place or object of artistic or historic interest…."

Hence in 1950 on the coming into force of all of the Constitution, the result was to treat monuments as mere buildings or objects of a chronological history and declare them by a law to be of national importance on the basis of their historic or artistic interest under Art. 49 or because these were ancient and historical under Entry 67 List I. The attributes of history, art or ancientness were to be decided by the ruling politicians or the Union Government and then put in a Bill before Parliament. Constitutionally, citizens would have the opportunity to participate in this process through their representatives in Parliament when the Bill would come up for discussion and enactment.

Now, no Bill would be required to be moved in Parliament concerning a monument proposed to be declared as being of national importance. The ruling politicians or the Union Government can simply declare by an executive order a monument under Art. 49 or under Entry 67 List I as being one of national importance. What under the original Constitution at its commencement was required to happen in public in Parliament would now happen behind the closed doors of the Executive called the Union Government, "under a law" passed by Parliament.

But the Declaration of National Importance Act, 1951, enacted under the "by law" original provision of Art. 49 and Entry 67 List I was still alive. So the second step was taken to make provision for notification by the Executive, of monuments to be declared as being of national importance and thereby completely wipe out a public debate on this through Parliament, as originally intended by our Constitution makers. The citizen was given the right to file objections to such intention and opinion of the Central Government within two months of the notification. The citizen, hence, lost the constitutional scrutiny of the executive's intention by the institutional mechanism called the Parliament and was left as an individual to scrutinize the action of the State expressed through the Central Government's notification.

5.3.4.7 Second Effect: Hollowing out Art. 49

The constitutional-cum-legislative coup, leaving an isolated citizen to scrutinize an action bearing the might of the Executive, was sealed by appropriating the content of Art. 49 into the new 1958 Act. This was achieved by providing in Section 2(a) a definition of ancient monument which included the word "artistic" from Art. 49 in relation to a monument. Only this word "artistic" distinguished the monuments of Art. 49 from those in Entry 67 List I, as this Entry does not have this word "artistic" in the "Ancient and Historical Monuments" covered by the Entry. The Directive Principle Art. 49 was now reduced to a mere constitutional obligation to protect every monument, since the subject matter of this obligation was now effectively transferred from Art. 49 to the Ancient Monuments Preservation Act, 1958. By virtue of Art. 37, this Directive Principle was fundamental in the governance of the country.

But the statutory provision defining ancient monument in the 1958 Act, so as to appropriate the Directive Principle monuments, is not fundamental in the governance of the country. That probably explains why the Director General ASI or the Director (Monuments) in the ASI, has not been made statutorily liable to ensure the protection of monuments of national importance. Thus, the abstract entity called the State is constitutionally obliged to protect monuments of national importance, but this has not been given any legal recognition in the Ancient Monuments Act, 1958 by imposing the obligation on any particular authority of the State and making such authority liable for the protection. In short, ruling politicians or the Union Government took statutory control of the declaration of monuments of national importance without any statutory accountability for their protection. This rendered the position of monuments to the same legal level as under the pre Constitution Ancient Monuments Preservation Act, 1904 which gave a similar definition of "ancient monument" and which in Section 3 empowered the Central Government to declare by a notification in the Official Gazette, an ancient monument to be a protected monument.

5.3.4.8 Third Effect: Converting Art. 29 into a State Right

In the first approach or Monuments as Objects Approach, the State takes this decision by itself, that is through ruling politicians, the culture bureaucracy and a notification in the official gazette, which no ordinary citizens reads, inviting objections to a proposal for recognizing a monument as one of national importance, without using any of the mass media to involve citizens. The State thereby practically takes over the fundamental rights of the citizens concerning their culture of monuments. The first approach leaves the monument cultureless as a mere object of the materials of its construction. In the decision of the State to convert by a Parliamentary law or by a notification under the Ancient Monuments Act, 1958, the monument of the culture of a section of citizens to a monument of national importance, the citizen has no role in such decision and then in the management of the monument. Under this approach the obligation of the State under the Directive Principle in Art. 49 is converted into a right of the State, which it is constitutionally not. This brings Indian citizens to the same legal position as in the pre independence Government of India Act, 1935, which under Section 100 read with Entry 15, "Ancient and historical monuments, archaeological site and remains" in List I of the Seventh Schedule to the Act, gave exclusive power to the Centre or the Federal Government to make laws concerning monuments, while not conferring any fundamental rights at all on Indian citizens. The existence of independent India's Constitution made no difference in the State's approach to monuments.

Accordingly, the fundamental right of citizens to their culture in Art. 29 has been converted into an exclusive right of the State or its ruling politicians to determine the status of monuments and to manage these through the Ancient Monuments Act, 1958. This has been achieved through a three step process of the Declaration of National Importance Act, 1951, the Seventh Constitution Amendment, 1956 and the Ancient Monuments Act, 1958.

5.3.4.9 Net Effect: Unaccountability & Lost Monuments

The political control resulting in unaccountability is self-evident from the fact that the Union Ministry of Culture has set up in August 2013 a special committee to look into the "lost" monuments of the ASI in Delhi only after the media reported two such monuments – the Lal Mahal and the Qudsia Garden monument. The Committee also stated as to how 1500 notices for unauthorised construction and 70 orders of demolition by the Director General ASI have not been implemented without stating the duration of non-implementation.[8]

So accordingly, the Union Government, following the first monuments as objects approach, enacted in 1951, the Declaration of Monuments of National Importance Act, 1951 with a Schedule for mentioning such monuments therein to start the process of takeover of the citizen's fundamental right to monuments as a cultural heritage. This culminated in the Ancient Monuments Act, 1958. It is the first non-Art. 29 approach that continues even after the 2010 amendments to the Ancient Monuments Act, 1958.[9]

---

[8] Times of India, Delhi, August 4, 2013, p. 8.

[9] *The Act seems to have spawned illegal occupation of land in the name of temples by a board being put outside such temples to call them ancient or Pracheen. The Act continues as a negation of what the 1992 Draft Approach Paper on National Cultural Policy had stated: "as far as possible the State should play only a catalytic role in the development and progress of culture, its role being what may be called 'arm's length intervention'."*

5.3.4.10 Ancient Monuments Act, 1958

The logic of following the non-Art. 29/second approach makes it understandable that the Act in Section 4 does not recognize Art. 29, associates no citizen with the process of declaring a monument to be of national importance and only gives a negative right to "any person interested" to object to the notified intention of the Central Govt. to declare a monument to be of national importance. In keeping with the legislative coup through the Seventh Constitution Amendment as mentioned above, by which the Executive or ruling politicians could do by an executive order under Art. 73(1), what Parliament can do only by enacting a public law, Section 4 does not require the notification to be even laid before Parliament. Hence the citizen loses the possibility of even a Parliamentary oversight over the manner in which the Central Government is exercising its discretion under Section 4.

Independence, the advent of the Constitution, the change in the legal status of Indian subjects to Indian citizens, the existence of Arts 29 and 49 made no difference, as the same approach of ignoring citizens and their culture had been manifested in the pre-independence Section 3 of the Ancient Monuments Preservation Act, 1904, which with effect from August 28, 1958 was replaced by the Ancient Monuments Preservation Act, 1958.

The Ancient Monuments Act, 1958, brought in the word preservation" and monuments of "archaeological interest," while defining "ancient" as a monument which has been in existence for not less than one hundred years. The word "preservation," which was put in the Act in place of the word "protect" in Art. 49 of the Constitution, remains undefined, as also any powers or duties of the State or its officers in this regard.

The introduction of the word "preservation" in the aforesaid statute was unnecessary, when the word "protect" in Article 49 provides the specific ends of protection as protection from "spoliation, disfigurement, destruction, removal, disposal or exports, as the case may be." A monument cannot be protected unless it is preserved against these enumerated specific ends in Art. 49. But in keeping with the legislative coup already executed by the Executive, this content of the constitutional provision under Art. 49 was also transferred from the substantive provision to the subject matter entry in Entry 67 List I by using the word "preservation" in the Entry which the Executive could appropriate "under" an Act.

The Act itself introduces another term for the word "preservation." It introduces the word "maintain" for protected monuments that have been acquired under the Land Acquisition Act, 1894 in terms of Section 13 or which have been purchased etc. by the Director General ASI under Section 5. "Maintain" has been defined under S.2(f) as including inter-alia "the doing of any act which may be necessary for the purpose of preserving a protected monument". Hence the end of maintaining a protected monument is preservation and the end of preservation is the constitutional goal of protecting such a monument, upon a harmonious reading of Art. 49, Entry 67 List I, Schedule VII r/w Art. 245(2) and the Ancient Monuments Act, 1958.

5.3.4.11 Consequences of Conversion

This legislative coup by the then ruling politicians, ended Parliament's control over the monuments selected by a Central Govt. for being declared as monuments of national importance. Accordingly, the pre Constitution Seventh Amendment Act, 1956 law, namely, The Ancient and Historical Monuments and Archaeological Sites and Remains (Declaration of National Importance) Act, 1951 was repealed by Section 39 of the Ancient Monuments Act, 1958 after deeming under Section 3 monuments of national importance under the repealed Act as such monuments under the 1958 Act.

No process is laid down in the Act, by which a section of citizens having a fundamental right to their monument under Art. 29, can have it declared as a monument of national importance. The Act also does not lay down any responsibility on the Archaeological Survey of India to track and record such monuments and thereby have a country wide list of monuments from which monuments can be considered for being categorized as monuments of national importance in a public hearing having a transparent process with the participation of the section of citizens whose monument is being considered. In short, the Act does nothing to effectuate Art. 29(1) of the Constitution.[10]

---

[10] *Article 29 (1) Any section of the citizens residing in the territory of India or any part thereof having a distinct language, script or culture of its own shall have the right to conserve the same.*

5.3.4.12 Amendments of 2010

By the 2010 Amendment and Validation Act concerning the Ancient Monuments Act, 1958, a flat ban on all constructions within one hundred metres of a monument declared to be of national importance, was imposed regardless of the effect or impact of the construction on the context, perspective, value, nature or line of vision of the monument. Even renovation, but no reconstruction, of existing buildings in the prohibited area can be done only with the prior permission of the National Monuments Authority constituted under Section 20F of the Act. There is no provision for any compensation to those who lose property rights in the prohibited area concerning the buildings and lands owned by them prior to the declaration of the area of one hundred metres from a monument of national importance as a prohibited area.

5.3.4.12.1 Citizens Shut Out

Accordingly, the functions of the National Monuments Authority constituted under Section 20F, are confined by Section 20I to grading and classifying monuments already declared by the ruling politicians to be of national importance, make construction impact recommendations, make recommendations for permission to construct within 100 to 200 metres of such monuments, suggest measures for the implementation of the Act and oversee the working of competent authorities. There is no statutory citizen's representation in or before the authority, or even of a State wherein the monument of national importance is located.

5.3.4.12.2 Parliament Scrutiny Disabled

Under Section 4A of the 1958 Act, there is neither citizens association nor even parliamentary control by way of a requirement on the Central Government to place before Parliament, the categorization done by it of monuments already declared by it to be of national importance. Therefore, the citizens even through their elected representatives cannot verify whether the categorization done by the Central Government is on the basis of the recommendation of the National Monuments Authority concerning such categorization or by having regard to the specific factors mentioned in Section 4A. The factors mentioned therein, which the Central Government must regard are: historical, archaeological and architectural. Historical and archaeological may be subsumed under the category of monument of 'historic' interest in Art. 49 and architectural may be subsumed under monument of 'artistic' interest in Art. 49. Parliament is disabled from ensuring that the Central Govt. is discharging its constitutional duty, which is fundamental in the governance of the country, of approving categorization of protected monuments of national importance according to the criteria laid down in Art. 49 and detailed in the Ancient Monuments Act, 1958. The Act achieves this disablement of Parliament by simply not providing that the categorization done by the Central Government under Section 4A of the Act, be tabled before Parliament. Yet citizens participation and Parliament's supervision is essential because Section 4A allows the Central Government a wide discretion of taking into account "such other factors as may be relevant for the purpose of categorisation." Under Section 4A(2) the public is to be informed of the fait accompli of the categorization done by the Central Government.

5.3.4.12.3 Oversight Disablement: Consequences

The sole constitutional purpose of categorization can be to classify nationally protected monuments according to their common and/or special features which therefore may require common/special protection. The protection and the funds for it can be varied, depending on such categorization. It is submitted Art. 49 does not permit degrees of protection to protected monuments of national importance divorced from the ends of protection as given in the Article itself. It mandates the same categorization of monuments according to the ends of protection on the scientific basis of a study of the nature and condition of the monument. Giving lesser or more protection according to any other basis of categorization of such monuments would be to create a class within the constitutional class of protected monuments when Art. 49 does not speak of any such sub classification of the class called monuments of national importance.[11]

---

[11] *It is significant that the Act does not mandate consultation with and reliance on the Union of India's National Research Laboratory for Conservation of Cultural Property at Lucknow (U.P.).*

This would only open the scope, by ruling politicians at the Centre to play with categorization and the funds for the protection of such monuments, depending on the relationship of the ruling political party at the Centre with the ruling party that is governing the State wherein the monument is located. Art. 49 does not permit such mischief of Central ruling politicians treating nationally protected monuments under the Constitution with an unequal hand. But the door for such mischief is left wide open by the non-Art. 29 approach under which ruling politicians at the Centre will categorise monuments for the purpose of protection without any scientific study and parliamentary oversight.

Under Section 20E the Director General of ASI must prepare heritage bye laws for each protected monument, on the basis of rules framed by the Central Government for the preparation of site plans for each such monument and according to the content specified in such rules. After approval by the National Monuments Authority, the fait accompli of such bye laws is to be laid before Parliament. The Section and the Act do not provide for the usual provision that Parliament can reject, modify or amend the bye laws laid before it. This enhances the oversight disablement.

The underlying problem is that even after the 2010 amendment of the 1958 Act there is no reflection in its provisions that a monument is the manifestation of a culture of its time and hence no reference to Art. 29 or the implementation of Art. 49 through an enactment, on the basis of Art. 29. The implications of all these aspects of the Ancient Monuments Act, 1958, from the constitutional perspective, are further examined in this research.

5.3.5 Second Approach

The second approach looks at monuments as part of a historical cultural heritage which involves citizens in deciding the national importance of monuments, since the culture and its heritage is that of the citizens under Art. 29 of the Constitution.[12]

---

[12] *The January 1959 International Commission of Jurists Conference at New Delhi, attended by 185 judges, practicing lawyers and teachers of law from fifty three countries emphasised that Rule of Law must make for the establishment of social, economic and cultural conditions which permit men to live with dignity and to fulfil their legitimate aspirations.*

But then what is culture?[13] According to the pattern theory of culture, "culture consists of patterns, explicit and implicitly acquired and transmitted by symbols, constituting the distinctive achievement of human groups, including their embodiments in artifacts; the essential core of culture consists of traditional[14] ideas and especially their attached values; cultural systems may, on the other hand, be considered, as products of action, on the other as conditioning elements of further action."[15] Monuments are not mere objects, historic objects or cultural objects. They are part of a continuously developing stream or pattern of culture[16] of various sections of citizens living in a political entity called the State.

The method of management of land/resources[17] and people by rulers of the State and the response there to by sections of citizens in terms of each of their cultures, together constitute the evolving identity of a country. Monuments are a part of this evolution of culture and

---

[13] *See the conversation on this issue between anthropologists, lawyers, businessmen, psychiatrists and biologists: The Concept of Culture, see* Ralph Linton edn, The Science of Man in The World Crisis, p. 78–106 (1980).

[14] *i.e. historically derived and selected.*

[15] A.L. Kroeber and Clyde Kluckhohn, after compiling several definitions of culture, proposed this definition of culture in their book, Culture: A Crucial Review of Concepts & Definitions, p. 181 (1952).

[16] James A. R. Nafziger, R.K. Paterson, Alison D. Renteln, Cultural Law, p.64, Cambridge University Press, (2010).

A working definition of culture states that cultural law embraces a panoramic range of human behavior, expressions, and activities pertaining to family and social norms, rules of etiquette, folklore, folk art. Religion, art, architecture, media, sports, recreation, music, language, literature, drama, dance, other performing arts, and significant relations among these phenomena.

[17] *The comment of the UN Human Rights Committee, on Art. 27 of the International Covenant on Civil and Political Rights (ICCPR), which monitors compliance with this Covenant of which India is a party, is that "Culture manifests itself in many forms, including a particular way of life associated with the use of land resources, especially in the case of indigenous peoples.... The enjoyment of these rights may require positive legal measures of protection and measures to ensure the effective participation of members of the minority communities in the decisions that affect them."*

identity. When local events have national effect then the monuments signifying these local events become one of national importance. Whether they are to be so recognized or not depends on whether they serve or do not serve the constitutional purpose of "unity and integrity of India," because if there is no India then there cannot be a national monument.

Hence, the impact on the nation of recognizing a monument legally as one of national importance has to be considered to protect the very nation of whose culture the monument is a part.

This decision of the State to recognize or not a monument as one of national importance, requires citizens' participation for two reasons. Firstly, the decision cannot be that of a transient five year rule of elected politicians who constitute the Union Government through direct elections every five years on the basis of adult suffrage.[18]

Monuments get deculturised if they become a political football. Secondly, the monuments are a culture of citizens of which the Union Government is only a trustee of a public resource called culture under Art. 29, as in the case of natural resources under the Public Trust doctrine declared by the Supreme Court to be part of Indian law.[19] The fundamental right under Art. 29 sums up the entire diversity of ways of life in India to show that culturally India's entire population is a sum of cultural minorities. This explains the shoulder heading of Art. 29, "Protection of interests of minorities". But there is no cultural law on the Indian statute book which enables citizens to execute their fundamental right under Art. 29 by giving an option to sections of citizens to document and register their way of life including their monuments.[20]

---

[18] Art. 81(1) (a), 75(3), 83(2) of the Constitution of India.

[19] M.C. Mehta vs. Kamal Nath, (1997) 1 SCC 388.

[20] *Nafziger at al in Cultural Law summarise the relationship between law and culture as a law which: embodies culture and formalizes its norms ; promotes, protects, conditions and limits cultural attributes and expressions; harmonises cross cultural differences, confirms cultural rights, establishes international standards; and a culture that: reinforces legal rules; conditions and constrains the adoption, interpretation and vitality of legal rules; cultural expressions and symbols which promote legal relationships.*

The research work points out that the second approach is required by the fundamental right under Art. 29 of "any section of citizen having a distinct culture of its own to conserve[21] the same."

5.3.5.1 Nation of Cultural Minorities

India being a constitutional State of cultural minorities under Art. 29 and a party to the International Covenant on Civil and Political Rights, it is bound both by its own Constitution and international law to adopt the cultural heritage approach.[22] Art. 27 of the Covenant declares "In those States in which ethnic religious and linguistic minorities exist, persons belonging to such minorities shall not be denied the right, in community with the other members of their group, to enjoy their own culture, to profess their own religions or to use their own language." Art. 29 recognises India as a nation of cultural minorities and accordingly uses the words "sections of citizens." India is committed under Article 1of the International Covenant on Economic, Social and Cultural Rights to allow its citizens to freely pursue their cultural development and under Art. 15 to take part in cultural life.[23] So monuments declared by Parliamentary law to be of national importance cannot be effectively protected by the State, in terms of the State's obligation under the Directive Principle of Art. 49, unless they are a part of the culture of sections of citizens who have a feeling for their monuments and so preserve these.

---

[21] Words & Phrases, Vol. 8A, Permanent Ed. p. 229: *The verb 'conserve' means to keep in a safe or sound state; to save; to preserve from change or destruction; its synonyms are "maintain," "sustain," "uphold," "defend," "protect," "guard," "shield" and "secure"; to conserve means to keep something especially institutions, prerogatives and conditions, unimpaired or sound; and the word stresses the idea of maintenance of an existing condition.see* Hill vs. Bank of San Pedro 107 P.2d 399, 404, 41 Cal. App2d 595.

[22] Directive Principle Art. 51(c) & Art. 253 of the Constitution of India.

[23] *India's monuments of national importance seriously fall short of ensuring Art. 30. of the 2007 Convention on the Rights of Persons with Disabilities, viz, "State Parties recognize the rightsof persons with disabilities to taske part on an equal basis with others in cultural life, and shall take appropriate measures to ensure that persons with disabilities enjoy access to monuments and sites of national cultural importance.*

5.3.5.2 Cultural Heritage Approach Ignored

The judiciary has nowhere taken the cultural heritage approach of Art. 29 or of the International Covenant on Civil and Political Rights, in any of the cases of monuments that have come before it. Hence the interpretation principle of reading the Constitution as a whole has not come into play in any of these cases, so as to interpret Art. 49 in the light of Art. 29 and the Preamble.

5.3.5.3 Fundamental Duty

This constitutional approach towards monuments has not been adopted by the Supreme Court even in the light of the Forty Second Amendment of the Constitution which has been brought into effect from January 3, 1977, by the Constitution Amendment Act, 1976, introducing through Art. 51A (f), a specific duty on citizens in Part IV – A of the Constitution, "to value and preserve the rich heritage of our composite culture." But along with this amendment there was no resonating amendment of Art. 49 or Entry 67 List I of Schedule VII, to state that monuments of national importance in Art. 49 or Entry 67 List I of Schedule VII, must reflect the composite cultural heritage.

The amendment also did not state that this duty of a citizen under Art. 51A(f) was enforceable in a court of law.

This distinguished it from the Directive Principles in Art. 36 to 51 of the Constitution, which in Art. 37 states that the Principles "shall not be enforceable in a court of law". This difference leaves a window for the courts to apply the Fundamental Duties in deciding cases. But the Directive Principles liberate themselves from their non-enforceability, by stating that the Principles are "nevertheless fundamental in the governance of the country and it shall be the duty of the State to apply these principles in making laws." The Fundamental Duties do not mention this liberating phraseology of the Directive Principles.

Despite this the Supreme Court has used the Fundamental Duty in Art. 51A(f) to hold that wild life is part of our cultural heritage and the Fundamental Duty in Art. 51A(g), to give directions to the Central Government on environmental education.[24] But none

---

[24] Animal and Environmental Legal Defense Fund vs. Union of India, AIR 1997 SC 1071; M.C. Mehta vs. Union of India, (1998) 1 SCC 471.

of these decisions were applied by the Supreme Court in the cases of monuments of national importance before it, either under the environmental approach to such monuments or under the cultural objects approach.

5.3.5.4 Rootless Monuments

The basic problem in the judicial approach to monuments of national importance has been the complete absence of a discussion as to what a monument represents. Does it represent a conquest on the one hand and a failure of the conquered on the other; or is it an expression of power of its times and of powerlessness; or the culture of the oppressor and of the oppressed; a divided culture or a united one, depending through whose eyes or standards one looks at a monument.

There were three possible approaches for the Supreme Court to choose from.[25] First, was the "clash of civilisations" approach based on the theory that conflict is basically cultural and not ideological or economic.[26] Hence when a national government gives official legal recognition as monuments of national importance to monuments of those who violently conquered, pillage and plundered India, to impose a State of a single religion on a multicultural civilization, then is recognition being given to such violent conquerors, instead of to the victims of such conquests? In the absence of a discussion to attempt to find an answer to this question, a major corpus of monuments of national importance that were recognised as such by the British and which continue to be so recognised in independent India, becomes rootless. People cannot relate to such monuments divorced of their cultural context. The monuments become an officially designated tourist cum picnic site and nothing more. This is to deprive people of a cultural understanding of what the monument represents – the vulnerable spots of their culture or the superior strength of a single minded culture that overtook theirs.

---

[25] Richard Falk, Lester Edwin, J. Ruiz & R.B. Walker edn, Jacinta O' Hagan, Conflict, Covergence or Coexistence? in The Relevance of Culture in Reframing The International Law, Culture, Politics, Routledge (2002).

[26] Samuel Huntington, The Clash of Civilizations, p. 22, vol. 72, Foreign Affairs, Summer (1933).

The second approach is a "convergent world order" view of culture or the Francis Fukuyama[27] "end of history" approach, in which Western liberal democracy is the norm towards which all other societies are moving by defeating all competing models. This model does not question as to how and for whom the convergence is being forged. Who pays the cost for the political economy of such a liberal democracy, is a question that remains unanswered among the debris of the failed attempts to get the leading nations of such democracies into environmental regulation for the benefit of all and not some nations. The failure is on the touchstone of the way of life or culture of such nations. The recognition of the monuments of erstwhile colonizers turned liberal democracies, as monuments of national importance is to again leave the monuments rootless. Such monuments only help to evade the essential question of a scientific comparison of the ways of life or cultures. Uncomfortable questions of per capita energy consumption, the economic efficiency of waste disposal systems and the conservation of resources by recycling, which should provide the 'way of life' context for such monuments, remain unanswered and render such monuments meaningless pieces of legal recognition.

The third approach, of Martin Wright, Hedley Bull and Adam Watson[28] is of multi-civilisational identities in which non Western societies are projected as less rational, less advanced and less capable than the West and the use of law, order and stability as legal tools to enable the West to control the political and economic affairs of the non-West. The use of law by the British to create poverty in India and then make India pay for the poverty that the British created,[29] shows the necessity of examining the culture of law itself and as to why India never sought reparation from Britain for the wealth carted away from India as shown by British official statistics themselves.[30]

---

[27] Fukuyama Francis, End of History and the Last Man', 'Simon and Schuster, United Kingdom (2006).

[28] Hedley Bull, Adam Watson (eds.), The Expansion of International Society, Oxford: Clarendon Press (1984); Martin Wright, Systems of States ed. Hedley Bull (Leicester: Leicester University Press (1977).

[29] Prasad Rajendra, Colonialism, Lumpenisation, Revolution, Vol I, Ajanta Books International, Delhi (1995).

[30] Bagchi Amiya, Colonialism & Indian Economy, P. xxxi, OUP, Delhi (2010).

After using the import export law, the taxation law and the land revenue law to destroy India's culture of livelihoods, the British started the work of recognizing and preserving India's monuments under Regulations, Archaeological Policies and the Ancient Monuments Acts. At no point were the monuments so recognised linked to India's culture or put in their cultural context, probably because the culture had been extinguished and its people subjected to famines.[31] After independence the British legal cum administrative system with its laws was continued as per Art. 372 of the Constitution and the Ancient Monuments Act, 1958 continued the British practice of monuments without a culture.

None of the railway museums of the Union Govt. show how the railways were used in India by the British colonial Government for exporting from village India the raw materials needed by British industry and for bringing in British goods the attractive rate of interest on the capital invested in the Indian railways by British citizens, the free land granted to such private railways and the entire risk of this private capital being borne by the British colonial government in India. As the people of colonial India got poorer, the railways kept on expanding.[32]

The Constitution of India did not put culture into Art. 49 but kept it in the separate compartment of Art. 29. A national government which recognizes as monuments of national importance British forts in Bombay, Calcutta and Madras, without contextualizing these in the British culture of law as practiced by them in India for destroying India and creating a permanent Macaulay class of Indians,[33] is to wipe out what

---

[31] R.C. Majumdar, History and Culture of the Indian People, p. 416, VOL IX, – *"In the first half of the Nineteenth Century there were seven famines with an estimated total of one million deaths. In the second half, there were 24 famines with an estimated death toll of 20 million."*

[32] Ibid Prasad Rajendra.

[33] *Macaulay's Minute on Education (1835)* "We must at present do our best to form a class, who may be interpreters between us and the millions we govern – a class of persons, Indian in Blood and Colour and English in Taste, Opinions, Morals and Intellect." On Oct 12, 1836, Macaulay wrote to his father, a die-hard evangelist, inter alia: "It is my firm belief that, if our plans of education are followed up, there will not be a single idolater among the respected classes of Bengal, thirty years hence."

such monuments represent. So while the Western liberal democracies could evolve their own respective cultures,[34] the Indian view remained officially shut out from monuments even after the commencement of the Constitution on January 26, 1950.

The Indian view based on the Rig Veda – Ekam sad, vipra bahuda vadanti – "Truth is one; sages call it variously" allows for peaceful coexistence of multicultural identities.[35]

Art. 29 provides the context for a culture of monuments and the citizen's duty under Art. 51A(f) provides the purpose along with the Preamble for such a culture of monuments. There cannot be a movement towards a composite cultural heritage of citizens as required of citizens under Art. 51A(f), if the State under Art. 49 has its own culture by legally shutting out citizens and citizens have their own cultures or sub-identities by which they live regardless of the State's will or executive action, which the State does not recognize. This approach to constitutional interpretation of Art. 49, leaves Art. 49 without context or purpose.[36] Yet, the Supreme Court in any of the cases of monuments of national importance has not adopted the approach of applying Art. 49 and applying it with Arts 29 and 51A(f).

This approach of the Supreme Court is borne out by one of the earliest cases of 1989, when while dismissing the public interest petition as non-maintainable, it held culture as a fundamental right of "life" under Art. 21 of the Constitution without any reference to Art. 29 which specifically dealt with the culture of the citizens.[37]

The Union Govt. seems to be on the same page as the Supreme Court about the role of Art. 29 of the Constitution, in relation to monuments of national importance. The Results Framework

---

[34] Milton Singer, The Concept of Culture in International Encyclopedia of Social Sciences Vol. 3, p. 527, Macmillan Co. & The Free Press, U.S.A (reprint 1985).

[35] Nirmal Kumar Bose, 'The Geographical Background of Indian Culture' in The Cultural Heritage of India, p.7, Vol.1, Ramakrishna Mission Institute of Culture, Kolkata (Reprint 2007).

[36] Senghas, The Clash within Civilizations, p. 170, Routledge & Routledge, London (2002).

[37] Ramsharan vs. UOI, AIR 1989 SC 549.

Document of the Union Ministry of Culture,[38] while spelling out the vision for 2013–14 and 2014–15, on the question of preservation of monuments, makes no reference whatsoever to understanding its obligation under Art. 49 in terms of Art. 29, even while stating at the outset that "an India where cultural diversity and heritage are important pillars of inclusive national development." This cultural diversity is recognised in the Constitution itself, wherein special provisions have been made for eleven States in Art. 370 and 371 A-J. These eleven States are: Gujarat, Maharashtra, Nagaland, Assam, Manipur, Andhra Pradesh, Sikkim, Mizoram, Arunachal Pradesh, Goa, Karnataka and Jammu & Kashmir.

5.3.5.5 Composite Heritage

It is this connected and holistic understanding of the fundamental rights under Arts. 29, 25 and 26 with the Directive Principle under Art. 49, weaving together culture, religion and monuments, that results in the fundamental duty of citizens under Art. 51-A(f) to "value and preserve the rich heritage of our composite culture".[39] The fundamental duty gives a right to citizens[40] that the Indian State under Art. 49 will only protect monuments of national importance in a manner that a composite culture is created by such monuments collectively. Hence while a religion may be important to understand a monument of national importance, the composite culture of all such monuments put together does not get defined by only one religion.

The necessary implication of this is that the process of recognizing monuments as being of national importance is a process that must involve people of all religions. So understood, the Constitution creates

---

[38] Results Framework Document (RFD) for Ministry of Culture, GOI (2013–14 and 2014–15).

[39] *The 2002 National Commission to Review the Working of the Constitution, declared in Chapter III, Para 33 while referring to Art. 49, that more than more than five decades of experience in the working of the constitution and the laws has shown that our national life must be accommodative of the myriad variegations that make up the unique mosaic of India's society.*

[40] M.C. Mehta vs. Union of India, (1998) 9 SCC 589.

Duty on State under Art. 47 and Art. 48-A in Part IV of the Constitution is to be read as conferring a right on citizens and therefore Art. 21 must be read to include these Articles.

an opportunity for making composite cultural heritage possible and communalization of monuments preventable.[41]

5.3.5.6 Citizen-Enabling Approach

Based on the aforesaid understanding, the second/cultural heritage approach becomes one of joining fundamental rights to the culture of monuments, to the culture of religion with the duty of the State under the Directive Principle in Art. 49 and with the duty of citizens in Art. 51-A(f).

The second approach determines the role of the State as a citizen enabler and not as a controller of monuments which form a part of the distinct culture of a section of citizens. In this approach, by virtue of their fundamental right to their culture of which their monuments form a part, the citizens participate in the decision of the State for declaring a monument to be of national importance and thereby inviting under Art. 49 its legal obligation to protect a monument so declared.[42]

5.3.5.7 Sustainable Tourism

The second approach of monuments as a cultural heritage creates the possibility of any tourism, to such people-preserved monuments, being controlled at levels that are sustainable for the monument.[43]

The first Approach or Monuments as Mere Objects Approach turns the tourism to a monument into a revenue machine or an industry

---

[41] *While the Constitution guarantees a secular state, it permits the State to regulate the secular aspects of a religion by distinguishing between what is an essential or integral part of religion from its other parts.* Commr. H.R.E. vs. Lakshmindra AIR 1954 SC 282; Acharya J. Avadhuta vs. Commr. of Police, AIR 1984 SC 51; Ismail vs. UOI, AIR 1995 SC 605; A.S. Narayana Deekshitulu vs. State of Andhra Pradesh, AIR 1996 SC 1765.

[42] Edward R.A. Seligman ed., 'Malinowski Bronislaw: Culture in Encyclopaedia of the Social Sciences', p. 621, 645, Macmillan, New York (1937):
'Man varies in two respects: in physical form and in social heritage, or culture.... This social heritage is the key concept of cultural anthropology. It is usually called culture in modern anthropology and social science.'

[43] Rakhaldas Sengupta, Preservation of Ancient Monuments, p. 871, Vol. 8, The Cultural Heritage of India, Ramakrishna Mission Institute of Culture, Kolkata (Reprint 2007); Creative Economy Report, Special Edition UNESCO and UNDP (2013).

as in the case of the Taj Mahal,[44] regardless of the sustainability of the tourist traffic by the monument. The Supreme Court has allowed the first approach to prevail and continue as it has not decided to give a final hearing to the pending application of the Amicus in the case W.P (Civil) 13381/84, for a direction to the Archaeological Survey of India (ASI) to determine the carrying capacity of the Taj Mahal and implement the plan put up with the application for crowd management. The application has been pending for over five years now. This logically flows from the Supreme Court's approach of completely ignoring Art. 29 in the context of monuments of national importance.

5.4 International Law Ignored

This de-facto movement of the Indian State from the de jure Art. 29 community-based recognition and preservation of monuments of national importance, at least through the people's representatives in Parliament, to an entirely State Executive based recognition, preservation and control, finds its parallel in the evolution of the international legal framework for the protection of monuments. The research shows how the international legal protection has moved from communities to the State and the sheer international despair[45] on the ever increasing threats to monuments, posed by modern "urban development."

In the cases arising before it of monuments of national importance, the judiciary has not referred to this international legal framework and despair at the threat from "economic development" to interpret the obligation of the State under Art. 49 of the Constitution to "protect" monuments of national importance.

This is so even though the Supreme Court has declared in Vishaka vs. State of Rajasthan[46] that it will rely on international treaties and

---

[44] MC Mehta vs. Union of India, AIR 1997 SC 734, *the Supreme Court of India declared that Taj is an industry, because of the revenue inflow from tourism.*

[45] *Preamble of ICOMOS Charter for the Conservation of Historic Towns and Urban Areas,* October 1987.

[46] Vishaka vs. State of Rajasthan, (1997) 6 SCC 241.

covenants to which India is a party so long as these are compatible with the Constitution of India.[47]

5.5 Economic Development vs. Protection

Accordingly, the problem of preservation of monuments of national importance or otherwise, is that of "modern economic development". But neither the Ancient Monuments Act, 1958 nor the Supreme Court or the high courts have taken cognizance of this internationally recognized problem of protecting and preserving monuments – the clash between the ever rising economic value of land and the cultural value of the monuments which stand on the land, including the value of the land surrounding the monument. It is a clash inherent in the necessity of a developing economy of a State directed economic development and the State takeover of the citizen's fundamental right to conserve their culture of monuments.

The economics of State directed national economic development, quantifies the value of the land on which the monuments stand. But the same State makes no attempt to quantify the cultural value of a monument on that land. Since in economics that which is not quantified does not exist, the monument becomes economically invisible while the land on which the monument stands becomes a visible economic product. India, in this context finds the shifting of international conventions from community-based protection to State based protection, congruent with its economic development programme. This congruence is expressed in India by the legal approach of the Ancient Monuments Act, 1958 of State takeover of the recognition and protection monuments of national importance in a manner that ignores the citizens fundamental right to conserve their culture (and not the State culture) of monuments.

---

[47] On the other hand the Supreme Court has interpreted and constructed the entire environmental law of India by an unquestioned reliance on international environmental law, customary international law and common law principles as in State of Himachal Pradesh vs. Ganesh Wood Products AIR 1996 SC 149; Vellore Citizens' Forum vs. Union of India, AIR 1996 SC 2715; Andhra Pradesh Pollution Control Board vs. M.V. Nayadu, AIR 1999 SC 812; M.C. Mehta vs. Kamal Nath, AIR 2000 SC 1998.

5.6 State and Culture of Monuments

The State takeover of the national culture of monuments under the Ancient Monuments Act, 1958, by ignoring the composite cultural heritage approach of the Constitution of India, built upon the fundamental right of sections of citizens to conserve their culture under Art. 29, runs counter to the entire evolution[48] from the villages upwards, of the international Anglo Saxon system, on which our legal system is claimed to be based. The Supreme Court has declared "Our legal system having been founded on the British common law, the right of a person to a pollution free environment is part of the basic jurisprudence of the land."[49] As Julius Stone has pointed out, this international legal movement has proceeded from the question as to how shall we justify the limitation on the freedom of individuals which we find ourselves compelled to impose to the question "On what principles should we grant power and control the powers we feel compelled to grant to public officials over the freedom of individuals."[50]

The Ancient Monuments Act, 1958 does not even address itself to this issue, as its source is the Constitution of India, which is all power and immunity without any effective ongoing accountability of the executive, legislature or judiciary on the basis of a fundamental right of citizens to be informed as to what the three organs of governance are doing in their name for their way of life.

5.7 Differential Application

By the application of the international principle of sustainable development, incorporated by the Supreme Court into Indian law in State of Himachal Pradesh vs. Ganesh Wood Products,[51] the Supreme

---

[48] Robert L Schuyler, Jonathan Cape edn, George Burton Adams: For evolution of the common law system in England see Constitutional History of England,, London (reprint 1956).

[49] In Vellore Citizens Forum vs. Union of India, (1996) 5 SCC 647.

[50] Julius Stone, Human Law and Human Justice, p.4–5, Universal Law Publishing Co.Pvt Ltd, New Delhi (reprint 2000).

[51] State of Himachal Pradesh vs. Ganesh Wood Products, AIR 1996 SC 149.

Court declared that there was no conflict[52] between development and environment. However, the Supreme Court did not apply this international law principle of sustainable development to resolve the problem of modern economic development threatening the monuments of national importance, even while taking an entirely environmental approach to the protection of such monuments against air pollution.[53]

The Supreme Court declared that environment, including clean air, water and health as its components are a fundamental right under the word "life" in Art. 21. It further developed environmental rights on the basis of international reports and conferences concerning the environment. But it did not do so in the case of protection of monuments of national importance, even though as far back as 1988[54] it had declared culture, including monuments to be a fundamental right under the same Art. 21.

The Supreme Court seemed to have completely missed the intrinsic connection between environment and way of life and culture of human beings.[55] A recognition of this connection would have brought upfront two key issues before the Supreme Court:

Firstly, whether any international or national environmental regime can succeed in terms of its own goals without tackling the way of life that produces an environment admittedly ruinous for human beings? Secondly, can monuments be protected legally from despoliation through such an environmental approach that ignores the way of life and culture

---

[52] The traditional concept that development and ecology are opposed to each other is no longer acceptable. Sustainable development is the answer…in Vellore Citizens Welfare Forum vs. UOI A'96SC2720-2727.

[53] Lyndell V. Prott & Patrick J. O'Keefe, (1992) International Journal of Cultural Property p.311: *"Heritage creates a perception of something handed down; something to be cared for and cherished. These cultural manifestations have come down to us from the past; they are our legacy from our ancestors. There is today a broad acceptance of a duty to pass them on to our successors, augmented by the creations of the present."* This is similar to the inter-generational equity principle of the Brundtland report *"Our Common Future"* concerning the world's environment.

[54] Ram Sharan vs. UOI, AIR 1989 SC 549.

[55] *Mahajan Krishan, Sustainable Development In a State of Unconstitutional Economics, 2014, NGT, International Journal on Environmental Law, Delhi, Vol. II, P.53.*

around a monument? A struggle to answer these issues can possibly rupture the international and national legal fantasy of environment and monument protection without examining the culture or way of life that makes such protection necessary.

This approach of the Supreme Court to the question of protection of monuments of national importance, while dealing with both monuments and the environment under Art. 21 was in stark contrast to its approach to environmental issues in environmental cases. This was so despite the fact that unlike "environment," Art. 29 specifically created in the Constitution a fundamental right to culture and India was a party to the International Convention on Civil and Political Rights (ICCPR), International Convention on Economic, Social and Cultural Rights (ICESCR) and the Convention on Persons with Disabilities (CPD), which legally bound India to recognize the cultural right to monuments of its citizens. Further India has ratified the 1956 Hague Convention for the Protection of Cultural Property in the Event of Armed Conflict which recognizes in its Preamble that cultural property belongs to people and declares it as a "cultural heritage of mankind." In not a single case on the protection of monuments has the Supreme Court referred to this Convention or the human right to monuments of national importance[56] as part of the preambular social justice in the Constitution of India.

5.8 Divergence on Fundamental Duties

This divergence between the approach of the Supreme Court in environmental cases and that in cases of monuments of national importance, even though the Supreme Court's main thrust in the latter cases has been environmental, comes out clearly in the manner in which Fundamental Duties of citizens in relation to environment and monuments have been dealt with by it.

In Virender Gaur vs. State of Haryana,[57] the Supreme Court for the first time brought in the Fundamental Duty Art. 51A (g) to read it

---
[56] People's Union of Civil Liberties vs. UOI, (1997) 1 SCC 301: *Art. 21 has to be interpreted in conformity with International Law as India is a signatory to the ICCPR, 1967.*
[57] Virender Gaur vs. State of Haryana, (1995) 2 SCC 577.

together with Directive Principles 48A as also 47, and marrying these to the Fundamental Right under Art. 21, to fasten a duty on the State "to shed its extravagant unbridled sovereign power and to forge its policy to maintain ecological balance and hygienic environment." Three years later in M.C. Mehta vs. Union of India,[58] the Supreme Court declared that the duties of the State under the Directive Principles 47 and 48A created rights in the citizens which were to be included in the fundamental right to environment under Art. 21.

However, in none of the cases before it on monuments of national importance has the Supreme Court read the duty of the State under the Directive Principle in Art. 49 as creating a right which is part of the fundamental right under Art. 29 or even under Art. 21, in terms of its 1988 judgment in Ramsharan.[59]

---

[58] M.C. Mehta vs. UOI, (1998) 9 SCC 589 at p. 591, para 5.

[59] Ram Sharan vs. UOI, AIR 1989 SC 549.

Chapter VI
THE CONSTITUTIONAL CLEAVAGE

6.1 Monuments: Whose Culture?

Monuments symbolize a country's cultural history and identity. They live and die to the extent that they are meaningful in the lives of people. Governments as trustees[1] of monuments have only one role – that of recognizing the culture of people in which the monuments exist, selecting monuments of national importance from this cultural ensemble and thereby ensuring their protection. So, monuments exist and continue to exist in a context – that of people's lives which constitutes their culture. Any attempt at protection bereft of this context only begs failure. Hence which monuments are protected and the effectiveness of the protection bespeak the current or extant culture of a State, its government and the manner of treating its people. This context is defined by the Eleventh Plan (2007–2012) which views culture as "Ways of Living Together."[2] With the takeover by the State after independence of the Art. 29 fundamental right of citizens to their culture and its monuments, as also all State Govts., which have simply replicated the Central, Ancient Monuments Act, 1958, the question arises that the existing monuments of national importance represent whose culture — that of the State or of its people who have been kept, by the aforesaid 1958 Act, out of the whole process of selection of monuments of national importance.

When the British Government in 1899, with the arrival of Viceroy Lord Curzon on February 1, 1899, took up earnestly and actively the

---

[1] *This is a consequence of Art. 29 Constitution of India, especially of orphan monuments which belong to no section of citizens but have palpable outstanding historic or artistic value.*

[2] Planning Commission, Volume II, p.51, Para 2.2.21.

conservation and protection of monuments both in British India and the Native Indian States,[3] it justified the takeover by the British Government.[4] Two grounds for this task were stated by Viceroy Lord Curzon in his 1900 speech to the Asiatic Society.[5] First as an "imperial obligation" and secondly unlike in Europe, there was no private body, funding or action to protect the monuments.[6]

But after independence under the Constitution of India, this situation could not have continued as culture had become a fundamental right of Indian citizens. The Government was no longer to be in control of the culture of the Indian people including their monuments. But as shown by the postindependence Ancient Monuments Act, 1958, the Union of India or the ruling politicians, did nothing to effectuate Art. 29 fundamental right of the Constitution and continued with the pre-independence control of the Government over culture. As in British times this gave rise to an official culture of India including its monuments and an unofficial or people's culture of India.

The constitutional question therefore arises, that the present artistic or historic monuments designated by the Union of India, either by the deeming legal route or otherwise, as monuments of national importance,

---

[3] *Marshall, J. H. (1902), p10, "Introduction" to the inaugural issue of the archaeological Annual publication of the ASI: The Foreign Department of the Govt. of India by an order dated June 4, 1901 directed the conservation and protection of monuments in the Native States by the Archaeological Surveyors of the respective British India circles to which the native States were attached, without doing anything to offend the Indian rulers of these States.*

[4] *Ibid p.9, In Jan 1878 Lord Lytton had recorded in a Minute that it is indefensible that the Govt. of India should divest itself of all responsibility for the preservation of monuments which "for variety, extent, completeness and beauty are unsurpassed, perhaps unequalled, in the world."*

[5] *The Story of Indian Archaeology, Oct 5, 1949, Publications Division, New Delhi: Sir William Jones, a puisne judge of the Calcutta Supreme Court founded the Asiatic Society for inquiring inter alia 'into the History.... the antiquities, arts, sciences and the literature of Asia.'. James Prinsep as Secretary of the Asiatic Society, while being the Assay Master of the Calcutta Mint from 1832–1840, discovered the alphabet of the Brahmi script in which were written the earliest inscriptions of India. He also deciphered the Khaaroshthi script then prevalent in the north-west of India. Description of many ancient ruins of India were published in its journal Asiatic Researches.*

[6] *Ibid. Speech of Viceroy Lord Curzon in 1900 to the Asiatic Society of Bengal.*

represent whose culture? That of the citizens or that of the ruling politicians. The first, exists constitutionally. The second exists officially and legally.

6.2 Culture: Citizen's Right & Duty

Art. 29(1) of the Constitution of India in the Fundamental Rights Chapter, declares that any section of citizens residing in the territory of India or any part thereof, having a distinct language, script or culture of its own shall have the right to conserve the same. The words "any section of citizens" and "distinct culture" in the Article recognize the vast diversity of the ways of living of Indian citizens and their consequent distinct life styles based on religion, caste, sub-caste, languages, livelihoods, rituals and rites of life's events, food, clothing, beliefs, faiths, festivals, prayers, celebration and mourning. This is the context in which people have a fundamental right to their monuments reflecting their past and present. Culture and monuments reflecting such culture belong essentially to the culture of India, constitutionally called "any section of citizens."

6.3 Constitutional Cleavage

The Constitution carries further this theme of culture as a property of the citizens by imposing on citizens a correlative fundamental duty under Art. 51A (f) to "value and preserve[7] the rich heritage of our composite culture". Hence the culture of India/Bharat is composed of the distinct cultures of its citizens. If they are enabled to value this then preservation follows on the simple human emotion of preserving what one values. This is how monuments are to be preserved – on an understanding of their value in the context of their distinct culture as shown by history, in the territorial ambit as shown by geography for protection against the threat perceptions as shown by the economy. This consequently defines

---

[7] McKeon vs. Central Stamping Co, C.C.A.N.J.264F.385; 387: *"Preservation is not creation. It is saving that which already exists, and implies the continuance of what previously existed." Also to maintain (as state of things) S.21, fourth IPC to keep safe from harm or injury,* S.168 of the Indian Contract Act, 1872, S.209 (4A) of the Companies Act, Art. 60 of the Constitution of India.

the role of the State under the Constitution, namely, that of governing monuments in a manner that citizens understand the composite culture of distinct cultures and that this constitutes a rich heritage.[8] While each section of citizens have a fundamental right to "conserve" their distinct culture, all sections of citizens together have a duty to "preserve" these cultures that represent the Indian identity under the Constitution. Government, therefore, must necessarily enable such conservation and preservation. Only such governance of monuments is constitutional.

As Rao Bahadur K.N. Dikshit, Former Director-General, Archaeological Survey of India, states, "It would be wrong to think, as many do, that the conception of the fundamental unity of India is only of recent growth. This idea can be traced to ancient periods by the use of the common name, Bharata Varsha, for the whole country, and the designation Bharati Santatih applied to the people of India." Thus we read in the VishnuPurana that 'the country lying to the north of the ocean and south of Himadri (Himalaya) is called Bharata Varsha (Land of Bharat)', for there lay the descendants of Bharata (Bharati Santatih) similarly, the conception of the political unity of India appears from references to 'thousand Yojanas (leagues) of land that stretch from the Himalayas to the sea as the proper domain of a single universal emperor', and the conventional description in literature and epigraphic records of imperial domains stretching from the Brahmaputra (or eastern ocean) to the seven mouths of the Indus (or western ocean).

As regards cultural unity, the find spots of Asoka's records prove that one language and one script were used, or at least understood by common people all over India in 3rd Century B.C. Since then the Sanskrit language and literature have throughout been a common bond of culture in addition to religious and social ideas and institutions.[9]

This chalks out the work-path of the Archaeological Survey of India and points to the kind of organization it necessarily must be: to survey,

---

[8] Ashworth, G, and Graham, B & Turnbridge J., Pluralizing Pasts: Heritage, Identity & Place in Multicultural Societies, Pluto Press, London (2007).

[9] R. C. Majumdar, Chapter III, General Review of Archaeological Explorations and Excavations in The History and Culture of Indian People, p.107, Vol. I, Bharatiya Vidya Bhavan, Mumbai (2010).

record and register these distinct cultures of citizens communities,[10] identify their monuments within this culture, to inform and educate citizens about the surveyed and recorded cultures, to communicate history or art parameters for selection of monuments of national importance from such surveyed and recorded cultures, to involve the citizens in such selection and then to preserve/protect such monuments along with their contextual language, script, way of life and the territorial complex which gives meaning to the monument.

The involvement of State governments is ensured in this process by virtue of the location of the monument and the citizens associated with it, in the territory of a State. The preparation of the cultural resource base, including monuments, of each State will be done by the State Archaeology Department. A vernacular publicized option to register a language script, culture and monuments therein joins citizens to this process. The exploration/excavation has to be evenly and fairly spread

---

[10] *As a colonial power the British looked upon monuments in India as serving them and their generations, but they pithily recorded the raison d'etre of preserving monuments. Viceroy Lord Curzon in his speech of the year 1900, to the Asiatic Society of Bengal declared: "In the course of my recent tour, during which I visited some of the most famous sites and beautiful or historic buildings in India, I more than once remarked in reply to Municipal addresses that I regarded the conservation of ancient monuments as one of the primary obligations of Government. We have a duty to our forerunners, as well as our contemporaries and to our descendants – nay, our duty to the two latter classes in itself demands the recognition of an obligation to the former, since we are the custodians for our own age of that which has been bequeathed to us by an earlier, and since posterity will rightly blame us if, owing to our neglect, they fail to reap the same advantages that we have been privileged to enjoy. Moreover, how can we expect at the hands of futurity any consideration for the productions of our own time – if indeed any are worthy of such – unless we have ourselves shown a like respect to the handiwork of our predecessors." In The Story of Indian Archaeology, p.4, October 5, 1949, Publications Division, New Delhi. The director general of ASI, J.H, Marshall in his Introduction to the 1902 archaeological Annual of ASI spelt out the implication of this speech inter alia as a duty of the ASI staff "to place before European scholars' material for elucidation." India and its citizens were nowhere in the mind of the British while setting up the ASI or outlining its functions of conservation, exploration and research and epigraphy or to "dig and discover, to classify, to reproduce, and describe, to copy and decipher and to cherish and conserve."*

among various communities or sections of citizens, transparency ensured in the process of application of parameters and selection through public hearings and single appeal, with faithfulness in recording and prompt declaration. Anger, doubts, suspicions and beliefs come out in the open in a legally disciplined manner, culture becomes a public debate and a public consciousness, while the winds of post-independence rule of law[11] blow through archaeology to discover the law and rules of the neglected area of custom or usage by which sections of citizens live their lives, to test the legal boundaries of public policy.

This legal process triggered by the Fundamental Rights in Arts. 29, 21 and the Fundamental Duty under Art. 51A (f) turns State archaeology into a hand maiden of churning and distillation of each Indian's identity to meaningfully secure Art. 29 and 49. Archaeology becomes the Indian cultural service from the local and the provincial to the national. Every Indian, every State and national Govt. and the Indian State, which are mobile cultural messages, more or less depending upon the extent of 'modernisation', becomes a constitutionally and legally recognised carrier of his or her culture. This should trigger a reasoned cultural economy of consumption of products and processes,[12] spin offs into patent, copyright, biological diversity and geographical indicators laws, a groundswell towards a cultural law and a kinetic process of constant evolution and development of ways of life to understand monuments as culture, instead of a herd mentality of a voyeuristic tourism of shabby ill-administered monuments under VIP quotas or moneyed special treatment.

---

[11] *Non-arbitrariness, no hostile discrimination, natural justice and fair, just and reasonable action, transparency under the Constitution.*

[12] *UNESCO's 2005 meet 'Asia Pacific Creative Communities: Cultural Industries for Local Economic Development" resulted in the Jodhpur Consensus which defined Cultural Industries as the use of creativity, cultural knowledge and intellectual property to produce products and services with social and cultural meaning. In 2005 the Planning Commission appointed a Task Force on Culture & Creative Industries to make suggestions for the 10th Five Year Plan. There was no reference to the Fundamental Right in Article 29 which arises from missing the continuation of child education that contains his/her culture to create a culture capital that ensures the constitutional value of equality of opportunity which constantly renovates the capital as part of livelihood.*

6.4 Constitutional Archaeology

Formal education from school upwards gets connected to life as it becomes a living experience. Other run offs are a competitive development of languages and employment. If nothing else the translation demand itself should produce a large number of jobs with backward linkages to educational jobs and forward linkages to publishing, products and media industries. The poor have a culture in which the rich do not want to share[13] and the rich have a culture which the poor cannot share even if they may want to. The State's duty is not to mediate by enacting institutionalized begging under a corrupt administration of the Begging Act,[14] but to ensure respectful sharing of ways of living, opportunities, skills and social mobility.

Archaeology then attains the constitutional goal of endeavouring justice social, economic and political. A constitutional vision of culture as a vehicle of emancipation, renaissance and jobs open to all citizens makes citizens and monuments belong to each other on a cultural understanding of monuments. A contrary approach, of treating monuments in isolation of the fundamental right of culture, does to monuments what has happened to secularism minus culture – an animal spirit of dominance or iconoclastic elimination by any means.[15] Hence the constitutional way is the orderly path to change the legacy of an India divided by language, education, dress and extinction of the Indian culture of local production and consumption left to us by the British, which they fashioned for their own purposes and with which we have continued so far, as shown by shutting out of citizens and of Art. 29, from the Ancient Monuments Protection Act, 1958 and its 2010 amendments.

---

[13] *The decline of the numbers of the rich eating with the poor in the 'gurudwara langars' despite the religious injunction of the rich eating with the poor.*

[14] *Report of Amicus Curiae, Dec 6, 1994, in the Delhi leprosy patients' case, Yashwant vs. Union of India CWP No. 10210/85, Supreme Court.*

[15] *Anti-Sikh Riots, 1984–11 Commissions and Committees including that under the Chief Justice of India, Justice Ranganath Mishra, could not effectively deal with the mass murder of Sikhs after the assassination of then Prime Minister, Mrs. Indira Gandhi.*

A similar process under the State Archaeological Departments is necessary to ensure citizens their fundamental right under Art. 29, concerning monuments in Entry 12, List II, VIIth Schedule or in Entry 40 List III of the VIIth Schedule.

6.5 Article 49, 29 and 51A(f) Cleavage

The fundamental right to conserve distinct cultures of each section of citizens in Art. 29 and the fundamental duty of all citizens to preserve all these cultures is the harmonious constitutional basis on which Parliament has been given the exclusive power under Entry 67 List I in the VIIth Schedule of the Constitution read with Art. 246(1) to declare by a law enacted by it as to which monument forming part of the fundamental right and the fundamental duty of citizens, is a monument of national importance. The entry also empowers the Union Government to do the same 'under a law' made by Parliament.

It is the second option that has been chosen and hence the Union Government in power in 1958 made a political policy decision to enact the Ancient Monuments & Archaeological Sites and Remains Act.[16] Section 4 of this Act empowers the Union Govt. to notify, after considering objections, if any, in a period of two months from the declaration of its intention, an ancient monument as one of national importance and therefore, a protected monument. S.2 (j). The Act defined in S.2 (a) an ancient monument inter-alia as any monument which is of "historical, archaeological or artistic interest" and which has been in existence for not less than one hundred years.[17]

6.6 First Cleavage: Art. 49 and 1958 Act

However, the Directive Principle in Art. 49, unenforceable in a court of law but fundamental in the governance of the country, limits the obligation of the Central Govt. under a law made by Parliament to protect

---

[16] *Hereinafter the 1958 Act.*

[17] *The date from which one hundred years are to be counted is not given in the Act and to this extent the Act suffers from the vice of vagueness.*

monuments of "artistic or historic interest" which are declared under such law as monuments of national importance. So the first cleavage is between Art. 49 and the 1958 Act inasmuch the Act puts in a category called monuments of "archaeological interest" when no such category exists in Directive Principle 49.

6.7 Second Cleavage: Art. 49, 29 r/w 51A(f)

Citizens have a fundamental right to "conserve" their distinct monuments representing their distinct culture. They have a duty to preserve all the distinct monuments representing all the distinct cultures. But the Central Govt. has a duty to "protect" only those monuments which have been designated by it as monuments of national importance, which may or may not belong to any of the conserved monuments of distinct cultures under Art. 29. There is thus a second cleavage: between the Directive Principle in Art. 49 on the one hand, and the fundamental right of citizens under Art. 29 as well as the fundamental duty of citizens under Art. 51A(f). The Directive Principle does not require that a monument to be protected by the State must have a direct link or nexus to the distinct cultural monuments that are being conserved by citizens as their distinct culture to form part of the composite heritage.

If Art. 49 is read in this stand-alone manner, instead of reading it with Arts 29 and 51A(f), then constitutionally what is protected by the Central Govt. under Art. 49 is not necessarily what is conserved by citizens under Art. 29.[18] It seems that in 1958 when it was decided to enact the Act, Art. 49 was read without Art. 29. A cleavage was created when by the well-established interpretation principle of reading legal text as a whole, Art. 49 ought to have been read with Art. 29. A Directive Principle could not have been applied in the making of a law (Art. 37) by ignoring the relevant fundamental right which is directly impacted by such a law.

---

[18] Oliver Mendlsohn and Upendra Baxi, Das, Veena: "Cultural Rights and the Definition of Community," in The Rights of Subordinated Peoples, OUP, New Delhi (1996).

6.8 The Ancient Monuments Act, 1958

6.8.1 Act Reflects the Cleavage

This constitutional cleavage which enables the ruling politicians of the Union of India, to have their own culture of monuments which it calls of national importance, as distinct from the culture of monuments which citizens have conserved, is fully reflected in the 1958 Act in various ways:

I. Citizens have been given no right to suggest to the Central Government that the monument of their distinct culture should be recognized as a monument of national importance. At the highest the citizens can only object to the notification of the Central Government within a period of two months of the notification declaring the intention of the Central Govt. to declare a monument as one of national importance. No duty is cast on the Central Govt. to adequately publicise its proposal throughout the country, especially in the various vernaculars, and invite objections. The citizens are not entitled to any hearing or to any reasons for the rejection of their objections. This make for a complete packet of partisan party politics and arbitrariness after every national election in the declaration of monuments of national importance. Citizens have a fundamental right to their distinct culture of monuments without any machinery for having their monuments in the Indian identity of monuments of national importance.

II. Citizens have been statutorily shut out by a deeming[19] provision, Section 3 of the 1958 Act, from questioning the basis of labeling monuments as monuments of national importance under the Ancient & Historical Monuments & Archaeological Sites and Remains (Declaration of National Importance) Act, 1951 and by Section 126 of the States Reorganisation Act, 1956. What a colonial government gave us when there was no Art. 29 for its subjects was continued by independent India's first Central

---

[19] Wayne E. Bagley: The Myth of the Taj Mahal and a New Theory of Its Symbolic Meaning, available at http://www.collegeart.org/pdf/artbulletin/Art%20Bulletin%20Vol%2061%20No%201%20Begley.pdf (last visited on 20.07.2017).

Govt. by shutting out the fundamental right under Art. 29 of its citizens and using a legal fiction to continue the colonial legacy of monuments.

III. Citizens can lose the monument of their distinct culture, because under the 1958 Act any private monument can be declared by the Central Govt. as a monument of national importance or a protected monument.

IV. In an exercise of legislative power of doubtful constitutional validity, the 1958 Act has added another category of monuments, those of "archaeological interest" to the two categories given in Art. 49, namely artistic or historic. This amounts to statutorily adding a new category of monuments of "archeological interest" to the categories of monuments mentioned in Art. 49 of the Constitution. It is therefore an amendment of the Constitution which an ordinary statute cannot do. The amendment of the Constitution can only be done by following the procedure under Art. 368(2). Since the procedure has not been followed, the statutory addition of monuments of "archaeological interest" seems to be unconstitutional. The special procedure under this Article was required to be followed as the statutory addition effectively amends Entry 67 of List I of the VIIth Schedule of the Constitution which mentions only two kinds of monuments "ancient and historical" and not monuments of "archaeological interest."[20]

Archaeological interest can be one of the factors determining the historical or the artistic interest of a monument. But this is not what the Act says. The Act creates a standalone separate category of monuments of archaeological interest, which the Constitution in Art. 49 does not mention. Even taking these three criteria into account, the Act did not require the Central Govt. to specify which

---

[20] The ICOMOS Charter for the Protection and Management of Archaeological Heritage (1990), *defines "archaeological heritage" as "that part of the material heritage in respect of which archaeological methods provide primary information, comprising all vestiges of human existence and consisting of places relating to all manifestations of human activity, abandoned structures and remains of all together with all the portable cultural material associated with them."*

of the three criteria is the basis of notifying a monument to be of national importance, and therefore a protected monument under the Act.

The Act is largely a copy of the British-period Ancient Monuments Act, 1904. Hence it is not surprising that it has been drafted as if the Constitution of India did not exist. The words monuments of "archaeological interest" are there in the definition of ancient monument in the 1904 Act. The same have been put in the 1958 Act definition regardless that this category does not exist in Art. 49 of the Constitution.

Once a private monument is declared to be a monument of national importance or a protected monument by a notification of the Central Govt., its owners/citizens are subject to the coercive processes of the Central Govt. for entering into an agreement with it for its maintenance, if the owners refuse or fail to enter into such an agreement.[21]

V. If in the judgment of the Central Govt. Section 13, there is an apprehension that a private protected monument is in danger of being destroyed, injured, misused or allowed to fall in decay, it can acquire that monument under the Land Acquisition Act, 1894. The protected monument becomes bereft of its culture and is treated like any other structure or building under the Land Acquisition Act.

VI. Citizens can sell, lease, gift, bequeath to the Central Govt., or put under the guardianship of the Central Govt. any private protected monument.

VII. The obligation of the Central Government to protect such monuments under the Directive Principle in Art. 49 is not stated anywhere in the 1958 Act. Hence, no one in the Central Govt. has been made legally responsible for the protection of monuments of national importance, defined in the Act as protected monuments.

VIII. In the determination of any excavation policy, the Act gives no place to citizens even though it is the composite culture which is to be enriched by a continuous discovery of the past. Hence,

---

[21] Section 9 of the 1958 Act.

excavations[22] remain subject to the Central Govt. or the decisions of the political party in power.

6.9 Consequences

(i) ASI – No Place or Duty in 1958 Act

The consequence of such a legal approach on the part of the Central Government has been that the sole professional agency, the Archaeological Survey of India (ASI), actually in charge of the around 3500 centrally protected monuments in the country finds no mention in the 1958 Act. Only the Director-General of ASI is mentioned as an agent of the Central Govt. in the context of private protected monuments. The colonial structure of the ASI into circles continues without any specification of the duties of the Superintendents of the Circles in terms of Art. 29 of the Constitution. There is no duty even to ensure that the circles are organized along the cultural belts of the country in terms of language, script and culture.

(ii) No Culture in Union Ministry of Culture

The legal approach of treating monuments as buildings combined with keeping out citizens of distinct cultures relevant to a monument and non disclosure of the historical or artistic or even the archaeological basis of notifying monuments of national importance, has made the ASI irrelevant to the discovery and understanding of the composite culture of India. Topography, population, its life styles of living with and not against nature, or production, distribution and consumption patterns, languages, faiths, beliefs, practices in life's events, commerce, communication, employment, family structures, hierarchies and community care, the management of land resources and people by the governed, or the entire cultural pattern of a monument has been ignored. In short, the context of a monument which alone gives meaning to it as a text, figures nowhere in the Act as a statutory duty of ASI as part of the three constitutional concepts of protection (Art. 49), preservation (Art. 51A(f)) and conservation (Art. 29) The concept of culture is missing from the Union Ministry of Culture and its operative arm the ASI.

---

[22] Sections 21, 22, 24 of the 1958 Act r/w 1959 Rules 11, 12 and 13.

6.10 CAG Report, 2013

This is confirmed by the Performance Audit Report No. 18 of 2013 by the Comptroller and Audit General which highlights that the Ministry of Culture has not conducted a comprehensive survey or review to identify monuments which were of national importance for inclusion in the list of centrally protected monuments or to identify those monuments which had lost this stature over a period of time. Despite the Union Minister of Culture heading the Central Advisory Board on Archaeology which makes recommendations on conservation and maintenance of centrally-protected monuments, there was no conservation policy for such monuments, ASI had no prescribed criteria for prioritization of conservation works resulting in arbitrary selection of monuments for conservation works. The ASI officials were not preparing inspection notes on the condition of monuments and basic records like log books and site registers were not being maintained properly. The draft policy on conservation is being drafted since August 2011. ASI is still using the 1923 Conservation Manual prepared by its the then Director General Sir John Marshall and published under the authority of the GOI. The ASI did not have a reliable data base of the exact number of protected monuments under it.

The result was that in joint physical inspections out of a sample of 1655 centrally-protected monuments, 92 monuments or six percent were not traceable. There was no central data base of the notifications of protected monuments even though it is the notification that provides the legal status and defines the area of a site for determining encroachments and unauthorised construction. The Union Ministry of Culture informed the Lok Sabha that as of January 1, 2018 out of the 3686 protected monuments 14 were affected by rapid urbanisation, 12 were submerged by reservoirs or dams and 24 it simply could not trace.

The National Policy on Excavation and Exploration had not been finalized by the Ministry in five years despite the Prime Minister's instructions to do so. The ASI did not have any standards of the acquisition, preservation, documentation and custody of objects possessed by it under the Antiquities and Art Treasure Act, 1972, there was no systematic maintenance of the accession register of such antiquities in the museums and the ASI did not maintain a database as the custodian of antiquities of the total number of antiquities in its possession and little or no monitoring of the ongoing projects of the National Culture Fund. Hence on finance, manpower, legislation and monitoring the governance by the Union Ministry of Culture was found deficient as it had ignored all the red signals from a host of Parliamentary committees and courts.

The ineluctable conclusion on the basis of the above report is that the Union Ministry of Culture has deliberately and consciously abandoned its constitutional and legal functions to the point that national cultural monuments and items become prone to loss by simply not keeping the legal records concerning the monuments. This of course is in keeping with the findings of the N.N. Vohra Committee report, extracted in Dinesh Trivedi vs. UOI[23] that a parallel machinery governs India.

6.11 Tourism Revenue Replaces Culture

Maladministration by the Union Govt. of monuments of national importance under a Constitution that does not require accountability of anyone for patent violation of constitutional norms and an Act that simply ignores the fundamental right to culture, has left a cultural vacuum. This vacuum has been filled in by tourism.[24] Consequently, protected monuments like the Taj Mahal, as the Supreme Court has pointed out, have become an industry. The ever rising tide of tourists is permitted into the Taj Mahal complex at the cost of the spirit of the monument, its carrying capacity and its security. Having fallen into the tourism trap, instead of sustainable tourism according to the purpose for which the monument was constructed, the ASI has gone so far as to propose before the Supreme Court the breaking of walls inside the notified Taj Mahal protected complex to facilitate tourist inflow.[25]

---

[23] Dinesh Trivedi vs. UOI, (1997) 4 SCC 306.

[24] Simon During ed., Adorno, Theodor & Horkheimer Max: Chapter 2 "The Culture Industry, Enlightenment as Mass Deception" in The Cultural Studies Reader, 2nd edn, Routledge, London (1999).

[25] I.A. 426/427 in C.W.P. 13381/84, Supreme Court.

That would have been done had it not been for a Supreme Court order directing that not a brick of the wall of the complex would be touched without the prior permission of the court and an oral undertaking by the ASI's counsel not to do so.[26]

However, by that time some damage had already been done inside the notified Taj Mahal protected complex, as the dilapidated servants quarters had already been demolished and rebuilt near the entrance to the Taj.

6.12 All India Cultural Heritage Service

Hence there is an urgent need to convert the ASI into an organization or constitute a new organization, with an All India Cultural Heritage Service, having a specialized wing on Monuments, which will:

1. Be an organization of cultural outreach.
2. Recognise monuments as part of a distinct culture of all sections of Indians which they are entitled to conserve.
3. Recognise that these distinct cultures sum up into the composite rich cultural heritage of India, that culture is a property of the citizens and monuments exist in this cultural context.
4. Preserve this rich cultural heritage by advice, guidance, education, training, media and minimal intervention.
5. Reveal the profession/technical basis in history, art and architecture for recognizing monuments of national importance with participation of citizens and State governments.
6. Protect these monuments instead of focusing on their usufruct like tourism, advertising and revenue.
7. Do all this in a transparent, participatory and fair manner.

The ASI needs to be placed in a framework of cultural heritage to enable and facilitate the actualisation of the Art. 29 fundamental right. The creation of an All India Cultural Service will require an amendment under Art. 368 (1), of Art. 312 of the Constitution.

---

[26] Order dated November 2004 in I.A. 426/427 in C.W.P. 13381/84.

Chapter VII
CONSTITUTIONAL CULTURAL HERITAGE APPROACH

The constitutional perspective on monuments of national importance, emanates from reading together Articles 29(1), 51A(f) and 49 of the Constitution of India. Article 29(1) grants to "any section of citizens residing in the territory of India," the fundamental right of a "distinctive culture." Article 51A(f) imposes a fundamental duty on all citizens "to value and preserve the rich heritage of our composite culture." The Directive Principle in Article 49 places an "obligation" on the State to inter alia "protect every monument…of artistic or historic interest declared by law made by Parliament to be of national importance, from spoliation, disfigurement, destruction, removal, disposal or export, as the case may be." Hence, these three Articles of the Constitution spell out an integrated constitutional scheme based on what sections of citizens of India recognize as their "distinct culture."

7.1 Cultural Fraternity, Identity and Unity

Accordingly, the starting point for recognition of monuments of national importance is the entire diversity of India captured in the fundamental right to a "distinct culture" of any section of citizens. The fundamental duty to preserve the rich cultural heritage of such monument and to protect the same follows from the stakeholders belonging to the artistic or historic interest of their monument. The distinct culture is of a section of citizens, but the duty to value to preserve this culture is that of all citizens. Cultural sections of citizens are joined to all citizens into a cultural fraternity by which, in terms of the preamble, each individual citizen has a cultural identity which collectively creates an Indian cultural identity as a base for the unity and integrity of the nation.

7.2 Constitutional Scheme

This is the cultural heritage approach to the question of monuments of national importance based on the monuments of each distinct culture of sections, of citizens. Thus, the Union of India's legislative power to enact a law under Article 49, read with Entry 67 and 62 List-I, Seventh Schedule of the Constitution and Article 246, must necessarily be exercised in the context of Article 29, to declare monuments of national importance. Bereft of these constitutionally relevant factors, such monuments become legally meaningless pieces of stone.

When viewed in this constitutional perspective, monuments as part of the fundamental right of each section of citizens of their "distinct culture" collectively create a national Indian identity based on the historic or artistic interest reflected by such cultures and declared to be national importance. It necessarily implies the creation of indicators of what is "historic," or "artistic" or both in the monuments of a distinct culture in terms of Article 49 read with Article 29, for it to become a monument of national importance. The leitmotif of composite cultural heritage in Article 51A(f), as expressed by monuments of national importance in Article 49, runs through the constitutional filters of "distinctive culture" in Article 29 and "artistic or historic interest" in Article 49.

This constitutional scheme, based on citizens and their fundamental right, as supplemented by the Directive Principles and Fundamental Duties, embraces environmental or any other threat to such monuments which must be protected by the State from spoliation, disfigurement, destruction, removal, disposal or export.

The protection is of a cultural heritage represented by monuments. Two more constitutional provisions clearly indicate the democratic, national and public interest validity of the aforesaid constitutional scheme which emerges on a reading of the Constitution as a whole.

7.3 Monuments as One Art. 25 Religion

Firstly, monuments as symbols of the distinct culture of citizens, normally reflect the religious culture of sections of citizens who through their distinct cultures sum up the diversity of India. In that sense monuments are an expression of their Article 25 fundamental right to "freedom of conscience" and to "freely profess, practice and propagate religion." This is a constitutional extension of their fundamental right to freedom of speech and expression in Article 19(1)(a). But this religious freedom in Article 25 has been specifically made subject to the other Fundamental Rights. This means that if monuments reflect religion, then that religion is subject to Article 29, i.e. religion in relation to monuments is not be seen as an independent entity but as a part of the "distinct culture" of a section of citizens.

Such an interpretation is democratic, since it furthers the freedom of citizens individually, in collectivities called "sections" in Article 29, the freedom of expression and the freedom of religion. This is in the public and national interest since it constitutionally entrenches religion by recognizing it as a culture of India, subjects religion to the same fundamental rights in Article 25 as other religions, enables the constitutional regulation of all religions in terms of: public order, morality, health; the economic, financial, political or other secular activity associated with any religion; the fundamental rights of all Indians and persons in India as human beings; the fundamental rights of special categories of Indians based on their histories – women, children, Scheduled Castes, Scheduled Tribes and Other Backward Classes. Monuments then become symbols of expression of distinct religious cultures to become monuments of national importance to the extent that their art, history or both represent this constitutional recognition of religion to form an Indian cultural identity out of the multiple and manifold distinct religious or cultural identities.

7.4 Panchayat to Municipality: Monuments Gather and Unite Religions

This constitutional framework of the recognition of religion, in which the culture or cultural activity, cultural aspects of India are embedded, applies equally to "ancient and historical monuments...other than those declared by or under law made by Parliament to be of national importance," mentioned in Entry 12, List-II, Schedule-VII of the Constitution. Ancient and historical monuments in each State, are subject to the same fundamental rights approach of cultural heritage as described above for the Parliamentary law on monuments of national importance. The Constitution in Articles 243G and 243W reinforces this cultural approach in each State of the Union of India by speaking on State laws only in terms of culture concerning the panchayats and municipalities in each State and not specifically of monuments.

Article 243G read with Entry 21 of the 11th Schedule of the Constitution enables the State Government to enact a law by which this cultural approach trickles down legally to self-governance by Panchayats, since the State law can contain provisions for the devolution of powers and responsibilities upon Panchayats with respect to "cultural activities." Similarly, Entry 13 in the XIIth Schedule of the Constitution, "promotion of cultural, educational and aesthetic aspects" read with Article 243W enables each State Government to enact a law by which the cultural approach trickles down legally to self-governance by municipalities. Article 243W(a)(ii) and 243W(b) permit such a State law to contain provisions for devolution of powers and responsibilities to municipalities in relation to Entry 13 in the XIIth Schedule. At the rural governance level of panchayats and the urban governance level of municipalities, monuments of a State, which must necessarily be located either in a village panchayat or an urban municipality, get submerged in the local cultural heritage and the distinct culture of that panchayat or municipality. Without this cultural frame monuments are mere geometric pieces of stone.

Accordingly, from the national to the smallest constitutional governance unit at the village and urban levels, monuments whether of national importance or of importance in each State, become part of the cultural heritage approach based on the distinct culture of their respective location.

7.5 Constitutional Architecture: Culture Subsumes Religion

Hence constitutionally, culture as the sum of distinct cultures of India which include within it religion, constitutes the composite cultural heritage that unites India into a fraternity with a cultural identity.

The fact that the constitutional scheme has not been worked that way does not in any manner take away or dilute the constitutional architecture of cultural unity created through the fundamental rights of Articles 29, 25, 26; directive principles of Article 39(b) and 49; fundamental duties in Article 51A(e) and (f); Article 243G in Part-IX, and Article 243W in Part-IXA and other provisions of the Constitution relating to the power to legislate with respect to Entry-67 in List-I and Entry-12 in List-II of Schedule-VII of the constitution.

Culture is the common thread that stitches these constitutional provisions into the garland of cultural identity of Indians and thus of India. The second constitutional provision which clearly indicates the democratic, national and public interest validity of the aforesaid constitutional scheme which emerges on a reading of the Constitution as a whole, is the preamble. The preamble underlines the aim of this constitutional scheme. The aim is to secure to citizens fraternity based on the dignity of the individual and the unity and integrity of the nation.[1] This aim is the constitutional paste that binds the diversity of distinct cultures of Article 29 manifested through monuments of national importance based on historic, artistic or both interests depicted by such monuments.

The constitutional scheme of a cultural heritage approach to monuments, therefore, builds a national identity[2] based on the country's cultural history, ensures democracy through the plurality of distinct

---

[1] *States Reorganisation Commission, 1955*: "It is the Union of India that is the basis of our nationality. It is in the Union that our hopes for the future are centred. The States are but the limbs of the Union, while we recognise that the limbs must be healthy and strong...the strength and stability of the Union...should be the governing consideration."

[2] Nehru J, The Essential Writings of Jawaharlal Nehru, OUP, New Delhi (2003).
The Ramayana and the Mahabharata were woven into the texture of millions of lives in every generation for thousands of years. I have often wondered if our race forgot the Buddha, the Upanishads and the great epics, what then will it be like. It would be uprooted and would lose its basic characteristics which have clung to it and given it distinction throughout these long ages. India, would cease to be India.

cultures[3] of any section of citizens and creates the public interest glue of unity and integrity of the political entity called India or Bharat. However, the making of a constitutional Indian identity based on the cultural heritage of "every monument, place or object of artistic or historic interest," must remain limited to tangible heritage. Article 49 and the Constitution of India generally, nowhere refer to any obligation of the state to protect the largest and probably the most valuable intangible cultural heritage of India – its language, music, resources, methods of prayer, of construction of houses, or preparing foods, clothing, living styles, its oral traditions of learning and embedding of this culture into religion to make it a habit, with that habit in perpetual adjustment to modern education, livelihoods and life styles. The Constitution envisaged a lively cultural secularism based on its citizens fundamental right to culture and not a cultureless secularism based on State controlled culture.[4]

---

[3] Tharoor S, The Great Indian Novel Penguin Books, New Delhi (1989).

How can one approach this land of snow peaks and tropical jungles, with seventeen major languages and twenty two thousand distinct dialects… Inhabited in the last decade of 20th Century by nearly 940 million individual of every ethnic extraction known to humanity? How does one come to terms with a country whose population is 51% illiterate, but which has educated the world's second largest pool of trained scientists and engineers, whose teeming cities overflow while four out of five Indians scratch a living from the soil? What is the clue to understanding a country rife with despair and disrepair, which nonetheless moved a Mughal emperor to declaim, 'if on earth there be paradise of bliss, it is this, it is this, it is this…' how does one gauge a culture that elevated non-violence to an effective moral principle, but whose freedom was born in blood and whose independence still soaks in it? How does one explain a land where peasant organisations and suspicious officials attempt to close down Kentucky Fried Chicken as a threat to the nation, where a former Prime Minister bitterly criticises the sale of Pepsi-Cola in a country where villagers don't have clean drinking water, and which yet invents a greater quantity of sophisticated software for U.S. computer manufacturers than any other country in the world? How can one portray the present, let alone the future, of an ageless civilisation that was the birthplace of four major religions, a dozen different traditions of classical dance, eighty-five political parties, and three hundred ways of cooking the potato?

[4] Braidel F.A., History of Civilisations, Penguin Books, London (1995).

"People have a psychological history which gives rise to a mentality that dictates attitudes, guides choices, confirm prejudices, and directs actions. The psychological history results from a distilled tradition to create a collective personality."

Chapter VIII

STATUTE VS. CONSTITUTION: MONUMENTS AS OBJECTS

Pursuant to Article 49, Parliament has exercised its legislative power under Article 246 read with Entry 67 List I, which reads as: "Ancient and historical monuments and records, and archaeological sites and remains declared by or under law made by Parliament to be of national importance." The exercise of the legislative power by Parliament resulted in The Ancient Monuments and Archaeological Sites and Remains Act, 1958 (the Act). The Act went against the constitutional manner of viewing monuments as a cultural heritage based on the "distinct culture" context of a section of citizens, by replacing this constitutional approach with a monuments as objects approach minus any reference to the cultural context or heritage.

8.1 Ignoring Difference between Monument and Object

The monuments as objects approach is self-evident from the opening recital of the Act which declares monuments as part of "other like objects." This approach of monuments as objects is confirmed by the definition of "ancient monument" in Section 2(a) of the Act. The definition enumerates monuments as one amongst the following objects: any structure, erection, tumulus or place of internment, or any cave, rock sculpture inscription or monolith. The definition, accordingly, completely fails to recognize the constitutional distinction made in Article 49 of the Constitution, pursuant to which the Act was enacted, between a "monument" of artistic or historic interest and an "object" of artistic or historic interest.

Article 49 obliges the State to protect every monument of artistic or historic interest declared by or under a law made by Parliament to be of national importance. In addition, it extends the same obligation of the State to "object of artistic or historic interest." The failure to note this distinction in Article 49, resulted in the Act recognizing in the definition of "ancient monument" only one aspect of historic interest of a monument of national importance, namely, the past time called ancient extending to one hundred years. But it ignored the other aspect namely the cultural history in which such a monument was situated. Accordingly, the Act in defining, "ancient monument" nowhere referred to the fundamental right of "distinctive culture" in Article 29 of which the monument forms a part.

8.2 Act Defeats Article 49

The legislative draftsman seemed to have introduced the word "object" in the recital of the Act, by picking it up from Article 49 and then enumerated the various objects covered in the definition of "ancient monument." This defeated Article 49 which specifically set monuments of artistic or historic interest apart from objects of artistic or historic interest. Hence the drafting of the definition of "ancient monument" as enacted in the Act, is without application of mind by the draftsman to Article 49, from where the word "object" seems to have been picked up. This is clear from the fact that the word "object" does not figure anywhere in Entry 67, List I, Schedule VII or in Entry 12, List II or in Entry 4, List III, which are the only Constitutional provisions relating specifically to monuments, archaeological sites, remains of records. It seems the attempt through the Act was to limit monuments to the "ancient and historical" stated in Entry 67, List I, as stated in the recital or preamble of the Act, and subsume the Art. 49 artistic monuments into the Act, to yield a definition of ancient monuments as one of the several objects of the recital.

This approach of shutting out the mind in the drafting of the Act is visible in the deeming provision of Section 3. This Section deems as ancient and historical those monuments declared to be of national importance in the Ancient and Historical Monuments and Archaeological Sites and Remains (Declaration of National Importance) Act, 1951 or by Section 126 of the States Reorganisation Act, 1956. Hence Parliament in its Statute never examined on the basis of the twin tests of "historical" or "artistic" interest in Article 49 of the Constitution, the national importance of such monuments declared till 1956. The tests in Article 49 are to be applied, not deemed away.

In any event, it is legally difficult to understand how a Parliamentary statute could deem away a constitutional provision like Art. 49. If this were legally permissible, then ruling politicians with a majority in Parliament could statutorily deem away any provision of the constitution for their political convenience. The legality of this statutory deeming device, to bypass a constructional provision, is made worse in the case of Art. 49, which the constitution declares to be "fundamental in governance of country" and which as a part of culture has been declared it to be a fundamental right by Supreme Court.[1]

8.3 Unconstitutional Definition: Ancient – An Undefined Century

The Act is legislated on the subject mentioned in Entry 67 List-I of the Seventh Schedule of the Constitution. The subject mentioned in Entry 67, List-I is "Ancient and historical monuments and records and archaeological sites and remains, declared by or under law made by Parliament to be of national importance." This subject matter nowhere mentions the word "object" and does not treat monuments as objects. Yet the Act enacted on the basis of the subject matter in Entry 67 List-I treats monument as objects. Accordingly, the definition of ancient monument in the Act travels beyond the subject matter on which the definition could be formulated. It is hence ultra vires the powers of Parliament under Entry 67 List-I read with Article 246(1) of the Constitution. Under the Ancient Monuments Act 1958 the definition of "ancient monument" is spelt out as a structure or a monument that is at least one hundred years old. The obligation under Article 49 is to protect "every monument" and not only "ancient monuments" as sought to be done by the Act. The width of the protection given by the substantive constitutional provision in Article 49 to "every monument" of artistic or historic interest cannot

---

[1] Ramsharan Autyanuprasi vs. UOI, (1989) Supp SCC 251 (Alternately referred to as "Sawai Man Singh II case).

be reduced by an Entry in one of the Lists of the Seventh Schedule of the Constitution to "ancient monuments" and then further reduced by defining "ancient monument" as those which are one hundred years old to freeze the protection to a century of history. Even this freezing is meaningless because it does not state the point of time from which one hundred years are to be calculated. Thus the statutory definition in Section 2(a) defeats the extent of the constitutional protection given to monument of national importance. This renders the definition unconstitutional as a statute cannot take away the protection granted by a constitutional provision.

8.4 Archaeological Interest

The definition in Section 2(a) of the Act is also unconstitutional because of the kind of monuments covered by it in contrast to the constitutional provision in Article 49 of the Constitution. Article 49 obliges the State to protect every monument of "artistic or historic interest." The definition, after restricting the protection to only century old monuments, expands the protection to the century old monuments by including monuments of "archaeological interest." Such monuments, specifically of archaeological interest, are not mentioned anywhere in Article 49. The same are also not mentioned in the subject matter of legislation in Entry 67 List-I of the Seventh Schedule of the Constitution, which mentions only "archaeological sites and remains" and not monuments of archaeological interest. The act itself distinguishes between monuments of archaeological interest in Section 2 (a) and "archaeological sites and remains," by defining the latter in Section 2(d). Thus neither Article 49 nor the legislative subject matter Entry in List-I, under which Parliament has enacted the Ancient Monuments Act, 1958, enable or empower the inclusion of monuments of archaeological interest in the definition under the Act meant to carry out the purpose of Article 49 for monuments of national importance. The Act to this extent is not a law on the subject matter mentioned in Entry 67 List-I since monuments of archaeological interest in the definition in Section 2 of the Act have no nexus to the legislative Entry. There being no constitutional basis whatsoever for expanding by statutory definition the constitutional protection, has no constitutional basis to the extent it includes monuments of "archaeological interest."

8.5 How Objects-Approach Destroys Article 49

Article 49 required Parliament only to declare the monuments of national importance on the basis of the criteria already given in the Article, namely "artistic or historic interest." This required Parliament to enact a law to define the words "artistic" and "historic" and to constitute a machinery for applying this criteria of "artistic" or "historic" interest for picking out monuments of national importance.

It also necessitated the recognition of the fact that a monument, for example the Taj Mahal, is part of monument complex and not a standalone monument. Hence protection of the monument necessitates defining a monument as meaning a monument complex which gives context and meaning to the monument. The law would hence require and interdisciplinary study based on history and geography to define in each case of a monument of national importance picked out on the basis of "artistic" or "historic" interest to define the complex. The absence of this approach in the Act enacted by Parliament is only destructive of Article 49 and the monument concerned, as:–

8.5.1 It tears the monument out of its original historical and geographical context. Just as an Act or a document should be read as a whole to understand its meaning, so also a monument needs to be understood in its historical and geographical context. This alone can be the foundation of any meaningful preservation and protection of a monument – the preservation of what it means. History and geography is what defines and protects the monument.

8.5.2 It makes the monument alone a target of tourists and tourism which becomes voyeurism of simply a look at the monument instead of an understanding of the monuments. The monument gets linked to the revenue and employment history, instead of to its geography and history, its/artistic/or/historic interest.

8.5.3 It gives rise to perennial security and protection/conservation problems focused only on the monument, instead of diffusing the problems away from the monument by distributing interest and intention of visitors to the complex of the monument.

8.5.4 Instead of remedying this in 2010, when the Act was amended, to limit monuments of national importance to the two categories of "artistic" or "historic" interest mentioned in Article 49, Parliament further expanded statutorily the constitutional categories. This was done by introducing in Section 4A, "architectural value and such other factors as may be relevant for the purpose of categorization" and classification by the Central Government, of monuments of national importance. Thus, classification of monuments of national importance was to be done on factors in addition to and different from the two specific factors mentioned by the Constitution in Article 49, namely, "artistic" or "historic" interest.

8.5.5 The amendment also reflected the legal thinking that there was no difference between monuments of national importance and archaeological sites of national importance, despite the two completely different definitions of "ancient monument" and "archaeological site" in Section 2(a) and 2(d) of the Act itself.

8.5.6 In the context of the aforementioned unconstitutional approach in the Act, the Act as enacted, empowers the Union Government to protect the monuments of national importance as objects and does not obligate it to protect the cultural heritage of the distinct culture of which the monument is historically a part and of which it is a symbol. This approach ensured that Parliament never examined these monuments from the integrated constitutional scheme of cultural heritage arising from "distinct cultures" and meant to foster the objective of the preamble of "fraternity assuring the dignity of the individual and the unity of the nation."

8.5.7 The amendments of the Act in 2010 brought about no change whatsoever in the 1958 approach in the Act of treating monuments as objects as against the constitutional approach of treating monuments as a cultural heritage. The amendments show non-application of mind, for the following reasons:–

8.5.7.1 The amendments continue with the blanket ban on all private construction, including of dwelling houses or any horizontal or vertical increase in the houses, falling within hundred metres from the protected area of a national monument. Application of mind by the officers of the Archaeological Survey of India is shut out as to whether such construction will in any way affect the monument. Even though the amendments provide for surveys, detailed site plans and classifications of monuments of national importance, none of these of these factors are to be applied to the no construction zone of one hundred metres from the protected area of such monuments. The blanket ban is contradicted by Section 20A(4) stating that from the date the Amending Act received the assent of the President, only exceptional permission shall be granted by the Central Govt. or the Director General ASI under Section 20A(3) for construction in a prohibited area for any public work or a project essential to the public. The blanket ban is further contradicted by Section 24(A)(3)(b) concerning construction of "Such other work or project," if in the opinion of the Director General or Central Government, such other work or project shall not have any substantial adverse impact on the preservation, safety, security of, or access to, the monument or its immediate surroundings.

The use of the word "such" in Sec. 24(A)(3)(b) that the project of or work to be constructed in the prohibited area of 100 metres from the monument may not be "essential to the public" but it must belong to the genus of "public work."

8.5.7.2 This constitutes a hostile discrimination against construction of private works or projects like that of Housing. Even if the private work or project like Housing or a personal house, being constructed in the prohibited area of one hundred metres, has no substantial adverse impact on the preservation, safety, security of or access to a monument, still it would not be allowed to be constructed because of the blanket ban in Section 19. This hostile discrimination against an "owner or occupier" in Section 19 makes the section unconstitutional not only on this ground of Art. 14, but also on the ground of the ban being unreasonable, unfair and unjust. The blanket ban lacks reason which is the basis of the rule of law.

8.5.8 The amendments create in Section 20F to 20N a National Monuments Authority, with the powers of a civil court to summon persons for examination on oath and discovery and production of documents. But it is a toothless body (Section 20-I) having only the function of making recommendations to the Central Govt. and the officers of the ASI. The Authority is bound by the directions of the Union Government on matters of policy and the Union Government's decision is declared to be final as to whether a matter is one of policy or not. The complete lack of any legal power in the Authority is further emphasised by Section 20M by which all ASI officers, as the competent authority under the Act, are bound by the written decisions of the Central Govt. in the discharge of their functions of preserving and protecting the monuments declared to be of national importance under the Act. This renders meaningless Clause(c) of Section 20-I which stipulates overseeing the function of these very officers, as a function of the National Monuments Authority. In any event it has no power to enforce anything against any of the ASI officers it is supposed to oversee.

8.5.9 The most significant aspect is that the amendments stipulate no duty on the Authority or the ASI officer to find out and preserve the cultural heritage of the monuments of national importance. The amendments do not empower the Authority to give any direction for finding out such heritage of the concerned monuments. Hence all monuments of national importance are still left bereft of their cultural heritage or the distinct culture which they denote or dignify. The amendments nowhere refer to the constitutional framework under Article 29 read with Article 49, Article 51A(f) and the Preamble of the Constitution. The constitutional aspect of a culture of monuments of national importance is ignored by the amendments to The Ancient Monuments Act, 1958, thereby defeating the aim of the Preamble as amended by the Constitution (42nd Amendment) Act, 1976, by inserting the words, the "integrity of the nation." These words were not there when the 1958 Act was enacted.

8.6 Judicial Approach

Given the constitutional framework analyzed above, two legal approaches or routes were available for adjudication by the judiciary, on the issue of monuments of historical or national importance and, therefore, protected monuments under Section 2(j) of the Ancient Monuments Act, 1958. The first legal approach was the cultural heritage approach under the Constitutional. The second was the objects minus the cultural heritage approach under the Ancient Monuments Act, 1958.

It is from this constitutional and legal perspective that the book analyses the judgments and orders of the Supreme Court and some High Courts on various monuments of national importance and especially those concerning the Taj Mahal, which has been the longest court monitored protected monuments of national importance.

Chapter IX

THE POLITICAL ECONOMY OF CULTURE VS. LAW

The deculturalisation of India started with the British rule and became entrenched during that rule through the British created Macaulay-class of Indians.[1] The British showed how law could be used in pursuit of a policy to kill native India while creating a parallel India which was quantified and governed by a British-system of Courts and various Acts passed by the British Parliament.[2]

9.1 Unquantified & Neglected

The economy so created as a parallel to the vast but ruined native economy recognized only that which was quantified and that which was in the English language. The vast native economy with its diverse ways of life or cultures, linked directly to the needs, climate and resources of a local area, remained unrecognized by the simple expedient that western economics deems that what is not quantified does not exist. Worse, again through the use of law, the British way of life and its language as also its 'modern products' became a psychological[3] symbol of superiority over the 'barbarian' native classes, languages, and their ways of life, especially since this superiority was initiated and reinforced by the British

---

[1] Nirmal Kumar Bose, 'The Geographical Background of Indian Culture' in The Cultural Heritage of India, p.7, Vol.1, Ramakrishna Mission Institute of Culture, Kolkata (Reprint 2007).

[2] Charters of 1601, 1609, 1612; Navigation Act 1660; Charter Acts of 1661, 1793, 1813, 1833, 1853; Act 11 of 1843; Between 1800 to 1815, one million Indians died in 7 famines; Between 1851 to 1875, 20 million died in 24 famines; 18 famines in 1876 to 1900.

[3] Braidel F.A. History of Civilisations, Penguin Books, London (1995).
"People have a psychological history which gives rise to a mentality that dictates attitudes, guides choices, confirm prejudices, and directs actions. The psychological history results from a distilled tradition to create a collective personality."

government in India, as also the Macaulay-class of Indians created by this government. The native ways of life and languages – not having any investment, official support or research – declined and stagnated as they no longer formed part of the British economy in India which had moved from colonization to colonialisation.[4]

Consequently, for morning ablutions, toothbrush, toothpaste, toilet paper and perfumed factory-made soaps replaced the open air defecation system of human waste disposal and the use of flowing water, the Neem twig and local cleaning agents for personal hygiene are cleanliness. The British trouser-shirt-tie-suit and shoes replaced the native, locally-made innerwear and outerwear, Industrial alcohol replaced the locally-fermented alcohol from natural grains. Unfortunately, this entire process of deculturisation was not recognized in the Constituent Assembly Debates during the framing of the Constitution of India. Instead, the British legal framework of Acts, Presidency Courts and separate Provincial Courts which had created this deculturisation process without of course specifically saying so in any British-period legal document, was continued after independence through Articles 372, 312(2), 313 of the Constitution of India. Hence, as silently as in the British-period, the British economics continued after independence in terms of its non-recognition of Bharat by keeping the components of its cultures or ways of life unquantified and unspecified despite Art. 29.

The entire independence movement had based its logic on the fact that India was poor because of British rule and therefore independence from such rule was a necessary condition precedent to the ending of India's poverty. Several leaders of the Indian National Congress had documented how India was kept poor by the British in terms of what the British regularly took away from India for Britain and thereby made India pay for the poverty created by the British.[5] Unfortunately, there was

---

[4] Prasad Rajendra, 'Colonialism Lumpenisation Revolution' in Societies of Calcutta and Shanghai 18501914, Vol. 1 p. 39–56,. Ajanta Books International, New Delhi (1991).

[5] Census of India Report 1911 Vol.1, p. 408 stated: *"the extensive importation of cheap European piece goods and utensils and establishment in India itself of numerous factories of western type has more or less destroyed many village industries. The high prices of agricultural produce have also led many village artisans to abandon their hereditary craft in favour of agriculture...the change is most noticeable in the more advanced provinces."*

no analysis whatsoever of how the British Acts had introduced a Rule of Law in India which not only legitimized what the British took away from their colonial country but ensured the continuation of such British economics which had legally created the economic system to destroy the composite cultural heritage of India by breaking up the entire village system,[6] the ruralurban exchange of goods and the imports-exports into/from India.

In the absence of a recognition and understanding of this politico-legal economy of British India, nothing was ever discussed in the Constituent Assembly debates to specifically reverse this politico-legal economy by altering the psychological superiority of the goods consumed by the Macaulay-class which continued the British economy and legal system in India. On January 26, 1950, the Constitution of India commenced by specifically declaring the continuation of this British legal system without any declaration on the need to alter legally the economics and the deculturisation of native India that had been the hallmark of British rule.

9.2 Six Consequences

9.2.1 First Consequence

The first consequence of this was the continuation in Indian economic planning of the British-time economics by which a country was advanced or backward according to the percentage of its population working in the agricultural sector.[7] Accordingly, the Planning Commission in independent India continued this economics with the continuance of the British legal system through Art. 375 of the Constitution of India. At no stage, the Planning Commission of India thought it fit to invest or plan a legal system in terms of its own five-year plans. A planned economy modernizing itself on British economics was not thought fit to need a planned legal system for such economy. Accordingly, there was no question of any recognition by the Planning Commission or the Union

---

[6] Act 11 of 1843.

[7] Kuznets Simon, Chapter 4: The Pattern of Shift of Labor Force from Agriculture, 1950–70, based on ILO estimates of the industrial structure of the labor force, in The Theory of Experience of Economic Development: ed by Mark Gersovitz Carlos & Others, p. 43, George Allen Unwin, London (1982).

Govt. of the unquantified legal cultures of Bharat and the unquantified ways of life or distinct cultures of Bharat of which these legal cultures formed a part.

9.2.2 Second Consequence

The second consequence was that Art. 375 not only put the same Macaulay-class in charge of Bharat by virtue of the constitutional continuance of the English language British legal system, but also fixed legally the future of India's population in terms of jobs, skills, and the continued superiority of western goods and the English language.[8]

9.2.3 Third Consequence

The third consequence was that without any law, order or notification, the Planning Commission silently set the path of India's economic development. This path in consonance with western economics chose to ensure the shifting of millions of villagers of Bharat, compelled to leave their hearth and home, to the cities. This phenomena known to economists as the inevitable result of shifting out people from agriculture in the move towards the advanced countries definition of western economics was done silently without any Act, Order, information or consent of those affected. They were an unquantified mass of Bharat and therefore they did not exist for the western economic-style of economic development. Consequently, as in British India, there were no legal systems, no legal organizations and no suo motu powers given to the courts by the law concerning these unquantified victims of economic development. The law in independent India simply fell in line with the economics of independent India. So, did political control of culture.[9]

---

[8] Articles 343 to 351 of the Constitution of India.

[9] The Department related Parliamentary Committee in its 201st Report said: *These Academies (Sangeet, Natak & Sahitya) are always mired in one controversy or the other. Our founding fathers gave them autonomy to keep politics away from culture but today politics seems to have crept into them from the back door."* But nowhere the relationship of the political economy to culture was examined.

9.2.4 Fourth Consequence

The fourth consequence of this was the conversion of this unquantified mass of Bharat pushed into the cities by economic planning without any law for the same, got converted into illegal personalities as trespassers on public lands freely, but illegally, using public goods like municipal water, electricity and whatever other public facilities they could manage. They also got converted into useful, recognized numbers as voters. The unquantified Bharat now became legally quantified and recognized players in the political system based on the constitutional principle of Adult Franchise with increasing illegal access to public goods and facilities under political patronage. They had now become quantified, useful and productive elements of the economic system and therefore got converted to the new way of life or culture of western-style goods and consumption along with a lingering residue of what remained of their native culture. The city culture of western-style consumption became the aspirational model, psychologically affirmed by the vernacular audio-visual media and advertising which overcame the English language and literacy barrier.

9.2.5 Fifth Consequence

The fifth consequence was to bring into sharp focus the virtual impossibility of any effective legal system of legal help for native Bharat who had been victimized and continued to be victimized by the politico-legal economic system since British times. Good governance as defined in the constitution by the Directive Principles and Fundamental Rights, the 1977 Fundamental Duties and the National Legal Services Act, 1987, remain laudable objectives on paper since none of these can be monetarily quantified for recognition by the existing economic system.

Accordingly, the Fundamental Right to Culture under Art. 29, the Fundamental Duties of developing a scientific temper and preserving the composite cultural heritage, remain unimplemented. This must continue because legal concepts like public interest, rule of law, democracy, free speech, humanism and culture are not recognized by western economics till they are quantified and their non-quantification is itself treated as a sign of backwardness. Only those portions of these elements of the legal system which have been quantified merit any allocation of state resources.

This is probably the reason why Parliament has not passed a law till date under Art. 32(3) of the Constitution to give quick and effective access to justice in terms of Fundamental Rights and Directive Principles to all citizens of India at the Taluka Courts which are the nearest courts to them. This also explains the complete lack of the Fundamental Right to be informed, of the absence of an All-India Lawyers Service for Legal Aid, of no accountability of the regulatory systems or any one holding legal power or authority, of no transparency in the functioning of govt. departments meant to serve the public and the lack of provision of adequate funds by Parliament for the necessary enforcement mechanisms while enacting new laws.[10]

9.2.6 Sixth Consequence

The final consequence is that a politico-legal economic system has been created in independent India in which native culture and cultural goods have no application of science, advertising, marketing against 'the modern goods' affordable by only about 300–350 million people out of 1.2 billion. This is best reflected by the fact that instead of putting science into the village open-air defecation system, which remains the most efficient and scientific way of disposing human waste and recycling it to fertilize the soil, the state is choosing to replicate the flush water system when there is simply no water quantitatively available for such treatment of the waste of 1.2 billion Indians.[11] Accordingly, there is no effort to understand and establish the scientific superiority of native India's ways of life and goods against the hegemony of a single uniform culture

---

[10] *As more and more new laws are passed and more and more actions are made criminal, there is no corresponding provision for funds and infrastructure for the Police and other enforcement agencies to implement these new laws. Most of the Bills for these laws carry no financial memorandum pointing out the increased monetary resources required for the implementation of the new proposed law.*

[11] *India simply does not have the water at the rate of about 3–5 ltrs per person for a single flush.*

based on chemicals, plastics, and value-added industrial processes ad infinitum. This is needed for example in areas like: Gur (Jaggery) instead of white sugar; of natural salt instead of iodised chemical salt; of natural water instead if packaged and municipal water; of handspun cloth instead of textile – mill cloth; of cotton instead of synthetic yarn; of natural manure instead of chemical manure; of vegetable dyes instead of chemical dyes; and of natural herbs instead of drugs.

9.3 Citizens Torn Away from Culture & Monuments

Monuments in India have no quantitative price and therefore do not exist for India's unconstitutional economic development system. This economic system while ignoring history, geography and the human activity in relation to a monument tears it out of its active locational context. State economic development tears the people whose cultural component the monument is, away from the monument.

The kind of economic development pursued by the State uproots millions and pushes them to slums without any information, consent, law, executive order, rule, regulation and access to justice, as a mass of unquantified people unrecognized by the economics of economic development since economics recognizes only those who are quantified and legal rights flow only to such quantification. The quantified persons of such economic development drive the quantified votes of the legal democratic process of representative government. So the Ancient Monuments Act, 1958, unconstitutionally tears away monuments from relevant factors of place by legally converting their place into quantified or measured space and the political economy of reducing numbers in agriculture to ensure a conscious and deliberate economic development uproots millions from their homes in villages to tear relevant people away from their culture and monuments.

It is done at the silent, invisible and unquantified cost of the entire evolutionary idiom of Anglo-Saxon law or the common law (limited government, constitutionalism, rule of law, public interest and human rights) which as per the Supreme Court forms the basis of our legal system.[12]

---

[12] Ram Jawaya Kapur vs. State of Punjab, AIR 1955 SC 549.

Chapter X

SELF-DEFEATING CONVENTIONS: THE INTERNATIONAL LEGAL FRAMEWORK FOR MONUMENTS

This inherent conflict between economics and law is not recognized in any of the international conventions, treaties, declarations on monuments even while recognizing economic development or modernization as a threat to monuments. Nothing is done to identify why economic development as a threat arises from the economics of such development and to legally tackle these causes. Whether it is international environmental law or international law movement on monuments, the common factor is the non-recognition of culture or way of life by the law and hence of countries like India consisting of a huge unquantified number of cultural minorities, having a fundamental right to their minority culture or the environment under the Constitution of India.

But the internal or national economic order and its political economy do not recognize this fundamental right in India.[1] This helps the international private economy of goods and services since these are made the aspirational alternatives to the domestic way of life or culture of the

---

[1] *Article 37 of the Constitution of India mandates that the Directive Principles providing for the fundamental right to a life of dignity under Article 21 of the Constitution are "Fundamental in the governance of the country." The Planning Commission which commands India's economic development through 5-Year plans and hence the use of India's resources has been constituted by an Executive order under List III, Entry 20 "Economic and Social Planning." However, the International Division of Labour Model followed by the Planning Commission has resulted in the social being disintegrated from the economic. Consequently, economic policy is in the teeth of the constitutional principles which are fundamental in the governance of the country. Accordingly, the constitutional result of Justice-Social, economic and Political has become a mirage for the majority of the population.*

developing countries which deny research, innovation and marketing to the products of their own culture.

But this puts the international legal order in a contradiction – the very culture, way of life or consumption of products of the Anglo-Saxon rule of law countries, (called advanced economies) which are responsible for the greenhouse effect, climate change and conventions/declarations on the same, are sought to be made the way of life in the interests of the private market economies of these countries. The environment so created takes its toll on monuments.

The net result is a helpless international law for preserving monuments in the face of economic development for the billions in countries called developing because the majority of their people do not yet have the advertised aspirational way of life of the developed countries in terms of products, processes and legal enforcement systems to ensure that such products and processes are safe for consumption and use.

10.1 Consumption Creates The Effective Legal System

But this aspect of consumption creating the effective legal system and the way of life that alienates people from their environment and monuments goes unaddressed in the law both within countries and in international legal systems concerning protection of monuments. Accordingly, Art. 1 of the 1964 Venice Charter, approved by the Second International Congress of Architects and Technicians of Historic Monuments, is the flutter of a moaning soul that is left with a monument after having lost its civilizational heritage, when it says that the "concept of a historic monument embraces not only the single architectural work but also the urban or rural setting in which is found the evidence of a particular civilization."

India, the second most populous nation with an Anglo-Saxon democratic legal system, has an Ancient Monuments Act, 1958 that does not recognize its own civilisation in terms of Art. 29 of its own Constitution even though as early as 1900, Viceroy Lord Curzon in his speech before the Asiatic Society of Calcutta had recognised the British Government's responsibility in India to set up a requisite establishment to "supervise the most glorious galaxy of monuments in the world" the preservation of which he had accepted on Feb 1, 1899 before the same Asiatic Society as "a part of our imperial obligation."[2]

The 1904 Ancient Monuments Preservation Act, its amendment by Act No. XVIII of 1932, nowhere mentioned the culture or the civilization of the monuments for which the Archaeological Survey of India had been now firmly constituted. The same situation continued in the 1919 and the 1935 Government of India Acts. Citizens of independent India got culture as a fundamental right in Art. 29 but like the British Acts of pre-independent India, their culture found no mention in The Ancient and Historical Monuments and Archaeological Sites and Remains (Declaration of National Importance) Act, 1951, in Section 126 of the States Reorganisation Act concerning monuments in Part C States, in the Ancient Monuments and Archaeological Sites and Remains Act, 1958 and in the 2010 amendments to the Ancient Monuments Act, 1958. The 1964 Venice Charter's concept of a monument as including its civilization went for a legal toss in independent India. In 2009, pursuant to Art. 5 obligations of State Parties under the World Heritage Convention which had been ratified by India on Nov 14, 1977, a bill called the National Commission for Heritage Sites Bill, 2009 was introduced in the Rajya Sabha as Bill No. VII of 2009. The Bill in its definition of cultural heritage included a monument which was defined inter alia as "architectural works which are of outstanding value from the point of view of history, art or science". The same monuments as objects approach of the Ancient Monuments Act, 1958 continued and civilization or Art. 29 found no place anywhere.

10.2 People are the Heart of Monuments

Two world wars impelled Europe to recognize monuments as a cultural heritage of mankind in which even monuments had to recognize community rights. This began as a private initiative in 1932 at Venice and sovereign States later followed as "wardens of civilisation" into formal legal Conventions. The movement to protect, preserve and conserve

---

[2] Marshall, J.H, "Introduction" to the inaugural issue of the archaeological "Annual," p.8–9, Archaeological Survey of India, (1902).

monuments crystallized into one of international cooperation under UNESCO. But throughout it has two cardinal principles anchoring it. Firstly, that people constitute the heart of protecting and preserving monuments. Secondly, that you cannot hope to protect and preserve monuments unless there is respect for these in people's hearts. On this basis, the legal pacts sought to create records, documentation, an interdisciplinary approach technical institutional, museums, the sharing of information and support to voluntary bodies to make protection and preservation of monuments operational.

10.3 Problematic Efficacy

The efficacy of this legal regime with State and NGO participation is problematic since the idea of protection and preservation defies life in many ways. Man's attempt to make monuments almost immortal defies his own mortality of all mater. It defied the planning and concern of people for their own lifetime instead of an infinite thereafter. It defies market forces by valuing the building or structure or than of the land on which it stands. It defies in relatively poor nations, having majority of the world's populations and monuments, the compelling drive to get out of poverty by turning monuments or their tourists to current cash account. It defies in such nations the "Soft State" wherein defiance of protection and preservation law is an affirmation of status and is lucrative since this feeds the extant cultural of politico economic power. If defies the absence of the very idea of a national history in such countries in a context of no national language, no national education an no ongoing compelling mechanism to turn the State into an instrumentality of ensuring a minimum national standard of life of dignity for all citizens. It defies the religions in these countries which daily revive the cultural fear from those living with them as a result of past conquests and the monuments signifying those conquests. It defies the social structures of these countries wherein by godly conviction majorities have not been and are not allowed to have an history or monuments manifesting that history as a part of a continuing history of the denial of freedom of expression it defies the unexpressed but State enforced international model of economic development by which whole populations are compelled to uproot themselves from their hearth, home, history and cultural to seek a living in the new State created culture of slums. It defies the compelled illegal urbanization of the majority poor turning them into squatters and trespassers as also the relatively small planned urbanization of the minority lower, middle and higher classes through legal and illegal colonization of fertile agricultural lands, the wholesale destructions of culture, and the enormous incentive for slums to graduate into this planned urbanization. In short, it defies change and the matrix of this change of the majority of people having the majority of monuments. It has no mechanism for recognizing inconvenient political, social and economic truth, which is the ambience in which monuments must be protected.

10.4 Athens Charter

The First International Congress of Architects and Technicians of Historic Monuments took place in Athens in 1931. Seven resolutions were made at this Conference. These constituted the Restoration Charter of "Carta del Restauro." The seven resolutions were:–

1. Establishment of international organizations on operational and advisory levels, for restoration work.
2. Proposed Restoration projects are to be subjected to knowledgeable criticism to prevents mistakes which will causes loss to character and historical values to the structures.
3. Problems of preservation of historic sites are to be solved by legislation at national level for all countries.
4. Excavated sites which are not subject immediate restoration should reburied for protection.
5. Modern techniques and materials may be used in restoration work.
6. Historical sites are to be given strict protection.
7. Attention should be given to the protection of areas surrounding historic sites. These resolutions were reflected in the seven paras of the General conclusions of the Athens Conference. These paras put people, their respect and attachment for monuments, as the centerpiece of the preservation and protection of monuments.

Para VII (b) declared "The Conference, firmly convinced that the best guarantee in the matter of the preservation of monuments and works of art derives from the respect and attachment of the people themselves." The onus for creating these feelings of respect and attachment was placed squarely on "appropriate action on the part of public authorities" and on education and educators.

Accordingly, it recommended that educators should teach children and young people to take a greater and more general interest in the protection of these "concrete testimonies of all ages of civilization," and to abstain from disfiguring monuments of every description.

The idea of people at the heart of saving monuments was also reflected in Para-II wherein the Conference recognized the "right of the community in regard to private ownership" and that the conflict between public opposition by keeping in mind three factors – local circumstances, the trend of public opinion and the sacrifices which the owners of property are called upon to make in the general interest.

For meeting change through buildings, the Conference laid down in Para-III that in the neighbourhood of ancient monument buildings should recognize the character and external aspect of cities in which they are to be erected, surroundings should be preserved through ornamental vegetation most suited to them. The effects of modernization were sought to be checked by recommending "the suppression" of "all forms of publicity, the erection of unsightly telegraph poles and the exclusion of all noisy factories and tall shafts in the neighbourhood of artistic and historic monuments." While recognizing in Para-V, the ever increasing danger to monuments from "atmospheric agents." The Conference found it impossible to lay down any general rule on this issue given the then state of knowledge and the complexity involved.

Preservation, protection, consolidation, partial restoration of monuments was to be based on:–

1. An inventory of ancient monuments.
2. Collaboration between architects, curators of monuments, archaeologists and specialists in the physical, chemical and natural science.

Self-Defeating Conventions: The International Legal Framework for Monuments | 179

3. Record keeping and a thorough analysis of the defects and nature of the decay.
4. Indispensable restoration due to the decay of destruction, should respect the historic and artistic work of the past without excluding the style of any given period.
5. The work of consolidating a monument should be concealed whenever possible to preserve the aspect and character of the restored monument.
6. Judicious use of modern materials and techniques in consolidating monuments.
7. In the case of ruins, whenever possible, the original fragments that may be recovered should be reinstated (anastylosis), the new materials used for this purpose should be recognizable and when preservation is found to be impossible the ruins be buried after taking accurate records of the ruins.
8. The occupation of buildings is to be permitted where it ensures the continuity of their life while using them for a purpose which respects their historic or artistic character.

In Article VII the Conference desired that States cooperate with each other in this work in the spirit of League of Nations through the Intellectual Cooperation Organisation of the League of Nations and the International Museums Office.

10.5 Roerich Pact to Hague Convention

Armed conflict situations had posed a grave threat to cultural property in the European wars and then is World War-I. The Hague Convention had tried to tackle this in 1899. On April 15, 1935 the United States and 20 Latin American countries signed the Roerich Pact or the Washington Pact entitled Protection of Artistic & Scientific Institutions and of Historic Monuments. These countries agreed that historic monuments, museums, scientific, artistic, educational and cultural institutional should be protected both in times of peace and war. Protection in wars was to be given to all those monuments identified by flying the Pax Cultura (Peace through Culture) emblem. The Soviet Union States, since it has been superseded by the Hague Convention of 1954. India ratified the 1954 Hague Convention and its Protocol on June 16, 1958.

10.6 1954 Hague Convention

This Convention for the Protection of Cultural Property in the Event of Armed Conflict came into force from August 7, 1956 and was guided by the principal of Hague 1899, 1907 Conventions and the Washington Pact of April 15, 1935. The definition of cultural property in the Convention had the following hallmarks vis-à-vis monuments:

1. It included immovable property of great importance to the cultural heritage of "every people."
2. It recognized cultural property "irrespective or origin and ownership."
3. It covered monuments of architecture, art or history "whether religious or secular."
4. It recognized centres containing monuments, i.e. areas having a large number of monuments.
5. The Convention confers immunity from any act of hostility by parties to the Convention during armed conflict between them, to monuments that have been entered in the "International Register of Cultural Property under Special Protection" and consistent with the interests of cultural property. Such personal must be respected. During an armed conflict such properties are marked with a distinctive emblem provided for under

Article 16 value of Article 17(4), can be placed on such monument only displaying simultaneously and authorization duly dated and signed by the competent authority of the contracting party. This immunity can be withdrawn under Article 11(2) in exceptional cases of unavoidable military necessity for such time as the necessity continues. Such necessity can be established only by an officer commanding a force of the equivalent of a division or a larger size. But the contracting party on whose behalf the immunity is withdrawn on such ground must inform in writing with reasons, as soon as possible, the Commissioner General for Cultural Property.

The Convention becomes a supplementary document for parties bound by the Conventions of the Hague concerning the Laws and Customs of War on Land (IV) and concerning Naval Bombardment in Time of War (IX). The Roerich Pact becomes supplementary to this Convention. Under Article 11(1) a violation of the Article 9 special protection by a contracting party releases the opposing party from the obligation to ensure the immunity of the cultural property till the violation lasts. Whenever possible, the party seeking releases shall first request the cessation of the violation within a reasonable time.

Like the Athens Charter, the fundamental axiom of the Convention is respect for monuments. Hence, there is a continuing recognition that the minds of people. Article 2 defines protection of cultural property as comprising the safeguarding of and respect for such property. Accordingly, in Article 7(1) Convention casts a duty on the contracting parties to "foster in the members of their armed forces a spirit for the culture and culture property of all peoples." This spirit is to be nourished in times of peace itself. Towards this end, three duties are cast on the constricting parties under Article 71(1) and (2).

10.7 Duties of Contracting Parties

10.7.1 First Duty

Firstly, the contracting parties undertake to introduce in time of peace into their military regulations or instructions such provisions as may ensure observance within their armed forces, in peace time, services or specialist personal whose purpose will be to secure respect for cultural property and to cooperate with civilian authorities responsible for safeguarding it.

10.7.2 Second Duty

Secondly, under Article 25, apart from the widest possible dissemination of the Convention by the contracting parties in their countries, the contracting parties undertake to include the study of the Convention in their programmers of military and, if possible, civilian training.

10.7.3 Third Duty

Finally, under Article 28, the contracting parties undertake to take all necessary steps within the framework of their ordinary criminal jurisdiction to prosecute and impose penal or disciplinary sanctions upon those persons, of whatever nationality, who omit or order to be omitted a breach by Article 19 as a minimum regulation even when the armed conflict occurring within the territory of a contracting party is not of an international character.

Under Article 18, the Convention applies to any armed conflict between the contracting parties, even if the state if war is not recognized by one of them. It applies also to territorial occupation of a contracting party's territory even if the occupation meets with no armed resistance.

The enforcement of the Convention is done under the umbrella of the Protecting Powers who shall also lend their good offices for conciliation under Article 22.

With this Convention UNESCO came to be the prime organization for the international protection of cultural property including monuments. The Director General UNESCO, under Article 22 can request the Protecting Parties to propose to the conflicting parties a meeting of their representatives. Under Article 27 he is bound to convene meetings of the representative if one-fifth of the contracting parties request him to do so. He also can convene a meeting on his own with the approval of the Executive Board. Within the limits of its programmed and resources, UNESCO is bound under Article 23(1), to accord assistance concerning this Convention, when requested by the contracting parties.

10.8 ICCROM

The ninth session of the UNESCO General Conference at New Delhi, on December 5, 1956, adopted the proposal for creating an intergovernmental centre for the study and improvement of methods of restoration. Accordingly, the Centre for the Study of the Preservation & Restoration of Cultural Property was set up in Rome, Italy, on the invitation of the Indian Govt. UNESCO and the Italian Government concluded on April 27, 1957, the agreement for the setting up of the Centre. Article 1 of the statute of the Centre described its functions as: to collect, study and distribute documentation concerning the scientific and technical problems of conservation and of restoration of cultural properties; to coordinate and encourage research in this domain confined to missions of experts, international meetings, publications and exchange of specialists; provide consultation and recommendations on matters of conservation and restoration of cultural property; organize bodies of researchers and technicians to raise the level of restoration. The Centre has a general body, a council and a secretariat. The Assembly consists of the adhering States and each State, as per Article 3, shall have one delegate. The Assembly meets every two years. It determines the directions of Centre, elects the members to the Council, names the Director on the recommendation of the Council; studies and approves the reports and activities of the Council; controls the finances and approves the budget' fixes the contributions of the Members and the associate members. The Council, under Article 8, executes the decisions of Assembly, studies and approves the work plan submitted by the Director. Under Article 10 the Secretariat consist of the Director and his assistants who appointed by Council on the recommendation of the Director. The Director and his assistants are all specialists in different disciplines.

India became a member of the Centre in 1961. In 1978, the Centre's name was abbreviated to ICCROM. It has developed the national conservation research centre in India, called the National Research Laboratory for Conservation of Cultural Property (NRICCP) at Lucknow.

10.9 Venice Charter: Integrity of Monuments

After the Athens Charter, the Second International Congress of Architects & Technicians of Historic Monuments took place in Venice from May 25–31, 1964. This Charter noted with satisfaction that the earlier Athens Charter had contributed to an extensive international movement resulting in the International Council of Museums, ICCROM and UNESCO's work like the Hague Convention. In a fresh look at the Athens Charter, the Venice Charter enlarged the earlier Charter into a new document.

The fundamental principle of respect for monuments was restated with a greater emphasis on history, context and evidence concerning monuments. Article 9 specifically required respect for original materials and authentic documents in all restoration work which must be preceded and followed by an archaeological and historical study of the monument. Any indispensable extra work must be distinct from the architectural composition and history and work on the basis of conjecture was prohibited in the name of restoration. Further Article 11 required that the valid contributions of all periods to the building of a monument must be respected, since unity of style is not the aim of restoration.

The revealing of the underlying state in a building having superimposed work of different periods is justified only when what has to be removed is of little interest and what lies underneath is of great historical, archaeological or aesthetic value and in a good enough state of preservation. Article 12 declares that restoration must not falsify the artistic or historic evidence.

This emphasis on history and evidence is summed up in Article 7 which declares that a monument is inseparable from the history to which it bears witness and from the setting in which it occurs. Article 3 states that the aim or intention in conserving and restoring monuments is to safeguard them no less as works of art than as historical evidence and Article 1 declares that the concept of a historic monument embraces not only the single architectural work but also the urban or rural setting in which it is found, the evidence of a particular civilization, a significant development or an historic event. Accordingly Article 4 states that the sites of monuments must be the object of special care in order to safeguard their integrity and ensure that they are cleared and presented in a seemly manner with work of conservation and restoration done on the basis of the preceding principles. In short monuments have an integrity which must be documented and preserved.

10.10 ICOMOS

The 1964 Venice Charter on the Conservation & Restoration of Monuments and Sites was adopted by ICOMOS, in 1965 at Warsaw, Poland, where the ICOMOS Statutes were adopted on June 22, 1965. Its Statutes were amended at Moscow by the 5th General Assembly of ICOMOS on May 22, 1978 and then by the 18th General Assembly on November 12, 2014 at Florence, Italy.

Article 4 states that ICOMOS shall be the international organization concerned with furthering the conservation, protection, rehabilitation and enhancement of monuments, groups of buildings and sites, at the international level. It advices UNESCO on World Heritage Sites. Towards this end under Article 5 ICOMOS provides a mechanism for linking public authorities, institutions and individuals concerned with the conservation of monuments, groups of buildings and sites, and ensure their representation with international organization; gather study and disseminate information concerning principal, techniques and policies for the conservation, protection, rehabilitation and enhancement of monuments, groups of buildings and sites; cooperate at national and international levels in the creation and development of documentation centers dealing with conservation and protection and with the study and practice of traditional building techniques; encourage adoption and implementation of international recommendations concerning monuments, groups of building and sites; cooperate with the preparation of training programmes for specialists and establish and maintain close cooperation with UNESCO, ICRROM and regional conservation centres sponsored by UNESCO and other international and regional institutional and organizations.

Its headquarters are in Paris and can be changed by the General Assembly. Article 9 makes the General Assembly the Sovereign body of ICOMOS consisting of individual, Institutional, Sustaining and Honorary members with the last two classes having no right to vote but the right to participate.

The General Assembly is convened every three years. Article 3(a) of the ICOMOS statute defines inter alia monument to include structure together with their settings and pertinent fixtures and contents which are of value from the historical, artistic, architectural, scientific or ethological point of view. It includes works of monumental sculpture and painting, elements or structures of an archaeological nature, inscriptions, cave dwellings and all combinations of such features. Article 3(d) excludes from the definition museum collections housed in museums; archaeological collections preserved in museums or exhibited at archaeological or historic site museums and open air museums.

There is an Indian Committee of ICOMOS headed presently by Dr. S.S. Biswas, former Director General of the National Museum.

10.11 International Convention on Economic, Social & Cultural Rights

On December 10, 1947 the Universal Declaration of Human Rights referred to culture in a limited way in Article 27, this article stated that everyone has the right freely to participate in the cultural life of the community, to enjoy the art and to share in scientific advancement and its benefits. Further everyone has the right to the protection of the moral and material interests resulting from any scientific, literary or artistic production of which he is the author. The legal unit of culture was the community. There was division of culture into specified objects, no territorial divisions into specified objects if national and less than national importance. On December 16, 1966 the General Assembly of UN adopted the UN International Covenant on Economic, Social and Cultural Rights which came into force on January 3, 1976, three months after the deposit with the Secretary General of the 35th Instrument of Ratification.

Article 1 of this Covenant declared that all people have the right inter alia to freely pursue their cultural development. For the first time there was an international legal right for each individual to cultural development which remained undefined. Article 3 declared that State parties to the Covenant undertake to ensure the equal right of men and women to the enjoyment inter alia of all cultural rights set forth in this Convention. Article 15.1 reiterated that State Parties to the Covenant recognize the right of every one to take part in culture life and in Article 15.3 to benefit from the protection of the moral and material interests resulting from any scientific, literary or artistic production of which he is the author.

Article 15.2 declared that the steps to be taken by the State Parties to the present Convent to achieve the full realization of this right shall include those necessary for the conservation, the development and the diffusion inter alia of culture. Article 15.3 recorded the undertaking of State Parties to respect the freedom indispensables for creative activity. Article 15.4 stated that State Parties to the Convenant recognize the benefits to be derived from the encouragement and development of international contacts and cooperation in the cultural field. Article 16 requires the State Parties to submit reports to the Secretary General on the measures which they have adopted and the progress made in achieving the observance of the rights recognized herein. Under Article 17.2 these reports may indicate factors and difficulties affecting the degree of fulfillment of obligations under the present Covenant. Where relevant information has already been submitted to the UN or its specialized agonies it is not necessary for the State Party to reproduce that information, but a precise reference to the information furnished shall suffice. These reports are to be furnished in stages, in accordance with a programme to be established by the Economic and Social Council within one year of the entry into force of the Covenant.

International Conventions and cooperation were specifically covered by Article 23. This states that State Parties agree that international action for the achievement of the right recognized in the present Covenant include such methods as the conclusion of conventions, the adoption of recommendations, the furnishing of technical assistance and the holding of regional meetings and technical meetings for the purpose of consultations and study organized in conjunctions with the Government concerned.

10.11.1 Accordingly, in 1970 came the **Convention on the Means of Prohibiting & Preventing the Illicit Import/Export & Transfer of Ownership of Cultural Property.** This first UN Convention dealing with the return of illicitly exported or imported cultural property to the source state was followed in 1978 by the UNESCO Inter-Governmental Committee for Promoting the Return of Cultural Property to its Country of

Origin or its restitution in case of Illicit Appropriation. This provides an international forum for negotiation, discussion and awareness in cases where the legal framework of the 1970 Convention does not apply.

10.11.2 In 1995 came the UNIDROIT Convention on Stolen or Illegally Exported Cultural Object pursuant to UNESCO commissioning UNIDROIT (Institute of the International Commission for the Unification of Private Law) to help in preparing stronger rules than the 1970 Convention. This requires the return of cultural property to the source State in Cases of theft and dispossession by private citizens across national borders.

10.12 Convention Concerning the Protection of the World Cultural & Natural Heritage

In its seventeenth session at Paris, from October 17 to November 1, 1972, UNESCO recognized the formidable phenomena of damage or destruction to monuments by changing socio-economic conditions, the consequent impoverishment of the heritage of all the nations of the world. Tit stepped in with this Convention for an effective system of collective protection of the "cultural and natural heritage of outstanding universal value" which is of "outstanding interest" and, therefore, needs to be preserved as a world heritage of mankind on a permanent basis and in accordance with modern scientific methods. This preambular declaration to the Article carried several messages. Firstly, that UNESCO had accepted that it could do nothing about the acknowledged socio-economic changes that were admittedly seriously damaging or destroying monuments. Secondly, that in this context monuments had to be classified for purposes of international action – those of outstanding interest or outstanding universal value for all mankind and the rest. This seemed to go against the Venice Charter's declaration in Article 1 of equality of treatment of all monument by which the concept of a historic monument, embracing not only the architectural work but also its setting "applies not only to great works of art but also to more modest works of the past which have acquire cultural significance with the passing of time." UNESCO's preamble seems to divide monuments into small man's monuments whose history must necessarily constitute the history of any country against the monuments and history of the powerful and rich whose monuments would command the resources for creation of works of universal values. It seems that UNESCO took the world's socio-economic and tried to salvage the monuments of the history of the rich and powerful while abandoning the rest of history and it monument to their predictable fate. It divided history and decided to take monuments out of the mainstream of the history of the people in a country. It also seemed to ignore the legal recognition by the Universal Declaration of Human Rights of the community as a unit of cultural life and, therefore, monuments of outstanding historical value to community instead of to the world as a whole since the setting of a monuments related directly to a community and its history and not to that of the rest of the world. The world "community" disappeared as a legal entity form the International Covenant on Economic, Social & Cultural Rights and community was replaced by the individual or "everyone" in relation to the human right of culture, international cooperation and resources would now be focused in saving monuments in each country of outstanding universal value of interest by warding off as long as possible the formidable socio-economic factors working for the destruction for the destruction and/or disappearance of all monuments.

Accordingly, Article 1 of this Convention defined monuments as those architectural works which are of "outstanding universal value from the point of view of history, art or science." Hence in Article 4 each State Party to the convention was to recognize that primarily it is its duty to ensure the identification, protection, conservation, presentation and transmission to future generation only of the monuments of outstanding universal interest or value situated in its territory. The problematic history of a country's development which constituted the formidable threat to all monuments due to the socioeconomic changes brought about continuously by such development was now to be ignored legally both at the national and the universal level. This was ensured by Article 8 setting up an Inter-Governmental Committee for the Protection of the Cultural and Natural of Outstanding Universal Value, to be called the World Heritage Committee. Under Article 11.2

this Committee would establish the criteria for "outstanding universal value" for a monument, which would be applied to select and put on the World Heritage List, monuments, out of the inventory submitted by a State Party to the Committee as being suitable for inclusion in the list. There would be and updated list every two years. Article 11.4 recognizes the socio-economic changes; man made changes and force majeure changes that could put only such monuments recognized by the Committee in danger by criteria to be established by the Committee for preparing the List of World Heritage in Danger. After having for universal are and rescue (Articles 13, 14.2, 15 to 17 and 23 to 26) the Convention in Article 12 makes a meaningless declaration the exclusion from the world Heritage List or the Endangered List "shall in no way be construed to mean that it does not have an outstanding universal value for purpose other than those resulting from inclusion in these lists." This segregation is reinforced through Article 27 requiring the State Parties to Endeavour by educational and information programmes to strengthen appreciation and respect for such selected monuments in their country. Article 27.2 makes the State Parties undertake to keep the public broadly informed of the dangers threatening this heritage and of activities carried on in pursuance of this Convention. Accordingly, these selected monuments become tourist industry economic centres turning these monuments into business of maximal turnover regardless of the wear and tear or the carrying capacity of the monument. The Convention becomes a means of defeating itself with the monument's loss of all meaning and identify by losing the community to whose history the monument belonged.

10.13 International National Trust Organisation (INTO)

INTO was launched on December 3, 2007 with its Charter. INTO was created to institutionalize the process of promoting networking among heritage organization and to encourage regional cooperation on heritage issues. This is civil society's response to the protection and conservation of cultural heritage. INTACH has been holding conferences of INTO in Delhi on themes such as Heritage and Development. The Conference Recommendations of the 12th International Conference show a keen awareness of what needs to be done. But what seems to be missing is the larger picture or history, the consequences for cultural heritage of the international economic development model that holds all post-colonial countries in their grip and the dangers posed by international conventions to which States become parties.

PART – II
JUDICIAL IMPLEMENTATION

Chapter XI

SUPREME COURT SAVES A PROTECTED MONUMENT

The judiciary's critical role in ensuring the physical existence of a monument is clearly seen in the case of the protected monument of national importance, the Taj Mahal. If a monument of national importance ceases to exist physically, then there is nothing left to protect in terms of Art. 49 of the Constitution of India. The Supreme Court orders ensured that the Taj Mahal continues to exist physically.

There have been five major assaults on the continued existence of the Taj Mahal. On all five occasions, the Supreme Court's monitoring committee discovered, reported and argued against these assaults. In all these five cases, the Supreme Court intervened to pass orders to save the Taj Mahal.

11.1 First Assault: Green Belt

The first assault was concerning the Green Belt around the Taj Mahal. On the basis of the July 1993 Report of the National Environment Engineering Research Institute (NEERI) and the Union Ministry of Environment and Forests and the Vardharajan Committee Report of April 1995, the Supreme Court had directed planting of a green belt around the Taj Mahal notified complex. This was the natural way to meet the onslaught of Sulphur Dioxide, Nitric Oxide and dust that continuously endangered the marble of the Taj Mahal due to the air pollution from factories around or near the monument, the traffic and the sand blowing in from the Rajasthan desert. When the highest bureaucrats of the Union Ministry of Environment told the Supreme Court on oath and in writing that a green belt of around 1 lakh trees has been planted already as required by the NEERI Report, the judges doubted the affidavit. They directed the Monitoring Committee to verify this.

After a physical verification, the committee reported to the Hon'ble judges that the bureaucrats had stated incorrect facts before the court since there was not a single tree or plant that had been planted in execution of the green belt project. The monitoring Committee members, two of whom were senior officers of the statutory Central Pollution Control Board under the administrative control of Union Environment Ministry, came under serious threat of the IAS bureaucrats of that ministry, concerning their jobs. The threats ceased only when the conduct of these bureaucrats was orally mentioned by the Amicus to the judges in open court and an oral warming was issued by the judges to the bureaucrats concerned.

The Supreme Court issued contempt notices to senior bureaucrats concerning their affidavits about the green belt in the context of the report of the monitoring committee. The bureaucrats initially told the court orally that the monitoring committee report was a "tissue of lies." When the Amicus heading the monitoring committee offered himself and his team members for cross-examination, the bureaucrats retracted. They then filed profuse apologies, appeared in person and asked to be forgiven by the Court. That was ultimately done. The clear message from the court was that in the matter of protected monuments of national importance, action would be taken against the highest bureaucrats for such conduct. This resulted in the actual execution of the green belt project.

However, what happened to the public funds, stated earlier by the bureaucrats to have been spent by the Union Environment Ministry on a non-existent green belt of around 1lakh trees, remains a mystery. The court did not pursue the matter further.

But today there is a green belt and opposite the backside of the Taj Mahal across the River Yamuna there is a park called the Mehtab Bagh. The Mehtab Bagh, planted under the orders of the Hon'ble Supreme Court and followed by the supervision of its monitoring committee, today protects the Taj Mahal from solid particulate matter. Archaeological excavations have uncovered some water systems on the opposite side of the Taj Mahal, in a line from the dead center of the Taj Mahal. Mehtab Bagh has been attempted to be developed on the pattern of gardens that existed there during the Mughal period.

11.2 Second Assault: Hotel Near the Taj Monument

The second assault was an attempt to construct a multi-storied hotel in the name of Mumtaz Mahal at a distance of less than 25 feet from the Taj Mahal monument itself. Extensive deep foundations had already been dug, inspite of the Supreme Court's order prohibiting any construction in a 200 metre area around the Taj Mahal. A hotel at this proximity would have visually ruined the Taj Mahal. It would have brought in tourists and traffic of the hotel so near to the Taj as to imperil it. In February 1996, at the request of the monitoring committee, the Supreme Court in a special hearing summoned the solicitor general and directed him to ensure all construction work concerning the hotel is stopped immediately. That was done and those behind the hotel project simply disappeared. There was no effort by the Court to direct the tracing out of those responsible for such digging. There was also no attempt by the Court to seek an explanation from the ASI Superintendent at Agra as to how he allowed the deep digging to go on for several days immediately behind the Taj walls without informing the Supreme Court.

11.3 Third Assault: YANNI'S Concert

The third assault was by holding Yanni's Concert at the Taj. Mr. M.C. Mehta, the petitioner in person, brought the concert to the attention of the court. The Supreme Court directed the two senior scientists of the monitoring committee to go to the concert and ensure implementation of the safeguards laid down by it for the concert. The concert site, on the bed of Yamuna River immediately behind the Taj Mahal, was made accessible to top-level politicians, the bureaucrats, businessmen and others by temporary roads and pontoon bridges prepared with the help of the Army personnel. In this construction, diesel driven trucks and earth moving machinery of the State was used, right next to the rear wall of the Taj Mahal. Uttar Pradesh is India's most populous state, having the largest number of seats in Parliament and hence critical for any government. That seems to be the reason why the central government actively associated itself in the blatant violation of the Supreme Court order prohibiting, any construction next to the Taj Mahal.

The two scientists gave their recommendation that in the future any such event be held at least 500 metres away from the Taj Mahal and only after an Environment Impact Study, that only non-polluting vehicles be allowed in the 500 metre zone around the Taj Mahal and any such event should have prior clearance from competent authorities.

On March 24, 1998, the Supreme Court declared that it "accepted the report." They did this in light of their earlier experience with the Union Ministry of Environment and Forests officials concerning their written report to the court about compliance with Supreme Court's order for green belt around Taj Mahal.

The two Senior scientists did not put in writing before the court how the State authorities tried to prevent them from carrying out the order if the Supreme Court that they should report back whether the concert had actually complied with the safeguards for holding the concert. They stated this orally before the court. Nothing was done by the court on their oral statement and on their report which had been accepted by it. However, some public interest was served when the Supreme Court directed the State of Uttar Pradesh to give its share of the proceeds from the concert to the Agra Heritage Fund alongwith the amount of income tax levied on such proceeds and refunded by the Union Govt., under Court's orders to the Union Govt.

11.4 Fourth Assault: Wrong Data to SC

The fourth assault was an attempt to undermine the entire environmental law effort of the Supreme Court to protect the Taj Mahal from industrial, traffic, diesel generator and dust pollution.

There were two pollution monitoring stations inside the Taj Mahal complex. The first had been set up by the ASI which is responsible, under the Ancient Monument s Act, 1958 for protection of Taj as a monument of national importance. This monitoring station was crucial because the wind from the smoke stacks of Agra's foundries blows directly towards the Taj Mahal and this station. As a result of the Supreme Court's orders, the smoke spewing foundries or other such industrial units were no longer supposed to exist.

The second monitoring station was being run by the Uttar Pradesh Pollution Control Board under The Air (Prevention and Control of Pollution) Act, 1981. The second monitoring station was vital because it faced the traffic and the city around the Taj Mahal. However, the Monitoring Committee inspection revealed that both these stations were either without any proper instruments or wholly malfunctioning instruments.

Yet, the two stations were reporting normal pollution levels on the basis of erratically kept readings of 24 hours pollution monitoring supposed to be done by the two stations. In the absence of scientific data on air pollution, there was no question of any steps being taken by the ASI or the Uttar Pradesh Pollution Control Board, to protect the Taj Mahal. Hence, the Supreme Court was being given wrong data about the air pollution effect on the Taj Mahal.

The Monitoring Committee submitted report after report on this issue to the Supreme Court. The Supreme Court issued order after order. The monitoring committee after each order went back to these stations to report on the implementation of these orders. The alarming state of scientific recording on both the stations inside the complex impelled the Supreme Court to direct the monitoring committee to go with the equipment and manpower from the Central Pollution Control Board and monitor the air pollution in Agra in terms of the effects on the Taj Mahal.

The Committee did the monitoring for 7 days in July 2000, 7 days in August 2000 and 21 days in September 2000. The committee suggested the setting up of monitoring stations of the Union Govt.'s Central Pollution Control Board at least at four places in Agra for 24-hour monitoring. It also pressed for directions on its earlier suggestions of a traffic plan, conversion to Compressed Natural Gas, no petrol or diesel driven vehicles except for Taj Ganj city dwellers, issuance of stickers by traffic police dept. to Taj Ganj vehicles, exploration of bypass road for the residents of Taj Ganj residents to avoid regular use of the road in front of Taj Mahal complex entry. The display of pollution levels at Taj Mahal itself, use of solar energy with help of union ministry of non-conventional energy resources, battery-driven vehicles for transporting tourists, creation of a new bus stand-500 metres away from the Taj Mahal, relocation of shops serving the tourists, vendors policy for vending in front of Taj entry gates, and a security-oriented sustainable tourism policy for the Taj Mahal.

24-hour monitoring stations of ambient air quality control started functioning in Agra under the control of Central Pollution Control Board because of Supreme Court orders and reports were being filed by the Board in the Supreme Court on the data from the four air monitoring stations.

The Supreme Court orders have resulted in closure of foundries using coal as fuel, relocation of shops, battery-driven buses to the Taj Mahal, security plans, replacement of Uttar Pradesh Police by the Central Industrial Security Force for internal security of the Taj Mahal and the stopping of the construction of a police station by the U.P. Police opposite Taj Mahal entrance. The issuing of directions by Supreme Court on other suggestions of monitoring committee still awaits a hearing in the Supreme Court.

The State Government contributed its own share towards legally allowing industries to pollute freely. Under the Air (Prevention and Control of Pollution) Act, 1981, air pollution violations can be punished only for areas which have been declared as air pollution control areas. The Chief Secretary of U.P. used this provision in a manner which would help the industry in the State and around the Taj to escape from the entire Act. He issued a notification by which only the area around the Taj Mahal was declared an air pollution control area and not the areas around it. Hence, the industries could go on polluting the air at their sweet will since their areas had not been declared as air pollution control areas. When the monitoring committee brought this to the attention of the Supreme Court and sought orders, the U.P. Govt. responded by declaring the whole of the State as an air pollution control area.

11.5 Fifth Assault: Taj Heritage Corridor Project

The fifth assault which would have blocked out the Taj Mahal itself came in 2003. The monitoring committee had been requesting the Supreme Court for a permanent body which would ensure a regular and faithful compliance of the several Supreme Court orders issued concerning the

Taj Mahal and the Agra city in which the Taj Mahal is located. This resulted in the Supreme Court suggesting that the Planning Commission set up such a body and give it sufficient funds for the same. The Planning Commission agreed to set up such a body and the U.P. Govt. constituted a Mission Management Board under its Chief Secretary.

The monitoring committee, on its usual three-monthly inspection as per the orders of the Supreme Court, was shocked to see in March 2003 that a massive operation of digging the bed of the Yamuna River was on round the-clock behind the Taj Mahal. The committee collected the entire documentation concerning this project called the Taj Heritage Corridor project.

The committee in its report informed the Supreme Court that this documentation showed that the top-most politicians in power and bureaucrats at the Centre and in the State were involved in diverting the River Yamuna to reclaim the land for creating commercial projects like Fun Cities, Food Plazas and Carnivals, right in the middle of the river next to the rear of the Taj Mahal.

Worse, a Central Govt. undertaking, the National Projects Construction Corporation was doing the construction behind the Taj Mahal, after writing on the board at the site that the work was being carried out on the directions of the Supreme Court. The committee sought an immediate stay on the execution of all civil works being conducted, by pointing out that the project and the funds had been approved by the Mission Management Board which was supposed to protect and preserve the Taj Mahal.

Ultimately, the Supreme Court recorded the undertaking of the U.P. Govt. that it will not carry out any further work. The Supreme Court directed the CBI to tender before it a preliminary report and on the basis of that report the Supreme Court ordered the registration of a First Information Report against Chief Minister Mayawati, her Principal Secretary, the Chief Secretary, the Principle Environment Secretary, the Union Environment and Forests Secretary and others.

The Supreme Court's direction to the Central Forensic Lab to examine the relevant government files sent to it by the CBI brought forth a report that the Union Environment and Forests Secretary had tampered with the records concerning the Taj Heritage Corridor project.

For the first time in the history of any constitutional democracy, based on the Anglo-Saxon legal system, the Supreme Court of a country became the complainant for registering the FIR. The FIR was got registered with the Central Bureau of Investigation in a complaint made by the Supreme Court's Assistant Registrar (Public Interest Litigation). The FIR mentioned offences under the Prevention of Corruption Act, Indian Penal Code and the environmental laws. The accused were the Chief Minister of Uttar Pradesh, Ms. Mayawati and her key secretaries.

The specific argument of the Amicus Curiae, that in the light of what had ultimately happened in the Jain Diary Hawala case,[1] which had been monitored by the Supreme Court, the Court should take the entire documentary evidence under its control by requesting the Comptroller and Auditor General of India to assist the CBI. This was orally rejected by the bench presided over by Justice M.B. Shah. The Supreme Court also rejected the specific argument of the Amicus that to ensure a fair and impartial enquiry the delinquent officials be suspended during the departmental enquiries ordered against them as these were officials at the top-most rung of the bureaucracy having direct access to the evidentiary documents. The suggestion of the Amicus was orally rejected despite pointing out the legal difference between a stigmatic suspension and a suspension to ensure a fair and impartial enquiry.

However the Taj Mahal was saved from being eclipsed by giant Circus Wheels in the proposed complex at its immediate rear in the bed of the River Yamuna. The proposed complex sought to copy the Fun City in South Africa. The Taj Mahal was saved not by the cultural heritage reasoning of the Constitution, or the monuments as objects approach of the Ancient Monuments Act, 1958, enacted pursuant to Art. 49 and Entry 67, List I of the Constitution. It was saved simply by adopting an environmental approach without stating any statutory provisions or giving any reasons or by pointing out the binding nature of the earlier orders passed by the Supreme Court.

The Supreme Court did not issue notice in any of these five assaults through the Secretary of the Union Ministry of Culture, the Director General of the Archaeological Survey of India (ASI), the Director

---

[1] M.C. Mehta vs. UoI, I.A. 376/2003 in W.P. (Civil) 13381/84.

(Monuments) ASI or the Superintendent ASI stationed at Agra. All these assaults constituted cognisable offences under Section 30(1)(i) r/w Section 32 of the Ancient Monuments Act, 1958. But then the Court never referred to the Ancient Monuments Act, 1958. It seems to have been fascinated by the environmental approach to the Taj Mahal and that too without the support of any specific provision under the environment statutory law.

Chapter XII

JUDICIAL PROTECTION OF MONUMENTS THROUGH THE ENVIRONMENT ROUTE

The Taj Mahal Monument case was launched by the Supreme Court as an environmental problem with the issue of notice on a legally feeble petition filed by advocate-turned-petitioner-in-person, Mr. M.C. Mehta. On September 3, 1984, the Supreme Court Bench of Justices A.P. Sen and V.B. Eradi issued notice to the Union of India and others of Mr. Mehta's petition, which generally complained about the yellowing of the white marbled Taj due to pollution. Four years later, on February 13, 1989, the Supreme Court Bench of Justices E.S. Venkatarmiah and N.D. Ojha admitted the petition for regular hearing.

12.1 Is Art. 32 for Monuments?

The Supreme Court opened a new arena – the assumed maintainability of Article 32 petitions against the effects of pollution on a monument and not on human beings. This was assumed since this issue was never raised by the then Solicitor General who appeared for the Union of India. Maybe it was assumed because of the international currency of the Taj Mahal monument. But despite the daily incremental effect of the environmental pollution on the monument, Mr. Mehta and his petition,[1] went into slumber for about four years after its admission by the Supreme Court.

12.2 The MC Mehta Petition

The petition nowhere stated as to how a fundamental right against environment pollution could be claimed for a monument. It completely

---
[1] Writ Petition (Civil) No. 13381 of 1984.

missed the constitutional position of a monument as a cultural heritage, the heritage link with human beings as part of their fundamental right to a life of dignity and thereby the absorption of the environment aspect as a part of the protection of cultural heritage. It also missed the cultural objects or monuments-as-objects approach of the Ancient Monuments Act, 1958. Therefore, it did not state that the Taj Mahal was a deemed protected monument of national importance, under Section 3 of the 1958 Act, that carried over the British appreciation of the monument[2] under the 1904 Ancient Monuments Act. The British Government had declared the Taj Mahal a protected monument under the 1904 Act, as expressed in Notification[3] dated December 22, 1920, from Allahabad issued by the Secretary to the Govt. United Provinces, Public Works Dept., Building & Roads Branch declaring the monument's legal status under the Ancient Monuments Act, 1904. Independent India was assumed, by the deeming clauses in the Ancient Monuments Act, 1958, to have accepted the British viewpoint and the Notification was bereft of the constitutional cultural heritage which alone would give meaning to the monument.

The environment petition missed the cultural environment of the Taj Mahal as part of the Islamic funerary architecture designed to ensure a serene calmness for departed souls where silence is broken only by the surrounding greens[4] and the waters of the River Yamuna. The petition nowhere adverted to this daily breach of the cultural environment by the Union Govt. or the ASI, by allowing unlimited hordes of visitors to enter the Taj Mahal and the need to preserve and protect this by sustainable tourism. The Supreme Court's legal trajectory was set in terms of only a monument and its physical environment – a body to be protected without the spirit of its cultural heritage.

---

[2] *The Taj Mahal is a funeral or a burial site which Hindus do not visit again and again and which they never consider as a tourist attraction.*

[3] No. 1645-H/1133.

[4] Crowe Sylvia, Haywood Sheela, The gardens of Mughal India, p.1170, Vikas Publishing House Pvt. Ltd. New Delhi (1973); *for europeanisation of the Mughal time gardens, see* Stuart C.M. Villiers, Gardens of the Great Mughals, p. 62 & 66 Cosmo Publications, New Delhi (1983).

History too was discounted. The Taj Mahal was not to be seen as a colonial symbol of the recognition of a monument constructed by a conqueror, and occupier who, who used the monies of India for a personal end. Only the monument was to be seen and not its context – the history of conquest and the helplessness of a conquered people. The British as conquerors themselves could be least concerned about the context of history or of culture. The Taj Mahal was an artistic structure of white stone and therefore had to be declared as protected.

12.3 On a Legally Rudderless Journey

From January 8, 1993 to December 30, 1996 the Taj case suddenly galloped under Benches presided over by Justice Kuldip Singh. For this bench, the end was clear — to get rid of the environment pollution affecting the Taj Mahal. The legal manner and means of achieving this end did not seem to be of much importance. The legal vehicle accordingly became Orders. This dispensed with the necessity of giving reasons, examining pleadings or even giving of an opportunity of having their say to those who were likely to be adversely affected by the Orders. Only on December 31, 1996 was a judgment[5] delivered in the Chambers[6] of Justice Kuldip Singh by Justice Kuldip Singh alone,[7] just before his retirement, in which he summarized all that he had tried to do through Orders.

12.4 A Unique Legal Journey Begins

The first Order on January 8, 1993 directed the U.P. Pollution Control Board, as the Taj Mahal is located in the State of Uttar Pradesh, to inform

---

[5] M.C. Mehta vs. Union of India, (1997) 3 SCC 715.

[6] *Justice Kuldeep Singh informed the handful of legal correspondents and lawyers present, that he had requested the then Chief Justice for opening of a court-room for delivering the judgment. But all the court rooms were locked. Dec. 31, fell in the winter vacations of the Supreme Court.*

[7] *Justice Singh stated before delivering the judgment in his chamber that he had taken the oral consent of his brother judge Justice Faizun-uddin on the bench, to deliver the judgment. The urgency was the imminent retirement of Justice Kuldeep Singh.*

the court on or before May 5, 1993 "of all the industries and foundries which are the sources of Pollution" in Agra region on the basis of a survey by the Board of the area. After this the Board was to "issue notice to all foundries and industries in that region to satisfy the Board that necessary anti-pollution measures have been undertaken by the said industries/foundries."

On May 5, 1993 the Board informed the Court that it had issued notice in local and national newspapers, calling upon all the 511 industries to install anti-pollution mechanisms or effluent treatment plants, if they have not already done so. The notice was to call for replies from these industries which were to be processed by the Board. If the Board desired to verify the correctness of any reply, it could inspect the industry concerned. On August 13, 1993, the Board was directed by the Supreme Court to categorize the industries into those which have set up an "effluent treatment plant" to the satisfaction of the Board (Category-A), those which were in the process of doing so and whose plants "are likely to show satisfactory result if given time" (Category-B) and those industries which have neither replied to the Board's notice nor set up any treatment plant (Category-C). A copy of the report of the Board relating to the relevant industry was to be supplied in case the industry approached the Board for it. These set of orders were unique as:–

1. The petition before the Court raised the issue of Taj Mahal being affected by air pollution. The Court did not refer to the legal status of the Taj Mahal under the Ancient Monuments Act, the constitutional[8] and legal duty of the Archaeological Survey of India (ASI), under the Union Ministry of Culture, to protect it and the duty of the Uttar Pradesh Pollution Control Board (UPPCB) as also the Central Pollution Control Board (CPCB) to ensure this protection in terms of the powers conferred on them under the Air (Prevention and Control of Pollution) Act, 1981 and the Environment Protection Act, 1986.
2. There was no reference in these Orders to any legal provision whatsoever, constitutional, statutory or otherwise, in terms of which the Orders were issued. Orders can be without detailed

---
[8] Articles 49, 29 and 54 A(f), S. 30 (1) (i) of the Ancient Monuments Act, 1958.

reasons and sometimes without any reason, depending on the nature of the order. But they cannot be without the law or a legal basis.[9]

3. None of the industries were given an opportunity for a hearing before the passing of these Orders. It was presumed that without any material before it about any industry, the Supreme Court, without asking the respective authorities as to how they had discharged their constitutional and legal duties to protect the Taj Mahal, could order blanket surveys and notices in any "region" wherein a protected monument of national importance was located. The Air (Prevention and Control of Pollution) Act, 1981 did not provide for any categorization of industries as done by the Supreme Court since under the Act an industry is prohibited from being established or from functioning without a prior consent certificate from the State Pollution Control Board.

4. The Court's orders had directed survey to be done by the UPCCB and then the issue of notices. No survey material was put before the Court with the names of the survey teams and their reports on each of the 511 industries to which notices had been issued. The industries were not informed of the basis on which notices had been issued to them in terms of the survey done. A mere list of industries with their names and addresses was put before the Court and the Court proceeded on the basis of such a list which had also been published in local newspapers.

5. The Supreme Court extended its anti-pollution drive to the entire "Agra region," without stating in the Orders any factual basis whatsoever for doing so in terms of the Taj Mahal. The issue before the Court was not general pollution in the Agra region but only that of pollution affecting the Taj Mahal in Agra, for which the Supreme Court needed to minimally have before it the geographical data on the location of industries and the wind

---

[9] Reliance Energy Ltd. vs. Maharashtra State Road Development Corporation Ltd., September 11, 2007, Supreme Court judgment in CA 3526/2007: *Standards applied by Courts in judicial review must be justified by Constitutional principles which govern the proper exercise of public power in a democracy.*

direction from these to the Taj Mahal. The data has always been available, but the Supreme Court in its unilateral environment drive over an undefined territorial area called by it the "Agra region," never sought it before or after the passing of the Orders mentioned above.

6. The Supreme Court had before it in relation to the Taj Mahal, five environmental reports already – the 1978 Vardharajan report, the 1982 CPCB reports, the 1990 NEERI report, the 1993 NEERI report and the 1995 Vardharajan report. None of these reports were ever put to the industries or the organised chambers of the industries that appeared before the Court.

7. These five reports clearly pointed out that the main problem was that of the fuel used for industries energy needs. This was coal/coke. The problem, therefore, was not existence of these industries but the fuel input. If that changed then the entire exercise ordered by the Court was avoidable, since a fuel like gas would have virtually done away with the need for installing any anti-air-pollution equipment by industrial units.

8. Under the Air Pollution Act and the Water Act no industry could have set up and operated a unit without the 'previous consent'[10] from the Uttar Pradesh Pollution Control Board (UPPCB). Hence, industries which had such previous consent were legally exempt. If most industries did not have this consent or had fraudulent consents, then that would have indicated to the Court the kind of UPPCB it was dealing with. In any event the fact that the UPPCB itself had now submitted a list of 511 industries operating without any effective anti-pollution equipment, clearly showed the kind of UPPCB, the Court had before it, since it is a mandatory duty of the UPPCB under the Air and Water Acts to prosecute such industries. Yet the Supreme Court relied on the list supplied to it, by such a UPPCB, of industries without any effective pollution control equipment and that too without any supporting documents of industry wise inspection by it as the basis of the survey, it had been

---

[10] S. 21, Air (Prevention and Control of Pollution) Act, 1981, S. 25 of Water (Prevention and Control of Pollution) Act, 1974.

ordered to do by the Court. The Court never asked the UPPCB to explain why it had not prosecuted the industries in the UPPCB list which had been functioning without 'previous consent' and without any pollution control equipment.[11]

9. Since the cultural heritage constitutional perspective was not even on the Court's thinking horizon, there was no move to find out whether any of the industrial units constituted a heritage from Mughal British times, especially the foundries. None of the private foundry owners would be interested in having their foundry declared as an "ancient monument or site or structure" under Section 2(a) of the Ancient Monuments Act, 1958, as that would permanently freeze the land on which the foundry has stood since Mughal times. So the owners would keep quiet. But the Court in its aggressive zeal to push its environmental agenda would not hear of the Ancient Monuments Act or the concept of technical and industrial heritage.

10. Although the petition before it related only to air pollution affecting the Taj Mahal, the Court in its August 13, 1993 order carved out Category-A from the UPPCB's list of 511 allegedly polluting industries concerning installation of an "effluent treatment plant," without giving any reason.

Hence the Supreme Court started without any legal compass on a legal journey concerning the protected monument of national importance, the Taj Mahal. The legal journey was without any legal basis in the relevant Articles of constitutional heritage under the Constitution of India, without the relevant provisions of the Ancient Monuments Act, 1958, without the relevant provision of the statutory provisions under the Air, Water and Environment Protection Acts. It started on the shoulders of the statutory UPPCB without any legal cross checks on its legal credibility or reliability after it had provided to the Court a

---

[11] Paryavaran Suraksha Samiti vs. UoI, judgment February 22, 2017 in WP (C) 375/2012, the Supreme Court while directing all industries to make 'fully operational' their effluent treatment plant on or before April 21, 2017, has not said a word on the accountability of the Pollution Control Board's Chairmen for not having taken action under the Environment Protection Act, 1986 against the industries concerned.

list of 511 polluting industries without any relevant legal documents. These major legal issues arising from such a legal journey remained unstated in the court. This process created vast business for lawyers. But no advocate, including Mr. M.C. Mehta, pointed out all this to the blitzkrieg proceedings daily launched in the court by the presiding judge, Justice Kuldip Singh. There was no question of pause for thought. The proceedings of the presiding judge must roll on. The amicus intervention on these issues was firmly rebuked. If any counsel of an industrial client, persisted in trying to argue, he was told, "What's gone wrong with you. Don't you have work in any other court."

12.5 Protection of Monuments – A Fundamental Right

Is the protection and preservation of monuments a Fundamental Right? The Supreme Court seems to implicitly say so as far as the environmental protection of legally recognized ancient monuments under the Ancient Monuments Act is concerned. In M.C. Mehta vs. UOI,[12] the Supreme Court declared, that it is the "primary duty of the Union Ministry of Environment & Forest to safeguard Taj Mahal from deterioration" from polluting industries in the Taj Trapezium Area.[13] It is on the basis of this presumed fundamental right of environmental protection of ancient monuments declared to be of national importance under the Ancient Monuments Act, 1958, that the Supreme Court passed orders on power supply, shifting of brick kilns, water supply through Gokul and Agra barrages, relocation of slaughter house in Agra ending of illegal

---

[12] M.C. Mehta vs. UOI, 1996 (1) Scale (S.P.) 16.

[13] The May 18, 1999, Gazette of India (extraordinary), Part II – Sec 3 – Sub-Section (ii), states, *"the geographical limits of the Taj Trapezium Zone have been defined in the shape of a trapezoid between 26 Degrees 45' N and 77 Degree 15' E to 27 Degrees 45' N and 77 Degrees 15' E in the west of the Taj Mahal and in the east of Taj Mahal between 27 Degrees 00' N and 78 Degrees 30' E to 27 Degrees 30' N and 78 Degrees 30' E."* This Notification constituted the Taj Trapezium Zone Pollution (Prevention and Control) Authority under Section 3(1) (3) of the Environment (Protection) Act, 1986. *See Annexure I for Portected Monuments in TTZ area.*

slaughtering and disposal of wastes, traffic control and construction in Agra.[14]

The unique aspect of these orders was the transition of the Supreme Court from environmental protection of the Taj Mahal under Art. 21 of the Constitution to orders restructuring and reorganizing the whole of Agra city. The Supreme Court claimed the power under Art. 21 which guarantees done protection of life and personal liberty, read with the Directive Principles in Articles 47, 48A and the fundamental duty in Art. 51A(g) of the Constitution. The Dec. 31, 1996, judgment made it clear that a monument declared as an ancient monument of national importance under the Ancient Monuments Act would be under the fundamental right of environment under Article 21 of the Constitution plus the Directive Principles of the Constitution and the environment statutes. There was no reference to the Ancient Monuments Act, the Archaeological Survey of India of the Union Government which is the legal custodian of the ancient monuments of national importance or its legal duty under the Act to protect such monuments against anyone who 'imperils' these under S. 30 (1) (i) read with S. 32 of the Ancient Monuments Act, 1958.

Accordingly, it was under this legal construct, of environment having been declared a fundamental right, that the environmental protection of ancient monuments of national importance was subsumed. Hence the 1996 judgment listed all the projects the court was monitoring in relation to the Taj: Hydrocracker unit to control pollution from the Mathura Refinery, a fifty bed hospital for those living in and around the Refinery, construction of Agra Bypass for traffic diversion, electricity supply projects for uninterrupted power supply to Agra to replace diesel generators, Gokul Barrage and Agra Barrage for drinking water, Agra Green Belt, shifting of emporia and shops outside the Taj, declaration of Agra as heritage city and the suggestion to the Planning Commission of a special cell for Agra under the Central Government.

The legal canopy of the environment for the environmental protection of an ancient monument of national importance under the Ancient Monuments Act turned full circle with the Supreme Court on

---

[14] M.C. Mehta vs. UOI 1996 (3) Scale (S.P.) 58.

September 18, 2003,[15] directing CBI to lodge an FIR against the then Chief Minister Ms. Mayawati of Uttar Pradesh and others in the Taj Heritage corridor project which was discovered, reported and argued by the Court's Monitoring Committee.

The Supreme Court directed "CBI to take into consideration all the relevant Acts i.e. IPC/Prevention of Corruption Act and the Water (Prevention & Control of Pollution) Act, 1974 etc." The environmental protection of the monument as the conceptual base for dealing with the protection of ancient national heritage monuments was reiterated and expanded further into the criminal law as well as the Taj Heritage Corridor Project. There was no reference to Sections 30, 31 and 32 of the Ancient Monuments Act, 1958 even though these Sections make it a cognizable offence to imperil an ancient national heritage monument.

---

[15] M.C. Mehta vs. UOI – I.A. 376/2003 in WP (Civil) 13381/1984.

Chapter XIII

JUDICIAL CLOSURE OF INDUSTRIES: THE LOSS OF REASON

On August 27, 1993, the Supreme Court was given by the UPPCB a list of 212 industries, which according to the Board had neither approached the Board (despite individual notice and the public notice in newspapers), nor had installed anti-pollution equipment. The records of the case show that the Court ordered the shutting down of these industrial units without giving these units a copy of the Board's list filed before the Supreme Court and without giving a notice to these industrial units to provide an opportunity for a hearing. The hearing was important since there was nothing on the record of the Court establishing a nexus between the pollution by each of the industrial units, separately or collectively, and any deterioration of the Taj Mahal marble. The UPPCB stated nothing about the pollution from each of the industrial units and the wind direction, whether towards or away from the Taj, from such units. No notice was issued to the expert body, the Archaeological Survey of India, for determining the nexus between the pollution by such units and any deterioration in the Taj structure or marble.

Even under the environmental approach to monuments adopted by the Supreme Court, S. 7 of the Environmental Protection Act, 1986 required the determination of the facts as to whether the industrial units were discharging any pollutant in excess of the standards specified industry wise in the Rules under the Act. No notice was issued to the Union Environment Ministry[1] or the UPPCB for determining this relevant jurisdictional fact. But the Court had been converted into a war

---

[1] 1996 (1) SCALE (S.P.) 16: it is the primary duty of the Union Environment Ministry to safeguard the Taj Mahal from deterioration.

theatre by the presiding judge in which he was the one man judicial army, to the point of completely ignoring his brother judge, which would brook no legal barrier in its clean-up march under the Taj Mahal banner. There was no place for what the Supreme Court had laid down in A'70SC1880, Budhan Singh vs. Nabi Bux — "Justice and reason constitute the great general legislative intent in every piece of legislation."

13.1 SC: Permission Giving Authority

For nine years the petition had slumbered in the Supreme Court from the date of issue of notice without any complaint, petition or application by the ASI that the Taj Mahal had deteriorated further in this period due to pollution from industrial units. But now the Court seemed to be in a tearing hurry, by dispensing with the elementary principle of natural justice and relying on a UPPCB affidavit which had no documents in support of its list of 212 industrial units. The Superintendent of Police and the District Magistrate/Deputy Commissioner Agra were directed to ensure that the shut-down order is complied with. UPPCB was directed to approach the Court for the reopening of these industrial units once it was satisfied that the units had installed the necessary air pollution control devices. Accordingly, the Supreme Court constituted itself into a permission giving authority for industrial units functioning in the Agra region by relying on the statements of UPPCB put on affidavit.

The Supreme Court constituted by its orders, the regulator UPPCB having a mandatory duty to ensure that an industry does not function without its consent, into an inspector of its own breach of such a duty under the Air and Water Pollution Control Acts. Worse, it empowered such a regulator to determine the fate of an industry with complete power of what to put about the compliance by the industry with the court's order in its report to the court and what to represent about the industry to the court through the U.P. Government advocate on record and the arguing counsel. The Supreme Court saw no conflict of interest in turning the UPPCB into an inspector of its own breach of duty or the dangers of creating the chain of inspectors and counsel. The industry became a prized catch.

13.2 Which Equipment

In its unreasoned hurry, the Supreme Court paid little heed to the plea of counsel for some of the industries that the UPPCB was "not in position to advise the industry as to which type of air pollution control device is to be set up." This became self-evident from the fact that despite recording this in its August 27, 1993 order, the Supreme Court directed that the Board's experts shall give advice to the industry which approaches it. No attempt was made to find out as to what specific kind of air pollution control equipment the Board had advised to specific industrial units or who were the "experts" employed by the board for this purpose. Instead the Court gave a costly and distant alternative for the mostly small scale industrial units, which virtually made it unworkable. This was that the industrial units could contact NEERI in Nagpur and get the advice against the payment demanded by NEERI for such advice. On September 17, 1993 the Court recorded the fact that most of these units are small scale industries. Yet, it did not modify its order asking the units to approach NEERI at Nagpur in Maharashtra and take advice against payment to NEERI.

13.3 Court: Incompetent and Then Competent

On September 3, 1993 counsel for the industries contended before the Supreme Court that their units were not polluting the air and pollution, if any, was within permissible limits. The reference herein was to the Schedule of Industries in the Environment Protection Act, 1986 which gave the permissible pollution limits industry wise. After recording in its September 3, 1993 order, this submission of the industries, the Court instead of dealing with the submission, stated: "Be that as it may, we are not in a position to examine the technical aspects pertaining of the installation of air pollution devices."

The question was not of anti-pollution devices. The question raised by the submission of the industries was the legal one, namely, whether the UPPCB could show any material to the Court that their industries were operating in violation of the industry wise pollution level laid down in Schedules under the Environment Protection Act, 1986 The question raised had nothing to do with the technical aspects of anti-pollution devices. The Bench of Justices Kuldip Singh and S.C. Agrawal reiterated in the August 27, 1993 order and affirmed that "the industries shall remain closed till we further order." Within a week of the September 3, 1993 order, by the Supreme Court declaring that it is not in a position to examine the technical aspects pertaining to the installation of air pollution devices, the Court on September 10, 1993 declared that it will consider the technical inspection reports of the Board concerning the installation of these devices. The order pertained to eighteen industries which had claimed that such devices had been installed.

13.4 The Journey's Methodology

From September 3, 1993 the Supreme Court initiated the following methodology: industrial units would apply to it for being allowed to function/operate; the Court would order the UPPCB to inspect by ordering suspension of the closure of the unit to enable the Board to inspect the effectiveness of the anti-pollution devices installed; the Board reports would be filed before the court as to whether the unit was compliant or not and the Supreme Court relying on such reports would order closure, more time or permission to function for that industrial unit. The Court, therefore, constituted itself into a permission giving authority industrial unit by industrial unit. Accordingly, the September 10, 1993 order set this methodology into operation for eighteen industrial units represented by senior advocate Mr. G. Remaswamy with advocate-on-record Mr. Sushil Jain, for 82 units represented by advocate-on-record Mr. K.C. Dua, for four units represented by advocate-on-record Mr. Sanjay Parikh and one unit represented by advocate-on-record Mr. Prashant Kumar. In each of these cases the UPPCB was directed to inspect the units and file a report "to be considered by this Court."

13.5 Reliance on Oral Statements

The September 10, 1993 order revealed another aspect of the Court's methodology. The UPPCB made an oral submission about an industrial unit. The Court passed orders on such oral submission without reference to any report, affidavit or anything in writing by the UPPCB.

The UPPCB counsel started by stating that the name of M/s Choubey Glass Works, Nai Basti, Firozabad, was wrongly included in the list of 'C' category industries. On this bald oral submission the Court ordered: "We delete the name of the said industry from the said list and suspend the closure order." Similarly, concerning four industrial units – M/s. Singla Pesticides, M/s. Allora Paper Products, M/s. Super Chem Industries & Allied Iron Steel Works the Court ordered suspension of closure for two months and a report by the Board, on the bald oral submission of the UPPCB counsel that he agreed with the counsel for the industrial units that these units had installed air pollution control devices.

Hence a precedent was set for the practice of mentioning industrial units orally, without any reference to any record before the Court, the Court relying on such statements and ordering reopening of these units. The implied message that went out was that if the units had the UPPCB counsel speaking for them, then they had a good chance of the reopening of their units.

The beleaguered small scale units of Agra, with no legal aid or legal literacy drive on pollution ordered by the Supreme Court through its country wide legal aid framework to help the units, had learnt fast the route of transactional efficiency in negotiating a legal system that they hardly understood in its content or language. Accordingly, the industrial unit owners considered it to be a waste of their resources to impugn in any way the unprecedented order of the Supreme Court passed on September 10, 1993 that the UPPCB was "not required to supply copies of any of the affidavits filed by it to the counsel representing the industries. If the learned counsel so desire, they can examine the records in the Registry." None of the unit owners or their counsel protested.

13.6 SC's Unit to Unit Permission

But the Supreme Court now had set the legal methodology concerning the industrial units. The units would through their counsel mention their matter before the Bench orally or through an application. The Bench would direct inspection of the unit/s by the UPPCB. The UPPCB would file a report of its inspection. The Court without any reference to the data in the inspection report and without any analysis of that data would direct the reopening of the units, or give them more time with a further inspection by the UPPCB. The UPPCB counsel could stand up and simply make a statement, not backed by any document, that the unit/s was a compliant one under the Air, Water and Environment Protection Acts without even mentioning these Acts or any provision from these Acts. The Court on the basis of this statement would order the reopening and operation of the units. The Court orders would make no reference to any provision of any Act. There would be no reference to the nature or quality of the anti-pollution equipment installed by the unit since no such data would be demanded by the Court. There would be no report of the UPPCB showing the legal parameters of compliance by the unit. Yet the Court's closure orders would be suspended and the unit allowed to operate. Relevant documents, relevant facts and relevant law were redundant. This is reflected in the orders passed by the Bench of Justices Kuldip Singh and S.C. Agrawal till November 26, 1993 and thereafter by the Benches of Justices Kuldip Singh and Yogeshwar Dayal till March 4, 1994 and then on March 31, 1994 of Justices Kuldip Singh and B.L. Hansaria till December 16, 1995, which continued this methodology.

The normal adversarial method was effectively abandoned in favour of a result oriented approach. This was further emphasised when on September 17, 1993, a direction was given to the UPPCB Board to open a technical office at Agra within a period of four weeks, after counsel for the industries stated that it was not feasible for the small scale industrial units operating in Agra to go every time to the UPPCB office in Lucknow and back. This direction was given without any notice to the UPPCB. Similarly, without any notice to the Govt. of India, a direction was passed that the Govt. will provide sufficient funds to the UPPCB so that it can cope up with the various directions issued by the Court from time to time. This part of the order concluded by saying: "Needless to say that as and when the Board approaches the Govt. of India, necessary funds will be provided." No reason was given as to why funding for a State Pollution Control Board was shifted from the State to the Govt. of India.

By September 24, 1993, the Supreme Court constituted itself into a permanent permission giving authority for the industrial units in Agra. The Supreme Court ordered "We direct the Board to keep on inspecting these industries at least once a month and send a report to this court." The Court never got to examining these monthly reports. The temporary order for opening the industry for a specified period to enable the Board to inspect concerning the working of the pollution devices installed, as stated by the Board, became a Supreme Court pass for permanent operation of the industrial unit.

From October 1, 1993, the Court dropped even the condition that the Board should file a report before it about its inspection of the pollution devices, after the withdrawal by the court of the closure order of the industry on the basis of the statement of the Board before it. The mechanism for industries in Agra now was: The Board would inform the Court as to which industry or industries had installed the pollution control devices. The Court never verified whether documents about such installation had been filed by the Board in support of its statement and, if filed, whether these showed what the Board was orally stating before it. The Court would pass an order withdrawing its orders to close the industry or industries so that the Board can inspect the pollution devices installed by the industry/industries. The Court's order no longer stated that the Board should file before the Court its inspection report. Hence, the Board would supply the information by way of a statement in its affidavit or sometimes without an affidavit. The Board would secure the permission from the Court for the industry to function for a specified period, the Board would inspect the functioning of the unit without the Board having to inform the Court about what it has found in its inspection. The unit will go on functioning till the Board reports against the unit. For the Agra industrialist the case resolved from the Board to the Board and all that had to do was to focus on the Board. The Supreme Court was irrelevant for their unit.

On October 1, 1993 Justices Kuldip Singh, S.C. Agarwal and S.P Bharucha passed such orders for 19 industries. On October 8, 1993 Justices Kuldip Singh and S.C. Agarwal passed a similar order for five industries. This time they had directed the Board to file the inspection report. The inspection report, if filed, never came up for examination by the Court. The same two Judges on October 15, 1993 passed similar orders for six industries with no direction to the Board to file an inspection report.

On November 5, 1993 the two Judges directed the Union of India to consider the possibility of supplying LPG/natural gas to the industries situated in Agra and Firozabad as a fuel in place of coal. This order rendered meaningless all the orders passed on the basis of the statements of the UPPCB giving permission to closed industries to function to enable the Board to test the anti-pollution devices supposedly installed by them, as since 1984, the Court had before it the 1978 report pointing out that the problem was not the industry but the fuel used by it, namely the coal. The Court also had before it the 1982 report of the CPCB, the 1990 NEERI report, the 1993 NEERI report and the 1995 Vardharajan report which had recommended the replacement of coal by gas. But, unfortunately the Supreme Court instead of following up these reports, ordered wholesale closure of industrial units on the basis of the Board's affidavits and for the reopening of these industrial units for which it constituted itself into a permission giving authority, unit by unit.

Chapter XIV

THE TAJ HERITAGE CORRIDOR: JUDICIAL ROLE IN USING CRIMINAL LAW

The Monitoring Committee appointed by the Supreme Court, headed by the Amicus Curiae, reported to the Supreme Court that the bed of the River Yamuna behind the Taj Mahal was being excavated round-the-clock by heavy-earth moving machinery for the Taj Heritage Corridor Project. The project consisted of creating a Fun, Food and Carnival City behind the Taj on the bed of a river and that too when the river had already been reduced to a slush drain. The project outlay of several crores had been sanctioned by the Mission Management Board[1] without any Environment Impact Assessment and without any consideration of its effect on the protected monument, the Taj Mahal. The Amicus had obtained the project documents and the same were submitted to the Hon'ble Court. The Amicus was directed to move an I.A. on the basis of the report.

Accordingly, the Amicus prayed in I.A. 376 of 2003 for an immediate stay of the construction work, a direction to the Comptroller and Auditor General to report on the financial aspects of the matter so that the court will have all the financial evidence before it and for the eco restoration of the damage done by the construction. The prayer for the Comptroller and Auditor General's intervention had been made keeping in view the lessons learnt from the Jain Diaries Hawala case which despite Supreme Court's monitoring of the investigation had resulted

---

[1] *The Uttar Pradesh Government by OM dated May 9, 1997 stated that the GOI proposed to spend Rs. 600 crore during the 9th Five Year Plan on projects prepared by various UP Govt. Departments for the environmental protection of the Taj Mahal. As required by the Planning Commission D.O. PE (P) 2195 LP dated April 7, 1997, a Mission Management Board is constituted for review of projects of different departments and for allocation of funds.*

in the acquittal/discharge by the trial courts, of all the accused for the lack of evidence. The lesson was that what should be ordered by the Supreme Court to be collected first, while monitoring the investigation in Prevention of Corruption Act matters, is the financial evidence in government files, followed by the financial rules and procedures and then the names of the specific public and private persons involved in each transaction. This would have shown as to how the Uttar Pradesh Finance Secretary and his department were completely by passed by the Chief Minister and her Principal Secretary. It would also have revealed as to how the Mission Management Board of Uttar Pradesh headed by the Chief Secretary of the State and constituted under Supreme Court orders for handling the money and the projects related to the Taj Mahal, put its stamp of approval on the spending of money for the projects like those of the Taj Heritage Corridor. At least a remedy for the future could be put in place. This the Supreme Court did not do even though it was requested to make the Finance Secretary a specific party to the proceedings before it. It also did not ask the Comptroller and Auditor General, a constitutional office, to do the needful, even though the Central Government's Planning Commission money financed the projects.

The several stages through which this case went in the Supreme Court shows the manner and method and thereby the role of the judiciary in the highest court concerning protected monuments, as reflected from the Court records.

14.1 Stages I–IV

Stage I of the case culminated with the unprecedented lodging of a criminal complaint by the Supreme Court itself concerning this project against the then Chief Minister Mayawati, her special secretary Mr. Punia, the Chief Secretary who headed the Mission Management Board and other officials of the Uttar Pradesh and the Union Governments. On the orders of the Supreme Court the FIR was lodged on October 5, 2003. The second stage culminated with the Supreme Court passing an order concerning the October 22, 2003 order of the Lucknow Bench of The Allahabad High Court, to which the accused had applied in WP 5300/2003 (M/B) with WP 5315 and 5341, for quashing the FIR ordered by the Supreme Court and for stay of any coercive action or arrest by the CBI investigating the case under the Prevention of Corruption Act, 1988. The third stage concerned the implementation of the orders of departmental inquiries ordered by the Supreme Court against the accused officials. The fourth and last stage was the October 10, 2007 judgement of the Supreme Court upholding in I.A. 465/2007 the refusal of the Uttar Pradesh Governor to sanction the prosecution and trial of the former Chief Minister and other officials on the basis of the final report filed by the CBI before the Special Judge Lucknow.

14.2 SC: Investigate Without an FIR: Stage I

The I.A. moved by the Amicus on the directions of Supreme Court made no prayer for the launching of a criminal investigation by the Supreme Court into the contracts given by the Uttar Pradesh Government for the project. The case concerning the Taj Mahal was a case covered by the Ancient Monuments Act. The Amicus drew the kind attention of the Supreme Court to Sections 30 and 32 of the Ancient Monuments Act which made it a cognizable offence to 'imperil' a protected monument. However, the court through it fit to suo motu summon the CBI and direct an investigation into the sanctioning of the project, and the manner in which contracts were given for the project to various firms.

14.3 SC Lodges a Criminal Complaint

When the senior police officer representing the CBI and appearing in person, told the court that he could not investigate in the absence of an FIR, he was reprimanded by the presiding judge, Justice M.B. Shah and told, "This is the problem. You are still thinking of the Cr.P.C. etc. You must understand that the Supreme Court is asking you to inquire and investigate." The CBI filed a series of confidential enquiry reports on the basis of documents obtained by it. The court ordered the Forensic Laboratory to give it a report about any interpolations made in the documents. After these reports, the court declared that there was enough credible material for an FIR and it ordered the registration of an FIR under the Prevention of Corruption Act, the Environment Protection

Act, and domestic enquiries against the accused officials. An assistant registrar (Public Interest Litigation Section) of the Supreme Court lodged the complaint on behalf of the Supreme Court for the implementation of its order that an FIR be lodged.

14.4 Amicus Prayers Ignored by SC

No orders were passed on the prayers of the Amicus for investigation under the Ancient Monuments Act concerning the Taj Mahal being imperilled as a protected monument and for making the Finance Secretary of Uttar Pradesh a party to the case in view of the court's enquiries being directed on the sanctioning of the money involved in the project. The court orally rejected the suggestion of the Amicus that the accused officials against whom domestic enquiries had been ordered should be suspended to ensure a fair and impartial enquiry.

The court brushed aside the prayer to make the Taj Trapezium Authority,[2] notified by the Union Government and headed by the Commissioner Agra, a party so that it should explain as to why it did not bring the activity in relation to the Taj Heritage Corridor project to the notice of the court.

The Authority was bound to ensure compliance with Supreme Court's orders, being under the supervision and control of the Union

---

[2] The May 18, 1999 Gazette of India (Extraordinary) Part II – Section 3 – Sub Section (ii), empowered the Authority within the geographical limits of Agra Division in the Taj Trapezium Zone in the State of Uttar Pradesh to monitor progress of the implementation of various schemes for protection of the Taj Mahal and programmes for protection and improvement of Environment in the above said area; exercise powers under Sec. 5 of the Environment (Protection) Act, 1986; take all necessary steps to ensure compliance of specified emission standards by motor vehicles and ensuring compliance of fuel quality standards deal with any environmental issue which may be referred to it by the Central Govt. or State govt. of Uttar Pradesh relating to above said area; exercise powers under Sec. 19 of the Environment Protection Act, 1986. These powers and functions shall be subject to the overall supervision and control of the Central Govt. and the authority shall furnish a report about its activities at least once in two months to the Central Govt. in the Ministry of Environment and Forests.

Government, in terms of the May 18, 1999 Gazette notification of the Union Government, which constituted the Authority.

14.5 CVC Bypassed

It was legally mandatory on the part of CBI to inform the Central Vigilance Commission (CVC) under the Central Vigilance Commission Act, 2003 about its investigation against Chief Minister Mayawati and others under the Prevention of Corruption Act, 1988 so that the CVC could, under S.8(1) of the Act, ensure a fair and impartial investigation. The CBI did not do this. Accordingly, the Amicus moved an application to direct the CBI to discharge its legal duty and inform the CVC. The Supreme Court directed the CBI to submit all the investigation papers to the CVC who informed the court that a prima facie case existed. Senior Counsel for Uttar Pradesh and Chief Minister Mayawati, Satish Mishra, opposed the taking on record by the Court of the CVC report. The presiding judge, Ms. Ruma Pal ended the matter by pointing out that the Court was entitled to seek all relevant help. The Court did not think it fit to ask the CBI to explain as to why in this particular case it had not informed the CVC about its investigation when as a matter of routine it had been doing so in all Prevention of Corruption cases, as shown by the annual reports of the CVC placed before the Court by the amicus.[3]

14.6 SC's Silence on Relief after Dismissal: Stage II

The former Chief Minister and other accused then moved a writ petition 5300 of 2003 (M/B) with 5315 and 5341 before the Lucknow bench of

---

[3] Under Section 8(1) of the Central Vigilance Act, 2003, the Commission must discharge the following two functions: exercise superintendence over the functioning of the Delhi Special Police Establishment (CBI) concerning investigation of offences alleged to have been committed under the Prevention of Corruption Act, 1988 or an offence with which a public servant under the Cr.P.C may be charged at the same trial; and give directions to the CBI for discharging its responsibility entrusted to it concerning the offences specified by the Central Government under the Delhi Special Police Establishment Act, 1946. However, the Commission is not to exercise its powers in a manner as to require the CBI to investigate or dispose of any case in a particular manner.

the Allahabad High Court for quashing of the October 5, 2003 FIR filed by the CBI pursuant to the Supreme Court's order. The division bench at Lucknow dismissed the petition and after dismissing it passed an interim order prohibiting the CBI from arresting the accused. The Amicus mentioned the matter before the Taj Mahal bench of the Supreme Court, which directed to mention the matter before the Chief Justice. The amicus then mentioned the matter before the Chief Justice V.N. Khare, who directed the amicus to collect the relevant papers immediately from the Lucknow bench and file an I.A. 14.6.1 Lucknow Bench & SC. The Amicus complied. While disposing of the I.A. 404 filed on its direction, the Taj Mahal bench of the Supreme Court consisting of Justices S.B. Sinha, S.H. Kapadia and D.K. Jain, finally did not set aside the order of the Lucknow Bench. It noted the contention of the Amicus about judicial discipline and stated that the order of the Lucknow bench had already worked itself out. The Court did not say anything on the specific plea in the I.A. as to how the high court could even entertain a petition against the orders of the Supreme Court and then pass an interim order staying arrest of the accused till the investigation is over after dismissing the petition impugning the Supreme Court's order.

14.6.1 SC & Final Report Saga: Stage III

The final report was not being filed by the CBI after its investigation since the investigation officer's report stating that a case under the Prevention of Corruption Act and I.P.C had been made out against the accused, was being debated in the CBI whose Director Prosecution on deputation from the Union Law Ministry apparently held a contrary view. The Amicus moved I.A. 431 before the Supreme Court for a declaration that the Director CBI or CBI official could not legally sit in judgment over the report of the Investigating Officer, since the Supreme Court as far back as 1955 had held that the report of the Investigation Officer is final. The CBI however argued for several days on this issue. The Supreme Court finally upheld[4] the position as already laid down by the Supreme Court judgment.[5]

---

[4] November 27, 2006.

[5] H. N. Rishbud and Inder Singh vs. State of Delhi, 1955 SCR (1) 1150.

The Supreme Court chose not to say anything on the plea of the Amicus that in terms of the Supreme Court's judgment in Vineet Narayan vs. Union of India,[6] laying down the steps to make CBI into an independent agency, there should be no officer on deputation from the Union Law Ministry to the CBI for handling the prosecution decisions of the CBI, as such an officer is the ruling party's Trojan horse that robs the CBI of its independent professional character for a fair and impartial decision on prosecution. If the CBI feels the need for legal advice for taking the decision to prosecute on the investigation evidence collected by it then it could do so on its own by approaching the Union Law Ministry or the Attorney General. Otherwise, this procedure meant the imposition of an administrative sanction by the Union Government through its officer prior to the S.197 Cr.P.C sanction and there was no statutory provision for such prior administrative sanction on CBI's investigation.

The CBI filed the final report of its investigation under the Prevention of Corruption Act against the Chief Minister, Ms. Mayawati and others, before the Special Judge, Lucknow. The Special Judge by order dated June 5, 2005 refused to proceed with the case unless the CBI obtained a sanction u/s. 197 Cr.P.C. of the competent authority for prosecution of the former Chief Minister and other accused. The CBI did not go in appeal against this order. It did not inform the Supreme Court of this development which directly affected the Supreme Court's orders on the filing of an FIR, the investigation and its monitoring of the case. Instead, the CBI moved the Governor of Uttar Pradesh for the sanction. The same was refused by the Governor.

The Amicus brought these events in I.A. 465 to the kind attention of the Supreme Court bench for the consideration of the Governor's order and whether the order should be set aside. The Amicus was orally told that this bench had no jurisdiction to hear such an I.A. and the same could be filed before any other bench. The Amicus was directed to file written submissions.

---

[6] Vineet Naryan vs. Union of India, AIR 1998 SC 889.

14.7 S.197 Cr.P.C. Sanction Refusal Defeats SC's Order

In detailed written submissions showing how the refusal of sanction was incorrect as in view of the Supreme Court judgment in State of Orissa vs. Ganesh Chandra Jew[7] it had been held that under the old or the new S.197 Cr.P.C., a public servant could not claim immunity from prosecution for lack of sanction "if he ceased to be a public servant on the date when the court took cognizance of the said offences." The Chief Minister and the Environment Minister were no longer Chief Minister and Minister when the Special Judge in Lucknow took cognizance of the case. In any event the CBI ought to have immediately informed the Supreme Court on the basis of the Supreme Court's own decision in the Ganesh Chandra Jew case, instead of straightaway complying with the order of the Special Judge that there could be no prosecution by the CBI for the offences under the Prevention of Corruption Act and other criminal offences till it had taken sanction under Section 197 Cr.P.C. from the Governor. Moreover, the CBI ought to have come to the Supreme Court, knowing that the Supreme Court was monitoring the case.

14.8 A Supreme Court of Benches

The Amicus pointed out that under the Constitution there was only one Supreme Court and not benches of the Supreme Court. Further the written arguments pointed out that this matter was not similar to the forest matters in T.N Godavarman vs. Union of India[8] as the forests were a renewable resource unlike a monument which cannot be replaced as an ancient heritage monument. In the bench of Justices S.B. Sinha, S.H. Kapadia and D.K. Jain, Justice Kapadia put forth the forest matter and bench to bench proposition several times.

The consequences of the bench to bench jurisdiction now being espoused by the Court was analysed to show that this would mean the end of a constitutional institution called the Supreme Court and in any event there was no legal basis for stating that this bench had no jurisdiction

---

[7] State of Orissa vs. Ganesh Chandra Jew, (2004) 8 SCC 40 at 51.
[8] T.N Godavarman vs. Union of India, W.P. No. 202 of 1995.

when all along this bench alone had handled anything related to the Taj Mahal. The Supreme Court in its final order rejected the I.A. of Amicus without referring to any of the written arguments filed on its own direction. Its order stated that this bench had no jurisdiction to hear the I.A. which can be filed before any other bench of the Court or any other court. No reason/s whatsoever were given for its order which finally ended what the Supreme Court itself had started on a CBI investigation ordered by it and on forensic reports obtained by it showing mala fide interpolations in the project record made by the Principal Secretary to the chief Minister, the Union Environment Secretary, by the U.P. Minister for Environment and the pressure brought by senior officers on the juniors to give statements and arrange records.

14.9 Domestic Inquiries

The fate of the domestic enquiries ordered by the Supreme Court against the U.P. officials – Chief Secretary D.S. Bagga, the Principal Secretary to the Chief Minister P.L. Punia, the Principal Environment Secretary R.K. Sharma and his successor Secretary Dr. V.K. Gupta, was no better. The original inquiry officer/s appointed were changed without informing the Supreme Court. Some of the accused during the enquiry were elevated to judicial positions on the Board of Revenue. The Amicus brought this to the attention of the Supreme Court and the U.P. Govt. reported that they had been removed from those positions.

14.9.1 Compulsory Waiting

Meanwhile the IAS officers involved were put on leave with pay and all allowances (compulsory waiting). The Court asked the U.P. Govt. to file the rules for such leave under which full pay and allowances are given without attending office or doing any work, which would not be the case if they were suspended. The same were never filed. No final consolidated update report about the status of the enquiries and no final enquiry report or the action taken thereon was filed.

The Chief Secretary and the Secretary Appointments of the UP Govt. informed that after receipt of the inquiry reports and the opinion of the highest law officer these delinquent officers had been reinstated. The inquiry reports were not annexed to the reply or filed before the Supreme Court.

An I.A. and a Short Note was filed by the Amicus before the Court analyzing these facts and the affidavits of the Chief Secretary and the Secretary Appointments. It was also pointed out that these affidavits disclosed that the then Environment Secretary R.K Sharma had obtained relief against his suspension order from the Allahabad High Court, The high court had held that in violation of Rule 8 of the All India Services (Discipline & Appeal) Rule, 1969 the suspension order had not been extended immediately after the expiry of the maximum period of 180 days of life granted to such an order. This high court judgment of Feb 14, 2007, held that the suspension after December 4, 2006 was invalid as also the extension of suspension by the order dated Dec 15, 2006. The filing of the petition by Mr. R.K Sharma, the judgment and the absence of an appeal against it by the U.P Govt. was not brought to the attention of the Supreme Court by the State of U.P. or the Union Government.

14.9.2 Let Time Pass

In response to the filing of the I.A. by the amicus and the Short note, the order of the high court and several other developments concerning the delinquents were brought out in the replies filed by the Chief Secretary and the Special Secretary (Appointments). The affidavits sought to seek cover under the opinion of the "highest law officer" without disclosing or annexing that opinion. The Supreme Court was presented with a fait accompli. The I.A. of April 13, 2004 and the Short Note of April 23, 2004 are still pending. The passage of time, it may be said, has solved the problem in the absence of any judicial action.

The Supreme Court was faced with the situation of this conduct of the State Government in the manner of the implementation of its order dated September 18, 2003 in I.A. 376 in CWP 13381/84 directing domestic inquiries against the delinquent officers in relation to the Rs.170 crore Taj Heritage Corridor Project in which apparently about 17 crores of public money had been disbursed at the first step of the commencement of the project. The domestic enquiries had been ordered on the basis of a direction to the CBI to submit self-contained Note I and Note II concerning what the investigation had revealed about the role of these officers. Only the Union Environment Secretary was compulsorily retired on the recommendation of the UPSC as also the MD of the GOI's National Projects Construction Corporation.

14.10 Disproportionate Assets Case Hived Off Suo Moto

The final closure of the Taj Heritage Corridor project prosecutions was the suo motu order of the Court by the bench headed by Justice Ruma Pal hiving off the disproportionate assets case under the Prevention of Corruption Act from her Taj Case bench, which had been specifically designated by the Chief Justice to hear the Taj Mahal matters, to any other bench. There was no application by anyone praying for this. The oral reason given for this suo motu direction was that this case had nothing to do with the protected monument. On this rationale, the entire criminal proceedings initiated also suo motu by the Supreme Court in the Taj Heritage Corridor matter should never have commenced, since the Taj Heritage Corridor Project had nothing to do directly with the Taj Mahal monument per se. The implicit test so far had been the impact of any act or omission on the protected monument. The implied message now was that the Supreme Court had shifted away from this test.

14.11 Eco Restoration

The Amicus moved an application I.A. 389/2003 for eco restoration by the ASI and other agencies on basis of the Monitoring Committee report concerning the mountain of mud piled up behind the Taj Mahal that had been dug up from the Yamuna river bed and piled on the river bank till the edge of the road behind the Agra Fort, another protected monument. In a joint inspection with the ASI Superintendent at Agra, a report was filed as to what was required to be done and the statement of the ASI was recorded agreeing that it would do the needful. After that the ASI did not do anything. The matter was brought to the kind attention of the Court but the court thought it fit not to give any directions to the ASI.

14.12 SC Ignored Ancient Monuments Act, 1958

1. The key question concerning the protected monument under the Ancient Monuments Act, 1958 was whether the monument was imperiled by the proposed project and its implementation by the U.P Govt. This was never referred to by the court and the Ancient Monuments Act finds no mention in the court's orders.
2. Relevant materials like the project reports on the Taj Heritage Corridor Project, placed before the Court were ignored and no reference to the reports were made by the court.
3. The environment approach of the court towards protected monuments was also given up and hence no assessment was done of the environmental impact of the large amount of excavation already done for the Taj Heritage Corridor project.
4. No one in the CBI was held accountable for not complying with the Central Vigilance Commission Act which required, as per the CBI's own normal procedures also, the Prevention of Corruption Act case and its investigation to be referred to the Commission.
5. No reference to any provision of the Constitution or of any statute was made while holding that a bench of the court did not have the jurisdiction to hear the plea against the rejection by the Governor of sanction for the prosecution of the accused under the Prevention of Corruption Act, in the criminal case suo motu registered by the Supreme Court itself. No reason was given as to why this bench of the court lacked jurisdiction on a criminal investigation and prosecution in relation to a project named after a protected monument, which had been initiated on the complaint to the CBI by the court itself assuming that it had jurisdiction.
6. No reference was made in any of the orders passed by the Supreme Court, to the cultural heritage approach of Arts 49, 29 and 51A(f) of the Constitution of India Even though the Supreme Court had directed action to be taken under the pollution control laws, while ordering the registration of an FIR against the Chief Minister and

others, yet no case was filed by the Union Government under the Prevention of Water Pollution and Air Pollution Act as also under the Environment Protection Act, 1986. The Supreme Court chose not to aske the Union Government as to why its order to file cases under these Acts had not been complied with.

Chapter XV

IS JUDICIAL SILENCE THE BEST ROLE? NEITHER SECURITY NOR PROTECTION

15.1 SC Allows Night Viewing

The Taj Mahal, a protected monument which is most visited by foreign and domestic tourists, constitutes a permanent security problem. So on the basis of intelligence reports about possible terrorist attacks on the Taj Mahal, night viewing at the Taj had been banned. This ban, after clearances by the Union Government, was lifted by the Supreme Court which permitted only two and half hours of night viewing for groups of fifty each for half an hour. The night viewing could be done only from the sandstone platform before the fountains and the gardens on either side leading to the white marble monuments in which were the tombs.[1] The security for night viewing was controlled by the CISF which has already been made responsible for the internal security of the monument by replacing the State police for this task. The external security of the monument remained the task of the State police.

15.2 Khawasspuras: Replaced by Facilitation Centre

The records of the Court show that during the night viewing an ad hoc center for screening and frisking the ticket holders had been set up by the CISF. Keeping this in view the Supreme Court permitted the creation of a Facilitation Center.[2] However, the ASI took this as a opportunity to demolish and rebuild the two "Khawasspuras" which are part of The Taj

---

[1] *The actual tombs are in the subterranean chamber of the Taj Mahal.*

[2] I.A.s 111 (Facilitation Centre for night viewing); facilitation centre for night viewing reiterated. See infra Para16.2.14 to 16.2.16.

Mahal Complex, that has been notified under the Ancient Monuments Act as a protected monument.

Both the notified Khawasspuras, at the western gate of the entrance to the notified Taj Complex called the Fatehpuri Gate courtyard and at the eastern gate called the Fatehabad Gate courtyard, housed the Khadims who took care of the tomb. The Taj Mahal represents Islamic funerary construction and the Khadims performed also the services related to such a funerary. The Khadims included the hafiz, staying in the same Khawasspuras. The hafiz job was to recite the Qur'an day and night to redeem the soul of the queen Mumtaz Mahal by asking for divine forgiveness on her behalf. In the outer southern corners of the Khawasspuras were larger rooms which gave access to the latrines, which were inserted in a narrow strip open to the sky between the backs of the outer wings and the enclosing wall.[3] The Khawasspuras symbolize a worldly residential transition zone before one walks to the formal funerary area.

From 1899–1900 till 2004–05 the ASI conserved the Khawasspuras in terms of its constitutional duty to protect this monument declared by Parliament to be deemed of national importance, even though the ASI was using the eastern Khawasspura as a stable for the bull used in pulling the lawn mower in the Taj gardens and the western Khawasspura was being used as a nursery for the plants in the Taj Mahal gardens.

15.3 Rebuilding – No Conservation Principle

Around 2004–05 the ASI entered into an agreement with the Tata Group by which it seemed the Tatas were allowed to advertise their Taj tea by associating it with the Taj Mahal by giving funds for the conservation of Taj Mahal. A foreign trained architectural planner was hired at considerable expense as a consultant and a plan prepared. The agreement is kept a closely guarded secret by the ASI. Seemingly under this agreement the Khawasspuras were completely redone without following any of the conservation principles of recording the necessity for redoing a monument as also the entire evidence in photographic and

---

[3] Koch Ebba, The Complete Taj Mahal, p.118 and 226, Bookwise (India) Pvt. Ltd., New Delhi (2006–07) [*hereinafter* 'Koch Ebba' *for brevity*].

written form of the original condition before starting such civil works.[4] The legal cover put out by the ASI for this purpose was the permission given for a facilitation centre for tourists in the context of the limited number of tourists allowed for a specified limited time in limited batches by the Supreme Court for night-viewing of the Taj Mahal.

15.4 ASI Hits a Protected Monument Wall

The ASI without applying to the Supreme Court extrapolated this to daytime visitors running into thousands who could stay in the complex for any amount of time. After the Facilitation Centers were constructed, the ASI and the Tata's consultant seemed to find that to allow the tourists to go from the eastern Khawasspura facilitation centre towards the white marble monument itself, required breaking a niche into the wall of the Khawasspura. Legally the khwasspuras could not be touched, except for their preservation in their original condition, as these were a part of the Taj Complex, notified under the Ancient Monuments Act as a protected monument of national importance under Art. 49 of the Constitution of India.

15.5 SC's Order – Prior Permission

The Monitoring Committee immediately reported this and the Supreme Court promptly passed an order that nothing in the monument complex would be touched by the ASI without the prior permission of the court.[5] The Supreme Court thus saved the breaking up of an ancient heritage monument legally declared to be protected, by the ASI whose legal duty was to protect the monument.

15.6 Questions Regarding Tourism

Two questions now arose concerning the ever rising numbers of tourists to the protected monument, especially on weekends, public holidays and the Urs of Shah Jahan.

---

[4] 1923, Conservation Manual.
[5] October 9, 2006 in I.A. 453.

15.6.1 First Question: Security

The first question was the security of Taj Mahal as part of the constitutional duty to protect the Taj Mahal as a protected monument of national importance.

15.6.2 Second Question: Carrying Capacity

The second was how to ensure the protection against the heavy but unquantified wear and tear of the Taj marble tomb monument and its marble stairs and platform, while providing facilities for the comfort of the approximately twenty lakh tourists visiting annually, who had to stand in long queues exposed to the elements for several hours while awaiting their turn to enter the Taj complex after having bought the entry ticket. The constitutional duty to protect the Taj Mahal, required a calculation of the carrying capacity of this protected monument.

If the number of tourists allowed entry to the monument were kept at the carrying capacity level, then there was no question of long queues of hundreds of persons waiting for entry. The numbers had to be calculated on the basis of the wear and tear of the entire complex and especially the marble platform, the stairs and of the marble monument itself. Apart from the constitutional duty to protect the cultural heritage, the Supreme Court's own environmental approach towards the monument required the application of the principle of sustainable development by treating the Taj Mahal as a finite resource and therefore necessarily limiting its touristic consumption on the principle of limited numbers for a limited duration. The environmental principles of a precautionary approach and treating a resource as a public trust also required the same.

The Delhi High Court had applied the principle of sustainable development in the case of Anju Johri vs. Union of India[6] in the matter of determining how many tourist guides should be licensed for a monument by stating at P.429: "There is substantial justification for the respondents to limit the number of licensed Guides, as the same is imperative to have sustained development of tourism."

---

[6] Anju Johri vs. Union of India, (2005) 118 DLT 418 at 429.

15.7 I.A. for Carrying Capacity

This entry to limited numbers for a limited time would solve the problem of crowd control outside and inside the monument as also make it unnecessary for the breaking of a niche in a wall of the monument complex for the exit of the tourists from the ASI's newly constructed Facilitation Centre in Khawasspura of the eastern gate entry to the Taj Mahal. Hence the Amicus moved an I.A. 460 for directions to the ASI to make arrangements for determining the carrying capacity of the Taj, e-ticketing and introducing an RFID system to ensure tourist and monument security. The ASI plea in response was that it had to explore foreign experts to determine the carrying capacity. After this the court did not take up the I.A. and the same is still pending. This left only the avenue of a facilitation or a tourist holding centre for any number of tourists.

15.8 Alternative Land for Facilitation Centre

During a hearing of Taj matters, I.A.s 444/2008 and 474 the Amicus stated that alternative land was available near the Taj Mahal for a facilitation centre. The court directed the local officials and the Superintendent Agra Circle of the ASI to meet and find out whether any land was available for a Facilitation Centre. In a meeting presided over by the Director General ASI, who in terms of the Court's order was not supposed to be a member of that meeting, it was decided that the Facilitation Centre constructed by the ASI within the Taj, would be appropriate. This put the whole issue of tourist management at the Taj Mahal back to square one, since the use of the newly made Facilitation Centre required the breaking of the wall of the protected monument complex to enable the tourists to exit from the Centre for proceeding to the white marble monument itself.

When the Amicus pointed this out to the Court, a direction was issued requiring the Amicus, the petitioner in person and ASI officials to visit the Facilitation Centre constructed by the ASI within the Taj Mahal and suggest any other land available for the Centre which was a fait accompli. The team requested the ASI's consultant architect, who had planned and supervised the 'conservation' work of creating the

Facilitation Centre within the Taj complex, to join in the inspection. During the inspection it was revealed by the consultant that the wall of the protected monument complex were to be broken at four places for access to and exit from the eastern and western gates of the Taj. The team pointed out that the Supreme Court had not been informed about this by the ASI during the several hearings that had taken place on this issue. The team then located for the Western Gate entry of tourists, a piece of land for a Facilitation Centre. This was being used as an open defecation area. For the eastern gate Facilitation Centre the team proposed the use of the open area of the ITDC Hotel which was hardly one hundred yards from the eastern gate.

15.9 ASI: Underground Passage to the Notified Taj Complex

In response the ASI informed the court that there was no question of breaking any wall of the protected monument complex. It filed a plan for underground access from the two gates of the Taj having Facilitation Centres and other facilities. The Amicus pointed out the 1996 order of the Supreme Court which did not permit any construction within 200 meters of the Taj, the problem of erratic electricity supply and hence the security/safety of the tourists in the underground Centres as also the cleanliness of the underground premises. The Supreme Court viewed a video of the ASI's presentation of this plan by the Director General and approved it in principle., without any reference to the pending application for determining the carrying capacity of the Taj, or to its own order prohibiting construction within two hundred meters or to the problems that such Centres would face due to erratic electricity supply.

There was also no reference to the basic issue as to what would happen when these Centres run out of their tourist holding capacity in the absence of a determination of the carrying capacity to protect the monument and the consequent absence of permitting limited numbers daily for a limited duration.

The court did not consider at any stage, before granting it's in principle approval, as to what would be the effect of the ASI' proposals allowing unlimited number of tourists to enter the monument, on the constitutional duty to protect the monument. The Supreme Court's order effectively made this constitutional duty subject to unlimited tourism of the protected monument. The International Cultural Tourism Charter (ICTC), 1999 of ICOMOS as also the constitutional cultural heritage approach, were simply ignored by the court. The ICTC's first principle states: "Since domestic and international tourism is among the foremost vehicles for cultural exchange, conservation should provide responsible and well managed opportunities for members of the host community and visitors to experience and understand that community's heritage and culture at first hand." A monument meant to be a place of peace, reflection and prayer was denied its inherent cultural environment of an Islamic funerary monument through unlimited tourism that negates its culture. Like a beautiful woman in a poor country, the Taj Mahal became a victim of its own attraction.

15.10 Question of Judicial Will: Security Issue

The issue of protecting the Taj Mahal, I.A.s 111, 453 and 457 of 2006, by ensuring its security and determining its carrying capacity came to the fore again to test the judicial will for enforcing the Supreme Court's own orders. This arose from the incidents at the Taj Mahal of August 6, 2006; August 24, 2006 reported in The Times of India dated August 7, 2006 and the Dainik Jagran dated August 28, 2006. These were brought to the attention of the Supreme Court which issued notices to the ASI, CISF and the U.P. Government. The main issue involved was the implementation or enforcement of the November 21, 2001 order of the Supreme Court concerning the security of the Taj Mahal in terms of the contingency plan filed before the court by the U.P. Govt. The order was passed by the Supreme Court after it had issued notices on The Hindustan Times Report of October 16, 2001 that a huge crowd had gathered outside the Taj Mahal, entered it and created mischief.

The November 21, 2001 order was meant to enforce the contingency plan so that any sudden influx of persons trying to enter the Taj Mahal, could be kept "at least 500 meters away from the main monument so that the crowd does not get unrestricted entry inside the Taj Mahal."

The Supreme Court took note of the contingency plan of the U.P. Govt. which stated that a Deputy Superintendent of the local intelligence unit (LIU) will gather advance information through this unit about the possibility of such crowds and specify the strength of personnel, drawn from the local police, the Provincial Armed Constabulary, the Military Police and the Tear Gas Squad at six specified points around the Taj Mahal. On this basis the Supreme Court ordered:

1. The concerned authorities are directed to implement the same at the earliest.
2. The SP Agra City is directed to ensure that in no circumstances unruly crowd be permitted to enter the Taj premises or gather near about.
3. The Additional Superintendent of Police (City) Agra will be responsible for the implementation of the above contingency plan, properly and well in time.
4. The Additional SP (City) will be responsible for proper rehearsal of this contingency plan and he will coordinate with the Archaeological Survey of India and Additional District Magistrate (City) Agra to ensure smooth implementation of the above scheme.

The U.P Govt. in its affidavit made it clear that the internal security of the Taj Mahal complex would be that of the Union Govt.'s CISF by stating: "for the security deployment it has been agreed that the Central Industrial Security Force (CISF) would take over the security of the Taj Complex from May 1, 2002." Hence the external security in terms of the contingency plan would be that of the U.P. Govt.

15.10.1 Four Questions for U.P. and Six for ASI

When the Supreme Court took notice of the August 6, 2009 report of the The Times of India that ten thousand namazees had entered the Taj Complex for offering the Friday prayers at the mosque in the complex, adjacent to the monument itself, four question arose for an answer by the U.P. Govt. and six questions arose for a response by the UOI/ASI/CISF.

Is Judicial Silence the Best Role? Neither Security nor Protection | 243

The four questions for a response from the U.P. Govt were:

1. In terms of the November 21, 2001 order of the Hon'ble Court did the Deputy Superintendent of Police gather advance intelligence of the influx and gathering of about 10,000 persons in Agra for offering the Friday prayers at the Taj Mahal mosque, especially when the normal attendance for the customary Friday prayer between 12.00 hours to 14.00 hours is 600–1100 people and the crowd on August 3, 2006 Friday consisted of those coming from Ajmer Sharif, that is from outside Agra?
2. If the intelligence was gathered and given to SP Agra or the Additional SP (City) Agra or the District Magistrate (Agra), then why this crowd was not halted at the barriers on the roads to Taj Mahal, and at least 500 meters away from the Taj Complex, in terms of the Nov 21, 2001 order?
3. Did the Additional SP (City) Agra inform the Superintending Archaeologist, ASI Agra, about this crowd on August 4, 2006 and coordinate with him in term of the November 21, 2001 order?
4. Did the Additional SP (City) Agra inform the District Magistrate Agra about this crowd and coordinate with him for complying with the Nov 21, 2001 order?

The six questions for the UOI/ASI/CISF that arose were:

1. Did the ASI and CISF inform the SP Agra and the District Magistrate Agra on August 4, 2006 about this sudden influx that had gathered at the Taj Mahal despite the November 21, 2001 order?
2. Why did the ASI permit about 10,00 people (7,000 according to the letter of the CISF to ASI, Annexure C, internal P.8 of ASI's affidavit of Aug 18, 2006) entry into the Taj Complex for the customary Friday prayers on Aug 4, 2006, when it has been admittedly allowing only 600–1100 person in terms of the January 5, 2001.
3. Notification of the Director-General, ASI, under the Ancient Monuments Act, allowing entry to the Taj Complex on Fridays only to "those offering customary afternoon prayers in the mosque in the Taj Mahal complex between 12.00 hours to 14.00 hours?"

4. Why did the ASI permit about 7,000–10,000 persons to enter the Taj Complex for the customary afternoon prayers on Friday Aug 4, 2006, when the known capacity of the mosque, where the prayer are offered, is a maximum of 1000 persons only?
5. Does ASI have a system of identifying those who have been normally coming for offering the customary afternoon prayers on Fridays at the mosque from the others, especially since the spirit behind the Notification has been to permit access to the local residents subject to the capacity of the mosque?
6. Does CISF have enough personnel and equipment to ensure the security of the Taj, if ten thousand or several times the normal number of 600–1000 do manage to enter the Taj Complex?
7. What is the follow up action taken by the ASI and the CISF to prevent the recurrence of such incidents/threats to the Taj Complex, notified as a protected monument, under the Ancient Monuments Act?

15.10.2 Judicial Silence on U.P.'s and ASI's Replies

The Secretary, U.P. Home Department in his reply affidavit of September 15, 2006 detailed the measures regarding the internal security of the Taj Complex instead of what had been done to comply with the November 21, 2001 order of the Supreme Court concerning external security and in that context how did the incident of August 4, 2006 occur, when about 7–10,000 persons could gather outside the Taj and then enter it. The reply did not advert to any of the four questions, concerning compliance that arose from the November 21, 2001 order.

The ASI in its reply affidavit did not advert to any of the six questions that arose concerning compliance with the November 21, 2001 order, it merely stated that seven thousand persons had entered the Taj Complex on August 4, 2006 for afternoon prayers when normally only 600–1100 persons enter the complex. Further, CISF had only 47 personnel to deal with the 7–10,000 crowd.

These ten questions were put on record by the Amicus. The Supreme Court did not ask UP Home Secretary or the UOI/ASI/CISF to answer any of these concerning compliance with its own order of

November 21, 2001. The judicial role in enforcing the constitutional duty to protect a monument of national importance by enforcing its own order for security of such a monument, seemed to have become of simply keeping quiet. Maybe the passage of time will automatically take care of the problem, as after more than seven years the matter is still pending.

15.11 Judicial Silence: Shoes on Graves

This judicial role seemed to be reinforced by the Supreme Court's response to the photographs and reportage in the Dainik Jagran of August 28, 2006 showing that during Shah Jahan's Urs, around 50,000 people had entered the complex, an aggarbatti (incense sticks) fire in a pot had been lighted right outside on the platform of the Taj Mahal monument itself, several of these persons were bathing and frolicking in the fountain waters, food packets were being distributed, shoes had been put on the graves and hence every violation of legal, ethical and religious norms had occurred despite the November 21, 2001 order of the Supreme Court. The court issued notice to the UOI and the State of U.P. while giving to their counsel in the court itself, the newspaper report and photographs.

Once again the U.P Home Secretary filed a vague reply affidavit and the Supreme Court asked him file a better affidavit. In the new affidavit the Home Secretary, probably learning from the Supreme Court's silence on the kind of affidavit filed earlier by the Home Department in response to the notice on the August 6, 2006 incident of the entry of 7–10,000 persons, once again did not say a word about the discharge of the external security duties in terms of the November 21, 2001 order of the Supreme Court, or as to how around fifty thousand persons could travel to, collect outside the Taj Mahal complex and enter the Complex, if the Nov 21, 2001 order on external security had been complied with by the U.P. Govt. in terms of the contingency plan filed by it before the Supreme Court. None of the four questions that arose in relation to the earlier incident were answered. Annexure 3 of the better affidavit filed by the Home, Secretary stated that 40–50,000 people had entered the Taj Complex.

The Superintendent in this note in the Annexure, sent to the Senior Superintendent, Agra, stated that what had happened that day were "stray incidents."

15.12 Sustainable Tourism

The Amicus accordingly moved an I.A. seeking the following directions from the Supreme Court:

1. The State of U.P (The Home Secretary, the SP Agra and the Addl. SP Agra (City) be directed to file replies to the specific four questions concerning their duties that arise from the duty to comply with the Supreme Court's November 21, 2001 order.
2. This ASI and the CISF Commandant at Agra be directed to file their replies to the six questions that arise concerning their duties that arise from the duty to comply with the Supreme Court order to November 21, 2001.
3. The ASI be directed not to permit the entry of more than 1,000 persons, as per the capacity of the mosque in the Taj Complex, for the customary prayers on Fridays or for the performing of any Urs.
4. The ASI not to permit every one hour during the hours of entry to the Taj Mahal Complex more than what is permissible in terms of the security and the carrying capacity of the Taj Mahal Complex.

The application sought enforcement of the Supreme Court's November 21, 2001 order, accountability for its non-enforcement and to end unrestricted exploitation of the monument as an "industry," by regulating the numbers of visitors that could enter the Taj Complex per hour in pursuance of the constitutional duty to protect a monument declared to be of national importance under the Ancient Monuments Act. The application is still pending and no notice on this has been issued by the Supreme Court, which has not found the time to even list this for a hearing. The judicial role in the enforcement of the Court's own orders to protect a monument of national importance is self-evident. Sustainable tourism for the Taj Mahal sleeps in the Supreme

Court which is monitoring the protected monument for more than two decades, since 1984.

15.13 Supreme Court's Waning Interest

These issues concerning India's internationally advertised protected monument, which the Supreme Court has recognised as an "industry" are pending. The protected monument seemed to have lost its priority in the highest court since the Special Benches constituted by Consecutive Chief Justices of India, which used to give daily hearings and then weekly hearings, started giving twenty minutes to half an hour hearing after long intervals and then almost no hearing at all.

The loss of interest of the Supreme Court in management of petitions concerning the Taj Mahal and their disposal by enforcing the Union Govt.'s constitutional duty to protect monuments of national importance through the Writ of Continuous Mandamus, becomes selfevident from the following cases:

15.13.1 The Agra Master-Plan

The Supreme Court's saga of dealing with protected monuments, which still continues in 2014, began with Civil Writ Petition 13381 of 1984 filed by the Petitioner in person, Mr. M.C. Mehta. The petitions did bring the issue of protection of monuments of national importance to the court's attention and through the accredited legal correspondents of the court, to the attention of the public.

The Supreme Court continued to entertain the M.C. Mehta style of applications in the Taj Mahal case. I.A. 470 of 2007, filed by Mr. M.C. Mehta, challenged the Agra Master Plan 2001–2020 (Master Plan 2021), six years after it had already been executed. The application did not explain this long delay and also as to why the petitioner in person had not approached the Agra Development Authority at the time that the draft Master Plan had been notified by the Authority to invite objections. The application did not state any law that had been violated, like the Urban Planning and Development Act, 1973 or the Zoning Regulations. The application did not state as to why the ASI had not examined the draft

Master-Plan when it had been notified to invite objections to it. The application mentioned two documents of ICOMOS without stating how these applied to the case before the Court.

The verification of the application was defective since it did not state para-wise the source of information. Even the photographs annexed to the application were averred by Mr. Mehta as true to the "best of my knowledge." The application did not state that Mr. Mehta had gone to Agra and had taken these photographs of the area shown therein.

The Amicus Curiae pointed out all this to the Court. But the Court in its wisdom ignored even the laches involved in the filing of the application.

The Amicus Curiae had suggested to the Hon'ble Court in the Master Plan 2021 I.A. that ASI should examine the Master Plan, when it was put out in a draft form by the Agra Development Authority. On this basis, the ASI could file objections to the draft Master Plan itself in terms of the effect of the Master Plan on Monuments of National Importance. Further, the ASI should object to any development plans proposed by the local authorities for spending the money collected through the Agra Path Kar Nidhi from the fee paid by visitors to the Taj Mahal. This sum was distributed by the Commissioner, Agra Division and during the Financial Year 2007–08, a sum of Rs. 39.68 crores was received by the Agra Development Authority from this Nidhi. The ASI should examine the development plans of local authorities based on this Nidhi.

However, the Supreme Court simply ignored all the factors pointed out above and issued notice to the authorities concerned only on one out of the nine prayers made in the Master Plan I.A. by these applications. It never asked Mr. Mehta to explain as to why he had delayed the filing of this application by about six years. The Supreme Court simply kept these applications pending.

15.13.2 More Applications by Mehta

Similarly, applications were filed by Mr. M.C. Mehta – I.A. 480 of 2008 concerning the shifting of a crematorium behind the Taj Mahal as also the buffalo dairies around the Taj.

I.A. 481 of 2008 relating to the purported 'Holy Kunds' of Mathura was filed by Mr. Mehta, even though the Supreme Court on August 19 2003 had disposed of a bunch of I.A.s[7] on the same issue by holding that the dispute was not required to be decided by the Supreme Court and Mr. Mehta could approach the appropriate forum for the redressal of his grievances. Yet, the Supreme Court entertained the I.A., without questioning the utterly defective verification of the I.A., especially since this I.A. repeated the prayer (g) in I.A. 470 concerning the Kunds.

15.13.3 Brick Kilns and Agricultural Top-Soil

The Monitoring Committee report of June 19, 2001 in I.A. 125 of 2001 showed how all authorities in Agra, the Panchayat offices and the U.P. Pollution Control Board had made a mockery of the May 10, 1967 order of the Supreme Court concerning brick kilns. The order had directed all brick kilns within 20 kms of the Taj Mahal and the Bharatpur Bird Sanctuary in the TTZ Area to be closed and stopped. However, the Supreme Court passed no orders at all on the report of the Monitoring Committee that had been constituted by itself.

In the June 19, 2001 report concerning brick kilns, the Monitoring Committee had pointed out that huge areas of agricultural land with rich top-soil, a precious resource, was being dug up by brick kiln owners and all authorities at Agra, the Panchayat offices, the District Industries Centre, were granting licenses to brick kiln owners for the brick kilns without examining this aspect at all.

Pursuant to the Supreme Court order, the Ministry of Environment and Forests on April 2, 2002 by Office Order No. Q-18011/2/2002-CPW constituted a ten member committee under the Special Secretary of the Ministry to study the manner in which "the rich and fertile agricultural top soil is being used for brick-making activities and other uses, thereby depleting a very precious resource and suggest appropriate measure to solve/mitigate the problem." The Office order required the committee to submit its report within six months.

---

[7] Taj Case, p. 353–356 and 365.

On July 26, 2004 the Amicus Curiae in his written submissions pointed out that the April 2, 2002 Expert Committee on top soil constituted by the MoEF was to give its report within six months. So far nothing had happened. On Jan 12, 2004, the CPCB replied In I.A.s 163–165, 172–174, 306–310 and other I.A.s that NEERI had been commissioned for this study. However no report was filed and the Supreme Court did nothing on this urgent issue concerning the country's agriculture.

15.13.4 SC: Kiln by Kiln Permission

The Amicus argued against the Supreme Court being turned into a permission authority kiln by kiln licensing and its time being taken up in I.A.s 163–165, 172–174, 306–310, 311–324, 364, 366–369, 391 & 394, filed by Brick – Kiln owners for licenses. The Supreme Court on September 11, 2003, directed the Central Pollution Control Board (CPCB) to set up a Committee to examine, investigate and pass orders on these applications of the brick kiln owners seeking permission to start or continue a brick kiln. Consequently, the CPCB by a letter dated October 20, 2003, B-PLS/Brick/03/20110 to 20117, constituted a Committee. The committee's Chairman was a Director CPCB and other members were from the UPPCB, MoEF and ASI Agra. The committee could investigate on the applications, hire experts to be paid for by the UPPCB and prescribe conditions for a brick kiln. The committee was to meet at Agra. The Supreme Court's orders enabled the legal construction of a regulatory regime for brick kilns which now have to comply with CPCB guidelines in the Comprehensive-Industry Document on Brick Kilns, May 1996; NEERI guidelines; Environment Rules, 1986 on stack height and emissions; consent from UPPCB under the Environment Act, Air, and Water Pollution Acts.

15.13.5 Functioning of the TTZ Pollution Control Authority

The Taj Trapezium Zone Pollution (Prevention and Control Authority) constituted[8] by the Ministry of Environment and Forests in the

---

[8] S.O. No. 350(E).

Gazette of India Notification dated May 18, 1999 was headed by the Commissioner of Agra Division as Chairman. The Authority was to monitor the progress of various schemes for the protection of the Taj Mahal and improvement of environment. Further, it was to exercise powers under S.5 of the Environment Act, 1986; Ensure compliance with Vehicle Emission Standards and compliance of Fuel Quality Standards et al. The Authority was to submit, once in two months, a report of its activities to the Central Government. In I.A. 69 and 71, the Supreme Court on May 2, 2000 directed the Commissioner of Agra Division to file a report as to what had been done under this notification and to give to the Amicus, CPCB counsel and Mr. M.C. Mehta copies of the reports filed with the Govt. and to file the same on or before July 15, 2000, before the court. The Commissioner never filed in the Supreme Court copies of the reports he was supposed to submit every two months to the Union Government. The amicus, Mr. Vijay Panjwani the CPCBN counsel and the petitioner in person Mr. M.C. Mehta pointed this out to the Supreme Court. Nothing was done by the Supreme Court on this and the matter remains pending.

15.13.6 Low-Sulphur Diesel

In I.A. 398/2004, Shri Gurbachan Singh through Secretary, Petrol Dealers Association Fatehabad, Agra. vs. Union of India sought directions for the supply of Low-Sulphur Diesel to Agra City in view of the Hiigh – Sulphur Diesel pollution affecting the Taj Mahal. The I.A. remains pending.

15.13.7 Shifting of Polluting Bus Stand at Bijli Ghar

The Supreme Court Registry received a letter pointing out how the Bus Stand at Bijli Ghar, half a Kilometre from the Taj Mahal was causing pollution. It also pointed out how the District Magistrate's order against the parking of buses at Bijli Ghar was being flouted by the U.P. State Road Transport Corporation buses themselves. The Amicus had orally prayed that the Traffic Police chief of Agra be called upon to explain the violation of the District Magistrate's order. However, the letter was not even listed for hearing by the Supreme Court.

Advocate Dr. (Mrs.) Vipin Gupta filed on January 4, 2006 an I.A. Ravinder Kumar Sharma vs. State of U.P. to implead the applicant as a local resident of Agra, affected by the pollution of the bus stand. The applicant sought directions that the bus stand located in the heart of Agra city and near the Taj Mahal Complex be shifted to the newly constructed Bus Terminus outside the city. This I.A. remained unlisted.

15.13.8 Night-View Monitoring

Pursuant to the November 25, 2004 orders of the Supreme Court, in I.A. 426 in I.A. 69 in CWP 13381/84, on the application of the UP Govt. to allow night-viewing of the Taj Mahal for five nights – 2 before Full Moon, 2 after Full Moon and on Full Moon night itself, every month (which the Supreme Court allowed for three months), the Monitoring Committee monitored the three night viewings allowed by the order on Dec 26, 27 and 28, 2004. As directed, it filed its reports with the District Judge at Agra to report any violations of the Supreme Court's order forthwith. The three reports for the three night viewings showed that from ticket distribution by the ASI to the putting up of public notices and the checks required to be done by the Supreme Court order dated Nov 25, 2004, all had been violated. The first report especially pointed out the threat to security which such a situation gave rise to, — anyone could get the ticket in the name of anybody and do the night viewing without check of cameras, purses, etc.

Earlier in their order dated May 2, 2000 in I.A. Nos. 69 and 71, the court had stated: "Having regard to the report of Mr. Krishan Mahajan of the event which took place during December 22, 1999 to December 24, 1999, we are of the view that the Govt. of Uttar Pradesh should come forward with a specific scheme to see that adequate security and pollution measures could be taken and properly implemented and that earlier orders of this Court are not violated. We find from photographs produced before us that several vehicles have been permitted to go within five hundred metres, including vehicles of VIPs. Further, Photography is permitted within five hundred metres of the Taj Mahal, which is contrary to our orders. No vehicle belonging to any person, including that of VIPs, will be permitted within 500 metres of the perimeter of the Taj Mahal."

On December 17, 1999, the U.P. Govt.'s application for night viewing had been rejected on the ground of security. On December 22, 1999, in I.A. 71/99, the Supreme Court allowed the night-viewing, although it allowed three night-viewings of the Taj Mahal against the five sought. This was on the basis that the Union Govt. had stated it had no objection to the U.P. Govt.'s proposal and also the fact that the brightest moon in 133 years would be visible on December 23, 1999. Night-viewing was permitted on December 22–24, 1999, from 8.30 p.m. to 12 midnight in batches of fifty persons for thirty minutes for each batch from the sandstone platform and no further.

Apart from reiterating this earlier order concerning vehicles, the Supreme Court took no action against officials pinpointed in the report. Now again in 2004 no action was taken against the officers concerned for violation of the Supreme Court order. The question that arises is that of institutional credibility.

15.14 Tourism Takes over Monument Protection

In the above mentioned context of the Supreme Court's steadily declining interest concerning the protection of a Monument of National Importance, the Taj Mahal, the Department of Tourism of Uttar Pradesh went into action by creating the Agra Heritage Project.

On March 24, 1998, in I.A. No. 38 concerning Yanni's concert, the Under-Secretary of the Uttar Pradesh Government had told the court that Agra Heritage Fund Rules had been framed by the State Govt. and a sum of Rs. 2,28,08,972/– from the concert was lying with the State Govt. which was proposed to be put in the Fund for beautification/maintenance of the Taj Mahal and for developmental activities to promote tourism. The Court expressed that the Committee should be more broad-based. Accordingly, a Memorandum was notified by the Office of the Governor of Uttar Pradesh.

15.14.1 Memorandum and Manual: Agra Heritage Fund

As per the notification by the Secretary to the Governor on June 20, 2000, the memorandum under the head Aims and Activities states:

Keeping the historic and cultural importance of Agra in mind, which has a history of more than 3000 years, in fields of art, literature, culture and traditions and that with a view that preservation of this tradition is of an absolute necessity, the Agra Heritage Fund Committee shall have the following aims:

> A. Preservation and maintenance and development of tourism facilities of three receptors of Agra viz. Taj Mahal, Agra Fort and Fatehpur Sikri.
> B. Preservation and improvement of environment of Agra.
> C. Maintenance and renovation of the monuments of Agra and development of necessary facilities for tourists.

Hence the main aim was tourism.

Under the Agra Heritage Fund Committee Manual, the above mentioned purposes were to be the purposes of the Board of Management of the Committee. The State Govt. was to review the work of the committee and give directions to the Chairman ex officio of the Committee, the Commissioner, Agra.

Before the Supreme Court in Yanni's I.A., tourism was not the first priority but it was the Taj Mahal. Now tourism per se had become the first priority.

On January 4, 2001, the affidavit by the Joint Director of Department of Tourism, on behalf of the State of U.P. stated that in compliance with the Supreme Court's order in Yanni, the committee had been made more broad based by including a representative each of INTACH and of the School of Planning and Architecture. Further the State Govt. had deposited a sum of Rs. 2,08,72,000/- in the Fund.

15.14.2 Solar Disappears

On April 29, 2002, the Joint Director of the Dept. of Tourism filed another affidavit called a short affidavit to state that in compliance with the Hon'ble Court's order dated April 11, 2002, solar energy projects amounting to Rs. 439.50 lacs for the Taj Ganj and nearby areas of the Taj Ganj would be taken. The agency for execution would be NEDA (Non-Conventional Energy Development Agency) and the upkeep/

maintenance of the projects would be done by NEDA/Agra Development Authority. The details of the project were put in Annexure I. however, till today there is not a sign of the solar project and diesel generators continue to run in Taj Ganj.

On November 29, 2000, the Supreme Court order noted that the U.P. Govt. had deposited in the Fund Rs. 4.56 Crores, sanctioned earlier for it. The Central Govt. refund of Rs. 140 lakhs under Income Tax Act under the Yanni Concert tax collection, was directed by the Court to be put in the Heritage Fund. The Court stated that bye-laws of the society have to be looked into and registration of the society will not be done till this court passes further orders. The Office report dated Jan 9, 2001 stated that nothing had been filed. Since then, the matter is simply pending.

15.14.3 Shah Jahan Park

The Supreme Court's waning interest in the issue relating to the Protection of Monuments of National Importance became clearer when the Court did not even list for hearing three reports filed by the Amicus on two monuments of National Importance in Agra and the threat to the largest green area adjacent to the Taj Mahal – the 106 year old 244.51 acre Shah Jahan Park,[9] opposite the Taj Mahal with one side along the entry to the Western gate to the Taj. The two reports on Monuments of National Importance related to Sikandra (January 2004), the final resting place of Akbar, and Ram Bagh (September 2004).

---

[9] December 2004 Report.

Chapter XVI

JUDICIAL ROLE: TOURISM VS. PROTECTED WALLS IN TAJ MAHAL COMPLEX

The Taj Mahal,[1] in about 17 hectares, is an Islamic funerary[2] architecture on a central axis with bilateral symmetrical construction on either side set amongst gardens[3] and flowing water to create an earthly paradise[4] for Shah Jahan and his wife, buried in the mausoleum. The entire 17 hectare complex of the Taj Mahal's[5] outer court, also called Jilo Khana or "the Bright Quarter" is 412 feet North and South, by 941 feet East and West, within Taj Mahal's high walls. It was formerly used both as a bazaar and a caravan serai (Rest House). At its North-East and

---

[1] *Syad Muhammad Latif Khan Bahadur, Agra Historical and Descriptive with an Account of Akbar and His Court And of the Modern City of Agra*, Printed at the Calcutta Central Press Company Ltd, 40, Canning Street, Calcutta. Available in the Library of the Office of ASI Superintendent Agra and the Central Library ASI, New Delhi (1896).

[2] Koch Ebba, p. 85–88 and 28.
On the controversy between orthodox Islamic law of the Sunni schools and the imperial desire, whether to have a minimalist open-to-sky cenotaph or one with a domed structure on it, as also that tombs were exempt from the legal rule of Muslim administration that no owner of land or gardens could pass it in inheritance but it reverted to the imperial estate.

[3] Gupta I P Urban Glimpses of Mughal India, Agra the Imperial Capital, 16th and 17th Centuries; Discovery and Transactions of the Archaeological Society of Agra, January and June 1874, p.24 and 55, published by Order of the Council, Delhi Gazette Press, Agra, MDCCCLXXIV (1986).

[4] The following passage is inlaid in black marble on the gate of the Taj Mahal: O thou soul of peace/Return thou into thy Lord, well pleased/and well pleasing unto Him/Enter thou among My servants.

[5] Verma Chob Singh, Monuments of Agra, p.82, published by U.P Tourism Development Corporation.

North-West corners are the closed courts of the same dimensions known as Khawasspura (Servants Quarters). Those on the South-East and South-West corners are the tombs of Sirhindi Begum and Satiunnisa Khanum respectively.

The court is entered by high massive gateways at its East, West and South Centres. The first being the entrance for the Fatehabad road, the second for the Taj Road and the third the Sirhi Darwaza or Step Gateway for Taj Ganj. The one at the North Centre is the main entrance to the Taj Mahal. The entire Taj Mahal complex,[6] enclosed in a perimeter wall, is notified as an ancient monument of national importance and hence a protected monument.

16.1 Khawassparas

In gross violation of its constitutional duty under Art. 49 of the Constitution, the ASI allowed tourism to take over to the extent that it completely reconstructed two sections known as Khawassparas.[7]

Khawassparas were servant quarters to which opened the doors at the East and West ends of the dalans that constituted the essential constituents of the architectural design of the Taj Mahal.[8] The Jilaukhana square is framed on the sides by the residential quarters for the tomb attendants (Khwassparas), Bazaar Street and the subsidiary tomb enclosures.

The Khawassparas consist of an open courtyard surrounded by the pillared verandahs and a series of rooms of different sizes behind them. The verandahs are fronted by three multi-cusped arches supported on typical shahjahani pillars and pilasters. The verandahs and chambers have flat ceilings. Court historian, Abd-al-Hamid

---

[6] *In 2000 the Supreme Court dismissed a petition claiming that the Taj Mahal was built by a Hindu King P. N. Oak vs. UoI WP (Civil) 336 of 2000. In 1983 UNESCO designated the Taj Mahal as a world heritage site. Its construction was commissioned by the Mughal Emperor Shah Jahan in 1631.*

[7] Nath R., Agra and Its Monuments, p.151 (1997).

[8] Dayalan D, Taj Mahal and its Conservation, p.21 (2009).

Lahori,[9] states that each of the Khawassparas contain 32 rooms with a portico in front. The pillared arcades are provided with a deep sloping chhajjas that sail out over the brackets. It is a typical Indian idea which adds a new dimension to the otherwise plain surface of Islamic architecture. The chajjas were used effectively as visual breakers to create a play of light and shadow on the facades.

The eastern Khawasspara (Fatehabad Gate Courtyard) was used by the ASI as a cow-pen and hence it is known as Gaushala, whereas the Western one, (Fatehpuri Gate Courtyard) was known as Glass House, as it was used by the Horticulture wing of the Archaeological Survey of India as a nursery and a glass chamber was erected in it to keep the tender plants. It had a spacious court, around which were small rooms and verandahs (dalans) for the residence of the attendant staff of the complex. For holding the tourist inflow, the ASI was ready to break down the internal walls to provide exits from these holding areas towards the monument. The manner in which this was sought to be achieved through the Supreme Court was dubious since all along ASI was saying orally that 'niche' in one wall was needed to be carved out. The end which was actually sought to be achieved — to break internal walls of the notified Taj Mahal complex — was illegal, being in violation of the constitutional duty to protect the notified monument complex, rather than facilitate tourism by breaking the walls of the notified complex.

16.2 Steps to Facilitate Tourism

The dubious manner of achieving this, which speaks for itself, consisted of the following steps:

February 5, 2002: On October 16, 2001, the Supreme Court suo motu took notice of a Hindustan Times, Delhi edition report that on October 14, 2001, a large number of persons entered the Taj Mahal complex and caused mischief. It issued notices to the Chief Secretary

---

[9] Abd-al-Hamid Lahori (Lahawari), The Badshah Nama, Two Volumes, 1867 & 1868, ed. Kabir al-Din Ahmad and Abd-al-Rahim, Printed under the Superintendence of Major W. N. Lees, Calcutta College Press.

U.P and the Director General ASI to state on affidavit as to what preventive steps were taken and would be taken in future to meet such an eventuality.

16.2.1 Notice in One I.A. and Reply in Another

The Director General mysteriously filed the reply on February 5, 2002, not in the I.A. concerning the suo motu proceedings but in an earlier I.A. 111 of 2000 filed by the ASI itself. In this I.A., the Supreme Court on November 8, 2001, had ordered the U.P. Provincial Armed Constabulary (PAC) out of the Taj Complex on ASI's plea that ASI was in charge of internal security and not the U.P Govt., that the use by the PAC of the Taj Mahal as living premises degraded the monument and the ASI would make alternative security arrangements including hiring of private security agencies.

16.2.2 Silence on Internal Security of the Taj Mahal

The reply by the Director General was in itself peculiar. It made no reference to the newspaper report on which the Supreme Court had sought an answer. It did not deny the report. It did not state what effort, if any, the Director General had made to find out how such an incident had happened inside the monument complex. It did not explain what security steps had been taken to deal with what had happened on October 14, 2001 and to prevent the same in future. There was no reference in the reply to ASI's own staff stationed inside the Taj Mahal complex and having an office before the open sky entry to the fountain pathway to the mausoleum itself. Nothing was stated as to what action the staff took, what security force existed and what this force had done to stop the mischief as reported in the press. The reply while asserting that ASI was responsible for internal security of the notified Taj complex did not mention that any inquiry was conducted or that any action was contemplated on the report. The Supreme Court in its wisdom did not pass any orders on these issues arising from the reply in relation to the October 16, 2001 order.

16.2.3 ASI Slips in a Facilitation Centre: The Taj Hotel's MOU

Without explaining any connection to the October 16, 2001 order and the fact of I.A. 111 mentioned in the reply, the Director General's February 5, 2005 reply, in Para 5 stated that it had been indicated "in the meeting with the then Chief Secretary U.P. and others that the ASI had entered into a Memorandum of Understanding with the Taj Group of Hotels to finance the ASI to prepare a Site Management Plan providing for a facilitation centre, rest rooms, installation of X-Ray machines entry through stile turn gates."

There was no explanation as to why the ASI had not informed the Supreme Court about this, when it knew that since 1984 the Supreme Court has been monitoring all aspects of the protection of the notified Taj complex. The fact that the MOU between ASI, The National Culture Fund and the Indian Hotels Co. Ltd (The Taj Group) had been signed on June 20, 2001, (about four years prior to the February 5, 2005 reply affidavit of the Director General ASI), was not stated and hence concealed in the reply dated February 5, 2005. There was also no explanation as to why no copy of the Memorandum of Understanding (MOU) itself had been annexed to the reply. That would have probably brought in the National Culture Fund.[10] It would have opened up an inquiry of the common persons between the Fund and the Hotels Group, as to how such member/s participated in the decision making on what was described as the Taj Mahal Conservation Collaborative, at the foot of the annexed plans and why for a mere sum of Rs1.87 crores, a Government of India organization like the ASI had to resort to such an MOU.

16.2.4 Fait Accompli of Prepared Plans

After reverting to the exit of the U.P. Police from the Taj Mahal complex and its replacement from April 1, 2002 by the CISF, the reply suddenly

---

[10] *The 1996 Scheme for the administration of the National Culture Fund after vesting the Fund with the Treasurer of Charitable Endowments under the Charitable Endowments Act, 1890, was notified on Nov 28, 1996 as S.O.832(E) – In Part 11 – Section 3 – Sub-Section (ii), Gazette of India.*

in Para 9 stated a further advance made under the MOU with the Taj Group of Hotels. It now stated that a plan had been already prepared with the Hotel group for the Visitor Facilitation Centre. Copies of the plans were filed with the reply as Annexure C. The plans showed that one Visitor Centre on the Eastern Gate through the Khawasspura area was to be used as a Visitor Facilitation Centre.

The pleadings and the Annexed plan did not mention anything about a second Facilitation Centre at the Western Gate of the Taj Mahal for which purpose the khwaspura on that side would be used. Instead the plan showed that it was to be retained as a nursery in a glass house for keeping the plants used by the Horticulture Wing of the ASI.

The pleadings and the annexed plan did not state or show or mention:

1. Anything about completely redoing the Eastern gate Khawasspura and having toilets, water coolers and other facilities in the redone Khawasspura.
2. Any exit from the proposed Eastern Gate Facilitation Centre.
3. Anything about breaking the walls of the Khawasspura on the Eastern Gate for creating a 'niche' or an exit from the Facilitation Centre towards the Taj Mahal marble monument.

16.2.5 ASI Suppresses Further Facts

By May 22, 2002 the ASI Agra Circle had prepared a detailed estimate of the Special Repairs to the Gaushala or the Eastern gate Khawasspura. The note under the Archaeological Works Code under Para 11.1.1 was prepared by the Superintending Archaeologist Agra and the estimate for the works of Rs. 48,70,226/- was prepared by the Senior Conservation Assistant. The note of the senior conservation assistant stated the works for which the provisions had been made in the estimate for converting the Eastern gate Khawasspura, being used as a Gaushala, into a Visitors Facilitation Centre: "Demolition of the later additions; re-plastering of walls; relaying of floors; restoration of broken/missing stone chhajas; restoration of damaged stone pillars; resurfacing of the walls."

On May 22, 2002, these papers were sent by the Senior Conservation Assistant to the Director General who communicated the same to an officer of the Taj Group of Hotels in the Taj Mahal Conservation Collaborative (TMCC).

The detailed estimate by the Superintending Archaeologist contained photographs of the existing Gaushala but did not contain a single reference, map or plan of the original or the existing Khawasspura and no history at all about it from any authoritative source. Under the head Special Repairs, the historical Khawasspura, which was part of the notified complex of the Taj Mahal, was to be converted into a Facilitation Centre for tourists and not to be conserved under Art. 49 to protect the complex.

These documents were hidden from the court and not even mentioned in any application or pleading by the ASI, even though it had filed in I.A. 111 a plan of the Eastern Gate Facilitation Centre for the court's approval.

16.2.6 Hospitality vs. Conservation

But the ASI went further. It now sought the opinion of a foreign expert for not only the plans for the Eastern Gate Khawasspura conversion to a Facilitation Centre but also the conversion of the Western Gate Khawasspura. The expert, Sir Bernard Fielden, Director-Emeritus ICCROM, concluded his opinion by thanking the Indian Hotels Co. Ltd (Taj Group Hotels) for their generous hospitality and stated that "The immediate proposals for the reuse of the Fatehpur (Western) Gate courtyards and the Fatehabad (Eastern gate) courtyards as visitor centers are excellent, as long as the two Centres remain the same in their content to ensure that tourists do not feel the need to visit both."

The Khawasspuras had been reduced to courtyards by the foreign expert. The viewpoint was tourists and tourism not conservation and protection of the notified Khawasspuras. There was no mention by the foreign expert of the original condition of the Khawasspuras or any attempt to find out their architectural or cultural significance. There was no reference to the fact that the Khawasspuras were legally part of the Taj Mahal complex, notified as a protected monument of national importance.

16.2.7 Tourism vs. Conservation

The expert's letter went further and stated "I have examined the plans prepared by The Taj Mahal Conservation Collaborative (TMCC) in consultation with ASI and CISF for the installation of new security equipment. This necessitates cutting through to access the outer courtyards, and fully agree that this is acceptable and necessary for security screening and visitor flows. In the long term this work is reversible, if it proves necessary." Hence once again with an emphasis on tourists and tourism and not on conservation and culture of the notified monument complex the cutting through of the Khawasspura Visitor's Centre was justified. Worse, the process of cutting up parts of the ancient monument complex and providing doors was held to be reversible. In other words, a reversible illegality was permissible.

16.2.8 Reversible Illegality Approved

It is significant that so far, the ASI's specific preparations, for redoing the two Khawasspuras for tourism and also cutting up their walls for exits from these, were not disclosed to the Supreme Court even though the matter was pending before it. The Project Implementation Committee headed by the DG ASI and including its Director of Monuments, the Member Secretary of the National Culture Fund, Officials of the Taj Group of Hotels and members of the TMCC, labeling themselves under a conservation title instead of a tourism title, approved in their meeting of December 4, 2002 what had been stated by the foreign expert, Mr. Fielden.

16.2.9 ASI Violates Its Conservation Manual

All this violated every principle of the Conservation Manual, 1923, (prepared by the then Director General of ASI) which applies to the ASI, as so far the ASI has not formulated any other Manual to replace the 1923 one.[11] Para 22 stood violated as there were no photographs showing the condition of the Khawasspuras from "all points of view," there were no scale drawings and sketches. Para 22 states under the head Special Works that "no work is to be put in hand without such particulars". Para 24 was violated as the historic importance and the architectural value of the Khawasspuras was not considered. The cardinal principle laid down in the Para that "historical value is gone when their authenticity is destroyed and that our first duty is not to renew them but to preserve them" was simply abandoned by the ASI.

16.2.10 Questions on TMCC's Certificate to ASI

On March 2003 the TMCC group, financed by the Taj Group of Hotels, published the Site Management Plan of the Taj Mahal. It gave a certificate on p.18 to the ASI that it has taken adequate measures to preserve and protect the monument without disturbing its originality. It did not ask as to why for 21 years the ASI had not prepared a Site Management Plan even though ICOMOS had recommended a Site Management Plan in 1982 while endorsing the nomination of the Taj Mahal as a World Heritage Site. It also did not ask as to how the originality of the notified monument complex was retained by the ASI when it had converted the Eastern gate Khawasspura into a Gaushala and the Western Gate Khawasspura into a nursery under a glass ceiling, thereby ignoring the original culture and construction of these notified quarters called by the ASI as "Servants Quarters" in its affidavits before the Supreme Court.

16.2.11 "Servants" vs. Monument Culture

According to the Plan itself at p.13," In its conception the Taj Mahal had inbuilt systems for its continuous life; during Shah Jahan's

---

[11] Indian Archaeological Policy, 1915, being a resolution issued by the Governor-General in Council on October 22, 1915, Pg. 18, Superintendent, Govt. Printing, India, Calcutta, (1916).

"...*The Government of India are fully alive to the deplorable harm that may be done in the name of restoration, and except in special circumstances, are opposed to its being undertaken...*"

lifetime there was an annual urs; even after Shah Jahan's death and his internment, there were regular Friday prayers and financial provision for Khadims to maintain the property from thirty revenue villages yielding money from the lands as well as shops and serais within the complex. The Khadims maintained the property for many generations. This clearly indicated that those living in the khwasparas were something more than what the word servant indicates. But the attitude of the ASI seemed to be as to how can servants and their quarters be culture.

In any event the legal position was that these khwasparas were part of the protected monument and were hence required to be treated in terms of the constitutional duty of protecting the monument like any other part of the monument.

But regardless of the legal position the ASI and the TMCC seemed to project the typical Indian attitude of designating those serving an entity as human beings of little or no importance and therefore labeled as servants. The cultural value of the khwaspuras is indicated by Ebba Koch at p.118 "Both the khwaspuras housed the people who looked after the tomb (the khadims) and those who performed the funerary services…. They introduce an intimate residential element in a part of the Taj Mahal complex which functions as a transitional zone between the formal funerary area and the worldly area."

16.2.12 Taj Mahal, Tourism and Toilets

The Site Plan on p. 66 stated that these two "courtyards" were "underutilized" and had tremendous scope for use as visitor centers… These will contain amenities such as toilets, drinking water etc. The effect of these on the architectural discipline of the monument as a funerary architecture was neither mentioned nor spelt out. The notified funerary complex conceived and executed to create an earthly paradise for the peace of the souls interred therein was now to be modernized by having toilets and drinking water coolers in the khwasparas It was not even thought, as to whether the spirit of the Taj Mahal's architecture and the purpose of its construction permitted so many visitors (about 20 lakh annually) in the first place. After the British takeover of the monument under Viceroy Lord Curzon, the gardens had been Europeanised[12] and troops had been stationed in parts of the notified monument complex. The Waqf intended to take care of the monument complex was abolished by the British in 1803.[13]

16.2.13 Showing Entrances without Exits to Supreme Court

But the map in the Site Management Plan at p.64 now showed two Visitor Facilitation Centres at the Eastern and Western gates of the Taj Mahal without showing any exits from these enclosed centres. The exits were shown only at p.70 as part of the Security Installation for the Eastern Fatehabad gate without mentioning anywhere that the walls of the notified khwaspuras would have to be cut to allow visitors in these proposed Facilitation Centres out on the pathway towards the Taj Mahal marble monument. The text of the plan nowhere stated the cutting of the Taj Mahal complex walls for the exits. It is significant that this entrance but-no-exit-plan was not disclosed by the ASI in the Supreme Court despite the ASI having taken Mr. Fielden's opinion that that the facilitation centers necessitated "cutting through."

This kind of Site Management Plan was formulated and approved by the ASI probably due to two reasons. The Plan while referring to a number of international charters and conventions did not mention Art. 29 of the Constitution anywhere. So the persons connected to the monument culturally and/or economically figure nowhere in the making of this Plan.

Secondly, culture seemed to be farthest from the minds of those associated with the Plan. Page 49 of the Plan made it clear that the whole idea behind the plan was the Taj Mahal as "an attraction for high-spending international tourists." As p.66 shows the focus was the visitor or the tourist not the monument's serenity and sanctity. The monument was to be disciplined instead of the visitor. This is justifiable logic for a hotel group or industry. But it is legally impermissible logic for the ASI

---

[12] For Europeanisation of gardens see p.16, Dylan.
[13] p.101, Ebba Koch.

charged constitutionally with the duty to protect the notified monument. From an ancient Taj Mahal of serene, funerary architecture to a new Taj of modern toilets seemed to be ASI's idea of conservation, preservation and protection of ancient monuments of national importance.

16.2.14 Undisclosed Entrance Construction without Exit

In the meantime on Nov 25, 2004 the Monitoring Committee was directed by the Supreme Court in I.A. 426 of 2004 in I.A. 69 in CWP 13381/84 to report compliance by all the authorities concerned with the Taj mahal night viewing order passed by it on the application of the Uttar Pradesh Government to permit night viewing of the Taj Mahal. The order contained detailed instructions on publicity, tickets, tourists and security. In this the ASI filed an affidavit of its D-G dated October 6, 2004 stating that security facilities like the x ray machine can "only be done after establishing the Facilitation Centre as submitted to this Hon'ble Court on an earlier occasion". The "earlier occasion" was the affidavit dated February 5, 2002, of the earlier DG in I.A. 111.

Hence once again the ASI sought to do two things which were not part of the I.A. 426 in I.A. 69 in C.W.P. 13381/84 on night viewing proceedings. Firstly, it now introduced the Facilitation Centre idea in night view proceedings after having made it earlier in I.A. 111 as part of Taj security proceedings. Secondly, it did not disclose what it had already done concerning the Facilitation Centre since 2001, including its proposal to break the walls and that it had already gone ahead with the actual construction of the Facilitation Centres and expanded its proposal from one to two such Centres in both the khwaspuras of the Taj Mahal complex.

16.2.15 Supreme Court Saves the Taj Mahal Complex

The Monitoring Committee was viewing the Taj by night to ensure compliance with the Supreme Court directions. It queried about the security equipment lying idle in the ASI Taj Mahal premises when the CISF actually needed the same. It reported on this and what it discovered in Dec 2004 in the Monitoring Committee report to the court as follows:

"Even for the frisking and physical checking the CISF is handicapped because the advanced equipment CCTV and Multi-zone Door Frame Metal Detector purchased for this purpose is lying idle.

The reason for this seems to be that under the private MOU with the Tata business group a contractor is supposed to be making a Facilitation Centre in the Taj for the final installation of this equipment. It is not understood as to how construction is going on in the monument premises." However the Supreme Court did not call the ASI to account on this part of the report.

But by now the Monitoring Committee on the basis of its contacts with several employees of ASI was sure that the ASI intended to break the walls for the egress of persons in the Eastern Gate Facilitation Centre. Hence on Feb 14, 2005 when issues of compliance with night viewing orders came up in IA426–427, the Supreme Court asked about the Facilitation Centre. The amicus mentioned that the ASI was planning to break the walls of the Khawasspura on the Eastern side of the Taj Mahal Complex for egress of visitors from the Facilitation Centre which it had completed without informing this court.

The court then ordered: "The order passed by this court on 25.11.2004 (night viewing) will continue for one year subject to the following: That the parties will comply with the directions if not already complied with. It is being made clear that Archaeological Survey of India shall start the Facilitation Centre as soon as possible but not later than two months from today. However, we make it clear that under no circumstances will any portion of the boundary of the Taj be interfered with without the leave of this court. Whatever norms are being followed by Archaeological Survey of India at present will continue to be followed."

16.2.16 *Helpless Disclosure by ASI*

The Supreme Court order saved the cultural property of the Taj from being violated brazenly by the ASI and hence stopped the breaking of the internal wall (mis-described as "boundary" in the Supreme Court's order, but clearly understood by the ASI and others present in the proceedings, to be the internal wall) for one Facilitation Centre at the Eastern Gate which had already been built without informing the Supreme Court…

This was so understood because the boundary wall made no sense in the context of the Khwassparas and the Facilitation Centre. The order effectively prevented the ASI from taking advantage of its conduct of assuming the sanction of the court for the kind of Facilitation Centres it was building for tourism without any care for its fundamental obligation to culture, since without an egress the Centre was useless.

However, an undeterred ASI treated the order as being a sanction for its other Facilitation Centre at the Western Gate which it had started without informing the court and without any sanction for the kind of Centre it was constructing. The covert operations of the ASI inside the Taj Mahal had become overt. It had failed in its attempt to present the court with a fait accompli. In terms of the court order, now it had to take its prior permission before it could operationalise the Facilitation Centres by breaking the internal walls of the Eastern and Western Khawasspuras inside the Taj complex, the whole of which is a protected monument under the Ancient Monuments Act, 1958.

Accordingly, the ASI, now left with no choice, filed I.A. 444 of 2005 dated Sept 13, 2005 praying that in terms of the plans annexed it be permitted "to provide access into and outside the courtyards." The prayer itself was misconceived because it created the impression that the court had granted it the permission to break or cut the walls of the khwaspuras, called by the ASI as courtyards. The prayer did not state that access was to be provided by breaking the internal walls of the Khawasspuras and did not seek permission for such cutting or breaking.

16.2.17 Bridge of Half-Truths

But again the ASI application was based on half-truths. It relied on the affidavit of its DG in I.A. 111 of 2000 to state in Para 7 of its I.A. 444 of 2005 that the plans filed with the then DG's affidavit "contemplated the establishment of Facilitation Centres and Entry through Fatehabad Gate Courtyard on Eastern side and Fatehpuri Gate Courtyard on the Western side of the Monument," knowing that this was factually incorrect. The plan as stated by the ASI itself already in I.A. 111, showed only one Facilitation centre on the Eastern Side with the original Nursery being shown on the Western Side. The plan in I.A. 111 of 2000 showed no exit and no breaking of walls required for that purpose. But the ASI tried to use I.A. 111 of 2000 and the affidavit of it's the then DG to bridge what it had failed to state in that I.A. and affidavit and what it had done without informing the court. The ASI tried to do this bridging function, by putting in Para 7 in its I.A. 444 of 2005 and not filing the plan it had filed in I.A. 111 of 2000 along with the affidavit of the then DG and yet relying on the then DG's affidavit in I.A. 111 of 2000.

16.2.18 Culture Buried

It still chose to bury the cultural aspect of the Khawasspuras, where it had built its Facilitation Centres, by calling these "courtyards," and not explaining that the Khawasspuras were part of the notified Taj Mahal Complex which the ASI was constitutionally obliged to "protect" under Art. 49 and that such legally-mandated protection was not done by cutting up or breaking what one was supposed to protect. The entire theme song of the application was tourists and visitors.

It did not file the May 22, 2002 detailed estimates of its Superintending Archaeologist at Agra for Special Repairs to the Khawasspuras which the Director General had seen and transmitted to the TMCC for execution. A copy of the MOU for this purpose with the National Culture Fund and the Taj group of hotels company, the Indian Hotels Co. Ltd, was also not filed.

Thus, the Court had no facts at all as to what kind of Facilitation centres with what kind of alterations to the notified cultural heritage it was supposed to protect, had been sought to be executed by the ASI.

The ASI did not file the March 2003 Site Management Report which would have shown the toilets and other modern facilities sought to be put into the Khawasspuras, sought to be converted into Facilitation Centres through Special Repairs.

All this was sought to be bridged by filing the two page letter dated Sept 7, 2002 of one Sir Bernard Fielden director emeritus of the ICCROM approving the plans of ASI to cut through the Khawasspuras to access the outer courtyards.

16.2.19 ASI's Truth, but Not the Whole Truth

Now in this I.A. 444 of 2005 the ASI for the first time, left with no option but to take the permission of the court in view of its Feb 14, 2005 order against touching any part of wall of the Taj without its permission, stated in Para 14 that for visitors entering the already constructed Facilitation Centre on the East or the Fatehabad Gate, "an access by opening a wall on the western side of the court yard" will have to be provided. Similarly in Para 15 for visitors entering from the Western or Fatehpuri Gate "an opening is envisaged by cutting a portion of the western wall."

Once again the priority was "visitors" not the constitutional and legal priority of conserving the ancient monument of national importance. But once again what was being stated in the I.A. under the September 13, 2005 affidavit of the Assistant Director of Monuments, ASI, was not shown in the plans annexed to the I.A., namely, the precise internal walls and the point/s on these internal walls that were proposed to be cut to provide an egress for tourists/visitors who entered the Facilitation Centre/s.

The petition also marked a significant departure as to the person filing the affidavits. It was no longer the Director General ASI as in the previous IAs. It was not even the Director (Monuments). The responsibility was sought to be thrust on a lower level official, the Assistant Director, under the Director General and the Director. The Annexures A1 and A2 to the petition, which did not show what was stated in Paras 14 and 15 of the I.A., were by the Taj Conservation Collaborative shown to be consisting of a private "Art Heritage Consultant," a private "conservation consultant" and a private "conservation architect" forming part of the Taj Conservation Collaborative. These persons did not file any affidavit about these annexures. The Assistant Director Monuments simply stated that the annexures are true copies of the originals without mentioning anything about their correctness. This legal strategy ensured that no one could possibly be held responsible on the difference between the content of the I.A. in Paras 14 and 15 on the one hand and the annexures on the other, which did not show anywhere the cutting in the walls of the Taj mentioned in Paras 14 and 15.

The ASI did not explain anywhere as to why, for a monument under its constitutional and legal protection, it chose to file these annexures of the Taj Conservation Collaborative, instead of its own annexures under the signature of its own officers.

16.2.20 SC's Committee Offers a Solution

The Facilitation Centres were a fait accompli. But they were dead modernized Centres in the notified area of the protected monument, the Taj Mahal complex, being without exits, to reach the Taj marble monument, for the visitors collected in these Centres. The ASI's priority was visitors or tourism and tourists, not the protection of the ancient monument. The question therefore was whether there was an alternative to ensure genuinely comfortable and secure environment to visitors, in terms of an Art. 29 citizens fundamental right approach, by examining who were the prime stakeholders in the primary constitutional function of the Union Ministry of Culture under Art. 49 to protect the monument.

This way within the constitutional framework, the Taj could be spared modern toilets in the Facilitation Centres within its notified complex for the daily 10–15,000 visitors, a new cultural experience over a wider area directly related to the Taj could be offered to the visitors and thereby also ameliorate the serious water, electricity and drainage problems of the population of around one lakh in the immediate vicinity of the Taj. The other issue was whether the Facilitation Centres, which the ASI had sought to ride on the shoulders of security, provided this security or its opposite.

The Amicus on October 19, 2006, suggested to the court during the hearing of I.A. 453 that alternative land/sites are available for accommodating the 10,000 or more visitors per day to the Taj while ensuring their actual security, comfort and contribution to the immediate local population. The Supreme Court directed the amicus as the court commissioner to proceed with the court appointed monitoring committee and submit a report to it.

In compliance with this order the monitoring committee was in Agra on October 22 and 23, 2006. It submitted the October 2006 report with copies to the ASI and others, suggesting the alternative sites.

16.2.21 Committee's People & Culture Approach

The Committee report says that it approached the problem or the task by looking at the protected monument, the Taj Mahal, from three points of view.

Firstly, that the notified Taj Mahal complex is not a stand-alone monument. It is a part of the areas in its immediate vicinity at its three entrances from the city — East Gate or Fatehabad entry, West Gate or Fatehpuri entry and the South Gate entry. These are historic areas[14] called Katras, coeval with the notified protected monument complex, having a population of over one lakh.

Secondly, the visitors to the Taj must have an enjoyable experience starting with the buying of tickets for entry and then the entry to the Taj Mahal complex itself. This means that they should not be made to wait in the scorching sun, rain, dust storm or in biting cold during summer, monsoon or winter seasons, for hours together in a queue, after the purchase of a ticket, without any place to sit or to have snacks with their children or families. This necessarily implied a waiting area for ticket holders outside the Taj complex and not inside as the ASI was seeking to do through the Facilitation Centres within the Eastern and Western gate Khawasspuras.

Thirdly, security should be ensured of the monument and the visitors with the minimum fuss both outside and inside the monument by regulating the maximum number of entrants or sale of tickets and staggering their entry after the purchase of the ticket.

With this three-fold objective in mind, the Committee inspected the historic areas around the notified Taj Mahal complex. The logic for doing this is best described in its own words in Para 1.3 of its report. This was done to find out the connection to the protected monument of those living in these Katras and of the nullahs, the paths and the staircases leading from the Katras to the gates of the Taj. These nullahs, paths and staircases right till the monument's gate are probably as old as the monument.

---

[14] *Supra* Chapter on "Correlation to History and Geography."

Para 1.3 then explains: "It meant meeting the people in these historic areas who are the stakeholders in anything that is done for the Taj Mahal and whose own lives must be made meaningful in terms of what is done for the Taj Mahal, by providing them basic amenities like water, sewage and electricity. A welcome environment and a happy tourist cannot result from unhappy stakeholders. It also required the Committee to interact actively with the Archaeological Survey of India, Agra and the security agencies, since the professional technical input can come only from the ground experience of the officers of these two agencies regarding the value of what Agra has in terms of its history and the protection of this value. Finally it required the Committee to physically inspect and measure the various land areas where facilities could be set up for visitors and security could be ensured while safeguarding local livelihoods."

The report pointed out that ASI should have done this work of inspecting and detailing the Katras, recording the oral history and collecting the ancient documents/objects available with some of the oldest families in the Katras, as part of its constitutional duty to protect the monument.

16.2.22 Committee's Alternative to ASI's Facilitation Centres

Accompanied by the Superintending Archaeologist, the Deputy Commandant CISF incharge of the monument's security, the local police chowki incharge, the ASI engineer and officials of the Agra Development Authority, the Committee located two sites as alternatives outside the protected monument complex, as alternatives to the ASI's Facilitation Centres within the monument complex. The first site at the Western Gate entry was that of the ample lawns and space around the Central Government's ITDC restaurant, hardly one hundred metres from the Gate. The land in between the Western Gate and the restaurant of barely hundred metres could be taken over by the Central Government under the Ancient Monuments Act as land adjacent to the protected monument and necessary for its protection, after consultation with the State Government. Since both the ITDC restaurant and the Taj Mahal notified complex were under the same Union Ministry, the takeover of the land would not be difficult.

This would give a comfortable space to the waiting visitors and their families, including the lawns, with the existing restaurant available for snacks and food. The two existing kiosks were to be shifted into the lawns for the convenience of the visitors and so the livelihoods of the owners of these kiosks would not be affected. The Western Gate ticket counter, illegally created in the wall of the notified Taj Mahal complex and having no space for the large numbers wanting to buy the tickets, could be shifted to this area along with creation of lockers for keeping the prohibited items and possessions of the visitors securely and safely.

The first search of the visitors here with metal detector doors and X-Ray machines, before entry to this area would have resulted in the collection of the prohibited items not allowed inside the Taj Mahal complex. Since the visitors would now go empty handed and minus all prohibited items, to the Western entry gate to the Taj complex, a second search before the entry at the West gate would be formal and quick as the visitors would be having nothing to delay or derail the process. This ensured a double security check and kept the waiting visitors away from the monument till their entry.

Similarly, on the Eastern Gate side the Committee found an area of two acres which had been given by the Uttar Pradesh government, under Supreme Court orders, to its Forest department as a green belt around the notified Taj complex. This land was also about hundred metres from the Eastern Gate. The land was covered with naturally growing shrubs and was being used as an open defecation area even though there was a nominally charging Sulabh Shauchalya available to the residents around this land. The same arrangements as suggested for the Western Gate would be organized on this land and the Eastern gate ticket office, illegally created in the wall of the notified complex, would be shifted to this land. The same benefits would be there as stated for the Western Gate. Since unlike the Western Gate area there is no restaurant here, a waiting or holding area would have to be created with provision for snacks, food and toilets, apart from the security arrangements. Again the land between this area and the Eastern Gate could be acquired by the Union Government in consultation with the State Government.

Both these waiting areas at the Western and Eastern Gates, outside the protected monument of the Taj Mahal Complex, could have audio visual facilities, business communication centres and digital display showing the ticket numbers that could proceed to the entry gate.

The South Gate lane which is adjacent to the Taj Complex boundary and which is the only gate that leads directly to the historic Katras surrounding the Taj complex, was a centre of illegality. The Agra Development Authority had allowed construction of commercial complexes and temples which blocked the view of the South Gate. The Agra Development Authority had not formulated any height and width restrictions even for these illegal new buildings. With the help of the accompanying officials the Committee found space next to the ticketing centre for the South Gate for the visitors to wait after buying the ticket and undergo security checks, as the ASI has vacant rooms on either side of the ticketing centre. This space is also outside the protected monument of the Taj Mahal complex.

The Committee requested that the court may direct the ASI to prepare detailed project report for the sites mentioned above and undertake construction only after permission of the court.

The Committee then gave details about the katras – Omur Khan, Resham, Jogidas and Pholail – which are older than the Taj Mahal and the ancient gates of which have been declared by the ASI as monuments of national importance by putting up the ASI plaques on these gates. On the basis of several interviews the Committee recorded the rich history of these Katras, the historical religious places within them and the historical documents in the private collections. The Committee suggested that the ASI act to preserve all this which has a direct nexus to the Taj Mahal notified complex.

The Committee reported to the court that on the basis of the official documents collected by it from the chief chemist and other officials of the Jal Sansthan, Agra, toxic water was being supplied by the Jal Sansthan and that in the absence of electricity the Katras used diesel generators. This information available to the Jan Sansthan from its own reports was not told to the residents of Agra who would be drinking and using this water supplied to them through the pipelines.

The Mission Management Board under the Chief Secretary of Uttar Pradesh, meant to deal with these infrastructure issues, had done nothing about these problems, which created pollution in the immediate vicinity of the notified Taj Mahal Complex. For this purpose the Board is funded by the Central Government specifically for the protection of the Taj Mahal notified complex, the Agra Heritage fund under the U.P Tourism Department meant for projects to protect the Taj Mahal to promote tourism, the statutory Agra Development Authority and the Taj Trapezium Authority empowered by the Environment Protection Act, 1986 under the Commissioner Agra. The notified complex it was pointed out is hardly hundred metres away from these Katras. Yet the aforesaid authorities had not even bothered to introduce solar energy in these Katras to save the notified complex from the regular pollution of the diesel generators which the inhabitants are compelled to use. Similarly the sewage lines laid under the Centrally-funded Yamuna Action plan were non-functional. The health of the people around the Taj Mahal and that of the Taj Mahal was tied together.

The Committee after traveling around the old nullahs and the underground staircases of red sandstone leading from these katras directly to the gate of the Taj Mahal, found that the local police in terms of security had no idea about these routes.

16.2.23 ASI Sticks to Its Facilitation Centres

The Supreme Court directed the ASI to respond to this report. The ASI called a meeting under its Director General at Agra with several officials. The Court was informed that the proposals in the Committee's report were not possible since the areas suggested and their distance from the Taj complex gates could not be "sanitised". Instead of dealing with the integrated report that had tried for a congruence between local livelihoods, security of the monument and tourist plus tourist comfort, only this objection was taken in addition to pointing out the Supreme Court's order prohibiting construction within 200 metres from the Taj. It reiterated the Facilitation Centres which had already been constructed by it fully on the Eastern side and partly on the Western side and which admittedly were of no use till the internal walls of the notified complex were broken to allow the visitors to exit from these Centres and move towards the main Taj Mahal monument.

16.2.24 SC's Mysterious Silence

On the basis of the report prepared by the Monitoring Committee on the directions of the Supreme Court, the Committee had sought that the court may direct the ASI: to prepare a detailed project report for the land areas located by the Committee by combining local livelihoods, security of the monument and the tourist as also tourist comfort. These areas would hold the tourists outside the notified monument complex in a larger, more open area and not inside the complex as the ASI's Facilitation Centres would do. Another direction sought was that the ASI submit a conservation plan for the katras around the Taj complex as also a project for recording the rich oral history available among the residents of these Katras, while preserving ancient documents available in the Katras by encouraging private local initiatives which the well-educated and well earning residents were prepared to do. A direction was sought to the Mission Management Board and the Taj Trapezium Authority for ensuring uninterrupted electricity supply to the Taj Ganj area surrounding the notified complex, to prepare an incentive scheme for adoption of inverters in place of the diesel generators used by those in Tajganj and a project on solar energy supply to reduce diesel generator use.

Lastly the Jal Sansthan, Agra be directed to restore the readily available Taj Ganj tank for supplying water to the over one lakh population which was now being admittedly supplied toxic piped water by the Agra Jal Sansthan, as per the data of its own chief chemist which was annexed to the Monitoring Committee report, and to at least inform the residents using this water for drinking purposes.

However, for reasons best known to it, the report which the Supreme Court itself had sought was not taken up by the Supreme Court for considering these specific directions that had been sought.

16.2.25 The Whole Truth from ASI

The ASI, seeing that no orders were forthcoming from the Supreme Court, on its I.A. 444 for enabling it to break the internal walls and provide exits from the Facilitation Centres constructed by it, then filed I.A. 474 of 2008, practically seeking to replace its earlier pending I.A. 444 of 2005 in which it had suppressed, as pointed out already, several relevant documents and facts. The new I.A. seemed to have been filed by the ASI for two reasons.

Firstly, it increased the number of places where the internal walls of the notified Taj Mahal complex were to be broken for using the Facilitation Centres. In para 19 it stated that two doorways were required to be opened and in Para 20 it stated that two doorways for exit (and hence for breaking of the internal walls) were required in the Eastern Gate facilitation centre with three breaking points of the internal walls for the three doorways for the Western Gate Faciltation Centre. It now declared that the Eastern Gate Facilitation Centre had been completed by calling the construction as "repairs" of the Gaushala (cow-pen) which it had been admittedly maintaining within the notified complex. In Para 12 ASI had stated that the "Gaushala" was developed into a Facilitation Centre at a cost of Rs. 1.25 crores".

The ASI did not explain anywhere in this I.A. or in the earlier ones as to how it was maintaining a cow pen inside the notified Taj Mahal complex under the Ancient Monuments Act, 1948, which along with Art. 49 of the Constitution mandated it to protect the notified monument in its original form. The ASI also did not explain as to how it had done construction within the notified complex when there was a Supreme Court order prohibiting all construction even within two hundred metres of the perimeter of the notified complex. It also did not explain how the Western Gate Facilitation Centre "restoration" had been started within the notified complex and which it now stated had been put on hold after the Court's order dated October 19, 2006 recording ASI's undertaking that "we are assured that no construction/breaking up of any wall would be carried out without express leave of this court."

The second reason seems to be put belatedly on record that the Supreme Court order, that any portion of the boundary wall of the Taj will not be touched was passed on a "false allegation." The attempt was to play on the mistaken use of the word "boundary" instead of "internal" in the order and thereby show by inference that the order was based on misapprehension. But the ASI clearly understood what the court order meant and had on October 19, 2006 given the undertaking to the court after admitting that its Facilitation Centre was nearing completion. The attempt seemed to be that the Supreme Court being a court of record, the ASI now could try to take away the factual basis of the Supreme Court's order. In any event there was no explanation as to why the ASI never moved an application before the court for a correction of this Feb 14, 2005 order which it was now questioning indirectly after more than three years, in the new I.A. 474 filed by it on May 9, 2008 and in which again it was not praying for a correction of this order.

The reason for raising a grievance on the basis that the Supreme Court had passed the Feb14, 2005 order on the basis of a false allegation and not praying for correction of the order was probably two fold.

Firstly, the Feb 14, 2005 order did not record any statement or allegation at all for passing the order: "It is being made clear that the Archaeological Survey of India shall start the facilitation centre as soon as possible but not later than two months from today. However, we make it clear that under no circumstances will any portion of the boundary of the Taj be interfered with without the leave of this court." So ASI would have been put to the arduous task of showing how it was stating that the order had been passed on a false allegation.

Secondly, it would have no explanation for the October 19, 2006 undertaking recorded by the court that ASI will not break down any wall of the notified Taj Mahal complex.

16.2.26 ASI's Novel Pleadings & Suppression

This was a new style of pleading by the ASI – of throwing doubt on a Supreme Court order by mentioning it in the body of the interim application without showing any basis for this and then not seeking any relief in the prayers against the order, while seeking the main relief of being allowed to break the walls and create exits for the Facilitation Centres constructed by it so as to completely alter its undertaking to the court, without stating that such an alteration in the undertaking was being sought or that the undertaking was now sought to be withdrawn.

16.2.27 Hiding UNESCO & ICOMOS Letters

Worse as in the earlier I.A. wherein it had suppressed from the court the relevant internal documents of the ASI itself on the Facilitation Centres, it suppressed the fact that it had obtained, vide letter WHC/APA/07/04/SF/SZ, dated January 16, 2007 addressed to Ambassador and India's Permanent Delegate to UNESCO, from Francesco Bandarin, "The position of the UNESCO World Heritage Centre and the International Council of Monuments and Sites (ICOMOS)" on this breaking of the internal walls of the Khawasspuras for creating the exits for the Facilitation Centres made by converting these Khawasspuras within the notified monuments. The letter calls this "planned intervention" and stated that UNESCO World Heritage Centre and ICOMOS "strongly support this planned intervention."

The factual basis on which this position was being taken was revealed in Para 2 of the letter. This para stated that the Director General ASI had informed inter alia that "a door is foreseen to be created in a historic annex building at a distance of approximately 100 metres from the Taj Mahal." Hence the ASI conveyed to UNESCO that the Khawasspuras, for breaking the walls of which it was seeking permission from the Supreme Court, were a mere historic annex instead of being a part of the protected monument under the Ancient Monuments Act, ever since the notification by the British in pre independence India.

The mentioning of the fact that this planned intervention is one hundred metres from the Taj Mahal shows that the Khawasspuras were treated as something distinct and separate from the main monument mausoleum in marble. This is legally surprising since the letter states that the comprehensive plan of the ASI, of which this planned intervention is a part, "has been subject to rigorous internal and external review and has received broad approval." Either such reviews of UNESCO and ICOMOS ignore their own law governing the monument under consideration by them or they choose to ignore the domestic law. There is no reference in the letter to the Ancient Monuments Act, 1958, and the Taj complex notification of Pre-independence British India which continues even today as the legal foundation for protecting not the

Taj monument alone but the Taj monument complex mentioned in the notification. Surprisingly there is no mention also of the pending Supreme Court proceedings on this issue in terms of the I.As filed by the ASI itself. This may explain as to why the ASI did not reveal this letter or the record of its correspondence with UNESCO and ICOMOS to the Supreme Court.

Once again in this I.A. the ASI used the cover of security for the notified Taj Mahal complex to justify the Facilitation Centres, admittedly constructed by it within the complex without explaining as to which law permitted it to carry out such construction inside the complex. The Monitoring Committee report of October 2006 had pointed out that the Facilitation Centres would create a threat to the notified complex since they would create an attractive target to any mischief monger by confining hundreds of tourists within the bounded confines of such Centres having only one entry gate and the one exit gate now sought to be created by breaking the ancient walls of these Centres constructed by converting the very use of the Khwasspuras of the protected monument — from a place meant to house what the ASI chose to call 'servants' to a place for hundreds of tourists.

16.2.28 Twenty Minute Hearings

By now the Supreme Court thought it fit to fix only twenty minutes after lunch for dealing with the large number of I.As and issues concerning what it was monitoring since 1984, namely, the protection of the Taj Mahal monument complex under the Ancient Monuments Act, 1958. So now I.A. 474 came up only in July 2008.

16.2.29 Issues Defined: Another SC Committee

On July 14, 2008, the amicus requested the Supreme Court for a final hearing of I.A. 474 seeking again permission to break the internal walls for providing the exits to the Facilitation Centres created by it inside the notified Taj monument complex by re constructing the Khawasspuras. Both the amicus and the petitioner in person Mr. Mehta informed the court that no written response was required from them in the matter as the matter could be argued on the materials already on the record. The amicus indicated to the court that the basic issue was whether ASI's acts of constructing Facilitation Centres with modern toilets and kiosks by converting the heritage Khawasspuras which constituted part of the notified Taj Mahal monument complex and its proposed breaking of the walls of these khwasparas for providing exits to tourists in the Facilitation Centres, could be treated as acts to protect the monument under Art. 49 of the Constitution of India. The Supreme Court directed that the Monitoring Committee should submit a report to the court on the Facilitation Centres.

Only July 16, 2008 the amicus asked by a written application the Director General ASI to give copies of the documents listed therein concerning the Facilitation Centres. Only some of the documents were made available and that is how the amicus discovered the several documents that had not been revealed to the Supreme Court and which have been mentioned above already.

This time the team for the inspection of the Facilitation Centres was not only the monitoring committee, but on the instructions of the Supreme Court, it consisted of the Amicus and Mr. Mehta, as the petitioner in person. The first visit of the team, on July 19, 2008, was with the Joint Director of ASI and his officials including the private conservation architect Mr. Navin Piplani who had supervised the construction of the Centres. The amicus with the petitioner in person and Mr. Piplani undertook a second inspection on August 21, 2008 by taking along with them the two members of the normal Monitoring Committee of the Supreme Court in these matters — a senior scientist, Dr. R.C. Trivedi and an additional director of the Central Pollution Control Board, Dr. S. Ghosh. The team submitted a two part report to the Supreme Court. The first part contained the report and the second part the photographic plates of the inspection of each of khwaspuras wherein the internal walls were proposed to be broken.

16.2.30 *Full Truth Tumbles Out*

The conservation architect had stated in the presence of the ASI officers that the Eastern Gate side or Fatehabad Facilitation Centre was being used as a Gaushala by the ASI. It was in a completely ruined and dilapidated condition. The Taj Collaborative as a part of the conservation programme had "restored" this place which used to be the place for the stay of the Khadims of the Taj Mahal, that is the servants and servers of the Taj Mahal.

Since this was being stated the team pointed out to Mr. Piplani, the ICOMOS Principles for the Recording of Monuments laid down by its eleventh General Assembly. This principle stated that recording of the physical configuration and condition at a point of time is an essential part of the conservation process. The team also pointed out Paras 22 and 24 of the Conservation Manual 1923 and of the Indian Archaeological Policy 1915 which pointed out the deplorable harm that can be done in the name of restoration. Accordingly, the team asked the conservation architect and the ASI officials to produce the following documents:

1. Showing that the Khawasspuras were being used as a place for the stay of the Khadims of the Taj Mahal. These were necessary since the team found that the cells, in the Khawasspuras in which the Khadims were supposed to have lived, were suffocating. None of these cells, both on the Eastern Gate side and the Western Gate or Fatehpur side, have any inlet/outlet for air in their walls or in the ceiling. The historical drawings of the Khawasspuras on the basis of which these had been "restored".
2. Inspection reports of the Khawasspuras showing their actual condition along with photographs of that condition before the restoration work was started.

None of these documents were produced.

The team in its inspection of the Eastern Gate Khawasspura found that the same had been fully constructed as was apparent from the new construction with planters placed in it. Then the conservation architect pointed out to the team the specific walls of the Khawasspuras which were intended to be "punctured" to provide an exit to the tourists collected inside each Khawasspura. It was found that the ASI intended to break the three walls of three cells of the eastern gate Khawasspura, after the conservation architect on being asked the meaning of the word "puncture" explained that the walls would be broken.

The first wall in a cell was a niche wherein the width of 0.89 metres and the height of 0.77 metres would be enlarged to 1.20 metres and 1.80 metres respectively. Since this would be the exit exclusively for the disabled tourists, a ramp would have to be built to permit them to enter the cell and reach the proposed exit. The second wall in another cell was to be broken to increase its width from 0.8 metres to 1.20 metres and its height from 0.67 metres to 1.80 metres. This exit would be for the general or able tourists. There is no air inlet or outlet in these cells.

The third wall in still another cell was an ancient lakhauri brick wall. This was to be broken to create an exit of 1.20 metres and a width of 1.80 metres. This was also for the general public, since the holding capacity of this Facilitation Centre would be 500 to 600 persons in its open area of 1727 square metres and two exits were thought to be necessary for these numbers.

At the exit of the cell for the disabled a ramp would have to be constructed above the lawn at the exit and continue till it meets the path from the present entry at the Eastern Gate. At the exit for the general public steps will have to be made and a path paved to enable them to go across the lawn to the path coming from the Eastern Gate. From here the tourists will proceed to the open-to sky forecourt, where tourists from all the three gates, the Eastern, Western and Southern gates mingle.

On the Western Gate side there is no separate entrance available as on the Eastern Gaushala side. So the tourists will enter through the normal entrance and then paved paths with steps will have to be made to allow the tourists to enter the two cells of the Khawasspura on the Western side. The cells are at a height of three feet from the ground. One cell will be exclusively for the disabled and the other for the general public. The first wall to be broken in a cell on this side to widen it from 0.8 metres to 1.20 metres and increase its height from 0.62 metres to 1.80 metres. In the second cell the wall will be broken to widen it from 0.8 metres to 1.20 metres and increase its height from 0.67 metres to 1.80 metres.

The tourists emerging from these cells, will have a choice of walking or the disabled travelling down this corridor in a wheel chair for a distance of 38 metres and then turning left to walk/travel a further distance of about thirty metres to reach the exit.

So after a walk or wheel chair travel of about sixty eight metres the tourists will reach where they would have reached directly from the normal or usual Western Gate entrance to the forecourt.

16.2.31 Findings of the SC Committee

The report pointed out that both the Centres seem to be futile and against the legal requirement of protection and preservation of the notified monument complex. Breaking walls and doing new construction not for the sake of the monument but for the sake of an official idea of facility for tourists cannot be part of protection and preservation of a monument. With the proposed provisioning of the two Centres by toilets, kiosks for snacks, audio visual materials and mementoes and air conditioned cells for exit, the authenticity of the monument is damaged. The monument is a royal funerary with tombs, gardens, a living masjid, and space to ensure peace and quiet amidst the waters of the Yamuna behind the monument complex. It is not a place for toilets catering to a daily tourist population of about ten thousand, kiosks and gathering of hundreds of persons in a confined space.

Changing the character and authenticity of one of the parts of the notified monument complex does not amount to preservation and protection of the complex under the Ancient Monuments Act, 1958.

The report pointed out that even from the security point of view it was futile to create these Facilitation Centres. The fundamental idea of the ASI that tourists should be protected from the elements after buying the ticket and then standing for hours with their families in long queues, especially on holidays, gets defeated. Each Centre can hold no more that 500 to 600 tourists in a confined area of about 1727 sq metres wherein there would be toilets, kiosks, coffee vending machines etc. The exits would allow only one person to go through at a time. There is no time limit on the stay of these tourists in the courtyard. With only five hundred tourists inside the majority of the tourists would still be waiting in a queue outside as at present.

The two security danger points, the tourist and the monument, get focused by confining five hundred tourists in a confined place, instead of their normal waiting outside the monument while being exposed to the elements and then walking in an open pathway to the forecourt.

Lastly, the report pointed out that an architectural tenet of the Taj Mahal monument complex is a bilateral symmetry on a vertical central axis in about 17 hectares of space enclosed on three sides by walls and by the Yamuna on the rear or the fourth side. This notified complex must be understood as one whole in which each part or component must be preserved, since the components add up to make the whole notified complex. Introducing a completely new bilateral symmetry of entrance but differential symmetry of exits with modern toilets and kiosks is to effectively de-notify these parts of the notified complex from the ambit of the protection and preservation of the notified monument which was declared a World Heritage on Oct 15, 1982.

16.2.32 ASI's Lingering Reply

When the ASI after several opportunities given to it did not file a reply to this inspection report and sought three weeks more time, the Supreme Court on March 16, 2009 allowed it the three weeks time after imposing costs on the ASI of Rs. 20,000/- to be paid to the Legal Services Authority. When the matter came up for hearing again the ASI counsel produced a receipt of Rs. 20,000/- showing that the money had been paid by him and not the ASI. The amicus pointed out that an order of costs of the Supreme Court could not be contracted out like this and the whole purpose of sending a message to the government department, in this case the ASI, would be lost. However, the Supreme Court told the amicus "How does this matter to you?" and proceeded to withdraw the order itself without any application, written or oral, by the ASI for such withdrawal, despite the amicus pointing out that the issue was not personal to the amicus but a question of the manner of institutional compliance with the orders of the Supreme Court. After this the Supreme Court did not list the inspection report for a hearing.

16.2.33 Another ASI Attempt & SC's Mysterious Silence

However, on April 16, 2009, the ASI filed another affidavit in I.A. 474 in I.A. 444 stating that as an interim measure the court permit it to operate the Eastern Gate Gaushala Facilitation Centre on a trial basis by using "wooden staircases" at the exits for the tourists. Implicit in this was that the internal walls be allowed to be broken for the exits in the Eastern Gate Khawasspura and instead of constructing stairs at the exits the ASI would place wooden steps.

The Amicus brought to the attention of the court the entire conduct of the ASI in this matter. The court had never in any order or proceeding suggested that a Facilitation Centre be built inside the notified monument complex or that it be built by demolishing the internal walls of the khwasparas which were a part of the notified monument complex and that this be done under the subterfuge of "conservation," "restoration" or "puncturing" of walls of the notified complex. This was in complete violation of ASI's own and internationally recognised principles of conservation of monuments especially for those which had been declared by UNESCO as a world heritage.

However, the constant attempt in the various IAs had been that no such Centre had been constructed, that it was constructed pursuant to court orders, that no walls of the notified monument will be broken for such centres, that walls will have to be broken for the already "developed" Centre on the Eastern Side and walls were proposed to be broken for the partially constructed Centre on the Western side.

The amicus pointed out that ASI's Horticulture Centre, right outside the notified complex, was available on the Western side for use instead of the Facilitation Centre but ASI still insisted on the Centre within the notified monument for the majority (about 65 percent) of the tourists visiting the monument and who enter from the Western gate of the notified monument.

This play with the court concluded by proposing wooden stairs at the exits presuming that internal walls could be broken. For reasons best known to it the court remained silent on this play by the ASI and did not consider the matter to be serious enough for a hearing.

16.2.34 Supreme Court Agrees to ASI's Underground Approach

On October 16, 2009, the ASI filed an affidavit with a CD and a large spiraled compilation printing the contents of the CD. This was a plan, incorporating elements from the various reports of the Monitoring Committee. It proposed visitors holding and security centres on the Eastern and Western Gates by demolishing the non-historic building of the ITDC restaurant on the West gate and the ASI's Horticulture office on the East Gate. After the demolition of the ITDC Centre a built up/holding area of 28,500 sq. ft. was proposed to be constructed seven feet above ground and going six feet below the ground. The portion above the ground would be camouflaged by landscaping. Similarly on the Eastern gate side after demolishing the ASI's Horticultural office, 28,500 square feet built up/holding area would be constructed partly over and partly underground with camouflage landscaping. It sought the court's permission to do this. The court on Dec 7, 2009 ordered the ASI to arrange for a visual demonstration on Jan 11, 2010 at 2.00 p.m. in the Judges Lounge.

The Amicus filed his objections to ASI's proposal on the grounds of security in an underground complex given the past history of breaches of security of the notified monument, hygiene in an underground complex where eateries would function with toilets for a large number of tourists and a complete change in the approach to the notified monument complex, which would totally alter the visual of the monument complex.

However, after the audio visual presentation by the Director General of ASI, the court on Jan 18, 2010 granted an in-principle approval to ASI's plan, but declared that no construction will take place till the project reports are submitted by the ASI to the court. Notice was directed to be issued to ITDC whose restaurant property was proposed to be demolished and the matter was directed for hearing on March 8, 2010.

In March 2010 ITDC filed its response stating that the proposal can go ahead provided the ownership of the land of the restaurant below the ground remains with the ITDC, the existing three souvenir shops are allowed to continue under ITDC either on the western or the eastern gate, the project must be time bound and additional toilet facilities more than the proposed ones for twenty tourists only at a time were needed.

After this no hearing was held on these proposals. The Union Government has so far not acted on this proposal for which it obtained an in-principle clearance from the Supreme Court.

Chapter XVII

JUDICIALLY PROTECTING MONUMENTS WITHOUT REFERENCE TO ANY LAW

In the case of Secretary and Curator, Victoria Memorial Hall vs. Howrah Ganatantrik Nagrik Samity,[1] the Supreme Court recognized and created a new type of monument called "Historical Monument" and declared its protection without any reference whatsoever to the Ancient Monuments Act, 1958 or Art. 49 of the Directive Principles. The category created and recognized by the Supreme Court, concerned the Victoria Memorial Hall in Calcutta, was new since the judgment nowhere stated that the monument was one of national importance which had to be protected by the State under Art. 49 of the Constitution.

17.1 Victoria Memorial Hall Case

The Supreme Court went further to formulate a new test for permitting construction within the Victoria Memorial Hall complex by stating that the question was whether permitting such construction would "by any means hamper the preservation and protection of the monument." So far, only those monuments had been given protection of the State which in terms of Art. 49 had to be declared to be Monuments of National Importance by or under a law made by Parliament. The only law made by Parliament for the purpose of Art. 49 is the Ancient Monuments Act, 1958. The Supreme Court nowhere in the judgment stated that the Victoria Memorial Hall had been declared a Monument of National Importance and therefore it was required to be protected by the State.

---

[1] Secretary and Curator, Victoria Memorial Hall vs. Howrah Ganatantrik Nagrik Samity, (2010) 3 SCC 732.

The question therefore that arises from the Supreme Court judgment is whether the Art. 49 principle for protection of monuments can be extended to structures like the Victoria Memorial Hall by declaring it to be a "Historical Monument" even though it is not shown anywhere in the judgment that the structure is a monument of national importance under the Ancient Monuments Act, 1958. The Supreme Court seems to have acted completely de hors Art. 49 and the Ancient Monuments Act, 1958.

On September 12, 2011, the Supreme Court in Friends of Victoria Memorial vs. Howrah Gantantrik Nagrik Samity passed an order in which it took jurisdiction over the monument because of its "Beautiful Architecture and Green Surroundings" The order nowhere stated as to the material on the record from which the court had concluded about the "beautiful architecture" of the Victoria Memorial Hall. The order relied on no provision of law or any facts whatsoever.

However, the Supreme Court seemed to continue either passing no orders concerning national monuments or doing so without any reference to any law whatsoever.

This becomes self-evident from two cases:

17.2 Baljeet Singh Malik vs. Delhi Golf Club[2]

The Lal Bangla in the Delhi Golf Club was a monument of national importance, according to the ASI. But no orders were passed for reporting its condition to the court.

17.3 Wasim Ahmad Saeed vs. Union of India[3]

In reference to the film shooting permitted by the ASI inside the mosque and the dargah of the nationally protected monument, Fatehpur Sikri, the Supreme Court directed that no such activity which is not connected with the affairs of the Jama Masjid or the Dargah should be permitted

---

[2] 1997 (1) SCALE (S.P.) 19.

[3] Wasim Ahmad Saeed vs. Union of India, 1997 (5) SCALE 451.
 Case concerning the Dargah and Shrine of Sheikh Salim Chisti and Fatehpur Sikri, Agra.

by the ASI inside the Mosque or the Dargah till further orders. The Supreme Court also directed alternative sites for the shopkeepers at the monument but there was no reference to any Act or law.

17.4 M.C. Mehta vs. Archaeological Survey of India[4]

The Supreme Court directed a befitting monument in the memory of Ghalib to be built on his tomb and ordered restoration of the grave of the poet Zauq which was buried under the M.C.D. toilets. The Supreme Court passed these orders without associating the ASI and without mentioning any law whatsoever as the basis for its orders. It observed "the least to say, it is highly defamatory and an utter disgrace to a great poet like Zauq who gave immortal poetry to the country. It is a pitty that poets like Ghalib and Zauq who brought glory to the country are being dealt with in such a shabby manner. The Supreme Court now extended its jurisdiction to making prima facie declarations of whether a monument was a nationally protected monument or not. This function has been given to the Union Government under the Ancient Monuments Act, 1958.

17.5 Wasim Ahmad Saeed vs. Union of India[5]

The Supreme Court directed ASI to start repair work at the Dargah and Shrine of Sheikh Chishti at Fatehpur Sikri, Agra which is a World Heritage and a monument of national importance.

17.6 Wasim Ahmad Saeed vs. Union of India[6]

The Supreme Court gave directions on the repair programme of ASI as also licenses to guides and photographers. The Court indicated that the

---

[4] M.C. Mehta vs. Archaeological Survey of India 1996 (8) SCALE (S.P.) 11.

Where the Supeme Court declared that prima facie it was of the view that the whole Nizamuddin Complex, Delhi should be declared a National Protected Monument in the context of Ghalib's Tomb.

[5] 1996 (1) SCALE (S.P.) 19.

[6] Wasim Ahmad Saeed vs. Union of India, 1996 (6) SCALE (S.P.) 11.

basis of its jurisdiction was not any law but "a broad consensus between the ASI and the Waqf Board in respect of the directions."

17.7 M.C. Mehta vs. Union of India[7]

The Supreme Court directed the Union Ministry of Environment and Forest and the U.P, Govt. to come out with a scheme to shift out all polluting industries in the Taj Trapezium Zone and it framed questions for a positive response from the "new Minister of Environment & Forests, Rajesh Pilot." Ministers are not the authorities mentioned in the environmental law Acts. The Court did not ask the notified and the constituted Taj Trapezium Authority[8] to prepare the scheme.

17.8 M.C. Mehta vs. Union of India[9]

The construction of the Mumtaz Mahal hotel, a few feet from the rear of the Taj Mahal complex was stopped by the Supreme Court till further orders. No legal basis was stated in the order.

17.9 M.C. Mehta vs. Union of India[10]

The Supreme Court issued notice to the then Union Minister of Environment and Forest, Kamal Nath and other officers of MoEF to show cause as to why they be not be held guilty of contempt of court concerning the implementation of orders for a green belt in the Taj Mahal area. The Supreme Court extended its orders from the Taj Mahal area to the Agra city by declaring that "apart from the Taj Mahal, the city is also to be made beautiful and attractive." The Supreme Court

---

[7] M.C. Mehta vs. Union of India, 1996 (1) SCALE (S.P.) 16.

[8] *The Taj Trapezium Zone (TTZ) Authority was constituted by the May 17, 1999 order under Section 3(1)(3) of Environment Protection Act, 19996 by the Union Ministry of Environment. It was headed by the Commissioner Agra Division. It was reconstituted on 30/04/2003 to be headed by the Principal Secretary Environment Uttar Pradesh.*

[9] M.C. Mehta vs. Union of India, 1996 (2) SCALE (S.P.) 88.

[10] M.C. Mehta vs. Union of India, 1996 (3) SCALE (S.P.) 56.

extended its jurisdiction from the protection of nationally important monuments to making cities beautiful and attractive, without stating any legal basis for it whatsoever. On what legal basis the orders were extended from monuments to the city remains unknown. The issue of Agra being declared as a Heritage city, wherein the Union Government has stated before the Court that the necessary requirements for this are absent from the city, is pending in the Supreme Court.

Chapter XVIII
PROTECTING MONUMENTS: ROLE OF HIGH COURTS

An examination of the judgments of various High Courts on the issue of protection of monuments under Art. 49 of the Constitution and under the Ancient Monuments Act, 1958, shows that no High Court adopted the cultural heritage approach required by the Fundamental Right under Art. 29 of the Constitution as also by Art. 51A(f) as Fundamental Duty, since March 1, 1977. The Delhi High Court, the Orissa High Court and the Calcutta High Court judgments clearly show this. The Supreme Court also did not refer to or apply the Cultural Heritage Approach in any of the appeals from the judgments of some of these High Courts.

18.1 Siri Fort Wall

In V.P. Singh vs. Union of India,[1] a prayer was made to the court to stop the vandalism of the Siri Fort wall and area in Delhi, since the wall was a protected monument under the Ancient Monuments Act, 1904. The vandalism complained of concerned the construction of a Delhi Development Authority officer's club and a banquet hall in the Asiad tower within the prohibited area of 100 metres from the protected monument.[2] The High Court censured the ASI by declaring that it had been failing in its duty and had woken up from slumber after the damage to a Protected Monument had been done. It also pointed out that the ASI was silent about the DDA officers club admittedly constructed within 100 metres of the site of the historic wall after the notification banning

---

[1] V.P. Singh vs. Union of India, (2003) 102 DLT 72.

[2] *On May 15, 1991, a notification was issued under Rule 32 of Ancient Monuments Act, 1958 stating that no construction activity was permissible with 100 metres of a protected Monument and that within 200 metres it could only be undertaken with the permission of the ASI.*

such construction. Yet, the High Court left it to the ASI to decide the question whether there is a wall or not and then to decide whether prima facie the DDA officers club was in violation of the law. Further, it directed the DDA to pass an order of demolition in case the construction was in violation of the law, without noting that no such demolition power had been given to the ASI under the Ancient Monuments Act, 1958. Hence, the court left issues to be decided by the very agency which it declared had failed to protect the monument. The court never thought it necessary to find out if the ASI had filed an FIR against the DDA officers club with the Delhi Police and as to why the affidavit of the Commissioner of Police before it did not state anything about this issue.

18.2 Bade and Chote Khan

In Ashok Kumar vs. Union of India and Ors[3] concerning construction within the prohibited area of 100 metres from the tombs of Bade Khan and Chote Khan, declared as Protected Monument under the 1904 Act, the High Court did not ask the ASI for an explanation as to why it had kept quiet about this construction till 2003.

18.3 Red Fort Meena Bazar

The case of Sudhir Goyal vs. Municipal Corporation of Delhi[4] concerned the shops on lease or license from the MCD and the Union Ministry of Defence in the Meena Bazaar of the Red Fort complex, Delhi. The Red Fort had been declared a Protected Monument under the Ancient Monuments Act, 1958 vide a notification dated July 31, 2002. The shopkeepers had challenged the eviction notices issued to them by the Union Ministry of Defence and the MCD on the ground that the Meena Bazaar was a part of heritage of Red Fort and the goods they were selling represented the Indian cultural heritage and ethnic values. Accordingly, the High Court held that the removal of the Meena Bazaar would be contrary to the intendment and very purpose of the Ancient Monuments

---

[3] Ashok Kumar vs. Union of India and Ors, (2004) 111 DLT 230.
[4] Sudhir Goyal vs. Municipal Corporation of Delhi, (2004) 112 DLT 249.

Act itself. The High Court relied on the Shahjahannama to point out the Meena Bazaar had been functioning for centuries in the Red Fort. It also relied on the Supreme Court judgment in Rajeev Mankotia vs. Secretary to the President of India[5] to hold that the Supreme Court itself was not adverse to the continuation of an activity that had been historically carried out in the monument in question.

The High Court never asked as to why the ASI had not initiated proper legal proceedings against the shopkeepers under the Ancient Monuments Act, 1958 and allowed instead the MCD to initiate eviction proceedings against the shopkeepers under the Public Premises (Eviction of Unauthorized Occupants) Act, 1971. The High Court specifically noted that the ASI had not challenged the findings of the Additional District Judge in the proceedings under the Public Premises Act that the Director General, ASI was not empowered by the Ancient Monuments Act to evict any person from the premises of a monument under the Act.

18.4 Church Cemetery

However, in Roseline Wilson vs. Union of India,[6] the High Court single judge did not examine the specific contention that the Ancient Monuments Act, 1958, did not empower the ASI to issue notices of eviction to those found in a protected monument and declared as encroachers within the protected area of the monument. The single judge also did not consider the specific contention that the protected monument in question, the Kishanganj Christian Church compound of the Protected Monument D-EREAMO Cemetery did not fall under the definition of Ancient Monument as given in 1958 Act.

18.5 Illegal Appellate Authority

In EMCA Construction Co. vs. Archaeological Survey of India,[7] the issue before the Court concerned construction within Prohibited Area

---

[5] Rajeev Mankotia vs. Secretary to the President of India (1997) 10 SCC 441.

[6] Roseline Wilson vs. Union of India, (2007) 139 DLT 462.

[7] EMCA Construction Co. vs. Archaeological Survey of India, (2009) 164 DLT 515.

of 100 metres from the Protected Monument of Humayun's Tomb. The High Court struck down the expert committee set up by the ASI as an Appellate Authority against orders made under the 100 metres (Prohibition of Construction) Rules, since the Committee had no legal basis whatsoever. The High Court referred to an earlier judgment of the same court in ASI vs. Narendra Anand[8] in which it had been suggested that a pragmatic balance between protection of monuments and development lies in the ASI reconsidering the 100 metres blanket prohibition against construction for a case-by-case approach.

18.6 Jantar Mantar, Delhi

The Narendra Anand judgment related to the Protected Monument, Jantar Mantar, in New Delhi. The Supreme Court in the Civil Appeal against the High Court judgment in the case of Narendra Anand set aside the High Court's suggestion for a reconsideration of the Central Govt.'s notification of June 16, 1992 imposing the blanket ban on construction within 100 metres of a Protected Monument, especially in view of the 2010 Validation Act[9] which converted the blanket ban imposed by a rule under the 1958 Act into a statutory provision, Section 20(A) in the Ancient Monuments Act, 1958.

18.7 Orissa: Churengagarh Fort

On March 9, 2011, the Orissa High Court dismissed the petition[10] of Orissa Industries Ltd. against the ASI for rejecting their proposal to construct commercial and residential buildings on unused vacant land of Orissa Industries where since 1949 it had been running two factory units. The rejection on 18/19 August 2009 by the Expert Advisory Committee of ASI was on the ground that the construction would take place within the Protected Area of the Protected Monument, the ancient

---

[8] ASI vs. Narendra Anand, (2007) 144 DLT 794.

[9] Ancient Monuments and Archaeological Sites and Remains (Amendment and Validation) Act, 2010.

[10] Writ Petition (C.) 20433/2009 (Orissa High Court).

fort at Churengagarh in the district of Puri and Cuttack. The fort was a Protected Monument under the Ancient Monuments Act, 1904 and then subsequently under the Ancient Monuments Act, 1958. The petition was dismissed on the basis of the Expert Advisory Committee records of reports, maps and other relevant documents. Nothing was stated in the order of the High Court as to what was there in these records due to which the petition had been dismissed.

An inspection of the records of the case showed that the High Court bench presided over by the then Chief Justice V. Gopala Gowda had completely ignored the following:

a. Permission could be refused only if the proposed construction was within the 100 metre no-construction zone from the Protected Monument. The Court's record showed that the superintending archaeologist had filed a detailed report which did not state the distance between the monuments and the site of the proposed construction. The report had two specific entries for showing this critical distance for determining whether the proposed construction fell within the 100 metres of the no construction zone. The first specific entry required the distance to be mentioned of the proposed construction from the monument. The second specific entry required the distance to be mentioned of the construction from the protected limit. Instead of mentioning any distance, the following statement had been put against the two specific entries – "not available (as it comes within the protected area)." The High Court completely ignored this strange report which showed a specific quantitative figure of measurement as not being available.

b. The High Court record further showed that this report at Page 86 of the case file had been sent on August 17, 2009, by the Superintending Archaeologist, A.K. Patel to the Expert Advisory Committee of ASI at New Delhi. The High Court record also contained a map dated 12 August 2009 filed by the Superintending Archeologist. This map stated that it was "not to scale" while showing the location plan of the proposed construction. This was also ignored by the High Court. The Court's order dismissing the petition completely ignored the "not to scale" map and consequently no question was asked as to why the map was not to scale and how the distance of the proposed construction site could be known or estimated in a not to scale map. This was more so in view of the fact as stated in (a) above that no quantitative measurement from the monument was mentioned against specific entries.

c. At Page 43 of the High Court record, there was a report of D.S. Consultants.[11] This was a surveyor's report which stated that the plots on which the construction was proposed were at a distance of more than 1,085 metres from the south-eastern point of the fortification wall of Churangagarh fort. Hence, the distance of the proposed construction site from the south-eastern point was far beyond the 100 metres no-construction zone. This document also was ignored by the High Court in its order dismissing the petition.

d. In light of the abovementioned documents, the question arises as to how the Expert Advisory Committee of ASI on 18 August 2009 came to the conclusion that the construction proposal is rejected since the construction is to take place within the Protected Area. However, since the High Court had ignored the abovementioned documents on the record before it, there was no question of the High Court asking the ASI to explain its conclusion.

---

[11] 502, Nilakantah Nagar, Nayapalli, Bhubaneshwar-751012.

Chapter XIX

AN ALTERNATIVE LEGAL APPROACH

We come to the end of our journey having analysed in detail the constitutional and statutory framework for the protection of monuments which is an obligation of the State under Art. 49 of the Constitution of India. The judicial implementation of this framework in the context of the operational judicial culture shows that the maximum judicial contribution has been by interim orders.

We have also examined the international legal framework to show how economic development has been recognized as the major threat to protection of monuments that ties in with our analysis of the kind of economic development adopted officially in India, its consequences on the lives of citizens and thereby the final consequence of monuments being torn out of their context and people being torn away from their monuments. The problem is the kind of city and the manner of creating it through the kind of economic development which brings only misery and illegality to the citizens in erstwhile colonial countries now launched on post-independence development. The Supreme Court and the High Courts have ignored this context in which monuments are to be protected. We have tried to explain the interface between a declining judicial culture and monuments.

19.1 Unconstitutional Economics vs. Cultural Heritage

An analysis of the constitutional provisions shows that the present economics based entirely on the western/international model of economic development constitutes unconstitutional economics resulting in the abandonment of the fundamental rights of citizens to their monuments as part of their distinct culture under Art. 29. This result necessarily makes it impossible for citizens to fulfill their fundamental duty of preserving the composite cultural heritage under Art. 51A (f) and for the State to fulfill its obligation to preserve every monument of national importance. We have also shown how the State has taken over the fundamental right of citizens under Art. 29 while implementing Art. 49 through the Ancient Monuments Act, 1958, and its various amendments. The State's entire exercise under Art. 49 and the amendments to the Ancient Monuments Act, 1958 has been to virtually eliminate the fundamental right of citizens under Art. 29 to their monuments as part of their distinct culture.

In this context the Supreme Court's approach has been everything but legal. This is especially so in the case of the Taj Mahal, which has already been monitored by the Supreme Court for almost thirty years. The Supreme Court's environmental approach towards these monuments of national importance has saved the bodies or structures of the monuments but not their spirit. It has ignored the concept of sustainable tourism, to ensure the spirit of the monuments, by not passing any orders and simply by keeping pending specific applications praying for directions on this aspect.

The net result of this examination has been that the Supreme Court basically adopted Monuments-as-Objects approach and sometimes monuments as cultural objects approach. It never adopted the cultural heritage approach as required by the Constitution of India, so as to recognize the intrinsic link between people, their land, and their way of life or distinct culture and monuments.

On the basis of the lessons learnt, from this exercise, an alternative legal approach has been suggested in which monuments are sought to be protected as part of Cultural Heritage. Under such proposed legislation, the western model of economics adopted in India can no longer ignore the cultural heritage and its people on the ground of the assumption of such economics that what is not quantified does not exist and what is not priced becomes common property for domestic and international pillage.

This is an effort to use the Constitution of India for an economic development and a culture that would be meaningful for the lives of the people and thereby for their monuments as part of their distinct culture which the State would enable the citizens to enjoy and treasure as a fundamental right.

This will probably make the Art. 29 fundamental right accessible to citizens, especially concerning their monuments, and thereby make Art. 49 and the subject matter of Entry 67 List I, meaningful in their lives as well as that of the country. Hopefully the composite cultural heritage that emerges will develop national unity, fraternity and an Indian identity.

19.2 Culture Since 1950

So how have Parliament, the Union Government and its Culture Ministry as also the Supreme Court treated the Art. 29 fundamental right of citizens to their culture, the duty of citizens in Art. 51 A (f) to preserve and value the rich heritage of our composite culture and the Art. 49 obligation of the State to protect monuments of national importance. Let us try to sum it up.

Parliament: Under our constitutional system, governments by virtue of commanding the majority of the members in Parliament, sit at the heart of Parliament. Except in the case of serious internal dissension and an Opposition that can effectively turn a government's majority to a minority on a proposed law, Parliament is the Union Government. Accordingly, the Union Government under Jawaharlal Nehru moved the Constitution Seventh Amendment Act, 1956 to amend Art. 49 and Entry 67 List I of the VIIth Schedule of the Constitution. The then Union Government used its majority to turn the constitutional provision of monuments of national importance, to convert the Parliamentary function of deciding monuments of national importance into a governmental or executive function. We examine this constitutional coup and the use of the legal technique of deeming.

We must be the only country in the world that celebrates its conquerors by accepting what the British declared as monuments of national importance. Parliament never chose to revisit the British declarations or notifications to put these colonial declarations of pre-independent India through the sieve of representatives elected because of an independent India's Parliament. Despite the presence of the founding fathers of the Constitution, including the Chairman of the Constituent Assembly, independent India's Parliament forgot the fundamental right of Indians to their distinct culture under Art. 29. Since the advent of the

Bhartiya Janata Party, the nation is grappling this very issue in finding the meaning of the three constitutional foundations of its culture and Indian identity — religion and custom, secularism and modernization or the scientific temperament, culture or the way of living together — to achieve the constitutional trinity of justice social economic and political.

A modernization achieved knowingly and unconstitutionally by breaking this trinity through learned and Western trained professional economists and statisticians of independent India's entirely government controlled Planning Commission, raises serious issues of the relationship of culture and monuments to economics. It compels us in this book to attempt to answer the question as to what is a monument. Was all this essential to ensure India's political or territorial unity.? Can the Western approach to culture and economics or the management of the country's resources preserve and protect monuments in a nation of awfully perpetuated inequality as compared to the Western nations whose modernization we choose to copy? Can the Western concept of human rights including that of monuments and culture, substitute the need for religious cum cultural renaissance towards human dignity, without the Western milieu of education, technological might and institutional infrastructure and learning lessons from the Christian religion's evolution in their own idiom for most of the citizens of Western countries? These are vast questions of national debate about shaping an Indian identity by diligently studying and shaping the logic of the past of a political economy for a defined India in today's world. In this study of monuments we could only touch some of these issues by studying monuments in relation to history, geography and economics.

Union Government: The Nehru government having achieved this constitutional coup, simultaneously moved administratively to take over culture. The Article 29 fundamental right of Indians to their distinct culture, which recognized India as a nation of cultural minorities and which the government was supposed to enable, was thereby effectively put to sleep without a need to amend or delete Art. 29. This maybe smart politics. But it found its logical result in a secularism that virtually eliminated the constitutional idea of India being the sum total of cultural minorities or different ways of living together — an ancient evolved tradition exhibited by sects and sub sects of every religion.

The Nehruvian era launched national modernization on a secularism filled with State culture instead of people's culture, ways of life and religion. Its economists, administrators and ruling politicians launched a modernization process that knowingly uprooted citizens sub-silentio, without information and consent, from their homes, culture and monuments to push them into city slums of value free religion that taught the practical of corruption as a way of life in a value free economic development wherein the non monetized being, culture or monument, do not even exist for the State. What is not monetized does not get constitutional or State protection. The planned modernization and city created value free men and women with value free opportunities for bringing up value free children smart enough to grab whatever they can howsoever. Such a value free model of economic development that broke up consciously the constitutional unity and trinity of ensuring justice social, economic and political, based on the unity of "economic and social planning" in Entry 20 of the Concurrent List of the Constitution, for the law and administration of the political economy of modernization, led to obvious consequences for monuments of national importance How this was done through the use of the legal process is examined in this book.

Modernisation through the planning process of the State was deliberate State administration, executed to create cities that ensured inequality of opportunities while depriving the migrant citizens of their cultural roots and monuments. The perfectly legal Indian was compelled to become an illegal city resident in which the political method and not the rule of law was the route to any semblance of human dignity.

The place of monuments in terms of the infinite vast canvas of history, geography and economics is attempted to be analysed in this book to show how modern religion became a route of land grab and even reserved – forest grab, as shown by the Supreme Court orders permitting Asaram's encroachment into the ridge forest in Delhi, backed by politically powerful lawyers of the Congress and the BJP. The Supreme Court did this despite a dissenting report by the third member of the three person committee, (which included the two politically powerful lawyers who also belong to the creamiest class of the legal practitioners at the Supreme Court) appointed by the Supreme Court to report to it on this Asaram venture on Delhi's ridge, for a large number of disciple lawyers.

The tragic irony was that this was done by the orders of a bench whose one judge had been projected by the media as India's environmental crusader. The same judge became the environmental crusader for the Taj Mahal through highly questionable court procedures vis a vis his own colleagues on the bench and the counsel appearing in the case.

The result was that on his last working day, when he wanted to deliver his judgment singly during the vacation of the court, the registry of the court did not oblige him by opening any court and he had to deliver the judgment alone from his chamber in the court. The orders on monument protection in this public display of judicial behavior became merely declaratory instead of enforceable fundamental rights under Art. 21 of the Constitution. Art. 29 found no mention in the judicial culture of shouting down from the bench any counsel or government official, with a contrary argument or thought. The administrators presiding over the violations have so far ultimately carried the day.

The Union Ministry of Culture, through the Archaeological Survey of India, has been in charge of the monuments of national importance. Their functioning which is the subject of several official reports reflects negatively on our proclaimed cultural pride. Minus a system to enable citizens to actualize their fundamental right to culture in Article 29, by making it possible to collect, document and study the trillion ways of living cultures from area to area, the emergence of an Indian entity will remain problematic. This approach could probably yield the desperately needed jobs and the meaningful economy of a trillion dollars that we seem to pursue by denying citizens their mother tongues and the examination of the cultures of their birth, as the cost of mastering the English medium and creating the hope of this mastery for a billion as the gateway for an aspirational so-called Western way of life translated as human rights regardless of the consequences of this way of life. We examine how in a step of doubtful constitutional validity, the States have chosen to copy the Centre's model of heritage monuments through local and municipal laws, to declare monuments in municipal areas as national heritage monuments, when the subject of such monuments of national importance is reserved by the Constitution only for the Union Government under Lists I, II and III of the VIIth Schedule to the Constitution of India.

Supreme Court: The highest court showed how the rule of law concerning monuments of national importance suffers at its hands. It ignored Art. 29 of the Constitution to proceed in cases of monuments of national importance before it as if these monuments did not exist in any culture of the people in and around the monument. Its valuable role was in saving these monuments physically by passing interim orders against emergent situations that seriously threatened the very existence of these monuments. This was especially so concerning the Taj Mahal, the case of which has been pending till today since 1984. But instead of taking a cultural heritage approach of Art. 29 of the Constitution, it took an environmental approach without even examining the nature of the monuments it was seeking to protect.

Despite applications and written submissions of the amicus as to how tourism was defeating the very founding logic of a monument like the Taj Mahal and what was required to be done, the court simply did nothing to call the Union Ministry of Culture or its Archaeological Survey of India to account. The judicial method and manner of doing this negated the elementary rules of fairness and non arbitrariness. The environmental principles developed by the court were not applied, even while adopting an environmental approach to the protection of monuments of national importance. The petitioner – in-person in the Taj Mahal case, kept quiet on issues of Art. 29, about the judicial method or the constitutional and the official political economy context in which monuments of national importance were required to be protected.

In the judge driven zeal, multiplied by the national media, to shut down the Mughal era foundries of Agra, despite official reports pointing out that coal fuel be replaced with gas to end the pollution caused by the foundries, the industrial and technological heritage of the Mughal era was effectively destroyed by the court.

When the culture of corruption caught up with the Taj Mahal through the Taj Heritage Corridor project, the court seemed to beat a retreat from its own orders, despite the excellent investigation reports filed before it by the CBI in tracing the money trail down to specific named persons and properties in relation to the accused Chief Minister. The Taj Mahal became a case study of a monument monitored for the longest time by the highest court of a country, which harmed the monuments, the rule of law in relation to these and the court itself as an institution meant under Art. 32 of the Constitution for the "enforcement" of fundamental rights. The opportunity to lay down a holistic constitutional basis for the meaning of a cultural India that enabled people to protect and enjoy their distinct languages, scripts and cultures, to channelize it to the values in the Preamble and to create an evidence – based cultural renaissance that would create thousands of jobs to make culture meaningful for the unity and integrity of India, seems to have been irretrievably lost by the Supreme Court despite the public time and money it has spent on the Taj Mahal and Fatehpur Sikri national monuments.

The book analyses the proceedings of the Supreme Court to make it the first attempt at writing on law and culture, based on the original materials of the Supreme Court itself. The book would have served its purpose if we learn our lessons from this so that the Supreme Court develops an institutional approach to the collection, analysis and protection of the meaning of culture to return the heritage to the citizens to whom it belongs and who do not even know the value of what they have since they daily live in a contrary constitutional culture. It is only then that they would realize the monetary value of what they are losing, understand the onslaught of modernization and be able to apply their mind to the elements of modernization that they need for their way of life. That should be the task of the Union and State Culture Ministries, Parliament and legislatures and in the last resort of the judiciary, as the carrier of constitutional values.

No Anglo Saxon nation, the legal systems of which we have copied and continue to copy, has developed a rule of law that is not rooted in its culture, ways of life, language and history. Can we in India create a rule of law by ignoring our culture of the datum (medicinal twig of a tree for cleaning teeth), jaggery, unpolished rice or dal and the use of traditional ingredients for the mortar for repairing ancient monuments. Does it make sense to spend money on restoring monuments and learn nothing of the ways of life of that era that maybe useful to us? In the absence of this the Supreme Court will be trying to save, at the most. the structures without their cultural spirit? We try in this book to find the answer that emerges from what the Supreme Court has done in the cases of monuments before it.

19.3 An Alternative Legal Approach

The previous analysis shows that both the environmental law and the Ancient Monuments Act approaches of the judiciary are not compliant with the cultural heritage approach of the Constitution of India. This is so because both the judicial approaches fail to take into account that the constitutional obligation of protecting monuments of national importance is a part of the fundamental right of each section of citizens of their distinct culture under Art. 29 so as to impose a fundamental duty on each citizen to value and preserve the rich heritage of our composite culture. Only this constitutional approach by reading Articles 21, 25, 26 and 29 together confers a constitutional purpose to the protection of monuments. This purpose is the achievement of the constitutional goals enumerated in the Preamble, outlining the kind of society India must be legally.

In the absence of this purposive constitutional cultural heritage approach, the constitutional goals of protecting monuments cannot be achieved because a purely environmental judicial approach or a purely Ancient Monuments Act approach ignores the community, the geography, the history and the economics of the society behind the monuments by looking at the monuments alone minus its context of time, location, livelihoods and people.

Hence there is a need for a different Ancient Monuments Act than the present one, which by ignoring the community or sections of citizens connected to the monument, their territory, their mores, styles of living and their religion, does nothing to protect the ambience or the spirit of monuments. Minus its ambience or context monuments become a purposeless edifice and hence meaningless. Accordingly, it becomes difficult to save them from encroachment, depredation and theft.

19.4 Steps for a New Law

The first step recommended for a new Ancient Monuments Act, is that of laying down a process for the determination of the monuments of sections of citizens which should be treated as monuments of national importance. As a prelude to this the Act must provide for the detailed documentation of the various monuments of various sections of citizens in terms of their history, geography, religion, livelihoods and mores of that time. This will recognize and promote India's unique oral history and the collection of materials related to it. This is long term work, which will require not only increasing the qualified manpower and infrastructure of the ASI but also remodelling ASI to mandatorily involve the relevant teachers, institutions, organisations and people of the area in which the monuments are located. The ASI with branch or camp offices in every district will be responsible for receiving applications from citizens of the jurisdictional area for a preliminary registration of their distinct culture or way of life, language or script and monuments. Following its professional methods it will decide to do a final registration, if necessary, after giving a hearing to the applicant/s.

Hence work can begin with some selected world heritage monuments which are protected monuments of national importance. Such drafting of the new Ancient Monuments Act will give back to the citizens their constitutional right to culture, religion and expression with a duty to protect what they feel is theirs and to which they are emotively connected.

Under the Constitution no right was given to the State concerning monuments. The rights and those too fundamental rights were given to citizens – of culture, of religion, of liberty to freely express themselves, of a life of dignity and constitutionally monuments are located among these rights. The Constitution only imposed an obligation on the State to protect monuments of national importance. Unfortunately, the Ancient Monuments Act converted this obligation of the State into a right by keeping out under the Ancient Monuments Act, people, the civil society and even the federal State units from the determination of monuments of national importance and then their protection.

The new Act should therefore lay down a system of finding out, protecting and preserving both the tangible and intangible culture of various sections of the citizens of India by involving each tier of constitutional governance from the Gram Sabha upwards, the civil society, the relevant teachers and institutions at each tier. In this sense the present Ancient Monuments Act suppresses the blossoming of India's cultural past to reflect the diversity of sections of citizens of India, captured succinctly in Article 29 of the Constitution.

This necessarily means in the context of monuments, taking the second step that ASI's plans for deciding applications and excavations be discussed publicly and the public be permitted to propose excavations with reasons given by the local multi-disciplinary teams constituted under the new Act. It is tragic that India's past under the present Ancient Monuments Act stands frozen at one hundred years, without a fixed point from where to calculate these hundred years.

The third step should be to deal with the reality of development vs. monuments. This is absent from the Ancient Monuments Act, 1958. Both development and protection of monuments means legal management of land, people and change brought about by people. Since the existing Act keeps out people, it has formulated a fixed and inflexible thumb rule of total mechanical prohibition of any construction within one hundred metres of a protected monuments and regulated construction within two hundred metres The result is a gross violation of this rule under the very nose of ASI which is toothless, since it does not have the power to issue cease and desist orders, to evict or to demolish after following principles of natural justice.

A new Act is therefore required in view of the following derivations from the Constitution of India:

i. Every monument in India represents the distinct culture of a section of citizen. That is, there cannot be a monument which does not represent a distinct culture of a section of citizens of India.

ii. The monuments culture of India consists of an inventory of the distinct cultures of sections of Indian citizens. Hence every monument is rooted in a distinct culture of Indian citizens. The distinct culture contextualizes or gives meaning to a monument. Each section of citizens becomes constitutional stakeholders in their respective monuments.

iii. The constitutional stakeholders in monuments and culture are also the stakeholders in the State organized economic development and social justice plans, programmes and schemes. Accordingly the distinct culture of citizens, which is a fundamental right, intrinsically forms an essential component of economic development and social justice. There cannot be social justice without economic development or vice-versa and neither can be culture neutral.

iv. The fundamental right to religion and religious denominations in Articles 25 and 26 is part of a larger fundamental right – that of the distinct culture of any section of Indian citizens. Religion is a cultural right. A monument as a part of this cultural right reflects the religion of a distinct culture of a section of the citizens of India. Each religion and religious denomination becomes a constitutional stakeholder in its monuments.

v. Such monuments constitute the pool from which monuments of national importance must be selected according to the constitutional criteria of "monuments of historic and artistic interest."

vi. Each section of citizen of India having a distinct culture become eligible to place before their panchayat or municipality not only the monuments of historic artistic archaeological or architectural interest with the history of their community but also any other intangible culture like their paintings, music, knowhow of growing up, conserving or preserving or processing any product or natural resource of their area or ways of living and practices related to it, which they would like to be recognized at the State and/or national level. The intermediate panchayat shall co opt one expert from the State Archaeology Department who is an archaeologist preferably with knowledge of the area, one assistant professor each of history, geography, economics, sociology, anthropology and law. Any dispute on this issue or process will go for resolution before the Nyayadhikari, under the Gram Nyayalaya Act.

vii. This will constitute the national pool of culture from which the Archaeological Survey of India must pick the culture of national importance.

viii. The monument recognition and excavation policy of the ASI must take this national pool of culture as an input in determining its policy.

ix. Monuments of national importance will be finally decided in a spirit of cooperative federalism, with resort to the

Inter-State Council under Art. 263 of the Constitution, whenever felt necessary by a State/s. This Council can inquire and advise on disputes, investigate and discuss subjects of common interest, make recommendations for coordination of policy and action on a subject. This will make for a live cultural federalism of India's cultural capital that lies as a wasted and depreciating asset with imminent risk of permanent loss.

x. Use what is discovered by feeding it into the school, higher and professional education official media, publications and specialised institution systems.

19.5 Creating Jobs

A new Act requires large scale inputs. For this pan India cultural studies would be needed. This would create thousands of jobs and make culture a source of livelihood. Culture as a creative economy requires an understanding and use of modern science, technology and innovation in a manner that does not destroy what we seek to protect and preserve. Culture could make modernisation actually serve the public interest and thereby Constitutional.

Culture and monuments are an ongoing process of mankind. Courts play an important role in the judicial governance of this process that affects monuments. The role is as effective as the implementation of the judicial orders. Hence, a major project can be the execution and impact of such orders. Execution will reveal the nature of political governance. Impact will reveal how judicial orders have actually captured the problem to which the judges have addressed themselves. Such feedback on monuments is missing at present. A country wide comprehensive time bound multi-disciplinary program is needed. Academic faculties, ASI and the Union Ministry of Culture need to be in active partnership with the HRD, Industries and Commerce Ministries.

A wider research is needed into the culture of the communities associated with the monuments. This can be a valuable input for a meaningful administration and judicial governance of monuments, since this will involve the protection of a monument on the basis of the concerned communities fundamental right to the distinct culture under Art. 29 of the Constitution.

A wider study of the ways of life of sections of citizens needs to be undertaken to realise the composite cultural heritage of our country. Such understanding can be a practical basis for legislation, executive action, judicial intervention and citizen participation, to create fraternity, unity and integrity – human and territorial.

Annexure I

LIST OF TAJ TRAPEZIUM ZONE (TTZ) MONUMENTS

Upon Hearing Counsel the Court Made the Following
ORDER
OFFICE REPORT DT. 1.10.96

ITEM 'A'

Pursuant to this Court's order dated September 4, 1996 Mr. P.K. Sharan, Deputy Superintending Archaeologist, Archaeological Survey of India Agra Circle, Agra has filed an affidavit. Para 3 of this affidavit is as under:-

"That almost whole of Agra district and parts of Mathura, Aligarh, Etah, Ferozabad districts of U.P. and a part of Bharatpur district of Rajasthan fall within Taj Trapezium Zone. A list of centrally protected monuments located within Taj Trapezium Zone is submitted herwith as Annexure No. 1. Among these monuments namely Taj Mahal, Agra Fort and Fatehpur Sikri are also designated as World Heritage Monuments. It is pertinent to mention here that A.S.I. protects monuments of National importance & not significant monuments."

Annexure '1' to the affidavit is a list of the Centrally protected monuments located within Taj Trapezium. This Court's order dated May 10, 1996 shall operate in respect of the monuments which are listed in Annexure '1'. Registry to give a copy of annexure '1' to the learned counsel for the brick kiln owners for their information and necessary records.

Mr. Pradeep Misra, learned counsel for the State of UP states that the matter concerning rehabilitating the brick kiln owners in under consideration of the Government. He further states that regarding the disposal of fly ash instructions have already been issued by the UP Government. He shall place on record an affidavit regarding the scheme to rehabilitate the brick kiln operators. He shall also file a copy of the instructions regarding the fly ash within three weeks from today. To come up on 24th October, 1996.

ITEM 'B'

Pursuant to this Court's order dated August 7, 1996, August 13, 1996 and September 12, 1996 regarding shifting of various shops/emporia from within the Taj premises Mar. Satendra Singh Yadav, Public Relation Officer, Agra Development Authority, Agra has filed an affidavit dated October 3, 1996. In para 2 of the affidavit the details of the sites available for the seven shops/emporia has been given. It is agreed by the learned counsel that the allotment of the space for relocation at the alternative site shall be done by way of draw of lots between them. This shall be done within one week from today. The allottees shall take over the possession within one week thereafter. All the allottees shall stop functioning at their present location on or before December 31, 1996. The Archaeological Survey of India shall take over possession of the area from the allottees on or before December 31, 1996. All allottees may remove their fixtures installed by them without damaging any part of taj premises.

List of Centrally Protected Monuments of National Importance

Agra District

1. Group of Agra Fort monuments, Tehsil Sadar.
2. Chhattries on the Yamuna Bank to the north of Ram Bagh, village Naraich, Tehsil Itmadpur.
3. Chauburji of the temporary burial place of the Emperor Babar together with the Chabutra on which it stands, Tehsil Sadar.
4. Chini Ka Rauza including well tank and cross fencing the river Yamuna, Tehsil Sadar.
5. City Wall on the west side of Agra Gate, Tehsil Sadar.
6. Dakhini Darwaza in Mohalla Taj Ganj, Tehsil Sadar.
7. Firoz Khan's Tomb, Tehsil Sadar.
8. Gateway at Pul Changa Modi, Tehsil Sadar.

9. Gateways in the interior of Taj Ganj, Tehsil Sadar.
10. Gumbad of Itwari Khan, Tehsil Sadar.
11. Inscribed Tablet in a piece of the old city wall of Agra 'Akbrabad' on the west side of the M.G. Road, Tehsil Sadar.
12. Itmad ud Daula's Tomb, Tehsil Sadar.
13. Great Idgah Katghar, Tehsil Sadar.
14. Jama Masjid, Tehsil Sadar.
15. Kans Gate, Tehsil Sadar.
16. Kiosk & Building other than the river side kiosk at or near Zohrabagh, Tehsil Sadar.
17. Mehtab Bagh on the river bank facing the Taj Mahal, Tehsil Sadar.
18. Maqbara called Kala Gumbad between Chini Ka Rauza & Bagh Vazir Khan Tehsil Sadar.
19. Old Delhi Gate of the city, Tehsil Sadar.
20. Pahlawan's Tomb near Cantonment, Gwalior Road, Tehsil Sadar.
21. Ram Bagh Gateways, Houses, kiosks terraces & Kstra adjoining the Zohra Bagh, Tehsil Sadar.
22. Rauza Diwan Ji Begum & Mosque, Tehsil Sadar.
23. Satkuiyan of seven Wells close by Ram Bagh on the Aligarh Road, Tehsil Sadar.
24. Small Chhatri, Sonth ki Mandi on Agra Mathura Road, Tehsil Sadar.
25. Statue of Akbar's House on the Agra Sikandra Road, Tehsil Sadar.
26. Taj Mahal Group of Monuments, Tehsil Sadar.
27. Takhat Pahlwan near Cantonment, Gwalior Road, Tehsil Sadar.
28. Two Gateways of early Mughal date at the north-east and north-west corner of Ram Bagh, Tehsil Sadar.
29. Well and Flight of steps in the Char Bagh, Tehsil Sadar.
30. Zohra Bagh and river side kiosk, Tehsil Sadar.
31. Kos Minar on Agra – Fatehpur Sikri Road Miles 9 11 12 15 Tehsil Kiraoli.
32. Kos Minar on Agra – Mathura Road Miles 4 6 9 12 Tehsil Sadar.
33. Tomb of Mahabat Khan's daughter Bagh Raj Pur Tehsil, Tehsil Sadar.
34. Buria-Ka-Tal, Tehsil Itmadpur.
35. Fatehpur Sikri Group of Monuments, Tehsil Kirsoli.
36. Tomb of Sadiq Khan, Gelana, Tehsil Sadar.
37. Tomb of Salabat Khan, Gelana, Tehsil Sadar.
38. Dhakri Ka Mahal, Gopalpur, Tehsil Sadar.

39. Jama Masjid, Tehsil Itmadpur.
40. Jagner Fort including the Gwal Baba Temple with stair way leading there to and the Baoli out side and below the main way of the Fort.
41. Two Gateways & the Mosque in the Jajau Sarai, Jajau Tehsil.
42. Humayun Masjid, Kachpura, Tehsil Sadar.
43. Barah Khamba, Kagarol.
44. Guru Ka Tal, Kakretha.
45. Fifty Two Bullock Well Khawaspur, Tehsil Sadar.
46. Kamal Khan's Dargah, Khawaspur.
47. Roman Catholic-Cemetery with all its tomb boundary walls Gateways and garden, Tehsil Sadar.
48. Mass of Rubble and concrete said to contain tomb of Ladli Begum & her two brothers Faizi & Abdul Fazal Mau Tehsil Sadar.
49. Itwari Khan's Mosque near Sikandra, Tehsil Sadar.
50. Jaswant Singh Ki Chattri, Rajwara, Tehsil Sadar.
51. Tomb of Sheikh Brahim, Rasulpur, Tehsil Sadar.
52. Akbar's Tomb, Gateways and walls round the ground, Sikandra, Tehsil Sadar.
53. Dalans of the east and south sides of the great south gate and domed structure on the west side of the said gate, Sikandra, Tehsil Sadar.
54. Kanch Mahal at the south east corner of Akbar's Tomb, Sikandra, Tehsil Sadar.
55. Mariam's Tomb, Sikandra, Tehsil Sadar.
56. Small mosque situated in the Church Missionary Society's compound, Sikandra, Tehsil Sadar.
57. Bara Khamba together with adjoining area comprised in part of survey plot no. 150. Tehsil Sadar.
58. Chhatri marking the site of the Empress Jodh Bai's Tomb, Tehsil Sadar.
59. Buri in Civil Court compound (Jhan Jhan Kotra).

Aligarh District

1. Monument near Kailash Railway Station, Hathras.
2. Remains of an old Hindu Temple inside the remains of Dayaram's Fort, Hathras Khas, Tehsil Hathras.

Mathura District

1. Pillar with Sanskrit inscription dated 8, 1666 in the flanking towers at the Bhanckher tank, village Barsana.
2. Temple of Govind Dec, Vrindavan, Tehsil Sadar.
3. Temple of Madan Mohan, Vrindavan, Tehsil Sadar.
4. Temple of Radha Ballabh, Vrindaban, Tehsil Sadar.
5. Ancient Sculptures carvings images bass-reliefs inscriptions stones and like objects, Mathura.
6. Kos Minar on the circular road, Mathura.
7. Sati Burj supposed to corroborate the Sati of the widow of Raja Biharmal of Jaipur erected by her son Raja Bhagwan Dass in A.D. 1570 Mathura Tehsil Sadar.
8. Kos Minar Mathura Delhi road Mile 3.
9. Kos Minar Mathura Delhi road Mile 11.
10. Kos Minar Mathura Delhi road Mile 13.
11. Kos Minar Mathura Delhi road Mile 16.
12. Kos Minar Mathura Dig road.
13. Temple of Jugal Kishore Vrindavan Tehsil Sadar.

Firozabad District

NIL

Bharatpur District

1. Akbar's Chattri, Bayana.
2. Ancient Fort with its monuments, Bayana.
3. Brahmabad Idgah, Bayana.
4. Islam Shah's Gate, Bayana.
5. Jahagir's gateway, Bayana.
6. Jhajri, Bayana.
7. Lodhi's Minar, Bayana.
8. Saraj Sad-ul-lah, Bayana.

Alipur District

1. Usa Mandir.
2. Delhi Gate outside the Bharatpur Fort, Bharatpur.
3. Fateh Burj near Anah Gate, Bharatpur.
4. Jawahar Burj and Ashtadhatu Gateway inside the Bharatpur Fort, Bharatpur.
5. Deeg Bhawans (Palaces), Deeg.
6. Looted gun, Deeg.
7. Marble Jhoola, Deeg.
8. Chaurasi Khamba Temple, Kaman.
9. Colossal image of Yaksha, Noh.
10. Lal Mahal, Rupvas.
11. Fort walls including Chowburja gate and approach bridges gate and approach bridges at the Chowburja and Ashtachatu gates. Bharatpur.
12. Moat-surrounding the Fort Wall, Bharatpur.

BIBLIOGRAPHY

A. Charters/Constitution/Statutes/International Covenants and Conventions

1. Discovery and Transactions of the Archaeological Society of Agra, January and June 1874 published by Order of the Council, Delhi Gazette Press, Agra, MDCCCLXXIV.
2. May 18, 1999, Gazette of India (Extraordinary), Part II – Sec.3 – Sub-Section(ii).
3. Gazette of India, November 28, 1996, S.O. 832 (E) Part II – Section 3 – sub section(ii) 1996 Scheme for the Administration of the National Culture Fund.
4. Act No. XVIII of 1932 amending the 1904 Ancient Monuments Preservation Act.
5. Air (Prevention & Control of Pollution) Act, 1981.
6. Ancient Monuments Preservation Act, 1904.
7. Ancient Monuments & Archaeological Sites & Remains Act, 1958.
8. Andhra Pradesh Urban Areas (Development) Act, 1975.
9. Agreement for Constituting under UNESCO the Center for the Study of the Preservation & Restoration of Cultural Property, 1957.
10. Ancient & Historical Monuments and Archaeological Sites & Remains (Declaration of National Importance) Act, 1951.
11. Athens Charter, 1931.
12. Bengal Regulation of 1810, Bengal Code.
13. Central Vigilance Commission Act, 2003.
14. Charters of 1601, 1609, 1612, 1661, 1793, 1813, 1833 and 1853.
15. Charter of International National Trust Organisation (INTO).
16. Charter on the Protection & Management of Underwater Cultural Heritage, 1996.
17. Citizens Charter, 2016–17, Union Ministry of Culture, New Delhi.
18. Companies Act, 1956.

19. Conservation Manual, GOI, 1923.
20. Constitution of India.
21. Constitution (Seventh Amendment) Act, 1956.
22. Constitution of the International Council of Monuments and Sites (ICOMOS).
23. Convention on the Protection of the World Cultural & Natural Heritage, 1972.
24. Convention on the Rights of Persons with Disabilities 2007.
25. Convention on The Means of Prohibiting and Preventing the Illicit Import, Export and Transfer of Ownership of Cultural Property, 1970.
26. Devolution Rules, 1921.
27. Development Control Regulations for Greater Mumbai, 1991.
28. Environment Protection Act, 1986.
29. Hague Convention for the Protection of Cultural Property in the Event of Armed Conflict, 1954.
30. Hyderabad Urban Development Authority Zoning Regulations, 1981.
31. ICOMOS Charter for the Conservation of Historic Towns and Urban Areas, 1987.
32. International Cultural Tourism Charter of ICOMOS, 1999.
33. Indian Contract Act, 1872.
34. International Covenant on Civil and Political Rights, 1966.
35. International Covenant of Economic, Social and Cultural Rights, 1966.
36. Land Acquisition Act, 1894.
37. Madras Regulation VII of 1817, Madras Code.
38. Maharashtra Regional Town Planning Act, 1966.
39. Model Heritage Regulations, 2011.
40. Model Heritage Guidelines, 2011.p.
41. Navigation Act, 1660.
42. Places of Worship (Special Provisions) Act, 1991.
43. Prevention of Corruption Act, 1988.
44. Regulation for the Conservation of Historical Buildings in Hyderabad City, 1995.
45. Roerich Pact, 1935.

46. States Reorganisation Act, 1956.
47. Taj Trapezium Zone Authority, May 18, 199.
48. UNESCO Recommendation on Participation by People at Largae in Cultural Life and Their Contribution, 1976.
49. UNIDROIT Convention on Stolen or Illegally Exported Cultural Objects, 1995.
50. Universal Declaration of Human Rights, 1947.
51. Venice Charter or the International Charter for the Conservation & Restoration of Monuments (ICCRON).

B. Case/Judgment Reporters

1. **All India Reporter**
2. **Supreme Court Cases**
3. **SCALE**

C. Dictionararies/Encyclopedias

1. Black's Law Dictionary, West A. Thomson Reuters Business (9th ed., 2009).
2. ENCYCLOPEDIA BRITTANICA, Vol. VI, Printed in U.S.A., 1956.
3. Encyclopaedia Britanica, online, available at: http://www.britannica.com.
4. Halsbury's Laws of England, LexisNexis Butterworths, United KINGDOM, (4th ed. 2010).
5. Halsbury's Laws of india, LexisNexis Butterworths, New Delhi, (Ed. Pp 2008).
6. Latin Dictionary, Oxford, Charendon Press, (1937).
7. Oxford Dictionary and Thesaurus, edited by Maurice Waite, Oxford University Press, 2007.
8. Stanford Encyclopedia of Philosophy, available at: http://plato.stanford.edu.
9. Steven H. Gifts, Law Dictionary, Barron's Legal Guides (5th ed. 2003).
10. The New Encyclopedia Britannica, Vol. 12, 15th Edition, edited by Robert P. Gwinn, Peter B. Norton and Robert McHenry, (1992).

D. Books

1. (1959) 2 Journal of the International Commission of Jurists.
2. "Frontiers of Legal Theory" 2010.
3. "The Problems of Jurisprudence," 2010.
4. 5,000 years of Indian Architecture, Publications Division, Ministry of Information & Broadcasting, GOI (Reprint March, 1992).
5. A Cultural History of India: A.L. Basham, Oxford University Press, New Delhi.
6. Achin Vanaik (General Editor), Political Science, ICSSR Research Service and Explorations, Vol. I (2013 OUP; Edited by Samir Kumar Das.
7. Adams, George Burton, revised by Robert L. Schuyler: Constitutional History of England, Reprint 1956, Jonathan Cape, 30, Bedford Square, London.
8. Adorno, Theodor & Horkheimer Max: (1999) "The Culture Industry, Enlightenment as Mass Deception."
9. Amartya Sen, On Interpreting India's Past, The Asiatic Society, Calcutta, 1996.
10. American Geography, Inventory & Prospect, P.4. Syracuse University, 1954.
11. Ashworth, G. and Graham, B. & Turnbridge J. Pluralizing Pasts: Heritage, Identity & Place in Multicultural Societies, London Pluto Press (2007).
12. Bagchi Amiya, Colonialism & India Economy, P.xxxi, 2010, Oxford University Press, Delhi.
13. Banerji Mridula, Colonial Architecture & Indian Rationalism, 2001, The History & Culture of the Indian People, 7th ed. Vol. 8, Bhawan's Book University, Bharatiya Vidya Bhavan, Mumbai.
14. Bardhan, Pranab The Political Economy of Development in India, 1984, Oxford: Basil Blackwell.
15. Blomley, N.K. (1989) "Text and Context: Rethinking the Law Space Nexus," Progress in Human Geography, Oxford.
16. Blomley, N.K. and Clark G.L. (1990) "Law, theory and geography," Urban Geography 11(5).

17. Braidel F.A. (1995) History of Civilizations, Penguin Books (London).
18. Census of India Report 1911 Vol. 1.
19. Central Pollution Control Board guidelines in the Comprehensive-Industry Document on Brick Kilns, May 1996.
20. Chapter III, General Review of Archaeological Explanations & Excavations (2010).
21. Chapter V. the Geographical Background of Indian History.
22. Clark, G.L. (1989) "The Geography of Law," in R. Preet and N. Thrift (ed.) New Models in Human Geography, London: Unwin Hyman.
23. Connerton, Paul, Reprint 1999: How Societies Remember, Cambridge University Press, United Kingdom.
24. Constitutional History of England, George Burton Adams (Revised by Robert L. Schuiler) (1956 Reprint) Jonathan Cape, London.
25. Crowe Sylvia, Haywood Sheela: The Gardens of Mughal India, 1973, Vikas Publshing House Pvt. Ltd. New Delhi.
26. Cultural Law, James A.R. Nafziger, R.K. Paterson, Alison D. Renteln, p.64, Cambridge Univerisity Press, 2010.
27. Culture: A Crucial Review of Concepts & Definitions, 1952.
28. Das, Veena: "Cultural Rights and the Definition of community," (1996) in Oliver Mendlsohn and Upendra Baxi, The Rights of Subordinated Peoples, Oxford University Press, New Delhi.
29. Dayalan D, Taj Mahal and its Conservation (2009).
30. Dr. R.C. Majumdar, History and Culture of the India People, Vol. IX.
31. E.H. Carr in What is History? Reprint 1990, Penguin Books, England.
32. Eagleton, Terry, Reprint 2000, Blackwell, U.K.
33. Ebba Koch, The Complete Taj Mahal, Bookwise (India) Pvt. Ltd, 2006–07, p. 118 and 229.
34. Economics, David Begg, S. Fischer and R. Dornbusch, 4th ed. Mcgraw Hill Companies, England.
35. Environment Rules, 1986 on stack height and emissions.
36. Europeanisation of the Mughal time gardens, Stuart C.M. Villiers, Cosmo Publications, 1983, New Delhi.

37. Five-Year Plans: 1st to 12th of Planning Commission, Government of India.
38. Frankel, Francine: India's Political Economy 1947–2004 2nd ed. Oxford University Press.
39. Freeman T.W. 1961: A Hundred Years of Geography, London.
40. Fukuyama Francis: End of History and the last Man, 2006, Simon and Schuster, U.K.
41. Gasper Des and St. Clair Asuncion Lera Ed. (2010) Development Ethics, Ashgate Publishing Ltd, England.
42. General Review of Archaeological Explorations and Excavations in The Histroy and Culture of Indian People, Vol. I, Bharatiya Vidya Bhavan, 2010, Mumbai.
43. Glacken C.J. "Man's Role in Changing the Face of the Earth," Changing Ideas of the Habitable World, in W.L. Thomas(ed), 1956, Chicago, University of Chicago Press.
44. Glacken C.J. Traces on the Rhodian Shore: Nature and Culture in Western Thought, from ancient times to the end of the eighteenth century, 1967, Berkley. University of California Press.
45. Griffith Taylor(ed.) Geography in the Twentieth Century, Reprint 1965, New York Philosophical Library, Methuen & Co, London.
46. Guide to the Taj Mahal, Verma Chob Singh, published by U.P Tourism Development Corporation.
47. Gupta I.P.(1986), Urban Glimpses of Mughal India, Agra the Imperial Capital, 16th and 17th Centuries.
48. Guttman A. (ed.), Multiculturalism: Examining The Politics of Cultural Recognition, 2nd ed. Princeton University Press, Princeton, USA.
49. Habermas, Jurgen: "Struggles for Recognition in the Democratic Institutional State," 1994.
50. Hedley Bull, Adam Watson(eds.), The Expansion of International Society (Oxford: Clarendon Press, 1984).
51. Hettne, B.(1990) Development Theory and the Three Worlds, London, Methuen.
52. Hobswam Eric and Ranger Terence, eds. The Invention of Tradition, 1983 Cambridge University Press, U.K.

53. Husain, S. Abid: The National Culture of India, National Book Trust, India.
54. ICOMOS, Heritage at Risk: Vernacular Heritage in The Story of Indian Archaeology, October 5, 1949, Publications Division, New Delhi.
55. International Encyclopedia of the Social Sciences, David L. Sils Ed, The Macmillan Company and The Free Press.
56. Jacinta O'Haga, Conflict, Convergence or Coexistence? In The Relevance of Culture in Reframing The International Law, Culture, Politics, Eds, Richard Falk, Lester Edwin J. Ruiz and R.B. Walker 2002, Routledge.
57. James P.E. and Martin G.J. 1981: A Histroy of Geographical Ideas (2nd Ed.) John Wiley, New York.
58. James, 1972: All Possible Worlds: A History of Geographical Ideas, Indianapolis, Odyssey Press.
59. Julius Stone: Human Law and Human Justice.
60. Kuznets Simon, The Pattern of Shift of Labour Force from Agriculture, 1950–70.
61. Lal, Vinay: The History of History, 2003, Oxford University Press, New Delhi.
62. Lyndell V. Prott & Patrick J. O'Keefe, (1992) International Report on Cultural Property.
63. Macaulay's Minute on Education (1835).
64. Malinowski Bronislaw, Culture, in Encyclopedia of the Social Sciences, 621, 645, Edward R.A. Seligman Ed. 1937.
65. Marshall, J.H. "Introduction" Inaugural Issue of ASI's Archaeological Journal "Annual"(1902).
66. Marin Wright, Systems of States ed. Hedley Bull (Leicester: Leicester University Press, 1977).
67. Matthew Fitzjohn: "The Use of GIS in Landscape Heritage and Attitudes to Place," Heritage studies, 2009, Marie Louse Stig Sorensen & John Carmann, Routledge U.K.
68. Milton Singer, The Concept of Culture in International Encyclopedia of Social Sciences Vol. 3, Macmillan Co. & The Free Press, U.S.A.
69. Muslim Architecture in India By Martin S. Briggs, Chapter 22.

70. Nath R.(1997), Agra and Its Monuments.
71. NEERI guidelines.
72. Nehru J, The Essential Writings of Jawaharlal Nehru, Oxford University Press, New Delhi (2003).
73. Nirmal Kumar Bose: The Geographical Background of Indian Culture, Vol. 1, p.7 in The Cultural Heritage of India, Ramakrishna Mission Institute of Culture, Kolkata, Reprint 2007.
74. Nowak, John E. & Rotunda, Ronald D. 1991 4th ed., Hornbook Series, West Publishing Co. Minnesota and Raymond Arsenault, ed. Crucible of Liberty, 200years of the Bill of Rights, 1991, The Free Press, Macmillan Inc., New York.
75. Parekh B, The Constitution As A Statement of Indian Identity, in Bhargava R., ed.: Politics and Ethics of the Indian Constitution, 2008, Oxford University Press, New Delhi.
76. Paul A Samuelson, William D. Nordhaus, Indian Adaptation 19th ed. McGraw Hill Education (India) Pvt. Ltd, New Delhi.
77. Peoples Union for Democratic Rights vs. Union of India AIR 1982 SC 1473.
78. Planning Commission, Volume II, Para 2.2.21.
79. Prasad Rajendra, Colonialism Lumpenisation Revolution, Vol. 1, Societies of Calcutta and Shanghai 1850–1914. Ajanta Books International, New Delhi.
80. R.G. Collingwood in 'The Idea of History'
81. Rabindranath Tagore, Nationalism, New Delhi Rupa Publishers (1994) p.77–99.
82. Rakhaldas Sengupta, Preservation of Ancient Monuments, page 863 at P. 871, Vol. 8, The Cultural Heritage of India, Ramakrishna Mission Institute of Culture, Kolkata, Reprint 2007.
83. Results Framework Document (RFD) for Ministry of Culture, GOI (2013–14 and 2014–15).
84. Richard A. Posner "Overcoming Law" 2007, Universal Law Publishing Co. New Delhi, 'In Law & Social Norms', 2009.
85. Romila Thapar in Essay 1-Ideology and the interpretation of early Indian History in History and Beyond, OUP (2010) New Delhi.
86. Rudolf Lloyd I & Rudolf Susanne Hoeber, 1987, In Pursuit of Lakshmi: The Political Economy of the Indian State, Chicago III. University of Chicago Press, 1987.

87. Satish Chandra, "Historiography, Religion and State in Medieval India" Reprint 2010, Har Anand Publications, New Delhi, p.14.
88. Semple E.C."Man is the Product of the Earth's Surface" in Influences of Geographical Environment, 1911, New York, Henry Holt.
89. Senghas, Dieter: The Clash within Civilizations, Routledge & Routledge, London (English translation), 2002 at page 170, for intercultural philosophy and the civilizational hexagon.
90. Simon During (ed.) 1999: The Cultural Studies Reader, 2nd ed. Routledge, London.
91. Spencer, J.E & Thomas W.L. Cultural Geography: As Evolutionary Introduction to our Humanized Earth, 1969, John Wiley & Sons, New York.
92. Stein Burton, "Cultural Changes, Education and New Classes," in A History of India, 1948 Oxford University Press, New Delhi.
93. Syed Muhammad Latif Khan Bahadur, (1896), Agra Historical and Descriptive with an Account of Akbar and His Court And of the Modern City of Agra, Printed at the Calcutta Central Press Company Ltd, 40, Canning Street, Calcutta.
94. Tharoor S, The Great Indian Novel (1989) Penguin Books, New Delhi.
95. The Concept of Culture, in The Science of Man in The World Crisis 78–106 (Ralph Linton ed. 1980).
96. The Cultural Studies Reader, 2nd ed. Simon During (ed.) Routledge, London.
97. The Geographical Background of Indian Culture, Vol. 1, Reprint 2007, The Cultural Heritage of India, The Ramakrishna Mission Institute of Culture, Kolkata.
98. The Geological Background of India History.
99. The History & Culture of the Indian People, Vol. I, Bharatiya Vidya Bhawan, 2010, Mumbai.
100. 1The People's Linguistic Survey of India conducted by the Gujarat based Bhasha Trust. 2014 Vol. 1 Orient Blackswan Pvt. Ltd. New Delhi.
101. 1The Story of India Archaeology, Oct 5, 1949, Publications Division, New Delhi.
102. 1The Theory of Experience of Economic Development: ed. By Mark Gersovitz Carlos & Others, George Allen Unwin, London.

103. 1United Nations Development Programme, Human Development Report, 2003, Oxford University Press, New York.
104. 1Words & Phrases, Vol. 8A Permanent Ed.
105. 1Zafarnama, Guru Gobind Singh, translated by Navtej Sarna, 2011, Penguin Books, New Delhi.

E. Reports

1. Census of India Report 1911, Vol. 1.
2. Indian Archaeological Policy Report, 1915.
3. The Indian Problem: Report on the Constitutional Problem in India (Part I) (1944).
4. The First Five Year Plan, 1951–56.
5. State Reorganisation Commission Report, 1955.
6. Report of International Commission of Jurists Conference (1959) at New Delhi.
7. Planning Commission Report of the Committee on Tenancy Reforms, 1961.
8. Planning Commission: Report of the Committee on Land Ceiling Holdings, New Delhi, 1961.
9. Report of the 1976 Recommendation on Participation.
10. International Report on Cultural Property 1992, Lyndell.
11. V Prott & Patrick J O' Keefe, 1992.
12. 1992 Draft Approach Paper on National Cultural Policy.
13. N.N. Vohra Committee Report, dated 5th October, 1993.
14. Report of Amicus Curiae, December 6, 1994, in the Delhi leprosy patient's case.
15. Socio-Legal Field Report, August 4, 1994.
16. Vardharajan Committee Report, 1995.
17. National Culture Fund Report 1996.
18. Report of the 2002 National Commission to Review the Working of the Constitution.
19. United Nations Development Programme, Human Development Report, 2003.
20. Supreme Court Monitoring Committee Inspection Report, dated February 25, 2004.

21. Law Commission, 230th Report, 2009.
22. State of India's Livelihoods Report 2010: The 4P report ed. Sankar Datta and Vipin Sharma, Sage Publications India Pvt. Ltd, New Delhi.
23. Moily Committee Report, 2010.
24. Union Ministry of Environment & Forests – Report No. 21, 2011 – 12, Water Pollution in India.
25. CAG Performance Audit on fire crackers, Tenkailasanath Temple, 2012.
26. Union Ministry of Women & Child Development – Report No. 22, 2012–13, Performance Audit of ICDS.
27. Union Ministry of Coal – Report No. 7, 2012–13, Performance Audit of Allocation of Coal Blocks.
28. Performance Audit on Preservation and Conservation of Monuments and Antiquities, Report No. 18 of 2013.
29. Union Ministry of Rural Development – Report No. 6, 2013, Performance Audit MNREGA.
30. UNESCO, Oct 17, 2013: Social Inclusion of Internal Migrants in India, New Delhi.
31. 2013 Report of the Comptroller & Auditor General of India.
32. Report of the Hi-Powered Committee on the Akademies, Union Ministry of Culture, May 2014.
33. The People Linguistic Survey of India, Bhasha Trust, Gujarat, 2014, Vol. 1 Orient Blackswan Pvt. Ltd., New Delhi.
34. May 16, 2014 note of Deputy Chairman of the Planning Commission to Prime Minister.

F. Journal and News Articles

1. Wangkeo Kanchana, Yale J, Int'l L. 183(2003) Monumental Challenges: The Lawfulness of Destroying Cultural Heritage During Peacetime.
2. Samuel Huntington, The Clash of Civilizations, 72, Foreign Affairs, Summer 1993.
3. Marshall, J.H.(1902) "Introduction" to the inaugural issue of the archaeological Annual Publication of the ASI: The Foreign Department of the Government of India.

4. Mahajan Krishan, Sustainable Development in a State of Unconstitutional Economics (2013), NGT International Journal of Environment Law, Vol. II.
5. Layar A. "Shopping in the Public Realm: A Law of Place," Journal of Law and Society 37, 2010.
6. Dipesh Chakrabarty: Bourgeois Categories Made Global: Utopian and Actual Lives of Historical Documents in India, EPW Vol. XLIV No. 25 June 20, 2009.
7. Times of India, Delhi, August 4, 2013 page 8.
8. E.A.S Sarma, The Indian Express, New Delhi, November 17, 2013.
9. The Hindustan Times, May 24, 2014, page 10.

G. Public Lectures

1. The Managing Director of IMF, Christine Lagarde at the Feb 4, 2014 BBC Richard Dimbleby Lecture, London.
2. Vajpeyi Memorial Lecture, April 1, 2013, Media India Centre for Research & Development, Gurgaon, Haryana.

www.ingramcontent.com/pod-product-compliance
Lightning Source LLC
Chambersburg PA
CBHW020723180526
45163CB00001B/86